John Curtin writes about walking, cycling and other outdoor pursuits in Britain and continental Europe. Occasionally accompanied by his wife, Jennifer, his spaniel and also sometimes a very slow but endearing wheaten terrier, his travels are limited only by the responsibility of providing a year-round supply of organic vegetables from his allotment garden at the foot of the North Downs Way in Albury, Surrey.

North Downs Way
First edition: October 2006

Publisher
Trailblazer Publications
The Old Manse, Tower Rd, Hindhead, Surrey, GU26 6SU, UK
Fax (+44) 01428-607571, info@trailblazer-guides.com
www.trailblazer-guides.com

British Library Cataloguing in Publication Data
A catalogue record for this book is available from the British Library

ISBN 1-873756-96-8
EAN 978-1873756-966

Editor: Anna Jacomb-Hood
Series editor: Anna Jacomb-Hood
Additional research: Jenny Hill
Layout: Anna Jacomb-Hood and Bryn Thomas
Proof-reading: Jane Thomas
Illustrations: pp46-8: Nick Hill; pp52-3 Rev CA Johns
Photographs (flora): bee orchid opposite p49, © John Curtin
all others © Bryn Thomas
Cartography: Nick Hill
Index: Jane Thomas

The maps in this guide were prepared from out-of-Crown-copyright Ordnance Survey maps amended and updated by Trailblazer.

Warning: **long-distance walking can be dangerous**
Please read the notes on when to go (pp19-21), and health and safety (pp60-2)
Every effort has been made by the authors and publisher to ensure that the information contained herein is as accurate and up to date as possible. However, they are unable to accept responsibility for any inconvenience, loss or injury sustained by anyone as a result of the advice and information given in this guide.

Printed on chlorine-free paper from farmed forests by
D2print (☎ +65-6295 5598), Singapore

NORTH DOWNS WAY

FARNHAM TO DOVER

planning, places to stay, places to eat
includes 80 large-scale walking maps

JOHN CURTIN

TRAILBLAZER PUBLICATIONS

Acknowledgements

Thanks to Bryn Thomas for commissioning the book, Nick Hill for the maps and illustrations, Jane Thomas for the index and Anna Jacomb-Hood for editing the text and everyone else at Trailblazer. Thanks also to Hazelle Jackson for helping me out on follies and Tony Gowers, Project Officer, North Downs Way National Trail, who generously shared his knowledge of the trail, and to Yoma for being a computer angel. The biggest debt of gratitude I owe is to my wife, Jennifer. It is no exaggeration to say that she made this possible; thank you. Apologies to Rufus and Lilly; this was work and you couldn't come but I'm ready to walk with you anytime you want.

A request

The author and publisher have tried to ensure that this guide is as accurate and up to date as possible. Nevertheless things change. If you notice any changes or omissions that should be included in the next edition of this book, please write to Trailblazer (address on p2) or email us at info@trailblazer-guides.com. A free copy of the next edition will be sent to persons making a significant contribution.

Updated information will shortly be available on the Internet at
www.trailblazer-guides.com

Front cover: St Martha's Church (see p82) has a commanding position at the top of St Martha's Hill. Also called the Pilgrims' Church it features in the opening scene of Powell and Pressburger's wartime film, *A Canterbury Tale*. (Photo © Jennifer Ullman).

CONTENTS

INTRODUCTION

PART 1: PLANNING YOUR WALK

About the North Downs Way
History 9 – How difficult is the North Downs Way? 9 – How long do you need? 10

Practical information for the walker
Accommodation 11 – Food and drink 14 – Money 16 – Other services 16
Walking companies 16 – Taking dogs along the North Downs Way 18

Budgeting 18

When to go 19

Itineraries
Suggested itineraries 24 – Which direction? 24 – Side trips 24

What to take
Keep it light 26 – How to carry it 28 – Footwear 28– Clothes 29
Toiletries 30 – First-aid kit 30 – General items 31 – Camping gear 31
Money 32 – Maps 32 – Recommended reading 32

Getting to and from the North Downs Way
Getting to Britain 34 – National transport 35 – Local transport 36

PART 2: ENVIRONMENT AND NATURE

Conserving the North Downs
Government agencies and schemes 41 – Campaigning and conservation organizations 43 – Beyond conservation 44

Flora and fauna
Mammals 45 – Fish 45 – Birds 46 – Reptiles 48 – Butterflies 48
Flowers 49 – Trees 51

PART 3: MINIMUM IMPACT WALKING AND OUTDOOR SAFETY

Minimum impact walking
Access 55 – The Countryside Code 55 – Economic impact 57
Environmental impact 58

Outdoor safety
Avoidance of hazards 60 – Blisters 61 – Hypothermia 61
Hyperthermia 61 – Sunburn 62 – Personal safety 62 – Other users 62

PART 4: ROUTE GUIDE AND MAPS

Using this guide

Trail maps 63 – Map keys 64

The route guide

Farnham to Guildford
Farnham 65 – Seale 72 – Puttenham 72 – Compton 72 – Shalford 74
Guildford 78

Guildford to Denbies Wine Estate and Dorking
Chilworth 82 – Albury 82 – Newlands Corner 84 – Shere 86
Gomshall 88 – Holmbury St Mary 88 – Ranmore Common 92
Westcott 92 – Denbies Wine Estate 92 – Dorking 94

Dorking to Merstham
Box Hill 98 – Box Hill Village 98 – Reigate Hill 98 – Redhill 100
Merstham 103

Merstham to Oxted
Oxted 108

Oxted to Otford
Westerham 111 – Knockholt 115 – Dunton Green 115 – Otford 118

Otford to Medway Bridge and Rochester
Kemsing 122 – Wrotham 122 – Borough Green 124 – Trottiscliffe 124
Ryarsh 128 – Cuxton 128 – Rochester 134

Medway Bridge to Hollingbourne
Aylesford 138 – Detling 140 – Thurnham 142 – Hollingbourne 142

Hollingbourne to Charing
Harrietsham 146 – Lenham 146 – Charing 148

Charing to Chilham
Westwell 152 – Eastwell 152 – Chilham 158

Chilham to Canterbury
Chartham Hatch 160 – Chartham 160 – Canterbury 164

Canterbury to Shepherdswell
Bridge 170 – Shepherdswell 176

Shepherdswell to Dover
Dover 180

APPENDIX: ALTERNATIVE ROUTE

Boughton Lees to Dover via Folkestone 183

INDEX 185

INTRODUCTION

The 131-mile (209.6km) North Downs Way, from Farnham in Surrey to Dover in Kent via Canterbury, winds its way through the protected landscape of two Areas of Outstanding Natural Beauty, the Surrey Hills and the Kent Downs. It coincides in places with the so-called Pilgrims' Way and the built environment is as interesting as the superb landscape. En route you can visit six castles, three cathedrals (modern and ancient), the ruins of four archbishops' palaces, three Neolithic burial sites, two vineyards, various WWII defences and one folly, while walking in the footsteps of pilgrims, drovers and traders. There are numerous medieval churches, Georgian towns, and an ancient port all waiting to distract the walker. The literary minded will appreciate the associations with Jonathan Swift, William Cobbett, Charles Dickens and Jane Austen.

Right from the start the North Downs Way gives walkers a taste of what the trail offers as it follows farm tracks, sandy bridleways and woodland paths to cross the first of five rivers, the Wey, south of Guildford, Surrey's county town with its modern cathedral and many significant historic buildings. The first climb is to the Pilgrims' Church on St Martha's Hill with wonderful views across the Downs on a clear day from where the route strikes out along the chalk ridge to Dorking. It's this ridge, topped with short shorn grass and dense woodland, which forms the backbone of the walk.

Crossing the River Mole and climbing to the chalk grassland habitat of Box Hill with its box, yew, beech and oak trees, the trail takes you through dense woodland to Reigate Hill affording skyline views high above a densely populated commuter area. Then it's on to Kent whose title the 'Garden of England' is soon evident in the arable fields glimpsed from the wooded ridgeline as the route passes near the Neolithic burial site, Coldrum Stones.

Though the industrial Medway towns lie at the foot of the escarpment the route feels wonderfully isolated as the trail makes its way to the busy Medway Bridge and the outskirts of Rochester from where it climbs through Shoulder of Mutton Wood to pass Thurnham Castle and on to Hollingbourne.

Following the path of the Pilgrims' Way, the trail divides at Boughton Lees, this guide taking the longer, northern loop to Canterbury and its cultural riches. From Soakham Downs there are excellent views over the Great Stour valley before you emerge from King's Wood and on to the well-preserved medieval square at Chilham. From here it's pleasant walking through Kent's apple orchards to Canterbury which deserves at least a day of your time. The final leg is across huge arable fields at Barham Downs, through sleepy Womenswold, on to Shepherdswell and finally to Dover.

Taking about a fortnight to complete at a leisurely pace, with over 500,000 day-visitors a year and more than 5000 completing it in stages, this is one of Britain's most popular national trails – and rightly so.

About this book

This guidebook is as practically useful, comprehensive and up to date as humanly possible. It is the **only** book you need; no phoning around for tourist brochures. You can find here everything for planning your trip including:

- All standards of places to stay from campsites and hostels to B&Bs, inns, guesthouses and hotels
- Walking companies if you want an organized tour
- Varied itineraries for all types of walkers
- Answers to all your questions: when to go, degree of difficulty, what to pack and how much the whole walking holiday will cost

When the date is set and you're ready to go, there's comprehensive information to get you to and from the North Downs Way and 80 detailed maps and town plans to help you find your way along it. The route guide includes:

- Walking times in both directions
- Reviews of campsites, bunkhouses, hostels, B&Bs, guesthouses and hotels on and near the path
- Cafés, pubs, tea-shops, takeaways and restaurants as well as shops and supermarkets for buying supplies
- Rail, bus and taxi information for all the villages and towns along the path
- Street plans of the main towns and villages en route: Farnham, Shalford, Guildford, Shere, Dorking, Redhill, Oxted, Westerham, Otford, Rochester, Lenham, Canterbury, Shepherdswell and Dover
- Historical, cultural and geographical background information

Minimum impact for maximum insight

Nature's peace will flow into you as the sunshine flows into trees. The winds will blow their freshness into you and storms their energy, while cares will drop off like autumn leaves. **John Muir** (one of the world's earliest and most influential environmentalists, born in 1838)

It is no surprise that, since the time of John Muir, walkers and adventurers have been concerned about the natural environment; this book seeks to continue that tradition. There is a detailed, illustrated chapter on wildlife and conservation on the North Downs as well as a chapter devoted to minimum impact walking with ideas on how we can broaden that ethos.

By developing a deeper ecological awareness through a better understanding of nature and by supporting rural economies, local businesses, sensitive forms of transport and low-impact methods of farming and land-use we can all do our bit for a brighter future.

As we work harder and live our lives at an ever faster pace a walking holiday is a chance to escape from the daily grind and the natural pace gives us time to think and relax. This can have a positive impact not only on our own well being but also on that of the area we pass through. There can be few activities as 'environmentally friendly' as walking.

Break clear away, once in awhile, and climb a mountain or spend a week in the woods. Wash your spirit clean. **John Muir**

PART 1: PLANNING YOUR WALK

About the North Downs Way

HISTORY

The North Downs Way was officially opened as a national trail in 1978 by the then Archbishop of Canterbury, Dr Donald Coggan. The route follows the chalk ridge that forms the North Downs between Farnham and Dover and the trail is jointly managed by both Surrey and Kent county councils and will be supported by, pending its formal establishment as a new statutory agency, Natural England (see p41).

The route also follows, in parts, the Pilgrims' Way, reputedly taken by pilgrims to the shrine of Thomas à Becket at Canterbury Cathedral, though its existence on maps only appeared from the late 19th century. In all likelihood prehistoric man used trackways along the North Downs which were also later used by drovers and traders keen to avoid toll roads. It is a natural route east to the Continent.

HOW DIFFICULT IS THE NORTH DOWNS WAY?

The North Downs Way is a well-signposted 131-mile (209.6km) walk over generally level and firm ground with very few steep ascents or descents. You do not need previous experience of long-distance path walking. What you do need is suitable clothing, money, time, a half-decent pair of leg muscles and a realistic assessment of your fitness. Remember you don't have to do it all in one go and because transport options are so good you can tackle it in bite-sized stages.

Fitter, more experienced, walkers up for a challenge can always adopt a fast pace and cover the ground in a week or less but that leaves little time to take in the sights or enjoy what the towns and villages of the North Downs Way have to offer. The main thing is not to push yourself beyond your ability. With a bus or train, village or welcoming pub seldom more than a mile or two from the trail it's easy to peel off if you feel you've had enough for the day. Despite this there are places on the trail where you can feel quite remote and isolated.

> **❑ Alternative route**
> The 'official' North Downs Way divides at Boughton Lees (see p152) and we take the longer northern route through Canterbury, across Kent orchard and hop country and on to Dover. The alternative route (see p183 for a brief outline) is less interesting, bounded by the busy A20 and the Channel Tunnel marshalling yards and it lacks the cultural riches that Canterbury offers.

It can be comfortably walked end to end in about a fortnight and there is something special about walking day after day, establishing a rhythm, getting fitter and travelling at a pace that lets you appreciate the countryside.

If you don't have the time or want to skip the less interesting parts where motorways intrude, there are excellent transport links to most parts of the North Downs Way from London and the South Coast making day and weekend trips easy (see Highlights p27).

Route finding

There is little chance of becoming lost as the trail is well signposted with the National Trail acorn symbol. New waymark posts have been erected throughout the Kent section. Posts may also be marked with a blue chevron indicating a bridleway, yellow for a public footpath, and red for a byway open to all traffic where there is a chance you may meet off-road vehicles.

Any slightly tricky directions not immediately obvious on the ground are noted on the appropriate **trail guide** maps in **Part 4** of this book. In most cases the path is obvious and well trodden and certainly on weekends there are bound to be other walkers about to point you in the right direction. A compass is not necessary.

Do remember that summer foliage may obscure signs or they may go missing so it's best to read ahead in the trail guide and refer to the maps occasionally to confirm your location.

HOW LONG DO YOU NEED?

You can do it in a week if you are determined to crack off the miles day after day and provided you are fit. But that really feels like a race against time. You can have an invigorating holiday easily completing the walk in 10 days, or 14 if you prefer a more relaxed pace.

Bear in mind that if you are camping carrying a heavier pack will slow you down and many of the official sites are well off the trail. Of course you may want to take a day off – you'll probably be tempted by Canterbury. Both Guildford and Rochester are worth at least half a day each and this will add to the time needed. Then again there are superb **day** and **weekend walks** (see p27) with easy access and excellent transport links.

Practical information for the walker

ACCOMMODATION

The **route guide** (Part 4) lists a comprehensive selection of places to stay along the full length of the trail and often in each town or village there are a number of options. The three main types are camping, staying in hostels/bunkhouses, or using B&Bs/hotels. In the ever-more populated and prosperous south-east low-cost accommodation is increasingly hard to find. Proximity to London, soaring property values and a healthy demand for rooms from business travellers drives prices up.

Camping

It isn't possible to camp all along the North Downs Way and few people probably would anyway – there is always the temptation to have a hot bath in a cosy B&B and rest your head on a feather pillow. You will be carrying a heavier pack and this can slow you down and could add an extra day and additional costs to your walk. You'll have to buy breakfast and won't have the fuel which a full English breakfast provides and you might buy more snacks and energy boosters as a result.

While on other trails you could expect to pay anywhere from £2-6 per camper, on the North Downs Way organized sites can cost as much as £12 for a pitch. A number of sites are a fair distance from the trail though some owners may be willing to come and collect you from the trail. Some sites have no facilities, others have coin-operated showers and laundry whilst others are swish holiday parks with some tent spaces.

Wild camping Camping on land that is not a recognized campsite is possible along the route and I've met several people doing it but you must obtain the landowner's permission first. The amount of cultivated arable land in Kent reduces the number of potential sites and Surrey is very wooded so I'm told the most versatile set up is a bivvy bag or lightweight tarp.

Wild camping is not permitted on National Trust (NT) land – this will usually be signposted as you enter NT Land. Expect wardens to be particularly alert to campers in Surrey where there have been problems with raves in the past. Wild camping is not for the faint hearted and you'll be carrying extra gear but it does add a sense of freedom and adventure. See also p59.

Camping barns/bunkhouses and hostels

There are two **camping barns** along the North Downs Way: one at Puttenham (see p72) and one at Coldblow Farm (see p142). These provide comfortable accommodation either on foam-lined wooden sleeping platforms or a bunk bed, with showers and electricity on meter and a basic kitchen facility. A sleeping

❑ Hostel dorms make way for houses

The hostel at Kemsing, a former vicarage, has just closed and is to be sold as the YHA tries to shore up its finances by cashing in a valuable property asset. It may be converted to a single family home, in a lovely setting at the foot of the Downs and as a rational response to a rising property market. Who can blame them? However, there is some good news: Holmbury St Mary, the Youth Hostel Association's first purpose-built hostel (1935), has been saved from closure by local efforts and a £750,000 fundraising campaign was under way at the time of writing.

bag is essential. Puttenham opened in April 2005 in a restored Grade II listed building and charges £9 per person. Booking is essential for both.

Youth hostels have come a long way since the days of crowded dorms and chores. Sadly only three **Youth Hostel Association** (YHA; ☎ 0870-770 8868, 🖳 www.yha.org.uk) hostels on this trail remain open: Tanners Hatch (see p92), Canterbury (see p164) and Dover (see p180); Kemsing (see box above) has just been closed. Holmbury St Mary Youth Hostel (see p88) lies a good distance off the trail but you can get to it by bus. Tanners Hatch at Ranmore Common is busier than ever.

The downsides of YHA hostels are that opening hours are often limited, the beds in the dorms tend to be short, so if you're tall you'll spend the night with your feet dangling off the end, and the chances are you'll end up next to a Vesuvial snorer so bring ear plugs. You don't have to be a member of the YHA to stay at their hostels but you will pay an additional £3 per night.

Membership is currently £15.95 per year (£9.95 for under 18s); if you pay by direct debit it's usually a bit less. You can book hostels online on the YHA website (see above) or by either calling the central reservations number (☎ 0870-770 8868), or the hostel direct.

There is a **Y Centre** (formerly YMCA) in Guildford providing very good accommodation at B&B prices and an excellent independent hostel, **Kipps** (see p165), in Canterbury, with prices from £14 and it has additional tent pitches.

B&Bs

The B&B is a British institution. Although normally a reserved nation, you're welcomed into people's homes as a guest, provided with a comfortable bed (usually) and sent on your way the next morning with an enormous full English breakfast – often bacon, sausages, eggs, sometimes baked beans, maybe black pudding, all fried and washed down with lashings of tea or coffee and of course accompanied by buttered toast and marmalade. It's great but two weeks of this and you're ready for the cardiac unit.

More and more B&Bs offer a lighter, kinder on the arteries, help yourself buffet breakfast of cereals, fruits, pastries and breads which comes as a welcome relief. Alternatively, and particularly if you are planning an early start, it may be worth asking if you can have a free packed lunch instead of breakfast.

Some B&Bs are charming, some luxurious, others are modest. Prices vary, the least expensive on this trail is £17.50 per person but reckon on spending at least £25-35 and up to £50 at the top end. The listings in this book concentrate on establishments close to the trail but you should be prepared to walk for up to a mile, sometimes more, descending off the North Downs ridge to the villages and towns below at the end of the day. Some B&Bs proudly display four stars, others no stars, some are vetted by Tourist Boards, for others it is a low-key sideline business. In my experience the number of stars is not a sure guide to quality and it'll all depend on how enthusiastic the owner is.

Rooms vary but in general you'll find few **single rooms**. **Twin rooms** usually have two single beds with a gap between the beds and a **double room** has one double bed but sometimes two single beds pushed together. **Family rooms** sleep at least three people – often a double and a single so check in advance if you would prefer three actual beds.

More and more B&Bs offer en suite facilities; these are often squeezed into the corner of an already tight room. It can take Houdini-like contortions to shower in a tiny cubicle fighting back a clinging shower curtain. Some B&Bs offer an evening meal, though often you need to book this in advance, and they may also make a packed lunch.

Owners may offer to collect walkers from the trail but do check when booking. It's an added service, so an offer to pay the petrol money will be appreciated. Your offer will probably be refused but it's a courtesy that doesn't cost much. Increasingly B&Bs ban smoking on their premises so check when booking if this is likely to be important to you.

Rates quoted in this guide are **per person** in a single (sgl), double (dbl), twin (twin) or family room (fml). Often the solo walker will pay a supplement (£5-15) to occupy a double or twin room when a single isn't available.

Pubs/inns

Many walkers write off pubs as noisy and perhaps not offering the best in the way of B&B. That's not been my experience. True they're sometimes less personal, but no worse for that and often a great deal less precious about muddy boots. I've got to confess the Devil's at my elbow and it's difficult to resist the sybaritic pleasure of bed, bath, booze and board under one roof at the end of a long day's walk. Prices per person start at £25. If you want to get an early start the next day, do check that this is possible – landlords tend to keep late hours.

❑ Booking accommodation in advance

Always book your accommodation and I suggest doing so several weeks before departure. Because the trail is close to London and major business arteries, a busy port, as well as two of the country's busiest airports and top tourist attractions it means that demand for rooms is always high. Also it doesn't take long for all beds to go if one of the major motorways is forced to close. The M25 shut down twice in the course of researching this book and within hours there was no room in any manger.

Booking in advance means you risk losing your deposit and tie yourself to a schedule but you'll be assured of a bed and have an idea of what to expect and know the price. If you do have to cancel a booking let the owners know as soon as possible so they can re-let the room.

Hotels

Generally not considered the first choice of billet for walkers but if you want a touch of luxury at the end of the day and you can afford it there's no harm in spoiling yourself. There are several hotel options along the North Downs Way, some very upmarket. Quite a number of business travellers use hotels during the week so you'll probably find some discounted rates at the weekend at several hotels on the trail.

FOOD AND DRINK

Breakfast and lunch

Breakfast is usually included when staying at B&Bs though some owners and pubs offer bed-only rates in larger towns where there are breakfast options nearby.

Hosts can usually provide a packed lunch for an additional cost but let them know in advance, though, there is really no hardship in preparing your own lunch. If you buy local produce (see box opposite) so much the better. Details of lunch places, tea shops, pubs and eateries are in Part 4 but for an overview look at the Village and Town Facilities table on pp22-3. Always bring some food with you and don't rely on making it to a pub for lunch – country pubs usually finish food service by 3pm at the latest and frequently close for the afternoon.

Evening meals

There is nothing like a pint at the end of a day's walking and many of the **pubs** on the North Downs Way can trace their origins back to the 15th and 16th centuries. However, most are now owned by one or other of the drinks conglomerates but by and large retain their individual character thanks to a resident landlord. Many have à la carte restaurants as well as a bar menu, which is usually cheaper, and some have become 'gastropubs' serving restaurant quality food in a pub environment, but often at near restaurant prices.

There is a wide choice of restaurants and takeaways in the larger villages and towns from Italian to Indian, burger joints to modern British, Asian fusion to fast food. Of course the Great British culinary institution, the fish 'n' chip shop, can also be found along the route – there's even one serving up deep-fried Mars Bars (see p166) – a culinary rarity down south.

Camping supplies

There are plenty of shops along the North Downs Way for you to buy food and there are outdoor shops in Farnham, Guildford, Dorking, Redhill, Canterbury and Dover where you can get gas and other essential camping supplies.

Drinking water

There are no drinking-water fountains along the North Downs Way so take plenty of water with you each day – at least a one-litre bottle or a pouch. I usually get through two in a day making sure to drink regularly **before** I get thirsty and dehydrated. There are five rivers on this walk and drinking water from those is not recommended. Even if you do purify the water using a filter or iodine tables you will not succeed in removing heavy metals or pesticides present from run-off from roads and agricultural use.

Luckily there are many tea shops, pubs and refreshment kiosks within easy access of the North Downs Way so buying bottles of water should not be a problem. You could always just ask the owner if they'd mind filling up your water bottle from the tap.

❑ LOCAL FOOD AND DRINK

Britain's food reputation has come a long way since the days of warm beer, surly service and chips with everything. More and more people are looking for fresh quality produce, locally grown.

Food

Surrey Gourmet (p94), in Dorking, specializes in locally produced food and drinks, just the place to pick up some Norbury Blue cheese and a bottle of ale from the Hogs Back Brewery (see below) for lunch.

Farmers' markets give local producers a chance to showcase their products and in a recent survey 70% of shoppers said they would buy local produce if they could identify it. These markets are also a fun way to fill the larder while at the same time cutting down the food miles travelled and getting tastier, fresher produce. Farmers' markets along the North Downs Way are held at:

- **Farnham** Central Car Park, fourth Sunday of every month (see p67)
- **Guildford** High St, first Tuesday of every month (see p79)
- **Dorking** St Martin's Walk, off High St, second Wednesday and fifth Saturday of the month (see p95)
- **Redhill** Town Centre, second Friday of every month (see p100)
- **Rochester** The Moat, Rochester Castle, third Sunday of every month (see p134)
- **Lenham** Lenham Sq, second Sunday of every month (see p146)
- **Canterbury** Station Rd, Tue-Sun, The country's first full-time farmers' market restaurant (see p166) with an ever-changing menu from the daily produce.

Drink

Farnham had five breweries and Guildford had nine during the heyday of brewing in the 19th century. But now most pubs and brewers are owned by one of the international conglomerates. **The Hogs Back Brewery** (☎ 01252-784485, 🖳 www.hogsback.co.uk) survives as a small independent brewery and has a thriving mail-order service for its bottle-conditioned ales. Particular favourites are the classic TEA (Traditional English Ale) at 4.2% and BSA (Burma Star Ale) at 4.5% but after a bottle of A-over-T at 9% it's difficult to put one foot in front of the other.

If you stop by the **Percy Arms** (see p82) in Chilworth or the **Drummond** (see p82) in Albury it's worth asking if Shere Drop is a guest beer. This local brew has the nice tartness of an India Pale Ale.

Denbies Wine Estate (see p92) is the largest in Britain and the winery tour and tasting is highly recommended. Their Surrey Gold is a delicate 11.5% white aperitif wine, perfect on a summer evening and you'll find fine apple juices at **Godstone Vineyards** (see p108), which also does a bargain cream tea for £2.95. When you reach Kent, sample Shepherd Neame beers from Britain's oldest brewer and still a family company.

MONEY

There are several **banks** and many **post offices** on or close to the trail, some of which have cash machines. Cash machines can also be found in local shops and at petrol stations but they may charge for withdrawals (about £1.75), though they have to inform you of this before you take your money out.

A large number of UK banks have an arrangement with the Post Office enabling you to withdraw cash from branches by debit card (with a Pin number); a few permit withdrawals using a chequebook and card. You can also get money in a shop by using 'cashback' where the retailer advances cash against your debit card. Usually there is a minimum purchase of £5 though some shops also charge a fee of up to £1.50. Not everybody accepts **debit** or **credit cards** as payment and that includes many B&Bs but you'll find that many restaurants and shops now do. As a result, you should always carry a fair amount of cash with you just in case; a **cheque book** from a British bank is a useful back up. **Travellers' cheques** can be cashed only at banks, foreign exchanges and some large hotels.

OTHER SERVICES

Most villages and towns have a **post office** (from where you can mail back unnecessary items if your pack is too heavy), a **public telephone** and most have a **food store** with at least basic supplies. Where there is a **public library** you will also find **free internet access** but usually you have to join the library system. This does not take long and you do not have to be resident in the county; just show two forms of identification such as a passport and driver's licence. There is a snapshot of **services and facilities** in towns and villages en route on pp22-3 and further details in Part 4.

WALKING COMPANIES

If all you want to carry is a day pack consider one of the following companies as they'll transport your bags, book your accommodation and generally keep an eye on your progress along the way. It's a good idea to call each of the companies and study their brochures and websites to get a feel for their style.

- **Contours Walking Holidays** (☎ 01768-440451, 💻 www.contours.co.uk; Gramyre, 3 Berrier Rd, Greystoke, CA11 OUB) Offers self-guided 11-, 12- and 13-night itineraries from £625 per person including B&B, en suite room where available, and daily door-to-door luggage transfer (one suitcase per person). They also have 6-night itineraries from Farnham to Rochester and Rochester to Dover via Canterbury for those who have less time and can do it in two stages.
- **Walk Awhile** (☎ 01795-533387, 💻 www.awhile.fsnet.co.uk; Mountgreenan, St Catherine's, Faversham, Kent ME13 8QL) Offers a six-night itinerary on the Pilgrims' Way from £285 for a B&B option and £382 for a hotel option with luggage transfer included. If you want a guided trip prices start from £483.

(Opposite) Top: Classic North Downs landscape near Thurnham. **Bottom:** Stepping stones across the River Mole at the foot of Box Hill. (Photos © John Curtin).

❑ Information for foreign visitors

- **Currency** The British pound (£) comes in notes of £100, £50, £20, £10, £5 and coins of £2 and £1. The pound is divided into 100 pence (usually referred to as 'p', pronounced 'pee') which comes in silver coins of 50p, 20p, 10p and 5p and copper coins of 2p and 1p.
- **Rates of exchange** Up-to-date rates of exchange can be found at 💻 www.xe.com/ucc.
- **Business hours** Most **shops** and main **post offices** are open at least from Monday to Friday 9am-5pm and Saturday 9am-12.30pm. Many choose longer hours and some open on Sundays as well. **Banks** are usually open 10am-4pm Monday to Friday. **Pubs** are usually open from 11am to 11pm Monday to Saturday, and 12noon-3pm and 7-10.30pm on Sundays as well. New licensing laws came into effect in England in November 2005. Since then pub opening hours have become more flexible so each pub may have different opening hours. However, it is likely that most pubs on the North Downs Way will not change their opening hours much, though a number of pubs in Guildford and Canterbury have successfully applied to stay open till 1am or later.
- **National holidays** The following are nationwide holidays in England: New Year's Day (1 January); Good Friday and Easter Monday (end of March or in April); May Bank Holiday (first Monday in May); Whit Weekend or Spring Bank Holiday (last Monday in May); Summer Bank Holiday (last Monday of August); Christmas Day and Boxing Day (25-26 December). Businesses generally close on these days and accommodation prices often increase and you may find it difficult to book somewhere for just one night.
- **School holidays** School holiday periods in England are generally as follows: a one-week break late October, two weeks around Christmas and the New Year, a week mid-February, two weeks around Easter, and from late July to early September.
- **Travel insurance** The European Health Insurance Card (EHIC) entitles EU nationals (on production of the EHIC card so ensure you bring it with you) to necessary medical treatment under the UK's National Health Service while on a temporary visit here. However, this is not a substitute for proper medical cover on your travel insurance for unforeseen bills and for getting you home should that be necessary. Also consider cover for loss and theft of personal belongings, especially if you are camping or staying in hostels, as there will be times when you'll have to leave your luggage unattended.
- **Weights and measures** Britain is attempting to move towards the metric system but there is much resistance. Most food is now sold in metric weights (g and kg) but many people still think in the imperial weights of pounds (lb) and ounces (oz). Milk is sold in pints as is beer in pubs, yet most other liquid is sold in litres. Road signs and distances are always given in miles rather than kilometres and the population remains split between those who are happy with centimetres and metres and those who still use inches, feet and yards.
- **British Summer Time (BST)** BST starts the last Sunday in March, ie the clocks go forward one hour, and ends the last Sunday in October ie the clocks go back one hour.
- **Telephone** The country code for Britain is ☎ 44, followed by the area code minus the first 0, and then the number you require. To make a local call you can omit the area code. It is cheaper to ring at weekends, and after 6pm and before 8am on weekdays. Mobile phone reception is generally good on the North Downs Way.
- **Emergency services** For police, ambulance, or fire dial ☎ 999.

(Opposite) Tudor gate to a former refuge, Detling (see p143), where pilgrims en route to Canterbury could find food and shelter. (Photo © John Curtin).

❑ Disabled access

Unfortunately most of the North Downs Way is inaccessible to disabled people but there are some areas where roads provide access to good views and stretches of the trail that can be followed, particularly at **Newlands Corner** (see p84) and **Blue Bell Hill** picnic site (see p138).

Disabled Ramblers (🖳 www.disabledramblers.co.uk, Little Croft, Guildford Rd, Shamley Green GU5 ORT) is a national charity of like-minded disabled people who enjoy being in the countryside and get about using a variety of mobility aids. They have a busy calendar of events including rambles along the North Downs near Guildford. Resisting being ghettoized and confined to areas catering to every conceivable need their rambles take them nationwide.

At Newlands Corner there are designated paths for the use of an electric off-road **Tramper buggy** specially designed for countryside use. This is available for hire free from the Countryside Centre most Sundays; pre-booking advised (☎ 07968-8325076, 🖳 john.neate@swtcs.co.uk).

By All Means (☎ 01474-364413) is a project funded by the Countryside Agency testing methods to encourage disabled people to visit and enjoy the countryside.

- **Xplore Britain** (☎ 01740-650900, 🖳 www.xplorebritain.com; 6 George St, Ferryhill, Co Durham DL17 ODT) Offers a 13-night itinerary from £735 and a seven-night itinerary Rochester to Dover via Canterbury and Farnham to Rochester from £396.
- **Tanners Hatch Youth Hostel** (☎ 01306-877964, 🖳 tanners@yha.org.uk, see p92) organize walking packages, on selected dates, from Farnham to Merstham with three nights accommodation at a camping barn, Tanners Hatch Youth Hostel and a local B&B at a cost of £50.

TAKING DOGS ALONG THE NORTH DOWNS WAY

The North Downs Way is dog-friendly but owners must behave in a responsible way; see p56-7. Dogs should always be kept under close control to avoid disturbing wildlife, livestock and other walkers. Man's best friend is not everyone's best friend and being territorial he may be uneasy and unwelcome in the presence of farm dogs. Check if dogs are welcome when booking accommodation. Not all pubs allow dogs; some inns and hotels charge extra and in my experience you may not get the best room. Also bear in mind that you will need to carry your dog's supplies, extra water and food.

Budgeting

England is not a cheap place to go travelling at the best of times and the North Downs Way with its proximity to London is in one of the most affluent areas in the UK. Add to this the demand from other tourists and business travellers and it is easy to understand why prices are high. Budget accommodation is at a premium, camping opportunities are at a minimum and hostel prices are at the higher end of the scale. After you've allowed for accommodation and food and the cost of getting to and from the start of the trail you'll have to allow for incidentals and unexpected expenditure: beer, snacks, bus and taxi fares, admission tickets, internet access and so on. It all adds up.

CAMPING

With some sites costing up to £12 and the cost of food and the effort involved in carrying all the gear, camping might not be the attractive option it is elsewhere. It's also unlikely you'll be able to camp all the way so you'll have to budget for some nights in a hostel or bunkhouse. In all, reckon on needing a minimum of £20 per day.

BUNKHOUSES AND HOSTELS

The least expensive YHA hostel on the route is £11 for members. Add £3 supplement for non-members or fork out £15.95 for a year's membership. You'll get a bunk at Puttenham camping barn for £9 which is astounding value for the area and private hostels charge, on average, £14. You'll have to buy breakfast, lunch and dinner and just getting by will set you back £20-30 a day. Buy a couple of beers as well and you're looking at £30-35.

B&Bs

The cheapest B&B on this walk charges £17.50 per person and breakfast isn't included though you have the use of the kitchen; most cost around £25-30 per person. Add on the cost of lunch, dinner and a couple of pints in the evening and you should reckon on about £45-55 minimum per day.

When to go

SEASONS

The old joke is Britain doesn't have a climate; it has weather and if you don't like it just wait five minutes. Walking the North Downs Way can be enjoyed year-round as long as you dress suitably and take it for granted that even in summer there may be parts of the trail that are muddy. However, severe conditions of heat, cold or rain seldom last for long.

You may get wet on the North Downs but you're unlikely to perish. Temperatures seldom dip below 0°C in winter or above 32°C in summer and the south-east tends to have the highest temperatures and the greatest number of sunshine hours in Britain. In summer it tends to be slightly cooler by the coast because the sea takes longer to heat up. Conversely in winter it takes longer for the sea to cool so it's milder by the coast because of the warming effect of the sea.

Spring

This is a great time of year for stands of bluebells and spring wild flowers along the Surrey sections of the North Downs Way. With the first leaf growth coming on there is a tapestry of green before the views become obscured later in the year. It's difficult to predict the weather from year to year but there's often a settled period of fine weather around mid-May. The trail is generally quiet but gets busier around the Easter and May holidays. Days are getting longer and temperatures are rising, pubs open beer gardens and a few brave souls turn their minds to BBQs.

Summer

June can start unsettled and blustery but later in the season it can get very hot on the Downs; we've had some scorching days in the past few years. Fortunately much of the Surrey section is wooded so while you may miss the views the worst of the heat is taken by the trees. The open fields of Kent can be like outdoor ovens so bring plenty of water with you. Expect the trail to be busier and you'll be competing for accommodation with other holidaymakers and those on their way across the Channel. With early dawns and long days there's little need to rush on the trail though you may find it dusty across the Kent arable fields as the farmers gather in the harvest.

Autumn

The weather is generally settled early in the season and everything seems to slow down after the August Bank Holiday. Children are back at school, holidays are over and it's easier to find accommodation. September is a wonderful time to walk. There can be crisp bright days with a slight chill in the air and later the vivid autumn colours emerge as the leaves begin to change and the nights start to draw in. Farmers will be ploughing so you can expect some tough-going over recently ploughed fields especially if it's been raining.

Winter

There is nothing like a bright, clear, frosty day to admire the views from the North Downs' ridgeline and we often get a spell of weather like that early in the New Year. But it's wet, relatively mild, damp days that are the norm. With good waterproofs there is nothing to hold you back from walking the North Downs even if it's a bit dispiriting. With the leaves off the trees the views on a clear day are uninterrupted. Most pubs and B&Bs remain open as their business here is year-round so it will be easier to find accommodation but do make sure you get an early start each day as the nights draw in quickly.

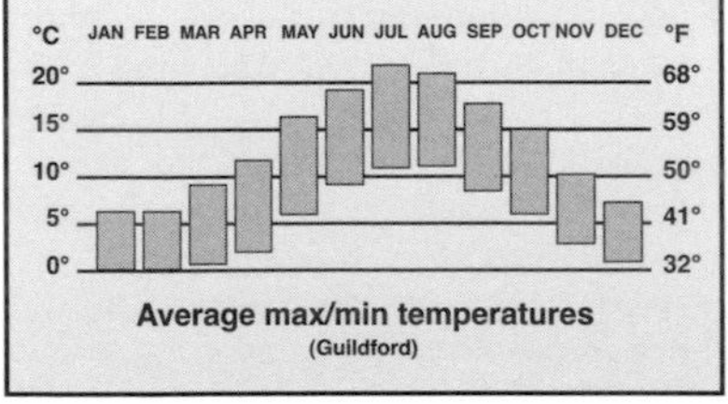

Average max/min temperatures
(Guildford)

TEMPERATURE

Temperatures are pleasantly warm during the summer and generally seldom drop below 0°C in the south-east in winter.

RAINFALL

Rain falls in every month of the year and is highest in winter as expected. England is affected by weather systems coming from the south-west containing a lot of rain.

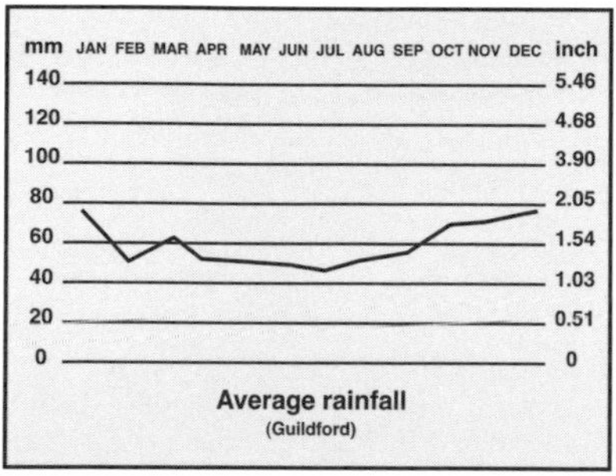

Average rainfall
(Guildford)

ANNUAL EVENTS

There are numerous village fêtes and fundraising events during the summer months and it's fun to go along if you happen to be in the village on the day.

But there are some annual events you should be aware of because it'll make finding accommodation difficult and prices usually go up.

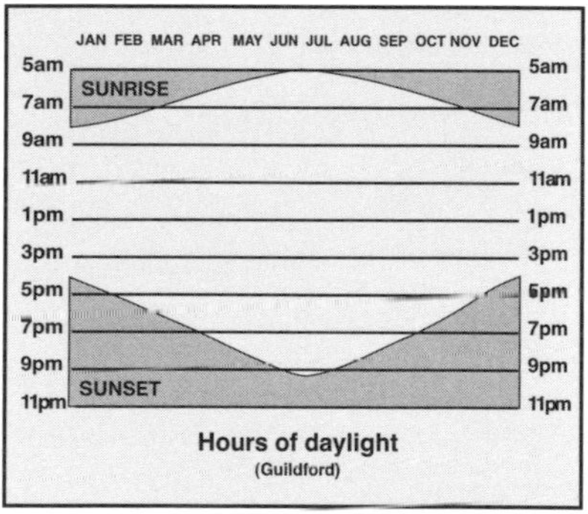

Hours of daylight
(Guildford)

- **Guildford** **Surrey County Show** (www.surreycountyshow.co.uk; Stoke Park; May Bank Holiday Monday) is a fine agricultural show with entertainment for all ages. **GuilFest** (www.guilfest.co.uk) the mid-July weekend three-day Glastonbury-like rock festival for respectable grown ups, a **book festival** (www.surrey.ac.uk) in October, and a **biennial international classical music** festival, the next in March 2007.

- **Detling** **Kent County Show** (www.kentcountyshowground.co.uk) This three-day show is held over a mid-July weekend. Show dates for 2006 are 14th-16th July. The showground is also home to the **annual country music festival** usually held in the first week of September.

- **Rochester** **Dickens Festival** (www.medway.gov.uk/tourism) Dickens' characters in period costumes flock to the streets of Rochester the first weekend of June and they're out again for a **Dickensian Christmas**, bah humbug, the first weekend of December. The city, quite the party place, has a **Son et Lumière** at the Castle and Cathedral the first week in September and a **food and drink** festival in October.

- **Canterbury** **Canterbury Festival** (www.canterburyfestival.co.uk) is a three-week celebration of the arts in the city and throughout Kent with over 200 events usually held in October attracting the likes of Van Morrison and Jo Brand.

VILLAGE AND

Place name (places in bold are directly on the NDW)	**Distance from previous place** (approx miles/km)	**Cash Machine/ Bank**	**Post Office**	**Tourist Information Centre (TIC)**
Farnham	0/0	✔	✔	
Seale	4.1/6.5 (.25)			
Puttenham	2.5/4			
Compton	1.7/2.7			
Shalford	2.6/4.1 (1.5)		✔	
Guildford	2.6/4.1 (1)	✔	✔	TIC
Chilworth	1.5/2.4 (1.25)		✔	
Albury	1/1.6 (1.25)		✔	
Newlands Corner	1/1.6			Countryside Centre
Shere	2/3.2 (.75)	Bank	✔	
Gomshall	1.1/1.7 (1.25)	✔	✔	
Holmbury St Mary	2/3.2 (2)		✔	
Ranmore Common	1.9/3 (.85)			
Westcott	1.9/3 (1.5)		✔	
Denbies Wine Estate	1.8/2.8			
Dorking	.7/1.1 (1.6)	✔	✔	TIC
Box Hill	1.1.6			Visitor Centre (NT)
Box Hill Village	1/1.6 (1)		✔	
Redhill	6/9.6 (1.8)	✔	✔	
Merstham	2/3.2			
Oxted	8/12.8	✔	✔	
Westerham	4.2/6.7 (1.4)	✔	✔	
Knockholt	2.7/4.3 (.25)			
Chevening	2.4/3.8 (.75)			
Dunton Green	.85/1.3			
Otford	1.8/2.8	✔	✔	
Kemsing	1.8/2.8 (.5)			
Wrotham	3.8/6	✔		
Trottiscliffe	2.6/4.1 (1.25)			
Ryarsh	2.1/3.3 (1.5)			
Cuxton	4.8/7.6		✔	
Rochester	2.3/3.6 (1.6)	✔	✔	TIC
Aylesford	4.6/7.3 (1.7)	✔	✔	
Detling	4.3/6.8		✔	
Thurnham	1.4/2.2			
Hollingbourne	3.9/6.2		✔	
Harrietsham	2.3/3.6 (1)		✔	
Lenham	2.5/4 (.6)		✔	
Charing	4/6.4 (.25)	✔	✔	
Westwell	2.5/4			
Eastwell	1.4/2.2			
Boughton Lees	.6/.9			
Boughton Aluph	1.3/2			
Chilham	4.4/7		✔	
Chartham Hatch/Chartham	3.6/5.7 (1.25)			
Canterbury	3.7/5.9	✔	✔	TIC
Bekesbourne	3.1/4.9 (.5)			
Bridge	.4/.6 (.5)	✔	✔	
Shepherdswell	6.8/10.8	✔	✔	
Dover	8.9/14.2	✔	✔	TIC
TOTAL DISTANCE	**131 miles/209km**			

Note: Places not in bold are a short distance from the path. Distances are given to the place on the path nearest to the village/town with the mileage from that point to the village/town in brackets

TOWN FACILITIES

Eating Place	Food Store	Campsite	Hostels (YHA/ YMCA – Y Centre)/ Camping barn (B)	B&B-style accommodation	Place name (places in bold are directly on the NDW)
✔✔✔	✔			✔✔✔	**Farnham**
✔					Seale
✔✔			B		**Puttenham**
✔✔				✔✔	**Compton**
✔✔✔	✔			✔✔	Shalford
✔✔✔	✔		Y Centre	✔✔✔	Guildford
✔	✔				Chilworth
✔	✔			✔	Albury
✔✔				✔	**Newlands Corner**
✔✔	✔			✔✔	Shere
✔✔	✔			✔	Gomshall
✔✔		✔	YHA	✔	Holmbury St Mary
		✔	YHA		**Ranmore Common**
✔✔	✔			✔	Westcott
✔✔				✔	**Denbies Wine Estate**
✔✔✔	✔			✔✔✔	Dorking
✔					**Box Hill**
✔	✔				Box Hill Village
✔✔✔	✔			✔✔✔	Redhill
✔✔✔	✔			✔	**Merstham**
✔✔✔	✔			✔✔	**Oxted**
✔✔✔	✔			✔✔	Westerham
✔✔					Knockholt
				✔✔	Chevening
✔✔	✔			✔	**Dunton Green**
✔✔	✔			✔✔	**Otford**
✔	✔				Kemsing
✔✔	✔	✔		✔✔✔	**Wrotham**
✔✔				✔	Trottiscliffe
✔				✔	Ryarsh
✔✔	✔			✔✔	**Cuxton**
✔✔✔	✔			✔✔✔	Rochester
✔✔	✔			✔✔✔	Aylesford
✔	✔				**Detling**
✔		✔*		✔✔	**Thurnham**
✔✔	✔	✔			**Hollingbourne**
✔	✔			✔	Harrietsham
✔✔✔	✔			✔✔	Lenham
✔✔	✔			✔✔	Charing
		✔			**Westwell**
✔				✔	**Eastwell**
✔					**Boughton Lees**
				✔✔	**Boughton Aluph**
✔✔	✔			✔✔✔	**Chilham**
✔✔	✔			✔✔	**Charham Hatch**/Chartham
✔✔✔	✔	✔	YHA	✔✔✔	**Canterbury**
✔					Bekesbourne
✔✔	✔			✔	Bridge
	✔			✔✔	**Shepherdswell**
✔✔✔	✔	✔**	YHA	✔✔✔	**Dover**

Note: * = at Coldblow Farm; ** at Hawthorn Farm, nr Martin Mill Railway Station

Eating place/B&B-style accommodation: ✔ = one place, ✔✔ = two or three, ✔✔✔ = four or more

Itineraries

Most people tackle the North Downs Way west to east and Part 4 has been written that way. It's perfectly possible to walk it in the opposite direction (the waymarking is in place) but there are advantages in doing it west to east (see below).

To help you plan your walk there is a **planning map** (see map opposite inside back cover) and a **table of village/town facilities** (see pp22-3); the latter gives a snap shot of the essential information you will need regarding accommodation possibilities and services. You could follow or adapt one of the suggested itineraries (see pp25-6) which are based on preferred type of accommodation and walking speeds. There is also a list of recommended linear **day** and **weekend walks** on p27 which cover the best of the North Downs Way, all of which are well served by public transport. The public transport map and table are on pp37-40. Once you have an idea of your approach turn to **Part 4** for detailed information on accommodation, places to eat and other services in each village and town on the route. Also in Part 4 you will find summaries of the route to accompany the detailed trail maps.

SUGGESTED ITINERARIES

The itineraries in the boxes on pp25-6 are based on different accommodation types (camping, hostels/bunkhouses and B&Bs), with each one divided into three alternatives depending on your walking speed. They are only suggestions so you can adapt them to suit your circumstances. Some accommodation and public transport options may be a considerable distance off the trail and where this is the case it is noted in Part 4 and on the maps where appropriate. Be sure to add travelling time before and after the walk. This is especially important in winter when there are fewer hours of daylight.

WHICH DIRECTION?

Most walkers tackle the path west to east. There are a number of advantages. The prevailing wind tends to be at your back as is the sun if you get a later start. As most others are going this direction, if you are walking alone but want some company you can fall in step with them. Also it's worth having a destination to look forward to and Canterbury, though not at the end, is a worthy penultimate goal. And like a river on its journey it seems natural to follow the route to the sea.

SIDE TRIPS

The North Downs Way is plenty long enough to satisfy energetic walkers. Yet the path cuts through a part of Britain that's packed with castles, grand country houses and sites of great antiquity. A glance at the Ordnance Survey map will

CAMPING

Night	Relaxed pace: Place	Relaxed pace: Approx Distance miles/km	Medium pace: Place	Medium pace: Approx Distance miles/km	Fast pace: Place	Fast pace: Approx Distance miles/km
0	Farnham*		Farnham*		Farnham*	
1	Compton*	8.3/13.2	Albury*	13.4/21.4	Ranmore Common (Cmn)	21.4/34.2
2	Shere*	8.1/12.9	Ranmore Cmn	8/12.8	Oxted*	20.5/32.8
3	Ranmore Cmn	5/8	Merstham*	12.5/20	Wrotham	17.5/28
4	Redhill*	10.5/16.8	Westerham*	12.2/19.5	Rochester*	11.8/18.8
5	Oxted*	10/16	Wrotham	13.3/21.2	Thurnham	11.4/18.2
6	Otford*	11.9/19	Rochester*	11.8/18.8	Boughton Aluph*	17.4/27.8
7	Wrotham	5.6/8.9	Hollingbourne	14.2/22.7	Canterbury	11.7/18.7
8	Cuxton*	9.5/15.2	Boughton Aluph *	14.6/23.3	Dover	19.2/30.7
9	Thurnham	13.7/20.8	Canterbury	11.7/18.7		
10	Dunn St	14.1/22.5	Shepherdswell*	10.3/16.4		
11	Chilham*	7.7/12.3	Dover	8.9/14.2		
12	Canterbury	7.3/11.6				
13	Shepherdswell*	10.3/16.4				
14	Dover	8.9/14.2				

* No campsite but other accommodation is available

STAYING IN B&Bs

Night	Relaxed pace: Place	Relaxed pace: Approx Distance miles/km	Medium pace: Place	Medium pace: Approx Distance miles/km	Fast pace: Place	Fast pace: Approx Distance miles/km
0	Farnham		Farnham		Farnham	
1	Compton	8.3/13.2	Albury	13.4/21.4	Gomshall	17.5/28
2	Gomshall	9.2/14.7	Dorking	10.5/16.8	Merstham	16.4/26.2
3	Dorking	6.4/10.2	Oxted	18/28.8	Otford	19.9/31.8
4	Redhill	8/12.8	Otford	11.9/19	Rochester	17.4/27.8
5	Oxted	10/16	Cuxton	15.1/24.1	Harrietsham	16.5/26.4
6	Otford	11.95/19.1	Hollingbourne	16.5/26.4	Canterbury	24/38.4
7	Trottiscliffe	8.2/13.1	Boughton Aluph	14	Dover	19.2/30.7
8	Rochester	9.2/14.7	Canterbury	11.7/18.7		
9	Thurnham	10.3/16.4	Shepherdswell	10.3/16.4		
10	Lenham	8.7/13.9	Dover	8.9/10.3		
11	Boughton Aluph	9.8/15.6				
12	Canterbury	11.7/18.7				
13	Shepherdswell	10.3/16.4				
14	Dover	8.9				

STAYING IN BUNKHOUSES/HOSTELS

	Relaxed pace		Medium pace		Fast pace	
Night	Place	Approx Distance miles/km	Place	Approx Distance miles/km	Place	Approx Distance miles/km
0	Farnham*		Farnham*		Farnham*	
1	Puttenham	6.6/10.5	Albury*	13.4/21.4	Ranmore Common (Cmn)	21.4/34.2
2	Guildford	4.3/6.8	Ranmore Cmn	8/12.8	Oxted*	20.5/32.8
3	Ranmore Cmn	10.5/16.8	Merstham*	12.5/20	Wrotham*	17.5/28
4	Redhill*	10.5/16.8	Westerham*	12.2/19.5	Rochester*	11.8/18.8
5	Oxted*	10/16	Wrotham*	13.3/21.2	Thurnham	11.418.24
6	Otford*	11.9/19	Rochester *	11.8/18.8	Boughton Aluph*	17.4/27.8
7	Wrotham*	5.6/8.9	Thurnham	11.4/18.2	Canterbury	11.7/18.7
8	Cuxton*	9.5/15.2	Charing*	11.6/18.5	Dover	19.2/30.7
9	Thurnham	13.7/21.9	Chilham*	10.2/16.3		
10	Charing*	11.6/18.5	Canterbury	11.6		
11	Chilham*	10.2/16.3	Shepherdswell*	10.3/16.4		
12	Canterbury	7.3/11.6	Dover	8.9/14.2		
13	Shepherdswell*	10.3/16.4				
14	Dover	8.9/14.2				

* No bunkhouses or hostels but other accommodation is available

give you some idea for side trips and possible walking trails to them as well as other long-distance paths such as the Greensand Way and Weald Way. A detailed description is beyond the scope of this book.

Those inspired to try more Downs walking may want to tackle the South Downs Way for which there is a Trailblazer guide (see p192). The Downs Link, a 32-mile bridleway utilizing a disused railway line links the North Downs Way at St Martha's (see Map 7, p83) with the South Downs Way, near Steyning.

What to take

What you take depends on personal preference and experience. As many walking the North Downs Way may be new to long-distance walking the suggestions below are a guide. What you must ensure is that you have all the equipment necessary to make the trip safe and comfortable.

KEEP IT LIGHT

There are a number of ways to do this. Buy the lightest equipment you can afford. Choose the smaller of pack sizes so you don't overpack (see p28).

❑ HIGHLIGHTS

There is nothing like walking the entire length of a long-distance path in one go but some people don't have the time and others want to experience only the best of what the trail has to offer. For details of public transport to and from the start and finish of each walk see pp36-40. The weekend walks can be split in two to suit day walkers, or combined and completed in a day by those who want a challenge. That would, however, leave little time for sightseeing which is a pity on this culturally rich route.

Day walks

- **Farnham to Guildford** 11miles/17.6km (see pp65-79) Walk through farmland, woodland and along sandy bridleways to Guildford where there is plenty of sightseeing. Visit the ancient burial tumulus at Puttenham Heath, itself geologically unusual in this area of chalk, and stop at the excellent Watts Gallery and the Cemetery Chapel, Compton (see p72), where you can also choose from 40 teas at Compton Tea Shop.
- **Guildford to Shere/Gomshall** 6½miles/10.5km (see pp79-88) A relaxed pace crossing the River Wey, the path climbs through woods (bluebell-filled in spring) to the top of St Martha's and Newlands Corner from where there are great views on a clear day. After 5½ miles there is the option to detour to Shere, Surrey's prettiest village, from where it's a short walk to Gomshall. Trains go from there to Guildford, Reading, Dorking, and Redhill.
- **Gomshall to Box Hill** 7½miles/12km (see pp89-98) Classic woodland walking emerging at Ranmore Common and the butterfly-/wildflower-rich habitats of the chalk grassland at Box Hill where two-thirds of all Britain's butterfly species (see p48 and p98) have been recorded. There are good train connections at Westhumble or return to Dorking.
- **Otford to Rochester** 17miles/27.2km (see pp118-34) Not the prettiest or quietest of sections and one of the longest but it passes through Kemsing Downs, a significant chalk grassland habitat, the woods of Trosley Country Park, with a short detour to see one of Kent's best-known megaliths, Coldrum Stones. Much of the walk is in woodland and surprisingly isolated from the industrial Medway valley towns to emerge by pretty Upper Bush into Cuxton before crossing the M2 and Channel Tunnel Rail link. Rochester is 35-40 minutes off the trail from where there are fast train connections to London, Canterbury and Dover. Consider an overnight stay there – the Norman Castle, England's second oldest cathedral, and Restoration House are well worth visiting.

Weekend walks

- **Farnham to Dorking** 24miles/38.4km (see p65-95) This is easy walking through farmland, heath and woodland to overnight in Guildford (11miles/17.6km). After a climb to St Martha's – the Pilgrims' Church – with wonderful views and a further climb across Albury Downs the path gains the ridgeline at Newlands Corner, and follows a mostly wooded drove road to descend through England's largest vineyard, Denbies Wine Estate, with views to Box Hill on the outskirts of Dorking (13miles/20.8km). Two castles, one cathedral, a gallery to eminent Victorian artist, George Frederic Watts, a Gilbert Scott church, WWII fortifications, good wine, and views that stretch for miles on a clear day – not bad for two days' walking.
- **Charing to Canterbury** 21½miles/34.4km (see pp148-64) Follow in the footsteps of pilgrims passing the ruined archbishop's palace in Charing to follow the Pilgrims' Way emerging from dense woodland into the tranquil landscape of Eastwell. Climb to Soakham Downs with extensive views over the Stour valley and emerge from the King's Wood to overnight in Chilham with its remarkably preserved medieval square (14¼miles/22.8km). The following day's walk is through Kent's orchard country before arriving at Canterbury, worth at least a day's exploration (7¼miles/11.6km).

Before packing lay out only what you deem essential. With the exception of the first-aid kit (see p30) ask whether or not you will use the item every day. If not, consider very carefully whether or not to pack it. Remember on the North Downs Way you are not so far away from a town or village that you can't get something you've forgotten even if it does mean interrupting your walk.

HOW TO CARRY IT

The size and type of **backpack** you carry will depend on how you plan to walk the North Downs Way. If you are day hiking or using a holiday service that transports your luggage at a minimum you should have a small **daypack** filled with those items that you will need during the day: water bottle, this book, a map, sun screen, hat, gloves, wet-weather gear, some food, camera, money, first-aid kit and so on.

If you are hiking the route end to end with no baggage service you will have to consider carefully the type of backpack you use. Its size will depend largely on where you plan to stay but do try to err on the smaller of sizes as it's so easy to overpack and thus overburden yourself.

With all backpacks make sure it is adjustable so you can fit it to your back length and body shape – there are both men- and women-specific fits now – and it should have adjustable chest and hip belts to distribute the weight and improve stability. Some shops allow you to take a pack home so you can try it out by filling it with what you intend to take; if it's not right you can then try a different model.

Campers bringing a tent, cooking equipment and food will probably need a 65- to 75-litre pack. Walkers staying in bunkhouses or hostels that provide bedding and cooking equipment will probably get away with a 40- to 55-litre pack and if you stay at B&Bs you should need no more than a 30- to 40-litre pack. A small daypack is useful so you can carry essentials on a day off around town or when leaving the main pack at your lodgings. Don't rely on manufacturers' claims to water resistance – it doesn't take a long shower to soak through most packs. Pack everything inside in **waterproof liners** or **canoe bags** or save weight and money by using strong plastic bags or bin liners.

FOOTWEAR

Boots

Quality is remembered long after the price is forgotten; invest in a pair of **suitable** boots. The North Downs Way has few sustained ascents or descents, is on a generally firm track with little rough or stony ground but it can be muddy. Therefore you do not need high, stiff-as-a-board boots that make you feel as if you're walking in a diving bell. My preference is for Lowa, a German brand mid-cut trail boot. They're waterproof (Gore-Tex lined) which is essential and provide sufficient ankle support but retain residual flexibility for comfort and don't require much breaking in. Also I like the fact that the fitting is wider than on other brands. If you are camping you may need to consider a boot with greater ankle support to cope with carrying a heavier pack. It is money well spent. When you go to try boots do so later in the day when your feet have swelled a little so you get a proper fit and also try on several brands. After completing the North Downs Way if you like the boots so much buy a second pair if you can afford it so you'll always have a spare. Manufacturers frequently change the last shape or style or discontinue a line.

Some people like to bring a change of shoes for the evening. If you are carrying all your own gear consider something lightweight like flip flops or **sports sandals**.

Socks

Modern hi-tech socks are very comfortable if you choose a high-quality pair designed for walking. Again don't stint on money – you are dressing the power house of the trail and the state of your feet is essential to your enjoyment. Others swear by a liner sock under a thicker wool sock – each to their own but the modern fibres dry quicker. Two pairs are fine, three are ample. You can wash socks each evening leaving them to dry overnight.

CLOTHES

British weather is notoriously changeable and you will need clothes that can cope with the sun, rain and cold. If you are a 'fashionista' you'll be glad to know that colours and styles in outdoor clothing change with the seasons and there's no limit to how much you can spend. But you needn't bankrupt yourself. You need clothes that are lightweight, durable, quick drying and that can keep you warm, cool and dry depending on the weather conditions. While you can get away with hiking in ordinary cotton-based clothes, provided you have a waterproof outer layer, you will feel more comfortable in specialized outdoor clothes – indeed they are even becoming street fashion. The number of retailers also means they have to work hard to keep prices keen.

On this trail you will encounter cyclists and horse riders and in the short sections which are by ways you may encounter off-road vehicles, though the state of the tracks suggests that this is not so common. You will also need to cross country lanes and roads at times so I go for bright colours, with the exception of trousers (see p30), so I'm as visible as possible to others; but this is a matter of personal preference.

Modern hi-tech outdoor clothes still follow the basic two- or three-layer principle, with an inner base layer to transport sweat away from your skin, a mid-layer for warmth and an outer layer to protect you from the wind and rain. A thin lightweight **thermal top** of a synthetic material is ideal as the base layer as it draws sweat away from your body keeping you cool in hot weather and warm when worn under other clothes in cold weather. Some walkers like to bring a **shirt** of synthetic material, giving coverage to the neck, and somewhere to pack small items in the pockets and they may want to smarten up in the evening. A light- to mid-weight **polyester fleece** over this will help keep you warm in cold weather. Fleeces are ideal trekking gear being light, fairly water-resistant, quick drying, remain warm when wet and pack down small in backpacks. A **waterproof jacket** is essential and 'breathable' jackets help to cut down the build up of condensation. In dry weather this layer can be worn to keep the wind out.

Leg wear

Most modern **trekking trousers** are a good investment providing a light, durable and quick-drying trouser. Go for a dark colour in trousers as this hides trail dirt much better. Jeans should never be worn as they are heavy and, when wet, cold and binding on the legs. A pair of **waterproof trousers** is essential and will help keep you warm on cold days, while on really hot sunny days you may wish you had brought shorts – some trekking trousers zip off and convert to shorts – but be warned parts of the North Downs Way can be overgrown in summer and stinging nettles a problem. Also if you are fair skinned you'll have to take extra precautions against sunburn. Thermal **longjohns** are useful if camping and could come in handy in winter.

Gaiters are not necessary but they provide extra protection when walking through muddy ground and when the vegetation around the trail is dripping wet after bad weather or early morning dew. They also help keep you looking presentable when you pitch up at the pub.

Underwear

Three changes of underwear are plenty and you may want to invest in the kind made from modern wickable fabrics that can be washed and dried overnight. Because backpacks can cause bra straps to dig painfully into the skin, women may find a **sports bra** more comfortable.

Other clothes

Don't leave home without a **warm hat** and **gloves** as you never know when you might need them. A sun hat is useful in summer – being fair skinned I always wear one – and carry a **swimsuit** if you intend to take a relaxing plunge at the end of the day. Public swimming pools are noted in Part 4 of this guide.

TOILETRIES

Once again, take the minimum. **Soap**, **towel**, a **toothbrush** and **toothpaste** are pretty much essential (although those staying in B&Bs will find that most provide soap and towels anyway). Some **toilet paper** could also prove vital on the trail, particularly if using public toilets (which occasionally run out of it). If defecating outdoors use a **lighter** for burning the paper and a **plastic trowel** to bury the evidence. Other items to consider taking are: **razor**; **deodorant**; **tampons/sanitary towels** and a high-factor **sun-screen** (especially if you are walking in the summer and/or are fair skinned).

FIRST-AID KIT

A small first-aid kit packed in a waterproof container could prove useful for those emergencies that occur along the trail. Carry some **aspirin** or **paraceta-**

mol in an old film canister for relief from mild pain; **plasters/Band Aids** for minor cuts; **'Second Skin'** or **'Compeed'** for blisters; a **bandage** for holding dressings, splints, or limbs in place and for supporting a sprained ankle; **an elastic support** for a weak knee, ankle or arches; a small selection of different-sized **sterile dressings** for wounds; **porous adhesive tape**; **antiseptic wipes**; **antiseptic cream**; **tweezers**; **scissors** and **safety pins** – useful also for attaching wet clothes to your backpack so they can dry as you walk. If you develop heat rash or suffer chaffing **nappy cream** works wonders. For information on outdoor safety, avoidance of hazards and dealing with emergencies see pp60-2.

GENERAL ITEMS

Essentials

Everybody should have a **torch**, at least a one-litre **water bottle or pouch**, **spare batteries** and a **penknife**. Carry a **plastic bag** for your litter. A **whistle** (see p60 for details of the international distress signal) can fit in a shirt pocket and carries further than any amount of shouting if attention is needed. Carry some **emergency food** such as raisins, prunes or dried apricots which will give an instant energy boost (see p60) and a **watch** with an alarm to get you up in the morning. Those with weak knees will find a **walking pole** or **sticks** essential. You may want to protect your eyes from the sun by wearing **sunglasses** (or clip-on shades if you wear glasses).

Some people find a **mobile phone** invaluable. There is reception throughout the North Downs Way and it is very useful to confirm bookings or directions to your accommodation or let them know, as a courtesy, that you are arriving early or late. But be considerate on the trail and consider switching it off. Walkers come to find peace and quiet and don't appreciate ring tones and one-way conversations about the latest footie results.

Usefuls

Some will think a **camera** is essential but a **notebook** may be a better way of recording your impressions; with a camera you often get too busy composing the picture and rarely appreciate the view. A **map** is a good idea if you are planning to explore off the North Downs Way. A **book** may pass the time on days off, or on train and bus journeys, but you'll have to consider how much extra weight you want to carry. Often a period of reflection as you write up your notes is time well spent. With **binoculars** you'll get a closer look at wildlife and trees but this adds extra weight.

CAMPING GEAR

Campers and those intending to stay in the camping barns en route will need a sleeping bag. A two- to three-season bag should suffice for summer. In addition, campers will need: a decent bivvy bag or tarp, if travelling light, or a tent; a sleeping mat; fuel and stove; cutlery/pans; a cup; and a scrubber for washing up if you intend doing any cooking.

MONEY

Cash machines (ATMs) are common along the North Downs Way; many post offices and shops along the trail have installed them. There are also plenty of banks with cash machines in the larger towns. Many restaurants and shops accept debit and credit cards but not all do, including many B&Bs. As a result, you should always have a fair amount of cash (at least £50) with you just in case and a **cheque book** from a British bank is a useful back up. See also p16.

MAPS

The hand-drawn maps in this book cover the trail at a scale of 1:20,000, better than any other scale currently available for the whole route and notes, tips and comments are written on the maps so you should not need any others if you are walking just the North Downs Way. But if you want to explore further afield it is a good idea to have **Ordnance Survey** (☎ 08456-050505, 💻 www.ordnancesurvey.co.uk) maps. The OS Landranger series (1:50,000) for this area are Nos 178, 179, 186, 187, 188 and 189 (£6.49 each). The larger-scale OS Explorer series (1:25,000) are Nos 137, 138, 145, 146, 147, 148, 150 (£7.49 each).

Harvey (☎ 01786-841202, 💻 www.harveymaps.co.uk) produce strip maps (1:40,000) covering the North Downs Way West (Farnham–Medway) and North Downs Way East (Medway–Dover) at £9.95 each.

While it is expensive to buy all these maps, members of the **Ramblers' Association** (see box opposite) can borrow up to 10 Ordnance Survey maps for a period of six weeks at 30p per map from their library.

RECOMMENDED READING

Some of the following books can be found in the tourist information centres and they may also have a number of books about the towns and villages en route, usually printed by small, local publishers.

General guidebooks

For general guidebooks, both Rough Guides and Lonely Planet publish guides to England. For a delightfully chatty read about the Downs habitat and British landscape in general with wonderful hand-drawn illustrations, obtain a copy of the out-of-print *Reading the Landscape of Europe* by May Theilgaard Watts through 💻 www.abebooks.com.

Other guidebooks

Other guides to the trail include Cicerone's *The North Downs Way* by Kev Reynolds and Aurum Press's *North Downs Way* by Neil Curtis and Jim Walker. For a thematic treatment of the North Downs through the eyes of painters, poets and novelists Kent County Council (☎ 08458-247600, 💻 www.kent.gov.uk) have produced a richly illustrated guide, *North Downs Way: An Inspirational Journey*, for a very reasonable £4.95. If you are inspired to try out other long-distance walks, check out the other titles in the Trailblazer series; see p192.

Flora and fauna field guides

The *RSPB Pocket Birds* is beautifully illustrated as you'd expect from a Dorling Kindersley publication and will help you identify any birds you're likely to see. It's light enough to bring with you as are the Collins Gem guides to *Trees* and *Wild Flowers*. The Field Studies Council (⊒ www.field-studies-council.org) publishes a series of *Identification Guides* (fold out charts) which are also practical. Otherwise make notes as you go and look up the species when you get home.

❑ SOURCES OF FURTHER INFORMATION

Trail information The latest trail information including any diversions to the route can be found on ⊒ www.nationaltrail.co.uk/Northdowns.

Tourist Information Centres (TICs) Many towns around Britain have a TIC which provides all manner of locally specific information for visitors and an accommodation-booking service (for which there is usually a charge). The TICs along or near the North Downs Way are at Guildford (see p78), Dorking (see p94), Rochester (see p134), Canterbury (see p164) and Dover (see p180).

Tourism South East (☎ 02380-625400, ⊒ www.visitsoutheastengland.com) There is a whole host of information on its website about accommodation, things to do and see, and upcoming festivals and events as there is also at ⊒ www.visitsurrey.com and ⊒ www.kenttourism.co.uk.

Organizations for walkers

- **The Long Distance Walkers' Association** (⊒ www.ldwa.org.uk) An association for people with the common interest of long-distance walking in rural, mountainous and moorland areas. Membership includes a journal, *Strider,* three times per year giving details of challenge events and local group walks as well as articles on the subject. Information on over 600 long-distance paths is presented in the LDWA *Long Distance Walkers' Handbook*. Membership is £13 per year. There is a memorial bench to LDWA co-founder Alan Blatchford at Tanners Hatch youth hostel (see Map 12, p91).
- **The Ramblers' Association** (☎ 020-7339 8500, ⊒ www.ramblers.org.uk, 2nd Floor, Camelford House, 87-90 Albert Embankment, London SE1 7TW) Looks after the interests of walkers throughout Britain. They publish a large amount of useful information including their *Yearbook* (£5.99 to non-members), a full directory of services for walkers. Membership is £24 for an individual; joint membership is £32.
- **The Backpackers' Club** (⊒ www.backpackersclub.co.uk) A club aimed at people who are involved or interested in lightweight camping through walking, cycling, skiing, canoeing, etc. They produce a quarterly magazine, provide members with a comprehensive advisory and information service on all aspects of backpacking, organize weekend trips and also publish a farm-pitch directory. Membership is £12 per year.

❑ GETTING TO BRITAIN

Air

There are plenty of cheap flights to London's airports: Heathrow, Gatwick, Luton, London City and Stansted. The most convenient for the trail are Heathrow, via the Rail Air Coach link to Woking and Guildford, and Gatwick Airport, with services to Redhill. You can also take the Heathrow Express train to Paddington and then London Underground to Waterloo and onwards to Farnham.

London City airport has good transport links on the Docklands Light Railway to Bank station on the London Underground with easy connections to London Waterloo and onwards to Farnham.

Far less convenient is Luton. There is a free shuttle from the airport to Luton Airport Parkway and Thameslink trains to London King's Cross Thameslink and then London Underground to Waterloo. Thameslink also stops at Redhill from where there are train connections to stations on the North Downs Way.

Easybus, National Express and Greenline coaches go to London Victoria from Luton. The quickest way from Stansted is to take the Stansted Express rail service to London Liverpool St and then London Underground to Waterloo and onwards to the start of the trail.

From Europe by train

Eurostar (🖳 www.eurostar.com), the high-speed rail link, travels between Paris and Brussels to London via Ashford International from where there are easy connections to stations along the North Downs Way.

The Eurostar terminal in London is currently at Waterloo station but is expected to move to King's Cross St Pancras station in summer 2007. Both Waterloo and King's Cross St Pancras have connections to the London Underground and to all other main railway stations in London. From Waterloo you can catch a South West Trains service to Farnham and the start of the walk. For more information contact Rail Europe (🖳 www.raileurope.co.uk).

From Europe by bus

Eurolines (🖳 www.eurolines.com) have a huge network of long-distance bus services connecting over 500 cities in 25 European countries to London. But when compared to the prices of some of the budget airlines and once expenses such as food for the journey are taken into account; the time it takes and the condition you're in on arrival having sat like a pretzel for hours, the rock-bottom prices may not be such a bargain after all.

From Europe by ferry and car

The shortest sea crossing from Europe is Calais–Dover and regular services are run by **SeaFrance** (🖳 www.seafrance.com), and **Hoverspeed** (🖳 www.hoverspeed.com); the journey takes about 40 minutes.

P & O Ferries (🖳 www.poferries.com) have a service twice weekly from Bilbao to Portsmouth (29 hours) and run frequent passenger ferries between Calais and Dover. The journey takes about 75 minutes. **Brittany Ferries** (🖳 www.brittany-ferries.com) sails from Santander and Roscoff to Plymouth as well as from Cherbourg and Caen to Poole and Portsmouth.

Eurotunnel (🖳 www.eurotunnel.com) operates the shuttle train service for vehicles via the Channel Tunnel between Calais and Folkestone. There are over ten ferry companies plying routes between all the major North Sea and Channel ports of mainland Europe and the ports on Britain's eastern and southern coasts.

Getting to and from the North Downs Way

Surrey and Kent have excellent transport services and with its proximity to London the North Downs Way is one of the most easily accessible national trails. Travelling to it by public transport is convenient, reasonably inexpensive and makes sense.

NATIONAL TRANSPORT

Train

You are only ever an hour or two from London on the North Downs Way with convenient and frequent train services to Farnham, Guildford, Dorking, Redhill, Merstham, Oxted, Otford, Rochester, Hollingbourne, Harrietsham, Lenham, Charing, Chilham, Canterbury, Bekesbourne, Shepherdswell and Dover. At a minimum you can expect at least one train an hour operating these routes and from some mainline stations up to four an hour. Trains to stations on or close to the North Downs Way depart from London Waterloo, London Victoria and London Charing Cross.

All timetable and fare information can be found at **National Rail Enquiries** (☎ 0845-748 4950, 24hrs, 💻 www.nationalrail.co.uk). Tickets can also be bought online at 💻 www.thetrainline.com and 💻 www.qjump.co.uk. Or you can look on the websites of the train companies concerned (see box below).

Coach

National Express (☎ 0870-580 8080, 8am-10pm daily, 💻 www.nationalexpress.com) is the principal coach (long-distance bus) operator in Britain. Coach travel is generally cheaper but longer than travel by train. Whilst there are

❑ **Train-operating companies serving stations on/adjacent to the NDW**

- **South West Trains** (☎ 0845-600 0650, 💻 www.southwesttrains.co.uk) Services to Farnham, Guildford, Dorking, Box Hill & Westhumble
- **Southern** (☎ 0845-127 2920, 💻 www.southernrailway.com) Services to Dorking, Box Hill & Westhumble, Oxted
- **South Eastern Trains** (☎ 0870-603 0405, 💻 www.setrains.co.uk) Services to Redhill, Merstham, Otford, Kemsing, Borough Green & Wrotham, Aylesford, Cuxton, Rochester, Maidstone East, Hollingbourne, Harrietsham, Lenham, Charing, Ashford International, Chilham, Chartham, Bekesbourne, Shepherdswell, Canterbury East, Canterbury West, Dover Priory
- **First Great Western Link** (☎ 0845-600 5604, 💻 www.firstgreatwestern.co.uk) Services to Shalford, Chilworth, Gomshall, Dorking West, Dorking Deepdene, Redhill, Gatwick Airport
- **Thameslink** (☎ 0845-330 6333, 💻 www.thameslink.co.uk) Services to Redhill and Gatwick Airport

excellent services between London, Dover and Canterbury – more than 15 departures daily – there is only one service at 6.30pm from London to Farnham and the start of the walk so you would then have the cost of an extra night's accommodation. But if starting at Guildford there are eight departures a day from London. There is one service a day from Portsmouth to Farnham (arriving at 8.05am). National Express also operates a Rail Air Coach link from Heathrow to Woking (daily, 2/hr). See public transport map and table pp37-40.

Car

The south-east of England is criss-crossed by roads and motorways and the North Downs Way itself crosses the M25, M20, M23 and M2 on its journey east to Dover. You can, of course, drive to the start of the trail but then you have the problem of safe parking and getting back to it at the end of the walk. With so many train services and the roads so busy do your bit for the environment and don't bother to drive.

LOCAL TRANSPORT

The number of train stations and bus services on or close to the route opens up the possibility of linear walks throughout the length of the North Downs Way lasting several hours or days without having to park a car, worry about it and then figure out a way of getting back to it.

The map on pp38-9 gives an overview of the principal direct routes of use to walkers and an indication of the frequency of services in both directions and who you should contact for further information. Both traveline (see below) and national rail enquiries (see p35) have a text-messaging service sending details of the next few departures from specific stops to your mobile phone. In both cases the service costs 25p plus of course the cost of sending a message. See the relevant websites for further details.

If the relevant operator's enquiry line is closed contact the information service **traveline** (☎ 0870-608 2608, 7am-10pm, 🖳 www.traveline.org.uk), which has public transport information for the whole of the UK. Alternatively try 🖳 www.transportdirect.info for a door-to-door journey-planning service. Tourist information centres along the North Downs Way provide, free of charge, a comprehensive local transport timetable. Route maps are also available online at 🖳 www.surreycc.gov.uk/passenger_transport and 🖳 www.kent.gov.uk/countrysideaccess.

One-way rural bus fares can be expensive and services sometimes infrequent so you may find it cheaper and more convenient to take a taxi for short hops, especially if there are two or more of you. Fares generally cost £3 minimum charge and £1 per mile thereafter. For a comprehensive listing of taxi services from train stations visit 🖳 www.traintaxi.co.uk.

Note that on many bus routes there is no Sunday service, or a limited one. Train services are better, Kemsing being the only station not to have any trains on a Sunday.

PUBLIC TRANSPORT TABLE

Surrey Hills Explorer Tours (☎ 01372-452048, 💻 www.nationaltrust.org.uk)
NT1 The Surrey Hills Explorer bus is a hop-on, hop-off service (£4/2 adults/children), operating between March/April and October, with a commentary along the route by a Blue Badge Guide. There are two routes – Vistas & Villages and The Heritage Trail. Contact them for a copy of the timetable and further information.
- **Vistas & Villages** Dorking South St, Dorking Station, Denbies Wine Estate, Burford Bridge Hotel, Polesden Lacey, Hatchlands Park, Newlands Corner, Shere, Abinger, Leith Hill (Broadmore Common), Westcott and back to Dorking (circular route), Saturdays and Good Friday 3-4/day
- **The Heritage Trail** The route is the same as above to Polesden Lacey then it goes to Clandon Park, Hatchlands Park, Ranmore Common and Dorking, Sundays and Bank Holiday Mondays 3-4/day.

Stagecoach Hants & Surrey (☎ 0845-121 0180, 💻 www.stagecoachbus.com)
46 Guildford to Aldershot via Compton and Farnham, Mon-Sat 8-10/day
X64 Winchester to Guildford via Farnham and Puttenham, Mon-Sat 11/day
547 Guildford to The Sands via Puttenham and Seale, Tue and Fri only 1/day

Surrey Connect Centra Passenger Services (☎ 01932-859250)
516 Dorking to Epsom via Betchworth and Box Hill, Mon-Sat 3/day

Arriva (☎ 0870-120 1088, 💻 www.arrivabus.co.uk)
21 Guildford to Strood Green via Shalford, Chilworth, Albury, Shere, Gomshall, Holmbury St Mary, Westcott Green, Dorking, Mon-Sat 5/day
24 Cranleigh to Guildford via Shalford, Mon-Sat 8/day
25 Cranleigh to Guildford via Shalford, Chilworth, Albury, Shere and Gomshall, Mon-Sat 6/day
32 Guildford to Redhill via Shalford, Chilworth, Albury, Shere, Westcott Green, Dorking, Strood Green, Betchworth and Reigate, Mon-Sat 8-10/day
70 Maidstone to Borough Green, Mon-Fri 1/hr, Sat 2/hr
135 Chatham to Maidstone via Rochester, Warren Wood, Burham, Eccles and Aylesford, Sunday 5/day (operated by Mann's Travel ☎ 01474 358194)
142 Kit's Coty to Chatham via Blue Bell Hill, Cookham Wood and Rochester, Mon-Sat 4/day
151 Chatham to West Malling via Rochester and Cuxton, Mon-Sat 1/hr, Sun 5/day
155 Chatham to Maidstone via Rochester, Borstal, Wouldham and Aylesford, Mon-Sat 2-3/hour
308 Sevenoaks to Bluewater via Borough Green, Wrotham, Vigo and Gravesend Mon-Sat 1/hr, Vigo to Bluewater via Gravesend only Sun 4-6/day
333 Maidstone to Faversham via Detling, Mon-Sat 1/hr
335 Maidstone to Canterbury via Detling and Sittingbourne, Sun 5/day
425 Sevenoaks to Kemsing via Seal, Mon-Sat 1/hr between 10am and 5pm
431 Sevenoaks circular route via Otford and Dunton Green, Mon-Fri 4-5/day, Sat 3/day
432 Sevenoaks circular route via Dunton Green and Otford, Mon-Fri 4-5/day Sat 3/day ie the same route as the 431 but in the opposite direction
433 Sevenoaks to Heaverham via Otford and Kemsing, Mon-Sat 3/day
434 Sevenoaks to Shoreham via Otford, Mon-Sat 2-3/day
703 Maidstone to Bluewater via Cuxton, Mon-Sat 2-3/day

(continued on p40)

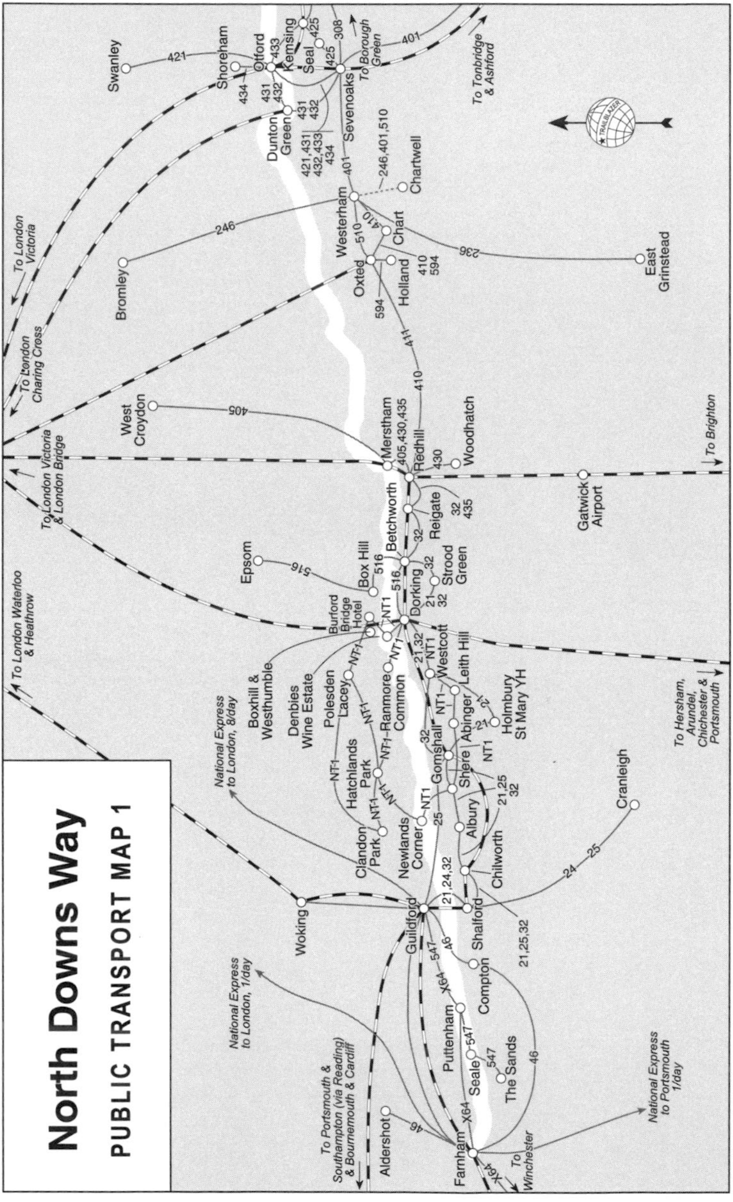
North Downs Way
PUBLIC TRANSPORT MAP 1
Swanley
Shoreham
Otford
Kemsing
Seal
Sevenoaks
Dunton Green
To Borough Green
To Tonbridge & Ashford
Chartwell
Westerham
Chart
Oxted
Holland
East Grinstead
Bromley
To London Victoria
To London Charing Cross
West Croydon
Merstham
Redhill
Woodhatch
To Brighton
Gatwick Airport
To London Victoria & London Bridge
Betchworth
Reigate
Epsom
Box Hill
Dorking
Strood Green
To London Waterloo & Heathrow
Burford Bridge Hotel
Boxhill & Westhumble
Denbies Wine Estate
Polesden Lacey
Ranmore Common
Westcott
Leith Hill
Holmbury St Mary YH
Abinger
Gomshall
Shere
To Hersham, Arundel, Chichester & Portsmouth
National Express to London, 8/day
Hatchlands Park
Clandon Park
Newlands Corner
Albury
Chilworth
Cranleigh
Woking
Guildford
Shalford
Compton
Puttenham
Seale
The Sands
National Express to London, 1/day
To Portsmouth & Southampton (via Reading) & Bournemouth & Cardiff
Aldershot
Farnham
To Winchester
National Express to Portsmouth 1/day
421
434
431
432
433
425
308
401
246,401,510
421,431 432,433 434
246
510
410
236
410 594
594
411
405
405,430,435
430
32 435
32
516
NT1
21 32
21,32
21
25
21,25 32
24
21,24,32
21,25,32
46
547
X64

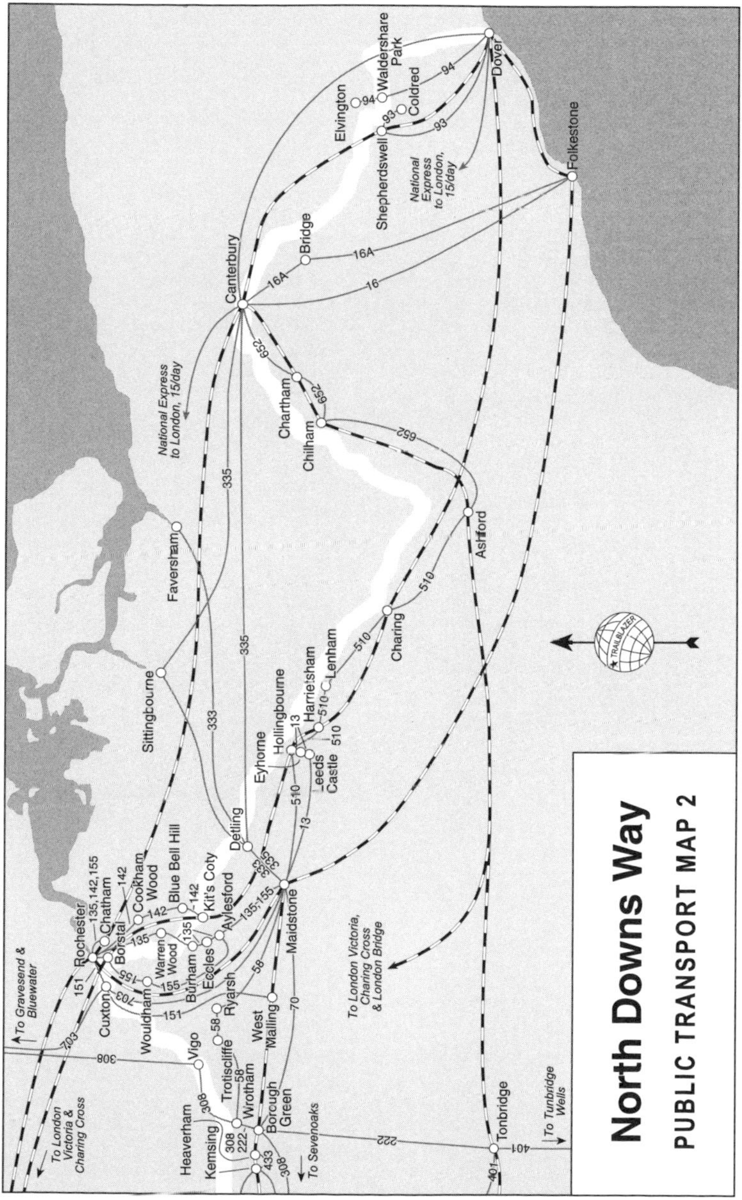
North Downs Way
PUBLIC TRANSPORT MAP 2
Rochester
Chatham
Borstal
Cuxton
Wouldham
Cookham Wood
Blue Bell Hill
Warren Wood
Burham
Eccles
Kit's Coty
Aylesford
Maidstone
Detling
Eyhorne
Hollingbourne
Leeds Castle
Harrietsham
Lenham
Charing
Ashford
Chilham
Chartham
Canterbury
Bridge
Shepherdswell
Elvington
Waldershare Park
Coldred
Dover
Folkestone
Faversham
Sittingbourne
Vigo
Trottiscliffe
Ryarsh
West Malling
Wrotham
Borough Green
Heaverham
Kemsing
Tonbridge
To Gravesend & Bluewater
To London Victoria & Charing Cross
To Sevenoaks
To London Victoria, Charing Cross & London Bridge
To Tunbridge Wells
National Express to London, 15/day
National Express to London, 15/day
TRAILBLAZER

PUBLIC TRANSPORT TABLE

(continued from p37)

Metrobus (🖳 www.metrobus.co.uk)

(Note: phone ☎ 01293-449191 for further information on service numbers followed by § and ☎ 01342-893080 phone for services followed by *)

236§ East Grinstead to Westerham, Mon-Fri 3/day

246* Bromley to Westerham via West Hill, daily 8/day; the Sunday service continues to Chartwell (see box p111) when the house is open (Mar-Oct)

401* Sevenoaks to Westerham, Mon-Sat 8/day; Tunbridge Wells to Westerham via Tonbridge and Sevenoaks, Sun 6/day. The Sunday service continues to Chartwell when the house is open (Mar-Oct) 4/day.

405* West Croydon to Redhill via Merstham, Mon-Sat 3/hr, Sunday 2/hr

410§ Redhill to Westerham via Old Oxted, Oxted, Chart and Westerham, Mon-Sat 12/day

411§ Redhill to Oxted, Mon-Fri 5/day mornings only

430§ Woodhatch to Merstham via Redhill, Mon-Sat 2/hr

435§ Reigate to Merstham via Redhill Bus station and South Merstham, Mon-Sat 2/hr, Sun 1/hr

594§ Holland to Chart via Oxted, Mon-Sat 3/day

421* Sevenoaks to Swanley via Otford, Mon-Sat 3/day

New Enterprise (☎ 01732-350509, 🖳 www.arrivabus.co.uk)

222 Tonbridge to Borough Green, Mon-Sat 6/day (2/day start from/continue to Wrotham)

Buses 4U Sunday Rambler

510 Oxted Station Rd East circular route via Westerham, Quebec House and Chartwell Car Park, mid-April to end Oct Sun only 7/day

Nu-Venture (☎ 01622-882288, 🖳 www.nu-venture.co.uk)

13 Maidstone to Hollingbourne via Leeds Castle and Eyhorne, Mon-Sat 4-5/day

58 Maidstone to Wrotham Heath via Ryarsh and Trottiscliffe, Mon-Sat 3-5/day

Stagecoach in East Kent (☎ 08702-433711, 🖳 www.stagecoachbus.com/eastkent)

16 Folkestone to Canterbury, Mon-Sat 1/hour

16A Folkestone to Canterbury via Bridge, daily 1/hr

93 Dover to Coldred via Shepherdswell, Mon-Sat 3-5/day

94 Dover to Elvington via Waldershare Park, Mon-Sat 1/hr

510 Ashford to Maidstone via Charing, Lenham, Harrietsham and Hollingbourne, Mon-Sat 6-7/day Sun 5/day

652 Ashford to Canterbury via Chilham and Chartham, Mon-Sat 8/day plus 3/day from Chilham to Canterbury only

Jaycrest (☎ 01795-438400)

335 Canterbury to Maidstone via Detling, Sunday only every two hours

PART 2: THE ENVIRONMENT & NATURE

Conserving the North Downs Way

Britain is an overcrowded island, and England is the most densely populated part of it. The south-east has suffered a great deal of pressure from both over-population and competition for land use. The landscape of the North Downs in Surrey and Kent is the levée holding back London's sprawl.

Thankfully there are a number of bodies at local and national level whose job it is to protect and conserve that landscape for future generations.

GOVERNMENT AGENCIES AND SCHEMES

Since 1 April 2005, the **Countryside Agency**, **English Nature** and the environment section of the **Rural Development Service** (RDS) have operated as a 'confederation of partners' with regard to responsibility for the protection and conservation of rural, urban and coastal areas in England. (Prior to this the Countryside Agency and English Nature were independent agencies, and the RDS was a core part of the Department for the Environment, Food and Rural Affairs.) This partnership became more formal on 30 March 2006 when the Natural Environment and Rural Communities Bill, became law. This new law means these three organizations will be united formally on 1 October 2006 with the creation of a new agency, **Natural England**. A new **Commission for Rural Communities** will also be established; its role will be to act as an independent adviser and watchdog for rural people, particularly communities suffering economic disadvantage.

Natural England

Natural England will be a single body responsible for identifying, establishing and managing National Parks, Areas of Outstanding Natural Beauty (both previously managed by the Countryside Agency), National Nature Reserves, Sites of Special Scientific Interest, and Special Areas of Conservation (all previously managed by English Nature).

The highest level of landscape protection is the designation of land as a **national park** which recognizes the national importance of an area in terms of landscape, biodiversity and as a recreational resource. At the time of writing there are nine national parks in England and the process for the designation of the South Downs as the next national park, which began in 2000, is nearing completion – a decision in principle is expected in late 2006. Designation of land as a national park does not signify national ownership and these areas are not uninhabited wildernesses so there is a lively debate trying to balance protecting the environment and the rights and livelihoods of those living in the parks.

❑ AONBs on the North Downs Way

The following bodies have lots of information on the landscape and villages on or near the North Downs Way.

- **Surrey Hills AONB** (☎ 01372-220653, 🖳 www.surreyhills.org)
- **Kent Downs AONB** (☎ 01303-815170, 🖳 www.kentdowns.org.uk)

The second level of protection is **Area of Outstanding Natural Beauty** (AONB), of which there are 37 in England covering some 15% of the country. The North Downs Way passes through both the **Surrey Hills** and the **Kent Downs AONBs** (see box above). Their primary objective is conservation of the natural beauty of a landscape and responsibility for this falls to the local authority within whose boundary they fall.

Other levels of protection are National Nature Reserves and Sites of Special Scientific Interest. **National Nature Reserves** (NNR), of which there are 215, are places where the priority is protection of the wildlife habitats and geological formations. They are either owned or managed by English Nature/Natural England or by approved organizations such as wildlife trusts. However, there are no national nature reserves actually on the route, though Wye Downs is on the alternative, shorter, loop. **Local nature reserves** (LNR) are managed locally.

The route also passes through other areas of protected land designated as **Sites of Special Scientific Interest** (SSSI); see for example Box Hill (p98) and Oxted Downs (Map 21, p109). There are over 4000 SSSIs in England (63 in Surrey and 102 in Kent), ranging in size from little pockets protecting wildflower meadows, important nesting sites or special geological features, to vast swathes of upland, moorland and wetland. At the time of writing SSSIs were managed by English Nature/Natural England in cooperation with their owners who are prevented from doing any work that is likely to damage the special features of the site. Many SSSIs are also either a NNR or a LNR.

Special Areas of Conservation (SAC) is an international designation which came into being as a result of the 1992 Earth Summit in Rio de Janeiro, Brazil. This European-wide network of sites is designed to promote the conservation of habitats, wild animals and plants, both on land and at sea. At the time of writing 236 land sites in England had been designated as SACs. Every land SAC is also an SSSI.

The main wildlife sites/local nature reserves along the North Downs Way are Cole Kitchen Down (off Map 10, p89), Ranmore Common, White Downs and Denbies Hillside (Map 11, p90 and Map 12, p91), Box Hill (Map 13, p93), Kemsing Downs (Map 28, p123), Shoulder of Mutton Wood (Map 36, p133) and Blue Bell Hill (Map 38, p139). Wye Downs (p183) is on the alternative route via Folkestone.

The **Environmental Stewardship Scheme** provides financial incentives to farmers to adopt low-impact agricultural practices. Particular priority is given to applications by farmers which will help conserve and restore chalk grassland

❑ **Statutory bodies**

• **Department for Environment, Food and Rural Affairs** (☎ 020-7238 6951, 💻 www.defra.gov.uk; Nobel House, 17 Smith Sq, London SW1P 3JR) Government ministry responsible for sustainable development in the countryside.

• **Natural England** (At the time of writing contact details for Natural England were not known; however, it is likely that the offices of the Countryside Agency and English Nature will be able to advise). **Countryside Agency** (☎ 01242-533222; 💻 www.countryside.gov.uk; John Dower House, Crescent Place, Cheltenham GL50 3RA) Statutory body charged with improving the quality of the countryside for everyone. Designates National Parks and AONBs; manages England's National Trails and provides most of the funding and resources for path maintenance. **English Nature** (☎ 01733-455000; 💻 www.english-nature.org.uk; Northminster House, Peterborough PE1 1UA) Government agency championing the conservation of wildlife, geology and wild places in England.

• **English Heritage** (☎ 0870-333 1181, 💻 www.english-heritage.org.uk, PO Box 569, Swindon SN2 2YO) Organization whose central aim is to make sure that the historic environment of England is properly maintained; it is officially known as the Historic Buildings and Monuments Commission for England. Dover Castle (see p180) at the end of the North Downs Way is an English Heritage site.

along the scarp of the North Downs Way (NDW) and between the NDW and the so-called Pilgrims' Way. Farmers are also encouraged (financially) to establish grass margins, protect historic field boundaries and create and enhance bird habitats with the assistance of the RSPB.

CAMPAIGNING AND CONSERVATION ORGANIZATIONS

These voluntary organizations started the conservation movement in the mid-19th century and are still at the forefront of developments. They rely on public support and can concentrate their resources either on acquiring land, which can then be managed purely for conservation purposes, or on influencing political decision-makers by lobbying and campaigning.

Managers and owners of land include well-known bodies such as the **Royal Society for the Protection of Birds** (RSPB) with their 150 nature reserves and over a million members, and the **Campaign to Protect Rural England** (CPRE) which exists to promote the beauty and diversity of rural England by encouraging the sustainable use of land and other natural resources in town and country. Action groups such as **Friends of the Earth**, **Greenpeace** and the **World Wide Fund for Nature** (WWF) also play a vital role in environmental protection by raising public awareness with government agencies when policy needs to be formulated.

Encouragingly, environmental issues are now part of mainstream politics locally, nationally and internationally.

❑ Campaigning/conservation organizations and charities

• The umbrella organization for the 47 wildlife trusts in the UK is **The Wildlife Trusts** (☎ 0870-036 7711, 🖳 www.wildlifetrusts.org), The Kiln, Waterside, Mather Rd, Newark, Nottinghamshire, NG24 1WT; two relevant to the North Downs Way are: **Surrey Wildlife Trust** (☎ 01483-795440, 🖳 www.surreywildlifetrust.com; School La, Pirbright, Woking GU24 OJN; looks after 60 sites in Surrey), and **Kent Wildlife Trust** (☎ 01622-662012, 🖳 www.kentwildlife.org.uk). Surrey Wildlife Trust manages Quarrey Hangers Nature Reserve; contact the trust for a free leaflet and map.

• **Campaign to Protect Rural England** (CPRE; ☎ 020-7981 2800, 🖳 www.cpre.org.uk; 128 Southwark St, London SE1 0SW) A charity whose members care about the countryside and campaign for it to be protected and enhanced. At the time of writing the CPRE are opposing plans for a gas-extraction site near Albury Downs.

• **National Trust** (☎ 0870-458 4000, 🖳 www.nationaltrust.org.uk; PO Box 39, Warrington WA5 7WD) A charity with 3.4 million members which aims to protect, through ownership, threatened coastline, countryside, historic houses, castles and gardens, and archaeological remains for everybody to enjoy. Box Hill (see p93) is managed by the National Trust as is much of the land through which the NDW passes from Brockham (Map 14, p97) to Reigate Hill (Map 16, p101).

• **Royal Society for the Protection of Birds** (RSPB; ☎ 01767-680551, 🖳 www.rspb.org.uk; The Lodge, Sandy, Bedfordshire, SG19 2DL) The largest voluntary conservation body in Europe.

• **Woodland Trust** (☎ 01476 581135, 🖳 www.woodland-trust.org.uk; Autumn Park, Dysart Rd, Grantham, Lincolnshire NG31 6LL) The trust aims to conserve, restore and re-establish native woodlands throughout the UK. You pass through a Woodland Trust project after Coldblow Farm (Map 41, p144).

• **British Trust for Conservation Volunteers** (BTCV; ☎ 01302-572244, 🖳 www.btcv.org; 163 Balby Rd, Doncaster, DN4 0RH) Encourages people to value their environment and take practical action to improve it.

• **Common Ground** (☎ 01747-850 8204, 🖳 www.commonground.org.uk) Organizes arts and environmental events believing that celebrations are the starting point for actions to improve localities.

• **World Wide Fund for Nature** (WWF; ☎ 01483-426444, 🖳 www.wwf.org.uk; Panda House, Weyside Park, Godalming, Surrey GU7 1XR) One of the world's largest conservation organizations, protecting endangered species and threatened habitats.

• **Friends of the Earth** (☎ 020-7490 1555, 🖳 www.foe.co.uk; 26-8 Underwood St, London N1 7JQ) International organization campaigning for a better environment.

BEYOND CONSERVATION

The fact that areas of Britain are designated as National Parks, AONBs, SSSIs, is an admission that many of our activities degrade and destroy environments we clearly think of as important for their own sake and for recreation. Walking in nature is an ideal teacher developing in us a deeper awareness of our natural environment so we care more about protecting it. We cannot be honest with ourselves if what we do off the trail is leading to the loss of countryside. Through supporting local businesses, eating seasonally, living a low-impact lifestyle we can do our bit for a brighter future. Rather than believing that we can contain and exploit nature we need to respect and learn to live in balance with it.

Flora and fauna

The North Downs teem with wildlife and walkers are lucky to travel at a pace which allows them to appreciate their surroundings. Wildflowers are particularly abundant on the Downs in spring, and trees provide year-round interest.

The following is a brief guide to the more commonly seen flora and fauna on the trail.

MAMMALS

Many are nocturnal and very shy so you may only see evidence of their existence from their tracks or scat but it would be very strange not to see a **rabbit** (*Oryctolagus cuniculus*) especially as the trail crosses several warrens (see Map 10, p89). You may see a **hare** (*Lepus europaeus*) which is bigger, has erect black-tipped ears, and is capable of running at speeds of up to 40mph/64km to escape its predator the **fox** (*Vulpes vulpes*), one of the more adaptable of Britain's native species. Generally nocturnal you may see them during the day. Now they are common in urban areas feeding well on our leftovers and scraps.

The **badger** (*Meles meles*) with its distinctive black and white markings is fairly common judging by the numbers killed crossing roads on their habitual routes called runs. They live in underground setts often dug next to a tree in the side of a bank. The **hedgehog** (*Erinaceus europaeus*) is fairly common and like the badger mostly seen as roadkill.

Of the 17 species of **bat** in the UK, the **pipestrelle** (*Pipestrelle pipestrelle*) is the most common and easy to spot flitting at speed over water and hedgerows picking off insects just after dusk. There are signs that the **otter** (*Lutra lutra*) is making something of a comeback in Surrey and this is a good indication of a healthy environment.

The North American **grey squirrel** (*Sciurus carolinensis*) is constantly rustling about in the woodlands along the trail but sadly the **red squirrel** (*Sciurus vulgaris*) has lost its habitat to the grey squirrel and you won't see it. There are also a number of species of mice, voles and shrew.

With all the woodland along the trail there's a good chance of seeing **roe deer** (*Capreolus capreolus*), a small native species that likes to inhabit woodland and sometimes can also be seen grazing in fields. Early mornings are best.

FISH

In rivers such as the Wey (Map 1, p69 and Map 6, p77), the Mole (Map 13, p93) and the Darent (Map 26, p119) you may see fish feeding. The waters along the trail are home to **trout** (*Salmo trutta*), **pike** (*Esox lucius*) and **roach** (*Rutilus rutilus*).

BIRDS

The landscape of the North Downs is ideal for a variety of birds – the woodlands are an obvious habitat but there are also species at home on the open downs.

In the woodland areas on the trail, look out for **treecreepers** (*Certhia familiaris*), **tits** (family *Paridae*, including blue, great, coal and long tailed), **nuthatches** (*Sitta europaea*) and **goldcrests** (*Regulus regulus*). These are tiny and you'll probably hear their high-pitched 'see see' call in the conifers along with **siskins** (*Carduelis spinus*). They'll be joined by **spotted flycatcher** (*Muscicapa striata*) in summer and **chiffchaffs** (*Phylloscopus collybita*).

Woodcock
L: 330mm/13"

You'll see a lot of **pheasant** (*Phasianus colchicus*) often bred by gamekeepers for shooting and you may even see the feeding hoppers or bins deep in the woods. This encourages the bird to stay in an area and come the season (it starts in October and continues until the beginning of February) the birds are driven from the woods by 'beaters' to fly over guns. The male has distinctive red head-sides and often a glossy green-black head, while the female is a dull brown.

The **woodcock** *(Scolopax rusticola)* with its long straight beak and plump body frequents damp woodland where it can lie hidden thanks to its leafy brown plumage. It is most easily sighted in the spring at dusk and dawn. This is when the males perform their courtship flight known as 'roding' which involves two distinct calls, one a low grunting noise, the other a sharp 'k-wik k-wik' call.

Barn Owl
L: 355mm/14"

The most frequently seen birds of prey are the **kestrel** (*Falco tinnunculus*) and the **sparrowhawk** (*Accipter nisus*), small and agile, well able to pursue prey through forests. If you hear a loud hooting and a sharp 'kewick' after dark the **tawny owl** (*Strix aluco*) is responsible and you may see a **barn owl** (*Tyto alba*) with its pale plumage, white breast and heart-shaped face, glide silently by as it hunts open country along the woodland edge.

The sight and sound of a **skylark** (*Alauda arvensis*) with its warbling song pouring out, getting higher pitched the further it spirals upwards specking out against a blue sky is a joy. A good place to see and hear skylarks is crossing Reigate Hill Golf Club (see Map 17, p104) but they are common along the open land of the North Downs Way.

SKYLARK
L: 185MM/7.25"

Although it's more common on the downland of the South Downs Way you may catch sight of the **stonechat** (*Saxicola torquata*), a colourful little bird with a deep orange breast and a black head. They are easily identified by their habit of flitting from the top of one bush to another, only pausing to call out across the fields. The call sounds much like the sound of two stones being struck together, hence the name stonechat.

STONECHAT
L: 135MM/5.25"

One of the most attractive birds the Downs walker might spot, usually seen feeding on open arable farmland, is the **lapwing** (*Vanellus vanellus*), which is also known as the peewit. It has long legs, a short bill and a distinctive long head crest. Sadly, this attractive bird is declining in numbers. The name comes from its lilting flight, frequently changing direction with its large rounded wings. It is also identified by a white belly, black and white head, black throat patch and distinctive dark green wings.

The **yellowhammer** (*Emberiza citrinella*), also known as the yellow bunting, can sometimes be seen perched on the top of gorse bushes. Most field guides to birds along with most old romantic country folk will claim that the distinctive song of the yellowhammer sounds like 'a little bit of bread and no cheese'. At a push they are right but the yellowhammer is certainly no talking parrot.

YELLOWHAMMER
L: 160MM/6.25"

If you see a **kingfisher** (*Alcedo atthis*) you are in for a treat. Likely places are along the river Wey and the Mole but don't blink – these vivid blue birds with a long spiked beak streak past just above the water when disturbed.

The **green woodpecker** *(Picus viridis)* is not all green, sporting a bright red and black head. Green woodpeckers are sometimes spotted clinging to a vertical tree trunk or feeding on the ground in open fields. The most common view, however, is as the bird flies away when disturbed.

LAPWING/PEEWIT
L: 320MM/12.5"

Green Woodpecker
L: 330mm/13"

The undulating flight pattern of the woodpecker is characterized by rapid wing beats as the bird rises followed by a pause when the bird slowly drops. This is accompanied by a loud laughing call that has earned the bird its old English name of yaffle.

REPTILES

Reptiles have had a bad rap ever since slithering into the Garden of Eden. Britain's only poisonous snake, the **adder** (*Vipera berus*) is recognized by its zig-zag body pattern. They pose very little risk to walkers but dogs can get bitten when snakes come out of hibernation to warm themselves, often on a sunny path. They only bite when provoked, preferring to hide instead, and the venom is designed to kill small mammals such as mice, voles and shrews, so deaths in humans are very rare (10 attributed to adder bites in the last hundred years) but a bite can be extremely unpleasant and occasionally dangerous for children or the elderly.

Adders are a measure of the health of an environment and the Kent Reptile and Amphibian group has projects in Kent along the Medway paths recording their distribution. Visit www.kentarg.org for more information.

The **common lizard** (*Lacerta vivipara*) may sometimes be seen basking in the sun and is harmless.

BUTTERFLIES

Two species that are dependant on the chalk grassland for their survival are the **Adonis blue** (*Polyommatus bellargus*) and the **Chalk hill blue** (*Polyommatus coridon*). Both feed on horseshoe vetch and August is a good time to spot them. The best butterfly spotting is on Box Hill where over two-thirds of the British butterfly species have been recorded; there is a very informative panel in the National Trust visitor centre (see Map 13, p93).

Two species you may see are the **Brimstone** (*Gonepteryx rhamni*) and the less common **White Admiral** (*Limenitis camilla*) which is in fact predominantly black with white banded wings. Look for it on woodland edges and in brambles where it feeds on honeysuckle. The male brimstone is easy to identify – it's bright yellow. The name butterfly may have come from this and it's said the brighter the brimstone the better the summer will be. Expect to see it along Albury Downs (see Map 8, p85). Chances are you'll see, at some point on the walk, the familiar orange-winged **Small Tortoiseshell** (*Algais urticae*) common in many gardens and urban parks.

Peacock
Inachis io

Small Tortoiseshell
Aglais urticae

Small Garden/Cabbage White
Artogeia rapae

Common Blue
Polyommatus icarus

Painted Lady
Cynthia cadui

Chalk hill Blue
Polyommatus coridon

Large Garden/ Cabbage White
Pieris brassicae

Red Admiral
Vanessa atalanta

Adonis Blue
Polyommatus bellargus

Brimstone
Gonepteryx rhamni

White Admiral
Limenitis camilla

Gorse
Ulex europaeus

Common Ragwort
Senecio jacobaea

Honeysuckle
Lonicera periclymemum

Tormentil
Potentilla erecta

Birdsfoot-trefoil
Lotus corniculatus

Scarlet Pimpernel
Anagallis arvensis

Yarrow
Achillea millefolium

Hogweed
Heracleum sphondylium

Ransoms (Wild Garlic)
Allium ursinum

Common Fumitory
Fumaria officinalis

Old Man's Beard
Clematis vitalba

Common Poppy
Papaver rhoeas

Silverweed
Potentilla anserina

Self-heal
Prunella vulgaris

Violet
Viola riviniana

Meadow Buttercup
Ranunculis acris

Primrose
Primula vulgaris

Cowslip
Primula veris

Dog Rose
Rosa canina

Common Hawthorn
Crataegus monogyna

Ox-eye Daisy
Leucanthemum vulgare

Foxglove
Digitalis purpurea

Early Purple Orchid
Orchis mascula

Bee Orchid
Orchis apifera

Herb-Robert
Geranium robertianum

Bell Heather
Erica cinerea

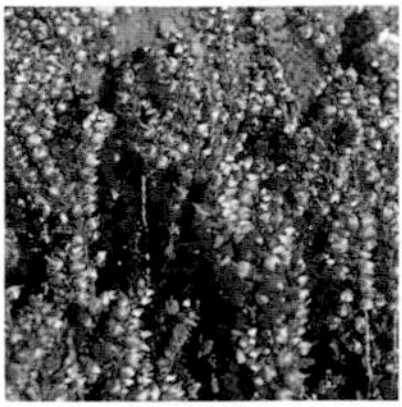

Heather (Ling)
Calluna vulgaris

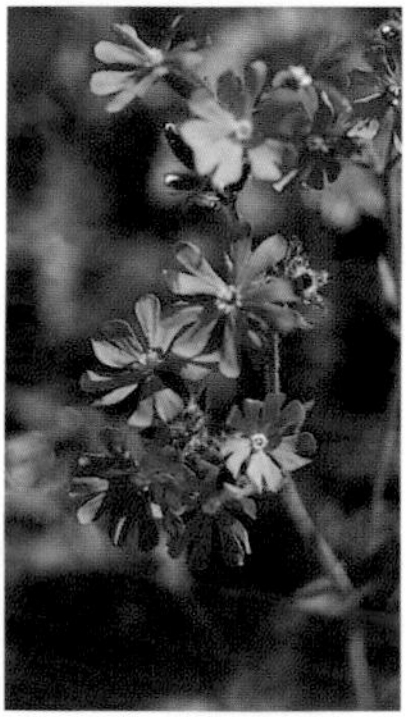

Red Campion
Silene dioica

Rosebay Willowherb
Epilobium angustifolium

Bluebell
Endymion non-scriptus

FLOWERS

Woodland and hedgerows

Spring is the time to come and see the rich displays of colour on the North Downs Way. From March to May **bluebells** (*Hyacinthoides non-scripta*) proliferate on the woodland floor along the North Downs Way forming large carpets of bright blue, bell-shaped flowers. Other common spring woodland flowers are the pink-tinged **wood anemone** (*Anemone nemorosa*) and the yellow clump-forming **primrose** (*Primula vulgaris*). The feathery **Travellers' Joy** (*Clematis vitalba*) with its pale-cream fluffy blooms in autumn, hence its other name **old man's beard**, twists through hedgerow and trees. Another climber is the **honeysuckle** (*Lonicera periclymemum*), a valuable butterfly food plant. A member of the carrot family, but not edible is **Queen Anne's Lace** or **cow parsley** with its white flowers covering banks and verges from early summer. **Red campion** (*Silene dioica*) is a decorative pinkish red flower with five petals and is common on the path edge between March and October. The pretty pink geranium **herb robert** flowers through to September.

At the woodland edge and in scrubland you will also find **bramble** (*Rubus fruticosus*), a common vigorous shrub; edible **blackberry** fruits ripen from late summer into autumn. They can be quite tart and very pippy with a free-running and staining purple juice. Fairly common in scrubland and on woodland edges is the **dog rose** (*Rosa canina*) which has a large pink flower, the fruits or 'hips' of which are rich in Vitamin C and were used to make rose-hip syrup during WWII.

Other flowering plants to look for in wooded areas and in hedgerows include the tall **foxglove** (*Digitalis purpurea*) with its trumpet-like flowers and **forget-me-not** (*Myosotis arvensis*) with tiny, delicate blue flowers.

Perhaps the most aromatic plant is **wild garlic** (*Allium ursinum*) whose broad pointed leaves release an onion bouquet when crushed. This plant carpets the verge of War Coppice Rd (see Map 19, p106) and is abundant in Marden Park and Church Woods (see Map 20, p107). Its early summer white, star-like flowers, held high on a stem, add a splash of colour to the woodland floor.

The chalk grassland

The flowers of the chalk grassland are a hardy group. A farmer tells me that to grow anything well there you'd need rain every day and a dose of manure on

> **❑ Unusual insects**
>
> Perhaps the most unusual insect on the North Downs Way is the **glow worm** (*Lampyris noctiluca*). It's not actually a worm but a beetle and related to the firefly. The best time to see these creatures is at night (10pm to midnight), between mid-June and mid-July, when the vivid glow of the female is used by her to attract males. The light glows like a luminous watch dial and is caused by a chemical reaction on the underside of the adult female. Unlike fireflies the glow can't be switched on and off instantly but takes minutes to turn on and off. A good place to see them is Box Hill (Map 13, p93); visit 💻 www.glowworms.org.uk for lots more information.

Ponder this while walking

- Britons have lost touch with where their food comes from – 20% don't know yoghurt is made from milk, more than 10% think rice is grown in the UK and 10% don't know that tomatoes and onions are grown in the UK
- We now import about 40% of our food supply; in the late 1980s we imported about 25%
- Since WWII we've lost over 300,000 farms; 70% of the UK land area is still farmed but the labour force employed has declined by 30% since 1990
- Fifty years ago farmers got 50p from every pound spent on produce, now it's 8p
- One and a half billion litres of fuel are used to transport food in the UK each year. Reduce these food miles by buying English varieties of apple from Kent – Lord Lambourn is deliciously crisp. Also buy in season – Kent cobnuts, a type of hazelnut, are freshest in August-October
- The area of land farmed organically has increased dramatically since the late 1990s to about 700 hectares in 2005 reflecting many farmers' desire to find alternatives to conventional production and an increase in payment rates under farm support schemes
- Plan to join a local box scheme when you return from the trail and have organic vegetables delivered to your door

Sundays. Battered by wind, grazed by sheep and rabbits they eke out an existence in a poor, thin chalk soil. The best way to look at them is up close and personal so drop to your knees at the top of Box Hill (see Map 13, p93) or on Oxted Downs (see Map 21, p109). They've all adapted to the poor soil and a relatively harsh environment. The dominant grass, **sheep's fescue** (*Festuca ovina*), has folded leaves to protect its delicate stomata, openings that allow carbon dioxide and light to pass through for photosynthesis, and the leaf is narrow to reduce loss of water.

The best defence against sheep and rabbits is to grow low to the ground and form a mat. So rosette leaves are common like those on the **cowslip** (*Primula veris*) anchoring the plant to the ground. Only the yellow flowers are held upright so the bees can pollinate. Tea made from the drooping flowers is said to cure insomnia. **Horseshoe vetch** (*Hippocrepis comosa*), an important butterfly food plant (see p47), bears its pea-shaped small yellow flowers on a dense close-fitting mat.

Other strategies are to put out roots wherever a stem touches the soil or to interweave a network of stems just below the surface as **birdsfoot trefoil** (*Lotus corniculatus*) does.

The tiny yellow flower of **tormentil** (*Potentilla tormentilla*) can be seen hugging the ground in short grassland. It gets its name from an age when it was used as a medicinal remedy for diarrhoea and haemorrhoids: the taste is so foul that it tormented whoever took it.

Another tiny flower that can also be found close to the ground is the **scarlet pimpernel** (*Anagallis avensis*), a member of the primrose family. The flow-

> **❑ Ray Mears – bushcraft survival and woodlore**
> Survival expert Ray Mears grew up on the North Downs which he describes as a unique habitat. Here he discovered a passion for the countryside and began to re-learn survival skills practised by our ancestors. Reckoning it's very important to learn from them, as it gives us some understanding of where we come from and hopefully rekindles a responsibility to maintain our fragile habitat, he is the author of several books on bushcraft and a TV presenter. When he's not away on expeditions he is leading survival skills' classes. Visit his website 💻 www.raymears.com.

ers are tiny at just 5mm in diameter but stand out from their grassy background thanks to its light red colour.

There are many **orchids** on the Downs and some are relatively common including the **early purple orchid** (*Orchis Mascula*), as its name suggests the first of the British orchids to flower from April onwards, and the widespread **bee orchid** (*Ophrys apifera*) which gets its name from the bee-shaped flowers (see photo opposite p49) produced in early summer.

The showiest plant is probably the **common poppy** (*Papaver rhoeas*) splashing colour, with its deep-red petals, on the open fields of the Kent landscape in late summer.

Heath

Puttenham Heath (Map 4, p73) is an isolated area of heath where acid-loving plants thrive on the greensand soil. The most common is **heather** (*Calluna vulgaris*), a versatile plant used for thatching, basket work, brooms and fuel for fires. You will also find a collection of acid-loving species about Hackhurst Downs (Map 10, p89).

Thorny **gorse** (*Ulex europeous*) bushes brighten up the summer with their small yellow flowers that burst open from February until June.

TREES

The number of trees and the amount of woodland along the North Downs Way is a striking feature of this walk. Surrey is England's most wooded county but since 1600 much of its ancient woodland has been felled for fuel and building material or cleared for agriculture.

In the last 50 years 88% of coppiced woodland has disappeared. But coppicing and old woodland skills are making a comeback and the north slopes of the North Downs Way remain heavily wooded.

> **❑ Can you see the wood from the trees?**
> - Surrey has about 50 times more trees than people
> - Nearly a quarter of the county is wooded making it the most wooded county in England
> - Surrey Hills AONB is the most wooded AONB in the country with 38.5% woodland cover

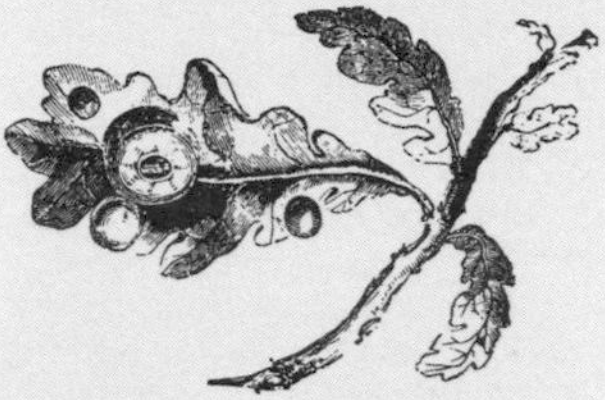

Oak galls

Oak trees support more kinds of insects than any other tree in Britain and some affect the oak in unusual ways. The eggs of gall-flies cause growths known as **leaf galls** (above). Each of these contains a single insect. Other kinds of gall-flies lay eggs in stalks or flowers, leading to **flower galls** (below), growths the size of currants.

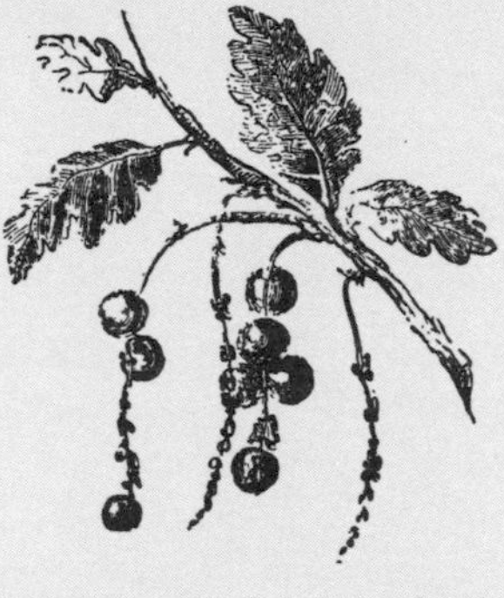

The **oak spangle** (below) is a flat circular disc, red and hairy, attached to the underside of the leaf. Each contains a single insect.

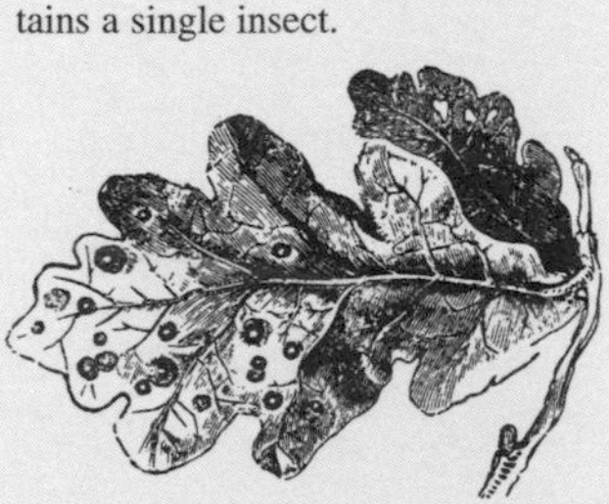

Much of the woodland is mixed deciduous made up largely of **oak** (*Quercus petraea*) and **ash** (*Fraxinus excelsior*). The **beech** (*Fagus sylvatica*) with its thick, silvery trunk is one of the most attractive native trees. It can grow to a height of forty metres with the high canopies blocking out much of the light. As a result the floors of beech woodlands tend to be fairly bare of vegetation. They favour well-drained soil, hence their liking for the steep scarp slope. In autumn the colours of the turning leaves can be quite spectacular.

Other trees that flourish include **silver birch** (*Betula pendula*) and **hazel** (*Corylus avellana*) which has traditionally been used for coppicing. There is frequent coppicing carried out in King's Wood (see Map 51, p157). The trees are cut off at ground level every few years yielding many slender, straight and pliable branches used for making charcoal, fences, hurdles, bean poles, barrels and by some as dowsing rods for water divining.

The **alder** is a tree which thrives near reliable sources of water and thus is often found along riverbanks. The River Mole is known for its picturesque stands of alders.

The **whitebeam**, though not a common tree, can be seen in parts of Surrey along the trail. It gets its name from the white mealy down which covers the undersides of the leaves; beam is Saxon for 'tree'.

Famous for its life expectancy, lasting for well over 1000 years in some cases, the **common yew** (*Taxus baccata*) is abundant in churchyards but there are also natural stands among beech woodland. The dark glossy needles are quite distinctive as is the flaky red bark of the often gnarled and twisted old trunks and branches. Do not be tempted to eat the bright red berries as they are poisonous. Taxine, this natural poison, has been used to make a drug for cancer treatment.

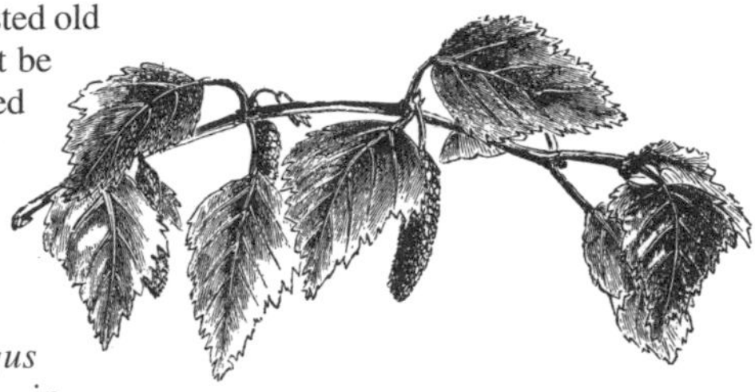

Birch (with flowers)

Hawthorn (*Crataegus monogyna*) is common in hedgerows and a valuable supply of berries for birds as is **holly** (*Ilex aquifolium*). Solitary hawthorn trees are also associated with spirits and fairies.

At Box Hill there are fine stands of **box** (*Buxus sempervirens*) after which it is named. This is one of the few places in Britain where the box grows wild: it's usually seen in a neatly-clipped state in a garden. Box is the hardest and heaviest of all European woods, the only one which does not float in water.

Many of the woods are owned and cared for by the National Trust, the most significant being Ranmore Common, Denbies Hillside and Box Hill (see Map 12, p91 and Map 13, p93). Kemsing Parish Council manages Kemsing Down Nature Reserve where in addition to woodland there are important chalk grassland and scrub habitats.

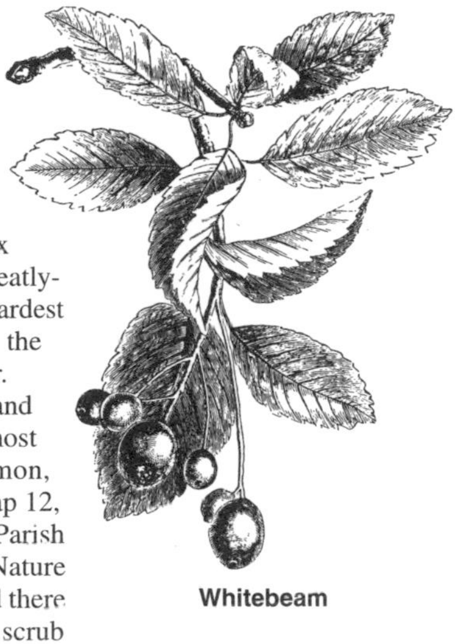

Whitebeam

Alder (with flowers)

Hazel (with flowers)

❑ Roman heritage

The Roman snail (*Helix pornatia*) is Britain's largest snail, up to two inches in diameter and was possibly introduced by the Romans as a food source. Its stronghold is the woods of the chalk downs and you may well see it near Tanners Hatch Youth Hostel (see p92).

PART 3: MINIMUM IMPACT WALKING & OUTDOOR SAFETY

Minimum impact walking

The south-east of England is a congested place and having protected landscapes such as the North Downs to get away to is a valuable resource. The countryside is becoming ever more popular for recreation and walkers should be aware of their responsibilities to help protect the countryside and minimize their impact on it.

By following a few simple guidelines while walking the North Downs Way you can have a positive impact, not just on your own well-being but also on local communities and the environment, thereby becoming part of the solution.

ACCESS

The right of access to open land under the **Countryside and Rights of Way Act 2000** (CRoW), dubbed 'freedom or right to roam' by the press and walkers alike, was first rolled out in the south-east in September 2004 and came into effect in full throughout England and Wales on 31 October 2005. Walkers now have the legal right to access on foot to defined areas of uncultivated open country, basically mountain, moorland, downland and heathland. What the act does not do is give walkers the right to wander willy nilly over private farmland, woodland, paddock or gardens.

So, when you are on the North Downs Way, keep to designated footpaths and follow the 'acorn' signs. There are, however, areas of open access land adjacent to the trail, notably land managed by the National Trust, the Forestry Commission and the Woodland Trust and areas of registered common land such as St Martha's Hill (Map 7, see p83) and Newlands Corner (Map 8, p85).

Rights of access have also been created over some new areas of land such as open land north of Hollingbourne (see Map 42, p145). But the effect of the Act on the North Downs is not as significant when compared to the large tracts of land now accessible in the Peak District or the opening up of land on the South Downs between Poynings and Upper Beeding which now have permanent access rights rather than permissive access which could be withdrawn at any time.

Visit 💻 www.countrysideaccess.gov.uk to see the areas of land covered by the freedom to roam and also any restrictions.

THE COUNTRYSIDE CODE

The countryside is a fragile place which every visitor should respect. The Countryside Code (see box p56) was revised in part because of the changes

❑ **The Countryside code**
- Be safe – plan ahead and follow any signs
- Leave gates and property as you find them
- Protect plants and animals, take your litter home
- Keep dogs under close control
- Consider other people

brought about by the CRoW Act (see p55) and was relaunched in July 2004. It seems like common sense but sadly some people still seem to have no understanding of how to treat the countryside they walk in. Everyone visiting the countryside has a responsibility to minimize the impact of their visit so that other people can enjoy the same peaceful landscapes. It does not take much effort; it really is common sense.

Below is an expanded version of the new Countryside Code launched under the logo 'respect, protect, enjoy':

Be safe – plan ahead and follow any signs

Walking on the North Downs Way is pretty much hazard free but you're responsible for your own safety so follow the simple guidelines outlined on pp60-2.

Leave gates and property as you find them

Normally a farmer leaves gates closed to keep livestock in but may sometimes leave them open to allow livestock access to food or water. Leave them as you find them and if there is a sign, follow the instructions.

Try always to use stiles and gates; climbing walls, hedges or fences will damage them over time.

Don't disturb historic ruins by scrambling over them – really all this is about being sensitive to the needs of others who work, live or visit the countryside.

Protect plants and animals, take your litter home

If you bothered to take it on the trail it should be easy to take it home with you – litter spoils the beauty of the countryside and can harm animals and spread disease so bring a plastic bag for cores and scraps (see p58), find a bin or take it home. Much of the North Downs Way is wooded and can be tinder dry so guard against all risk of fire – it can be devastating to wildlife, habitats and people. That means never lighting a camp fire, extinguishing cigarette butts if you smoke (bring them home) and exercising care with stoves.

Give livestock plenty of space when crossing fields, sheep are always nervous, cattle and horses are often curious and may follow you; keep an eye on them as they can behave unpredictably.

Keep dogs under close control

You don't have to have your dog on a lead on a public path but he's likely to be under control if he is. Don't let him be a danger or nuisance to other animals and people – game keepers won't be too happy if he disturbs pheasants causing them to fly about in panic. If a farm animal chases you and your dog it's safer to let your dog off the lead.

Remember that it is a legal requirement to **keep dogs under close control** on Rights of Way. It is particularly important to keep your dog on a lead when crossing farmland with livestock in it. Though there are not too many sheep on the North Downs Way you need to be especially vigilant around lambing time and from March to July when ground-nesting birds are busy laying and hatching their eggs. Incidents of dogs worrying sheep do nothing to endear dog-walkers to farmers and a farmer can legally shoot a dog that is apparently worrying livestock. Also take care around crops. Dogs that run through and flatten fields of wheat, barley and hay are affecting a farmer's livelihood. **Carry a 'pooper scooper'** or plastic bags to remove waste if your dog fouls on the path.

Consider other people

'Do unto others as you would have them do unto you…' would, if followed, make the world a better place and it's no different on the trail. If you have to use a car, park with care ie don't block driveways or gates. Slow down on country roads and if you have to walk along them face the oncoming traffic and carry a torch when it's getting dark. Don't make unnecessary noise – people come for the peace and solitude. Support the communities you travel through – buy local (see below).

ECONOMIC IMPACT

Buy local

Whether in a shop or restaurant look and ask for local produce – it helps to boost the local economy and creates a local food culture.

Shops such as **Surrey Gourmet** (see p94) and restaurants like the **White Horse Inn**, Bridge (see p170), proudly list their local suppliers. There are frequent **farmers' markets** (see box p15) and it's possible to buy **locally produced beer** and **wine** along the trail. Buy produce that's in season and you'll further cut down on the amount of pollution and congestion that the transportation of food creates and you have the satisfaction of knowing you're supporting local farmers and producers. If you can find local food which is also organic so much the better; if insects won't eat vegetables sprayed with pesticide why would you?

Support local businesses

Money spent locally has a multiplying effect: every £10 spent in a local business yields a £25 investment locally but £10 spent in a chain store only yields £14 investment locally – most of the money leaves the local economy and goes to pay for transport, good and profits elsewhere. In short the more you spend locally the more circulates locally and that supports local businesses.

Applying the same multiplier effect as above, if every household in Surrey spent £1 extra a week on local produce, that could mean an extra £57m generated locally.

Encourage local cultural traditions and skills

As you walk, look at the local architecture, the farm buildings, how the fields are laid out and used, observe how place names are pronounced and visit the local museums and heritage centres. No part of the countryside looks the same. Buildings, food, skills, and language evolve out of the landscape and are moulded over hundreds of years to suit the locality. Discovering these cultural differences is part of the pleasure of walking in new places. Visitors' enthusiasm for local traditions and skills brings awareness and pride, nurturing a sense of place; an increasingly important role in a world where economic globalization continues to undermine the very things that provide distinctiveness and a feeling of belonging.

ENVIRONMENTAL IMPACT

By choosing a walking holiday you are taking a positive step towards minimizing your impact on the environment. The following are some ideas on how you can go a few steps further while walking the North Downs Way.

Use public transport whenever possible

Public transport to and along the North Downs Way is generally excellent with just about everywhere served by at least one bus or train; see p36-40 for more details. Public transport is always preferable to using private cars as it benefits everyone: visitors, locals and the environment.

Never leave litter

Leaving litter shows disrespect for the natural world and others coming after you. As well as being unsightly litter pollutes the environment and can be dangerous to farm animals. **Please** carry a plastic bag so you can dispose of your rubbish in a bin in the next village. It would be very helpful if you could pick up litter left by other people too.

• **Is it OK if it's biodegradable?** No. Would you like to see litter at your picnic spot? When was the last time you saw a citrus grove on the North Downs Way? It spoils the natural beauty of the trail. Apple cores, banana skins, orange peel and the like are unsightly, encourage flies, ants and wasps and ruin a picnic spot.

• **The lasting impact of litter** A piece of orange peel left on the ground takes six months to decompose; silver foil 18 months; a plastic bag 10 years; clothes 15 years; and an aluminium can 85 years.

Erosion

• **Stay on the main trail** The effect of your footsteps may seem minuscule but when they are multiplied by several thousand walkers each year they become rather more significant. Avoid taking shortcuts, widening the trail or taking more than one path; your boots will be followed by many others. This is particularly true on the North Downs Way which is heavily used by local day walkers.

• **Consider walking out of season** It's possible to walk the North Downs Way at any time of year but it's particularly popular in spring and summer. Consider walking at less busy times – autumn and mid-winter can be just as enjoyable and sometimes afford better views. And it may be a more relaxing experience with fewer people on the path and less competition for accommodation.

• **Respect all wildlife** Care for all wildlife you come across along the path; it has as much right to be there as you. Tempting as it may be to pick wild flowers leave them so the next people who pass can enjoy them too. If you want to identify them make a note or photograph them. Don't break branches off or damage trees in any way.

If you come across wildlife keep your distance and don't watch for too long. Your presence can cause considerable stress, particularly if the adults are with young, or in winter when the weather is harsh and food is scarce.

Young birds and animals aren't usually abandoned – just leave them alone and their mothers will return.

The code of the outdoor loo

You're never far from a proper toilet on the North Downs Way be it in a village or at a café or refreshment kiosk but the chances are you will need to 'go' outdoors at some point. Judging by the scraps of toilet paper you see about so have many others. In some parts of the world walkers and climbers are required to pack out their excrement. We haven't reached that stage but you need to be as sensitive as possible towards others.

- **Where to go** Wherever possible **use a toilet**. Where there are public toilets on the trail they are marked on the trail maps in this guide and you will also find facilities in pubs, cafés and campsites along the North Downs Way. If you do have to go outdoors choose a site at least 30 metres away from running water and 200 metres away from the trail. Use a trowel or stick to **dig a small hole** about 15cm (6 inches) deep to bury your excrement in. It decomposes quicker when in contact with the top layer of soil or leaf mould. Do not squash it under rocks as this slows down the composting process.
- **Toilet paper and sanitary towels** These take a long time to decompose whether buried or not and may be dug up by animals and then blow into water sources or onto the path. To avoid this **pack them out**: put the used items in a paper bag which you then place inside a plastic bag (or two). Then simply empty the contents of the paper bag at the next toilet you come across and throw the bag away.

Wild camping

There is no general right to camp on land in England. You must first obtain the permission of the landowner and in the absence of this you may be trespassing. Camping outside official sites on National Trust land is against its bye-laws. Much of the North Downs Way is heavily wooded and most open land is private farmland and much of this is arable cropland. The opportunities for wild camping are therefore limited.

But wild camping provides the walker with a uniquely fulfilling experience of living in a simple and sustainable way in which the habitual activities of cooking, eating, washing and sleeping take on greater importance.

Follow these suggestions for minimizing your impact and encourage others to do likewise:

- **Be discreet** Camp alone or in small groups, spend only one night in each place and pitch your tent, tarp or bivvy late and move off early.

- **Never light a fire** The deep burn caused by camp fires, no matter how small, damages the turf which can take years to recover. Cook on a camp stove instead.
- **Don't use soap or detergent** There's no need to use soap; even biodegradable soaps and detergents pollute streams. You won't be away from a shower for more than a day or so. Wash up without detergent; use a plastic or metal scourer, or failing that, a handful of fine pebbles or some bracken or grass.
- **Leave no trace** Learn the skill of moving on without leaving any sign of having been there: no moved rocks, ripped up vegetation or dug drainage ditches. Make a final check of your campsite before departing; pick up any litter that you or anyone else has left, so leaving the place in a better state than you found it.

Outdoor safety

AVOIDANCE OF HAZARDS

The North Downs Way is not a difficult or dangerous walk and with common sense as well as good planning and preparation most hazards can be avoided. This information is just as important for those out on a day walk as for those walking the entire trail. To ensure a safe and stress-free trip **follow the countryside code** (see p56) and:

- Before going out **get information** about where and when you can go by eg visiting 💻 www.countrysideaccess.gov.uk.
- Check **weather forecasts** before you leave by listening to the radio or TV, or visit one of the online forecasts at: 💻 www.metoffice.gov.uk, 💻 www.weathercall.co.uk, or 💻 www.bbc.co.uk/weather. Telephone forecasts are available from Weather Call (☎ 0905-062 0539; calls cost 60p/minute. Then plan accordingly;
- Make sure that **somebody knows your plans** for every day you are on the trail. This could be a friend or relative whom you have promised to call every night, or the owners of the B&Bs that you plan to stay in at the end of each day's walk. That way, if you fail to turn up or call that evening, they can raise the alarm;
- **Stick to the path** and avoid old quarries or taking shortcuts on steep sections of the escarpment;
- **Check your location** regularly on the map; it's unlikely that you'll lose your way on the Downs but it'll save you missing a turning to a village and the frustration of retracing your steps at the end of a long day.
- Always fill your **water** bottles/pouches at every available opportunity and drink regularly;
- Make sure you have some **high-energy snacks** – fruit, nuts, or chocolate – to keep you going on the last few miles of a long day or in an emergency;
- Always carry a **torch** and **whistle** (the international distress signal is six blasts on the whistle or six flashes on a torch); a compass is not vital on this trail;
- Wear strong **boots** with good ankle support and a good grip, not trainers and have **suitable clothes** including wet-weather gear (see pp28-30).

- Be extra vigilant with **children**;
- Take a **first-aid kit**. If there is a casualty use basic first aid to treat the injury to the best of your ability. Work out exactly where you are. If possible leave someone with the casualty while others go to get help if you are not able to summon help via a mobile. If there are only two people, you have a dilemma. If you decide to get help leave all spare clothing and food with the casualty. On this trail you are never far from a road, village or farmhouse where you can summon help;
- In an emergency dial ☎ 999.

BLISTERS

It is important to break in new boots before embarking on a long trek. Make sure the boots are comfortable and try to avoid getting them wet on the inside. Air your feet at lunchtime, keep them clean and change your socks regularly. If you feel any hot spots stop immediately and apply Compeed or Second Skin before the blister develops. Applied at the right time it's magic stuff. If you've left it too late, do not burst the blister as this can lead to infection; dress it with any blister kit to protect it from abrasion. If the skin is broken keep the area clean with antiseptic and cover with a non-adhesive dressing material held in place with tape.

HYPOTHERMIA

Also known as exposure, hypothermia occurs when the body can't generate enough heat to maintain its normal temperature, usually as a result of being wet, cold, unprotected from the wind, tired and hungry. It is usually more of a problem in upland areas such as in the Lakes and on the moors than on the North Downs Way.

Hypothermia is easily avoided by wearing suitable clothing, carrying and eating enough food and drink, being aware of the weather conditions and checking the morale of your companions.

Early signs to watch for are feeling cold and tired with involuntary shivering. Find some shelter as soon as possible and warm the victim up with a hot drink and some chocolate or other high-energy food. If possible give them another warm layer of clothing and allow them to rest until feeling better. If allowed to worsen, strange behaviour, slurring of speech and poor co-ordination will become apparent and the victim can quickly progress into unconsciousness, followed by coma and death. Quickly get the victim out of wind and rain, improvising a shelter if necessary. Rapid restoration of bodily warmth is essential and best achieved by bare-skin contact: someone should get into the same sleeping bag as the patient, both having stripped to their underwear, placing any spare clothing under or over them to build up heat. Send urgently for help.

HYPERTHERMIA

Hyperthermia is the general name given to a variety of heat-related ailments. Not something you would normally associate with England, heatstroke and heat exhaustion are serious problems nonetheless. Symptoms of **heat exhaustion** include thirst, fatigue, giddiness, a rapid pulse, raised body temperature, low urine output and, if not treated, delirium and finally a coma. The best cure is to drink plenty of water.

Heatstroke is another matter altogether, and even more serious. A high body temperature and an absence of sweating are early indications, followed by symptoms similar to hypothermia (see p61) such as a lack of coordination, convulsions and coma. Death will follow if treatment is not instantly given. Sponge the victim down, wrap them in wet towels, fan them, and get help immediately.

SUNBURN

It can easily happen even on overcast days and especially if you have a fair complexion. The only surefire way to avoid it is to stay wrapped up, but that's not really an option. What you must do, therefore, is to smother yourself in sunscreen (with a minimum factor of 15) and apply it regularly throughout the day. Don't forget your lips, nose, ears, the back of your neck if wearing a T shirt, and even under your chin to protect against rays reflected up off the ground.

PERSONAL SAFETY

This is an issue usually raised by women walking or travelling on their own. The North Downs Way is much safer than any city and you are more likely to twist an ankle and have to hobble painfully to the nearest village, than become a crime victim. However, if you do walk on your own it's all the more important to make sure someone knows your plans for the day (see p60), and take all the usual precautions such as keeping an eye on your belongings at all times.

OTHER USERS

About 19% of the North Downs Way is bridleway and about 12% is classed as a byway or road used as a public path. So you may encounter off-road vehicles. Most of the by-ways are in Kent. The petrol heads I've met, and luckily it's not many, have stopped their engines and let me pass. Whatever you think about them in the countryside, and I don't like it, those I've met have been courteous and they were riding where they were allowed. When it comes to horses I've had many encounters with riders who are clearly over-mounted as they grimly try to control the equine equivalent of an F1 racing car. Give them a wide berth. Mountain bikers are allowed to use bridleways and you just have to keep an eye out for the fast youthful types – usually their girlfriends following behind sheepishly apologize. Most though are a decent bunch. Hot spots are Newlands Corner through to Dorking.

PART 4: ROUTE GUIDE & MAPS

Using this guide

This trail guide has been described from west to east and divided into 12 stages. There is excellent access by public transport if you're doing the walk in day stages but it is not the only way to structure the 131-mile (209.6km) walk. Much will depend on the speed you walk at, your interests and where you stay. See pp25-6 for some suggested itineraries.

TRAIL MAPS

Scale and walking times

The trail maps are to a scale of 1:20,000 (1cm = 200m; 3⅛ inches = one mile). Walking times are given along the side of each map and the arrow shows the direction to which the time refers. Black triangles indicate the points between which the times have been taken. **See note below on walking times.**

The times are there as an aid to planning your walk not to judge your ability. There are many variables which will affect your speed including weather, ground conditions, whether you are walking alone or with company and how interesting you find parts of the landscape.

Up or down?

Other than when on a track or bridleway the trail is shown as a dotted line. An arrow across the trail indicates the slope; two arrows show that it is steep. Note that the arrow points towards the higher part of the trail. If, for example, you are walking from A (at 80m) to B (at 200m) and the trail between the two is short and steep, it would be shown thus: A- - - - >>- - - -B. Reversed arrow heads indicate downward gradient.

Accommodation

Accommodation shown on the maps is either on the trail or within easy reach of it. Some owners are prepared to collect walkers from points on the trail where

Important note – walking times

Unless otherwise specified, **all times in this book refer only to the time spent walking**. You will need to add 20-30% to allow for rests, photography, checking the map, drinking water etc. When planning the day's hike count on 5-7 hours' actual walking.

To research this book I walked alone so kept a faster pace than if I were walking with companions. Most health and fitness professionals calculate average walking speed at 2mph/3kph. After a few days you will hopefully know how fast you walk compared to the time bars and can plan your day more accurately.

Trail map key

Path	Hedge	Boggy / Wet Ground
Other Path	Trees	Building
4WD Track	Fence	Accommodation
Tarmac Road	Stone Wall	Campsite
Steps	Water	Church
Stile	Sand	Public Toilet
Gate	Boulders	Public Telephone
Bridge	Cliffs	Bus Stop
2 Map Continuation	Stream	Golf Course
	River	CP Car Park

Town plan key

	Bank	Camping site
Place to stay	Museum	Bus stop
Place to eat	Library	Bus station
Post Office	Internet	Other
Tourist Information	Church	

the accommodation is a mile or two off the path and it is worth asking if this is possible when booking. An offer to pay petrol money will generally be appreciated for this added service.

Details of each place are given in the accompanying text. The number and type of rooms is given after each entry: S = single room, T = twin room, D = double room, F=family room sleeping at least three people. **Prices given are per person** and are summer high-season rates unless otherwise stated. As an example: £45sgl/30dbl means the prices are £45 for a single room and £30 per person for a double room. Don't bank on negotiating a discount in the off-season. Year-round demand from business travellers, holiday makers and weekenders for accommodation along and near the North Downs Way keeps prices high. But some of the larger establishments catering to business travellers may offer a lower weekend rate. It's worth asking when you book. See pp18-19 for more details on prices.

Other features

Features marked on the maps are pertinent to navigation but, to avoid clutter, not all features have been marked.

The route guide

FARNHAM [MAP 1a]

Situated roughly halfway between Winchester and London, Farnham made its money from trade in wool, then corn and in the 19th century its wealth came from brewing. Now it services well-off commuters but it also has a vibrant arts scene, a wonderful museum housed in a Grade I listed building and a fine medieval street pattern with a well-preserved Georgian streetscape in Castle St, West St and the Borough. There are guided tours of the 12th-century castle and the reputed birthplace of William Cobbett, the 18th-century politician and author of *Rural Rides*, in which he writes glowingly of the area covered in the first stage of the North Downs Way, is now a pub.

Services

The tourist information centre closed in March 2006. Since then information has only been available online (🖳 www.farnham.gov.uk).

The **railway station**, on Station Hill, is about five minutes away with hourly services to Guildford and London Waterloo, and to Portsmouth (change at Woking). National Express **coaches** drop off at the bus stop on the Borough and pick up from the stop on South St. The Stagecoach **bus service** No X64 from Guildford stops on East St; services from Winchester stop on the Borough; the service runs via Puttenham (up to 11/day, Mon-Sat only); the No 46 departs for Guildford from Farnham Station (up to 10/day, Mon-Sat); see the public transport map and table, pp37-40.

For **taxis** try Station Rank (☎ 01252-735735) or Home James (☎ 01252-722296).

There are branches of Alliance & Leicester, Barclays, NatWest, HSBC and Nationwide with **cash machines** on the Borough as well as a main **post office** (Mon-Fri 9am-5.30pm, Sat 9am-12.30pm); there is another post office on Station Rd. Sainsbury's **supermarket** (☎ 01252-734077; Mon-Sat 7am-8pm, Sun 10am-4pm) is on South St and there is a Boots **pharmacy** (Mon-Sat 9am-5.30pm, Sun

10am-4pm) on the Borough. Also on the Borough are two **outdoor shops** for last-minute gear purchases: Breaking Free (☎ 01252-724347; Mon-Sat 9am-5.30pm) and Millets (☎ 01252-711338, Mon-Sat 9am-5.30pm, Sun 10am-4pm).

Where to stay

Close to the railway station and just north of the start of the North Downs Way is ***The Exchange Hotel*** (☎ 01252-726673; 6T/3S); rates for B&B are £47sgl/35dbl. ***Meads Guest House*** (☎ 01252-715298; 1S/3D/6T), 48 West St, sandwiched between an Indian restaurant and a hairdresser, and close to the centre charges £40sgl en suite, £30 shared bathroom, £30dbl en suite, £25 shared bathroom.

For a great location and lodgings in an historic property at a fair price it's hard to beat ***1 Park Row*** (☎ 07880-541120, 🖳 www.1parkrow.com; 6D en suite or private bathroom, £47sgl/35dbl). It's just off Castle St and next door to the popular Nelson Arms (see column opposite); you may even find the keys left for collection behind the bar. The owners have arranged a 20% discount on food at the pub.

If you can face the 1½-mile walk uphill from the station consider ***15 Vicarage Lane*** (☎ 01252-723047; 1F). Mrs Burland, a friendly grandmother, charges £18 per person for an en suite room with a double and a single bed. About the same distance from the centre is Mrs Sherratt (☎ 01252-725793; 2S), ***12 Hillary Rd***, offering room only at £17.50. You can use the kitchen but she insists on a minimum two-night stay.

On the way you'll pass the well-kept ***Sandiway*** (☎ 01252-710721, 🖳 john@shortheath.freeserve.co.uk; 1D/2T), 24 Shortheath Rd, where rates are £30/25sgl/ dbl. There is no avoiding the uphill on the way to ***The White Lodge*** (☎ 01252-734166, 🖳 gill.stovold@virgin.net; 1S/1D/1T plus one king-sized room) on Lodge Hill Rd. A large, white Regency house with beautiful gardens and a refined sense of style; rates are £35 per person. Some rooms are en suite and some have a private bathroom; there is also a drying room.

About 500m further down this road, at No 73, is the spacious ***High Wray*** (☎ 01252-715589, 2T) charging £30 per person.

If location, not price, is your mantra try the 17th-century former coaching inn, ***Bush Hotel*** (☎ 0870-400 8225, 🖳 www.bushhotel.co.uk; 5S/45D all en suite) on the Borough at £112 per person Mon-Thu, from £62 per person Fri-Sun; however, rates are often discounted. They also have rooms with king-sized beds and suites.

Where to eat

The ***Q8*** (daily 6am-10pm) shop at the petrol station does snacks and drinks and is handily located for the start of the walk. If you skipped breakfast try ***Lucy's Lunchbox*** (☎ 01252-727519, 🖳 www.lucyslunchbox.co.uk; Mon-Fri 6am-4pm. Sat 8am-5pm) with all-day breakfasts from £2.50 and jacket potatoes with fillings from £3.90.

Fish and chip fans, and many walkers are, should make for ***Traditional Plaice*** (☎ 01252-718009, Mon-Sat 11.30am-2.15pm, 5-10pm), at 50 Downing St; haddock, chips and peas cost £6.95.

A couple of doors away ***Taste Buds of Farnham*** (☎ 01252-711602; Mon-Sat 8am-3pm), formerly The Stirling Sandwich, has generously filled baguettes, bagels and baps from £2.10; you can satisfy your summer-berry smoothy craving for £2.25. ***Maison Blanc*** (☎ 01252-821606, Mon-Sat 8am-6pm, Sun 9.30am-5pm), on the Borough, does delicious sandwich fillings; a goat's cheese, roast aubergine and baby spinach leaves' sandwich is £3.85 but it's fair to say portions are not huge.

The chain restaurants are here if you are looking for consistency: ***Café Rouge*** (☎ 01252-733688, 🖳 www.caferouge.co.uk; Mon-Sat 9am-11pm, Sun 10am-10.30pm) on the Borough does its interpretation of the French bistro with steak frites for £11.85 and it's usually jam packed.

Café Uno (☎ 01252-721193; Mon-Sat 10am-11pm, Sun 10am-10pm) has lunch offers from £4.95 and ***Pizza Express*** (☎ 01252-733220, Mon-Sat 11.30am-10.30/11.30pm, Sun noon-10.30pm), on Castle St, collars the Italian theme with pizza from £5.75.

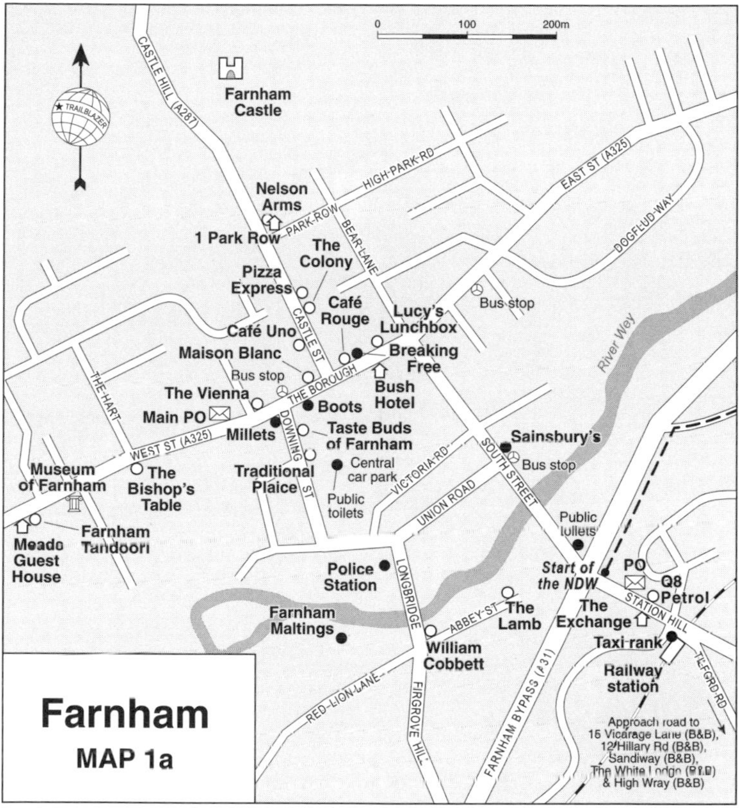

The ***Nelson Arms*** (☎ 01252-716078; food served Mon-Sat noon-10pm, Sun noon-9pm), on Castle St, is a low-beamed gastropub given the contemporary treatment with off-white walls, chunky chairs and zinc table tops. Sirloin steak is £13.95.

At 68 Castle St ***The Colony*** (☎ 01252-725108; Mon 6-11pm, Tue-Sat 12noon-2pm and 6-11pm) offers a taste of the East (prawns in oyster sauce £6.80), or try the ***Farnham Tandoori*** (☎ 01252-711860; daily noon-2pm/6-11.30pm, to midnight Fri & Sat), 47 West St next to Meads Guest House (see p66), with the ubiquitous chicken tikka masala at £8.45. For a formal dining experience try ***The Bishop's Table*** (☎ 01252-710222, 🖳 www.bishopstable.com; Tue-Sun 12.30-1.45pm & daily 7-9.45pm), at 27 West St. Start with braised pig cheek at £7.50 followed by cushion of veal for £17.20 or line-caught sea bass £18.95. There is a decent wine list quickly rising from £19 to £30 a bottle and beyond but the house red is £11.40.

At ***The Vienna*** (☎ 01252-722978; Mon-Sat noon-2pm/6-9pm, Sun noon-2pm), 112 West St, lots of attention is given to ingredients catering for nut free, vegetarian and gluten free diets. Starters such as yellow fin tuna (£7.95) to mains of Indonesian steamed sea bass (£17.95) feature.

As a former brewery town you'd expect to find a number of pubs: the ***William Cobbett*** (☎ 01252-726281; see p65) is worth a visit for its range of ales and ***The Lamb*** (☎ 01252-714133), also on Abbey St, serves lovely Spitfire ale from Shepherd Neame. It does what it says in the advertisement: No Fokker comes near it for sure.

What to see and do

If you have the time follow the comprehensive **Farnham Heritage Trail**; a free leaflet may be picked up from places such as the library, The Maltings, The Exchange Hotel or downloaded from 🖳 www.farnham.gov.uk.

Alternatively, for local lore from experienced guides, join **Farnham Town Walks** (Mr Pittuck; ☎ 01252-718119; first Sunday of every month, Apr-Oct 3pm, Nov-Mar 11am, £2 donated to charity). These walks last about 1½ hours and are commissioned by the local council.

If you are time poor visit **Farnham Castle** (☎ 01252-721194, 🖳 www.farnhamcastle.com; guided tours on Wed 2.30-3pm and also on Fri Apr-Sep, £2.50). Overlooking the town, construction was commenced in 1138 under Henry de Blois and it provided accommodation for the bishops of Winchester until 1955. Mary Tudor stayed here on her way to marry Philip of Spain in Winchester and Elizabeth I visited several times. The residential part is now occupied by Farnham Castle International Briefing and Conference Centre. The **fortified keep** is managed by English Heritage (☎ 01252-713393; Apr-Sep, Fri-Sun and Bank Holidays noon-5pm, £2.80).

Do visit, even if only briefly, the **Museum of Farnham** (☎ 01252-715094, 🖳 www.farnham.gov.uk; Tue-Sat 10am-5pm, free admission). It's located in Wilmer House, West St, a graciously proportioned Grade 1 listed building dating from 1718 with a pretty garden and the exhibits are well displayed.

There is a monthly market at **Farnham Maltings**, Bridge St (☎ 01252-726234, 🖳 www.farnhammaltings.com; first Sat in the month, 9am-4.30pm), which is also the focus of a thriving music and arts scene, and a **Farmers' Market** (☎ 01252-712667, 🖳 www.farnham.gov.uk), on the fourth Sunday of every month (10am-1.30pm), in the Central Car Park, off Victoria Rd.

FARNHAM TO GUILDFORD [MAPS 1-6b]

This **11mile/17.6km** stage is generally easy walking through a mixture of woodland, farmland and heath. The trail is mostly level with the only sustained climb just before Puttenham, home to a sensitively converted camping barn, a major benefit to walkers on a budget.

After an unpromising start to the walk at the junction of the B3000 and the busy A31, the noise soon recedes as the trail crosses the River Wey and passes along footpaths, tracks and sandy bridleways with some connecting minor roads. Seale (see p72) lies just off the trail and is worth a visit for refreshments. Allow time to visit the Watts Gallery and the Watts Cemetery Chapel at Compton, both of which really are must sees, before pushing on to the outskirts of Guildford which lies 15 minutes north of the River Wey towpath and Shalford which is 25 minutes to the south. *(cont'd on p72)*

❑ Important note – walking times

Unless otherwise specified, **all times in this book refer only to the time spent walking**. You will need to add 20-30% to allow for rests, photography, checking the map, drinking water etc. When planning the day's hike count on 5-7 hours' actual walking.

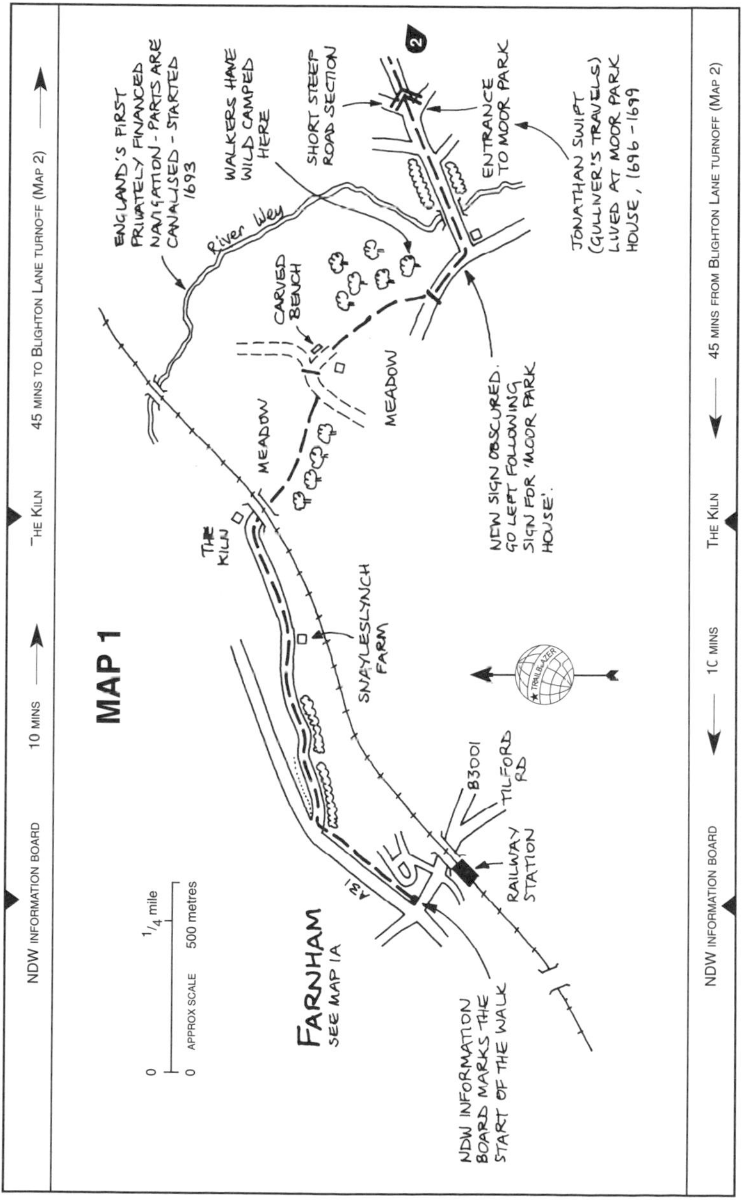
NDW INFORMATION BOARD
10 MINS
THE KILN
45 MINS TO BLIGHTON LANE TURNOFF (MAP 2)
MAP 1
0
1/4 mile
0
APPROX SCALE
500 metres
FARNHAM
SEE MAP 1A
A31
NDW INFORMATION BOARD MARKS THE START OF THE WALK
RAILWAY STATION
B3001
TILFORD RD
SNAYLESLYNCH FARM
TRAILBLAZER
THE KILN
MEADOW
MEADOW
CARVED BENCH
NEW SIGN OBSCURED. GO LEFT FOLLOWING SIGN FOR 'MOOR PARK HOUSE'.
River Wey
ENGLAND'S FIRST PRIVATELY FINANCED NAVIGATION - PARTS ARE CANALISED - STARTED 1693
WALKERS HAVE WILD CAMPED HERE
SHORT STEEP ROAD SECTION
ENTRANCE TO MOOR PARK
JONATHAN SWIFT (GULLIVER'S TRAVELS) LIVED AT MOOR PARK HOUSE, 1696-1699
2
NDW INFORMATION BOARD
10 MINS
THE KILN
45 MINS FROM BLIGHTON LANE TURNOFF (MAP 2)

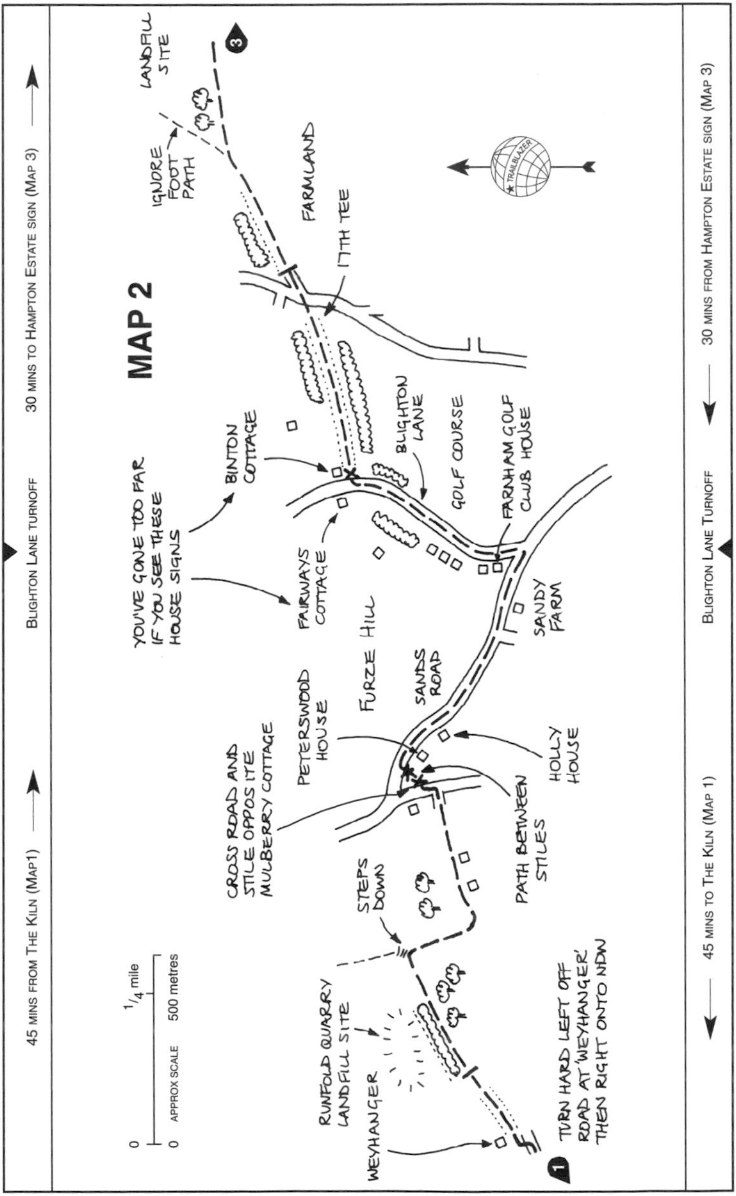
45 mins from The Kiln (Map1)
Blighton Lane turnoff
30 mins to Hampton Estate sign (Map 3)
MAP 2
0 1/4 mile
0 APPROX SCALE 500 metres
TURN HARD LEFT OFF ROAD AT 'WEYHANGER' THEN RIGHT ONTO NDW
WEYHANGER
RUNFOLD QUARRY LANDFILL SITE
STEPS DOWN
CROSS ROAD AND STILE OPPOSITE MULBERRY COTTAGE
PATH BETWEEN STILES
PETERSWOOD HOUSE
HOLLY HOUSE
FURZE HILL
SANDS ROAD
YOU'VE GONE TOO FAR IF YOU SEE THESE HOUSE SIGNS
FAIRWAYS COTTAGE
BINTON COTTAGE
SANDY FARM
FARNHAM GOLF CLUB HOUSE
GOLF COURSE
BLIGHTON LANE
17TH TEE
FARMLAND
IGNORE FOOT PATH
LANDFILL SITE
TRAILBLAZER
45 mins to The Kiln (Map 1)
Blighton Lane Turnoff
30 mins from Hampton Estate sign (Map 3)

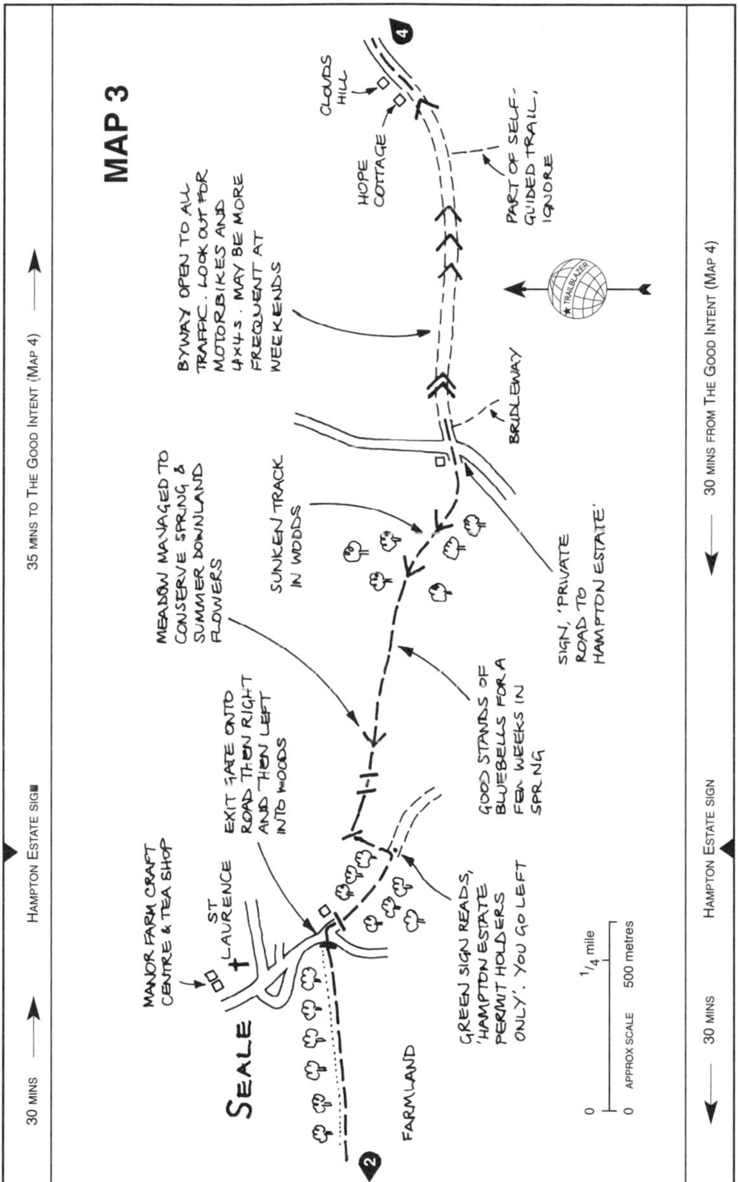
MAP 3
30 MINS →
HAMPTON ESTATE SIGN
35 MINS TO THE GOOD INTENT (MAP 4) →
← 30 MINS
HAMPTON ESTATE SIGN
← 30 MINS FROM THE GOOD INTENT (MAP 4)
SEALE
MANOR FARM CRAFT CENTRE & TEA SHOP
ST LAURENCE
FARMLAND
EXIT GATE ONTO ROAD THEN RIGHT AND THEN LEFT INTO WOODS
GREEN SIGN READS, 'HAMPTON ESTATE PERMIT HOLDERS ONLY'. YOU GO LEFT
GOOD STANDS OF BLUEBELLS FOR A FEW WEEKS IN SPRING
MEADOW MANAGED TO CONSERVE SPRING & SUMMER DOWNLAND FLOWERS
SUNKEN TRACK IN WOODS
SIGN, 'PRIVATE ROAD TO HAMPTON ESTATE'
BRIDLEWAY
BYWAY OPEN TO ALL TRAFFIC. LOOK OUT FOR MOTORBIKES AND 4x4s. MAY BE MORE FREQUENT AT WEEKENDS
TRAILBLAZER
HOPE COTTAGE
CLOUDS HILL
PART OF SELF-GUIDED TRAIL, IGNORE
0 1/4 mile
0 500 metres
APPROX SCALE

SEALE [MAP 3]

A five-minute detour will bring you to this hamlet with its attractive church, St Laurence, and the great-value ***Manor Craft Centre and Tea Room*** (☎ 01252-783661; Tue-Sun and Bank Holiday Mondays 10.30am-5pm). Set in a converted milking parlour with a wood-burning stove to take the chill away in winter, choose from tea (80p), soup of the day (£2.20), filled rolls with salad (£2.50), or big slices of home-made cake, up to five choices at £1.30 per slice; any of which will set you up for the climb before Puttenham.

The only **bus** service is Stagecoach's No 547 and that is only once a day on Tuesday and Friday; it stops by the church.

PUTTENHAM [MAP 4]

This long village is lined with pretty brick, stone, timber and tile-hung cottages. Unfortunately the village shop and post office have closed but Puttenham retains two pubs and walkers will benefit from ***Puttenham Camping Barn*** (☎ 01306-877978, 🖳 www.puttnhamcampingbarn.co.uk; open 5pm-10am, up to 11 spaces, prior booking essential), which opened in April 2005 and provides budget accommodation for £9 per person. The barn is a listed building restored over a period of ten years using sustainable materials and solar energy. Sleeping accommodation is on a three-section foam-lined wooden platform; sleeping bag essential.

The ***Good Intent*** (☎ 01483-810387; food daily 12noon-2pm, Tue-Sat 7-9.30pm) is a popular low-beamed pub with inglenook fireplace and does a good line in food. Fish and chips night is Wednesday night with the unusual offering of bull huss in addition to cod and haddock at £6.95.

Stagecoach's **bus** X64 (Mon-Sat only) and No 547 (Tue and Fri, 1/day) stop here by the Good Intent; see the public transport map and table, pp37-40.

Leaving the village the trail passes opposite the ***Jolly Farmer*** (☎ 01483-810374; food served daily noon-10pm), part of the Harvester chain, and continues through woodland bordering Puttenham Heath, geologically unusual in this area of chalk before reaching the outskirts of Compton.

COMPTON [MAP 5]

The village of Compton is busy with traffic because of the nearby A3 and has no obvious centre but it does have a collection of 19th- and 20th-century cottages and the **parish church of St Nicholas**, dating from the 11th century, is worth a visit particularly to see the two-storey sanctuary with a magnificent vault and nine-arch balustrade above it.

The ***Harrow Inn*** (☎ 01483-810379) serves lunches 12-3pm (12-4pm on Sunday). There's no food available on Sunday evenings. The Withies (see p74) is closed on Sunday evening so bear this in mind if you plan on staying the night here. You may want to press on to Shalford or Guildford.

Stagecoach **bus** No 46 (to/from Guildford and Farnham, Mon-Sat only, 8-10/day) stops on Down Lane; see the public transport map and table, pp37-40.

❑ Puttenham Heath

You may be surprised to come across this large area of heath filled with heather, an acid-loving plant in this area of chalk. That's because you're walking next to an area of greensand rock which is acid and porous. Plant material that decays forms a dry peat and the soil is then occupied by small-leaved acid-loving plants equipped for retaining moisture.

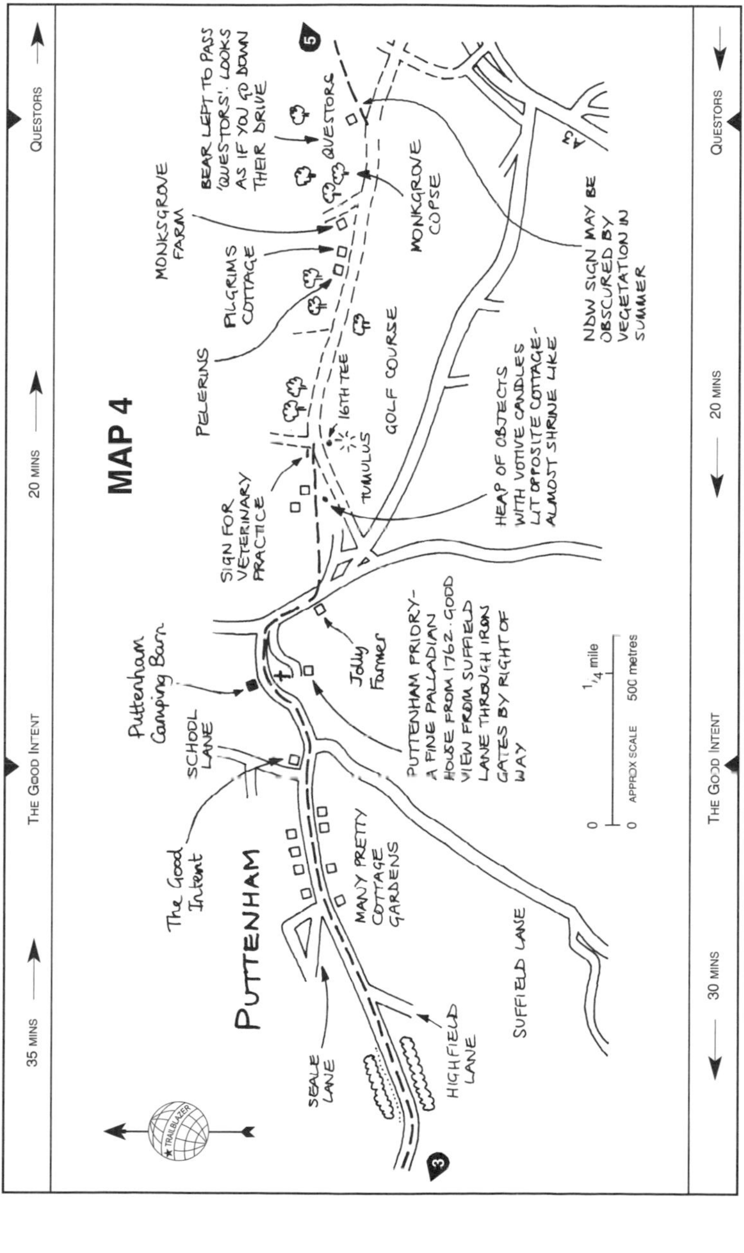
MAP 4
35 MINS
THE GOOD INTENT
20 MINS
QUESTORS
30 MINS
THE GOOD INTENT
20 MINS
QUESTORS
TRAILBLAZER
PUTTENHAM
SEALE LANE
HIGHFIELD LANE
The Good Intent
SCHOOL LANE
Puttenham Camping Barn
MANY PRETTY COTTAGE GARDENS
SUFFIELD LANE
PUTTENHAM PRIORY- A FINE PALLADIAN HOUSE FROM 1762. GOOD VIEW FROM SUFFIELD LANE THROUGH IRON GATES BY RIGHT OF WAY
Jolly Farmer
SIGN FOR VETERINARY PRACTICE
HEAP OF OBJECTS WITH VOTIVE CANDLES LIT OPPOSITE COTTAGE- ALMOST SHRINE LIKE
TUMULUS
16TH TEE
GOLF COURSE
PELERINS
PILGRIMS COTTAGE
MONKSGROVE FARM
MONKGROVE COPSE
BEAR LEFT TO PASS 'QUESTORS'. LOOKS AS IF YOU GO DOWN THEIR DRIVE
QUESTORS
NDW SIGN MAY BE OBSCURED BY VEGETATION IN SUMMER
A3
0
1/4 mile
0
APPROX SCALE
500 metres

The trail emerges below **Watts Gallery** (☎ 01483-810235, 🖳 www.watts gallery.org.uk; Mar-Oct Mon-Sat 2-6pm, Wed & Sat 11am-1pm, Oct-Mar 2-4pm, closed Thursday all year, admission free), an intimate space exhibiting works of the Victorian artist and sculptor George Frederic Watts, which is well worth a visit. The building which is in need of repair was a finalist in the BBC's *Restoration Village* programme putting it in line to raise substantial funds needed for roof repairs. Next door, in the former pottery workshop of the Compton Potters Guild, is the ***Compton Tea Shop*** (☎ 01483-811030; open daily 10.30am-5.30pm, closed Dec 24th-Jan 5th), just the place for gooey Welsh rarebit (£3). With over 40 green, black and flavoured teas it'll satisfy those who want anything from Darjeeling to blackberry and nettle. Also on Down Lane is the red-brick **Watts Cemetery Chapel** (open daily but locked at dusk; admission free), built by Watts's wife. His remains are interred in the cloister nearby. Irish yews line the path up to the chapel and the floral forms, tendrils and crosses on the exterior reveal the art nouveau, Celtic, Romanesque and Egyptian influences. Some may need to continue walking and recover their balance after seeing the dazzling interior decorated with red, silver and gold images and angels.

About 10 minutes east of Watts Gallery on the North Downs Way take the bridleway signed right and you will emerge by ***Little Polsted*** (☎ 01483-810398; 1D/1T) an attractive cottage with parts dating from the 16th century. B&B is £45/40 sgl/dbl. If they are full ***Mrs Arnold*** (☎ 01483-417313; 1S/1D private bathroom), 4 Tuttocks Cottage, Withies La, may have rooms at £20sgl/dbl. Within stumbling distance is ***Withies Inn*** (☎ 01483-421158; bar food Mon-Sat noon-2.30pm and 7-10pm, Sun noon-2.30pm only), which in summer has a very attractive beer garden, perfect for sinking a local brew from the Hog's Back Brewery, and serves a thick-cut gammon sandwich for £4.50.

The trail passes above **Littleton** and the church of St Francis (see Map 6 p77) to emerge at ***Ye Olde Ship Inn*** (☎ 01483-575731; food served Mon-Sat noon-3pm/7-11.30pm) on the outskirts of Guildford. A large sign asks patrons to switch off mobile phones so presumably they have to rely on semaphore. There are plenty of wines by the glass to go with pizzas from the wood-fired oven, £5 for a basic tomato and basil, or create your own from over 25 toppings at £1/1.20 a topping.

On reaching the River Wey you can either turn right (south) to Shalford or left (north) to Guildford along the towpath.

SHALFORD [MAP 6a]

Shalford has an attractive village green complete with cricketers most of the summer, a church with a **John Bunyan** connection, a National Trust **restored mill** and the remnants of some **WWII defences**. It's also home to **Ambient Picnic**, a one-day, car-free, family-oriented music and arts festival with poets, healers, jugglers and all manner of green interests; the festival is usually held annually (at the end of July/early August) but did not happen in 2006.

Services

Shalford Pharmacy (☎ 01483-561975; Mon-Fri 9am-1pm/2-6pm, Sat 9am-1pm/2-5pm) is at 7 Kings Rd. Further along, the **Total Garage and Shop** (Mon-Sat 7am-9.50pm, Sun 8.30am-8.50pm) has snacks, water and basic food provisions and the **post office** (Mon-Fri 9am-5.30pm, Sat 9am-12.30pm) is just beyond that.

A branch line service operates from the **train station** to Guildford (Mon-Sat 1-2/hr,

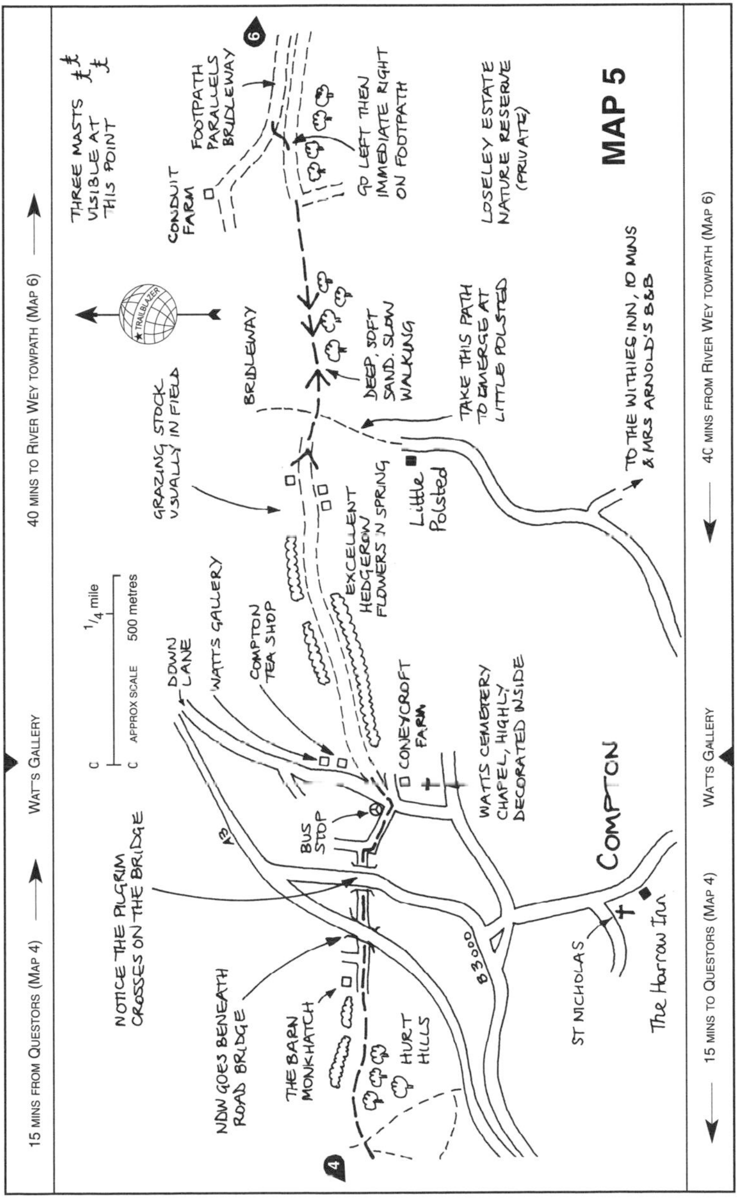
15 MINS FROM QUESTORS (MAP 4) →
WATTS GALLERY
40 MINS TO RIVER WEY TOWPATH (MAP 6) →
← 15 MINS TO QUESTORS (MAP 4)
WATTS GALLERY
← 40 MINS FROM RIVER WEY TOWPATH (MAP 6)
MAP 5
4
6
APPROX SCALE
0
1/4 mile
0
500 metres
TRAILBLAZER
NOTICE THE PILGRIM CROSSES ON THE BRIDGE
NDW GOES BENEATH ROAD BRIDGE
THE BARN MONKHATCH
HURT HILLS
A3
B3000
BUS STOP
DOWN LANE
WATTS GALLERY
COMPTON TEA SHOP
CONEYCROFT FARM
WATTS CEMETERY CHAPEL, HIGHLY DECORATED INSIDE
COMPTON
ST NICHOLAS
The Harrow Inn
EXCELLENT HEDGEROW FLOWERS IN SPRING
Little Polsted
GRAZING STOCK USUALLY IN FIELD
BRIDLEWAY
DEEP, SOFT SAND. SLOW WALKING
TAKE THIS PATH TO EMERGE AT LITTLE POLSTED
TO THE WITHIES INN, 10 MINS & MRS ARNOLD'S B&B
THREE MASTS VISIBLE AT THIS POINT
CONDUIT FARM
FOOTPATH PARALLELS BRIDLEWAY
GO LEFT THEN IMMEDIATE RIGHT ON FOOTPATH
LOSELEY ESTATE NATURE RESERVE (PRIVATE)

Sun one every two hours. Arriva **bus** Nos 21, 24, 25 and 32 operate 5-10/day, Mon-Sat only – they depart from the railway station and serve Guildford, Albury, Chilworth, Gomshall, Holmbury St Mary and Dorking; see the public transport map and table, pp37-40.

Where to stay

Parrot Inn (☎ 01483-561400, 🖳 www.parrotinn.co.uk; 2D/2T/1F all en suite), with B&B for £50sgl/£32.50dbl or twin / £28.30 fml, is just off the River Wey towpath over the bridge on Broadford Rd and is very popular for its food (see below).

The cats at ***The Laurels*** (☎ 01483-565753; 1T/1D), 23 Dagden Rd, are used to welcoming walkers. Tea always seems to be on the boil and B&B is £25 per person. At ***No 2 Northfield*** (☎ 01483-570431; 1T en suite), the Mordens offer a spacious room in an immaculately kept house for £20 per person, £22.50 single occupancy. They will collect you from the towpath at Broadford Bridge and other nearby points, and will drop you off in the morning.

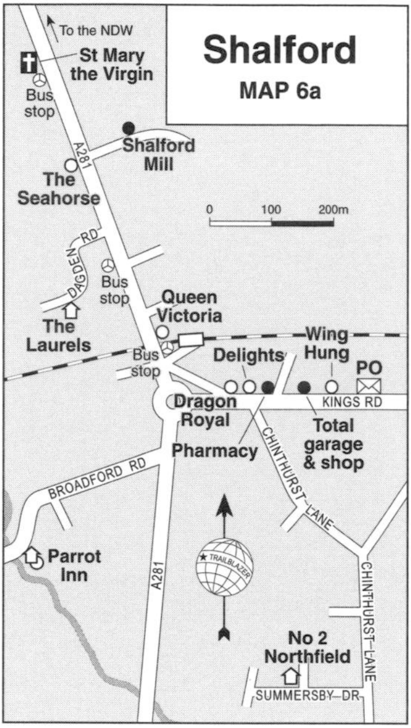

Where to eat

If you stay at The Laurels (see above), ***The Seahorse*** (☎ 01483-514351; food served daily noon-9.30pm) is conveniently around the corner off the busy Shalford Rd. Cheese and chutney sandwiches will set you back £3.95, and calves liver, bacon and sage mash is £9.25. The ***Parrot Inn*** (see above) attracts large crowds for the likes of grilled whole sea bass (£9.20), and steak and kidney pie (£7.90). Sunday lunch is very busy and there is no food service on Sunday evening when the pub is closed for a well-earned rest. The ***Queen Victoria*** by the train station does pub grub.

Wing Hung (☎ 01483-567111; Tue-Sat noon-2pm, daily 5-10pm, to 10.30pm Sun & Mon, to 11pm Fri & Sat) does Cantonese and Szechuan cuisine – specials include stir-fried mussels in black bean sauce at £4.80 – as well as fish and chips. The ***Dragon Royal Restaurant*** (☎ 01483-452550; open daily noon-2.30pm/6-11pm) serving Thai and Vietnamese cuisine has a loyal following for its Sunday buffet (noon-3pm at £10.90 per person).

Delights Sandwich Bar (☎ 01483-303038; Mon-Sat 7am-4pm) will fill your lunch box.

What to see and do

If you do detour to Shalford read the plaque on the wall at The Seahorse marking the location of a **WWII road block**, the last ditch defence against an expected German invasion in 1940. Opposite is the lane to **Shalford Mill** (☎ 01483-561389; Wed & Sun 11am-5pm, Mar-Oct, £2.50/1.25 adult/child). The timber-framed mill was given to the National Trust in 1932 by anonymous benefactors calling themselves Ferguson's Gang.

Further along the A281 is the parish church of **St Mary the Virgin** where a large embroidery work by the Women's Institute depicting **John Bunyan's**

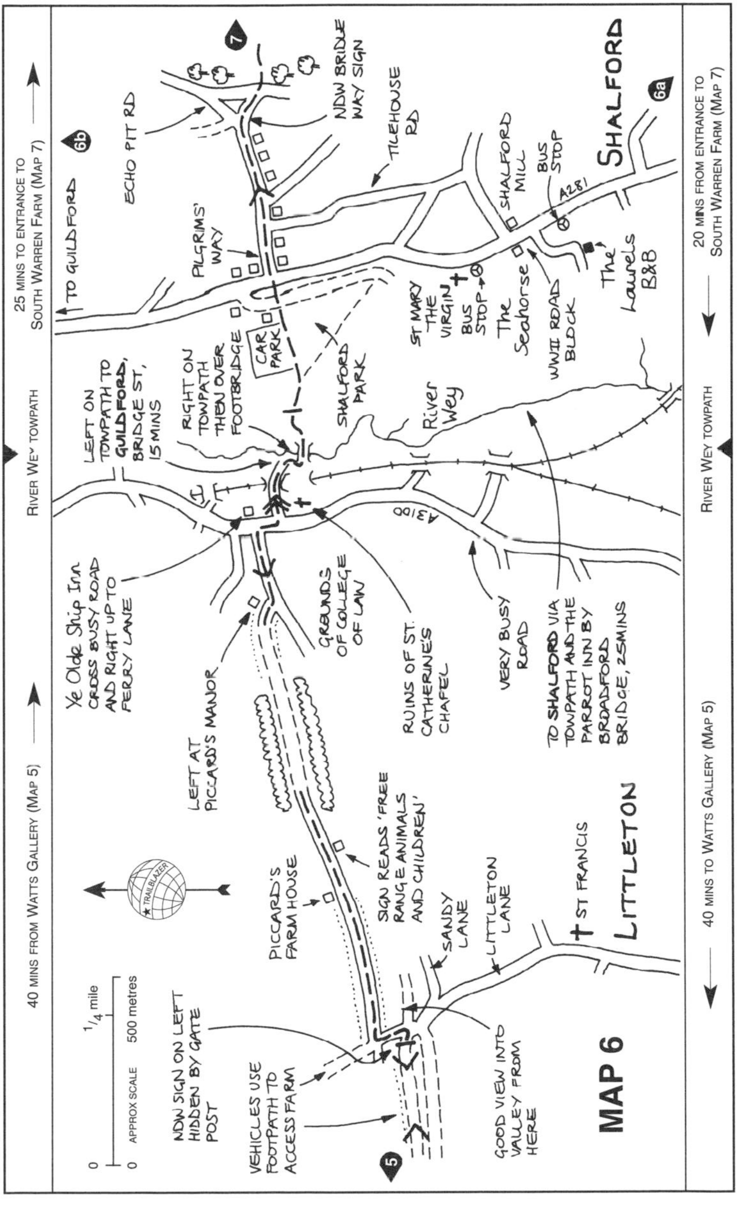
MAP 6
APPROX SCALE
0
1/4 mile
0
500 metres
40 MINS FROM WATTS GALLERY (MAP 5)
40 MINS TO WATTS GALLERY (MAP 5)
25 MINS TO ENTRANCE TO SOUTH WARREN FARM (MAP 7)
20 MINS FROM ENTRANCE TO SOUTH WARREN FARM (MAP 7)
RIVER WEY TOWPATH
RIVER WEY TOWPATH
TRAILBLAZER
5
6b
7
6a
NDW SIGN ON LEFT HIDDEN BY GATE POST
VEHICLES USE FOOTPATH TO ACCESS FARM
GOOD VIEW INTO VALLEY FROM HERE
PICCARD'S FARM HOUSE
SANDY LANE
LITTLETON LANE
ST FRANCIS
LITTLETON
SIGN READS 'FREE RANGE ANIMALS AND CHILDREN'
LEFT AT PICCARD'S MANOR
Ye Olde Ship Inn
CROSS BUSY ROAD AND RIGHT UP TO FERRY LANE
GROUNDS OF COLLEGE OF LAW
RUINS OF ST. CATHERINE'S CHAPEL
VERY BUSY ROAD
TO SHALFORD VIA TOWPATH AND THE PARROT INN BY BROADFORD BRIDGE, 25MINS
A3100
LEFT ON TOWPATH TO GUILDFORD, BRIDGE ST, 15MINS
RIGHT ON TOWPATH THEN OVER FOOTBRIDGE
CAR PARK
SHALFORD PARK
River Wey
ST MARY THE VIRGIN
BUS STOP
The Seahorse
WWII ROAD BLOCK
The Laurels B&B
PILGRIMS' WAY
TO GUILDFORD
ECHO PIT RD
NDW BRIDLE WAY SIGN
TILEHOUSE RD
SHALFORD MILL
BUS STOP
A281
SHALFORD

Pilgrim's Progress hangs on the south wall. Bunyan's book is an allegory of Christian life where the main character Christian sets off on a journey from the city of Destruction to the Celestial City with countless temptations placed in his way on the road to Salvation. Bunyan allegedly came to the Surrey Hills when his preaching got him in trouble. Some claim that the boggy ground on Shalford Common inspired the description which has entered the English language: the Slough of Despond.

GUILDFORD [MAP 6b]

Guildford is the lively county town of Surrey and an ideal access point to the North Downs Way with good public transport links, plenty of accommodation, a wide range of restaurants and lots to see and do. There are many significant historic buildings – the **Guildhall** with its projecting town clock, the one surviving **coaching inn**, The Angel Posting House, and the **almshouses** of Abbot's Hospital – and the car-free cobbled High St is criss-crossed by alleys and lanes.

Much of the town is given over to shopping and nightlife, but whether wandering through the Shambles, a maze of narrow alleys, around the Castle or along Tunsgate take time to look up and admire the facades and get a sense of the town's Medieval, Jacobean and Regency market town past.

Services

The **tourist information centre** (TIC; ☎ 01483-444333, 🖳 www.guildfordborough.co.uk) is through the Regency arch at 14 Tunsgate; it is open May-Sep, Mon-Sat 9am-5.30pm, Sun 10am-4pm; and Oct-Apr, Mon-Sat 9.30am-5pm. There is an accommodation-booking service. The **public library** (☎ 01483-568496; Mon/Fri 9.30am-8pm, Tue/Thur 9.30am-5pm, Wed 9.30am-1pm, Sat 9.30-4pm), 77 North St, has **free internet access** once you've joined the Surrey library system; just bring two pieces of identification such as a passport, driver's licence or utility bill. If you want to soothe tired walking muscles there is open-air swimming at the 50-metre **Lido** pool (☎ 01483-444888; Apr-Sept, daily 10.30am-6.30pm, £4.70). **Spectrum** (☎ 01483-443322) near to the Stoke Rd B&Bs has an indoor pool open year-round.

If you've forgotten any essential kit **Blacks** (☎ 01483-506432, 🖳 www.blacks.co.uk; Mon-Sat 9am-5.30pm, Thurs until 7pm, Sun 11am-5pm), at Phoenix Ct, should be able to help out. Or at the far end of the High St try **Field&Trek** (☎ 01483-573286; Mon-Fri 9.30am-6pm, Sat 9am-6pm, Sun 11am-5pm).

There is a **post office** (Mon-Fri 9am-5.30pm/Tue 9.30am opening, Sat 9am-1pm) at 171-3 High St and plenty of banks with **cash machines** on High St and North St as well as a **cashback** facility at **Sainsbury's** supermarket, High St; there is also a Boots **chemist** (Mon-Sat 8am-6pm/Thurs 7pm, Sun 11am-5pm) and a **bureau de change** at Marks & Spencer if the banks are not open.

The **bus station** for local services is Friary Bus Station by the eponymous shopping centre. Arriva Bus's Nos 21, 24, 25 and 32 serve variously Shalford, Chilworth, Albury, Shere, Gomshall, Westcott, Holmbury St Mary, Dorking, Betchworth and Redhill (5-10/day, Mon-Sat only). Stagecoach's No X64 and No 46 go to Farnham, the latter via Compton. National Express **coaches** drop off and collect at Egerton Rd; to get there walkers will have to turn off Farnham Rd at Guildford Park Rd.

The **train station** has mainline services to London Waterloo (2/hr daily) and Portsmouth (direct 2/hr daily) as well as services to Gatwick Airport via Redhill and Heathrow via Woking and the Railair coach link (2/hr) – note that the service to Gatwick on Sundays may be by bus if engineering works are being carried out; expect three departures per hour Mon-Sat, 2/hr Sundays; see the public transport map and table, pp37-40.

There is a **taxi** rank at the station and another at the foot of the High St; alternatively call City Cabs (☎ 01483-539393) or Guildford Radio Cabs (☎ 01483-567110), both operate 24 hours.

Where to stay

The ***Y Centre*** (☎ 01483-532555, 💻 www.guildfordymca.org.uk; 114S/3T shared bathroom/3T en suite) is on Bridge St. Centrally located it's about four minutes from the High St and two minutes from the railway station and right next to the towpath leading to the North Downs Way. A clean, comfortable single room with a shared bath and toilet between two rooms is £36; a twin with shared bath is £50, en suite £54. One drawback is it's close to Guildford's raucous bar and nightclub scene (see box p81) so get home before closing time.

Elevated above the town is the walker-friendly ***No 18 Harvey Rd*** (☎ 01483-534946, 💻 www.bedandbreakfasts-uk.co.uk/visitpatcham; 1D en suite shower/1T private bathroom) offering an attractive rate of £27.50dbl/twn, £35 single occupancy.

Patcham (☎ 01483-570789; 1S/2T), 44 Farnham Rd – look for the white squirrel on the gatepost – is a comfortable place less than ten minutes to the west of the train station costing £24sgl/24 shared bathroom/27twin en suite, with continental

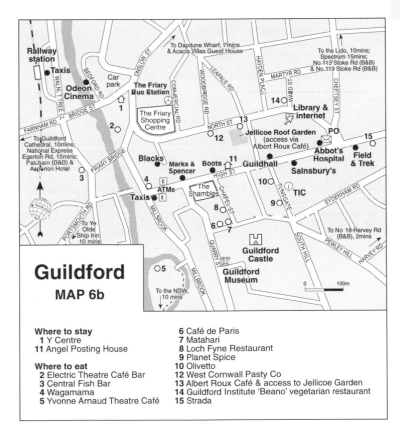

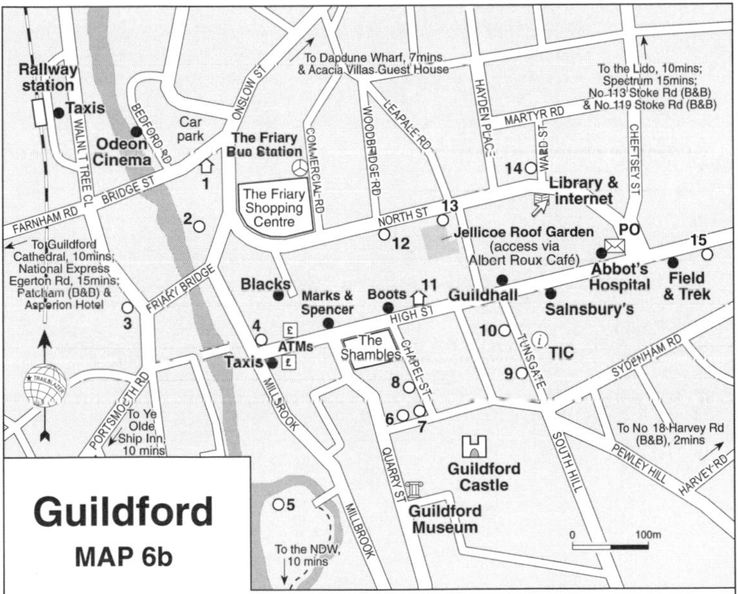

Where to stay
1 Y Centre
11 Angel Posting House

Where to eat
2 Electric Theatre Café Bar
3 Central Fish Bar
4 Wagamama
5 Yvonne Arnaud Theatre Café
6 Café de Paris
7 Matahari
8 Loch Fyne Restaurant
9 Planet Spice
10 Olivetto
12 West Cornwall Pasty Co
13 Albert Roux Café & access to Jellicoe Garden
14 Guildford Institute 'Beano' vegetarian restaurant
15 Strada

breakfast. Across the road is the ***Asperion Hotel*** (☎ 01483-579299, 🖳 www.asperion.co.uk; 4S/11D, singles have private bathroom, remainder en suite) with singles starting at £50 and doubles from £37.50 to £45 per person depending on the room size. Formerly the Crawford House Hotel the personable new owners have transformed it with a complete makeover and stylish contemporary furniture. They offer an organic breakfast and it's no smoking throughout.

About ten minutes north of the High St on Stoke Rd are several traditional older-style B&Bs but their prices have kept up with the times: ***No 113*** (☎ 01483-453025, 🖳 www.stokehouse.net; 3S/2T) costs from £35 single with shared bath or £32.50 for a twin en suite; ***No 119*** (☎ 01483-532200, 🖳 www.abeillehouse.co.uk; 2S/2T) charges £40/30sgl/twin and £42.50 for twin en suite. Close to the cricket ground and next door to the Tong Tong Chinese takeaway on Woodbridge Rd is ***Acacia Villas Guest House*** (☎ 01483-458884; 2T/2S/1F) where room only is £35/25/25 sgl/dbl/fml; breakfast costs £3 per person.

If you feel you are carrying too much weight the ***Angel Posting House*** (☎ 01483-564555, 🖳 www.angelpostinghouse.com; 21D all en suite), on the High St just below the Guildhall, will lighten your wallet with rates from £155 per room even for single occupancy. You get to stay in the last surviving coaching inn in England; there is Jacobean timber framing behind the Regency façade and a restored Medieval undercroft or basement.

Where to eat

On the way into town from the North Downs Way is the ***Yvonne Arnaud Theatre Café*** (☎ 01483-569334; Mon-Sat 10am-8pm, 4.30pm if no evening performance) offering sandwiches (from £2.50), salmon salad (£6.95), or just a refreshing cup of tea (£1.20). The ***Electric Theatre Café Bar*** (☎ 01483-444786; Mon-Sat 10.30am-11pm or 5pm if no show), on Onslow St, is a hipper outfit as befits the art-house cinema. The light and airy bar and the water's edge terrace is pleasant in summer. Spanish tapas start at £5.95, tarts of roasted tomato, onion and haloumi cheese are £4.75, while a traditional rib eye steak is £8.50.

For a bite on the go try ***West Cornwall Pasty Co*** (Mon-Sat 9am-5pm, Sun 11am-4pm) on North St, or for fish and chips ***Central Fish Bar*** (Mon-Sat noon-2.30pm, 5.30pm-12midnight, Sun 5.30-11.30pm) on Park St.

Wagamama (☎ 01483-457779; Mon-Sat noon-11pm, Sun 12.30-10pm), at the corner of High St and Friary St, does good-value noodle dishes served at long, shared refectory tables. A filling chicken chilli noodle soup (*ramen*) is £7.65 and tasty fried dumplings (*gyoza*) are £4.25.

For Japanese/Thai dishes try ***Matahari*** (☎ 01483-457886, Mon-Fri noon-2.30pm & 6-11pm, Sat/Sun noon-11pm), 10-11 Chapel St, for an assorted sushi lunch (£9.90).

A couple of doors down is the upmarket fish restaurant and oyster bar ***Loch Fyne Restaurant*** (☎ 01483-230550, 🖳 www.lochfyne.com) where you can tip back a dozen slippery molluscs for £13.95.

The bistro setting at ***Café de Paris*** (☎ 01483-534896, 🖳 www.cafedeparis-guildford.co.uk; Mon-Sat noon-2.30pm/6-10.30pm) is attractive. There's a fixed price menu (£12.50 for two courses) if seated by 7pm, or choose á la carte: rabbit is £9.50 and Isle of Lewis lamb rump, £19.50.

Curry lovers will appreciate ***Planet Spice*** (☎ 01483-306222; daily noon-2.30pm/6-11.30pm) and the prices are reasonable; a zesty trout curry is £7.95. It's almost opposite the TIC in Tunsgate. Also on Tunsgate is ***Olivetto*** (☎ 01483-563277; Mon-Sat noon-2.30pm, 6-10.30pm, Sun noon-8.30pm). Housed in an old Tudor dis-

---

(**Opposite**) Just outside Guildford, the terracotta-tiled Watts Cemetery Chapel (**top**; see p74), designed by Mary Watts and built using clay from her garden, stands in grounds still used as the village cemetery. The stunning gesso murals (**bottom left**) in the small vaulted interior were completed in 1904. The entrance door (**bottom right**) shows Celtic and Art Nouveau details. (Photos © Jennifer Ullman).

❑ Guildford – roll out the barrel

It might be part of the leafy stockbroker belt but there is a drinking culture in Guildford with plenty of pubs offering doubles for an extra pound, two-for-one deals, or 'flirty Fridays'. So finding a pub serving a quiet pint is difficult.

The area around Bridge St, Onslow Rd and Millbrook is a magnet for clubbers and young bar hoppers – the popular venue ***The Drink***, on Onslow St near the corner with Bridge St, just about sums it up. But for more civilized surroundings try Ye Olde Ship Inn (see p74) just out of town on the Portsmouth Rd, or enjoy a glass in the contemporary surroundings of the Electric Theatre (see p80).

pensary this cozy Italian restaurant and wine bar serves starters of asparagus wrapped in ham (£4.95) and classics such as veal marsala (£12.85). There is a pizza menu (from £6.90) but it's not available Friday or Saturday nights.

But ***Strada*** (☎ 01483-454455, 💻 www.strada.co.uk; daily noon-11pm, to 10.30pm Sun), 222 High St, promise 'designer pizza in an effortlessly chic setting' all week long.

If you want a great view join the ladies who lunch at ***Albert Roux Café*** (☎ 01483-534599; Mon-Sat 9am-5pm, Sun 11am-4pm), 4th floor at House of Fraser, High St. Sleekly groomed waiting-staff will guide you to the curved purple banquettes. Sandwiches start at £7.50 and a chicken *bois boudran* (that's marinated chicken to you and me) will set you back £9.95 but the real attraction is the restored Jellicoe Roof Garden (see column opposite).

The vegetarian restaurant ***Beano*** at the Guildford Institute (☎ 01483-562142, Mon-Fri plus first Sat of every month 12 noon-2pm, booking advised), on Ward St, is a busy good-value lunch spot. Two courses are £5.95, or you can have soup of the day (£2.10), or chickpea ratatouille for £2.95.

What to see and do

It's easy to go from Medieval to Modern so rich is Guildford's architectural history despite the best efforts of 1960s' planners and busy roads scything close to the High St. The **Guildhall** (☎ 01483-444035, 💻 www.guildford.gov.uk; tours Tue/Thurs, 2pm & 3pm) was built in 1683 and its bracket clock jutting over the High St is the town's symbol.

Further east is **Abbot's Hospital** almshouse still providing accommodation for the elderly poor. Access is limited but you can peer into the courtyard and admire the fine Jacobean brickwork. **Guildford Castle** (☎ 01483-444750; Apr-Sep daily 11am-6pm, closed Dec-Feb, otherwise Sat & Sun 11am-4pm) dates from the 13th century. There are spectacular displays of bedding plants in the grounds in summer.

Guildford Cathedral (☎ 01483-303350, 💻 www.guildford-cathedral.org; daily 8.30am-5.30pm) overlooks the town from its commanding position on Stag Hill. Movie buffs will recognize it from the 1976 classic *The Omen*. Italian marble floors and Somerset sandstone grace the pale interior of the first post-Reformation cathedral to be built on a new site.

If you stay at the Y Centre or Acacia Villas the National Trust's **Dapdune Wharf** (☎ 01483-561389, 💻 www.nationaltrust.org.uk; Apr-Oct, Mon & Thur-Sun, 11am-5pm) is nearby telling the story of England's first privately financed navigation – the River Wey.

The Jellicoe Roof Gardens at the House of Fraser (see Albert Roux Café column opposite) was refurbished in 2000-1

(Opposite) Top: With twenty per cent of the route bridleway, chances are you'll meet people out riding as here on Albury Downs (see p85). **Bottom**: A view over Dorking (see p95). (Photos © John Curtin).

and access is via the café. Designed in 1958 by landscape architect Sir Geoffrey Jellicoe, the circular planters were inspired by the launch of the Russian satellite Sputnik. It's a remarkable example of 1950s' elements which do not appear dated. Have lunch there if you scrub up well or ask nicely at the café to see it.

There is also a **farmers' market** on the High St on the first Tuesday of every month. If you want to rest your legs you might to like to go to a show at the Yvonne Arnaud **theatre** (☎ 01483-440000, 💻 www.yvonne-arnaud.co.uk) – a lot of the productions are pre West End – or see a **film** at the Odeon cinema.

GUILDFORD TO DORKING [MAPS 6-12a]

This **13mile/20.8km** day begins with a climb to St Martha's Hill and a further, gentle, climb along Albury Downs to gain the North Downs Way ridgeline at Newlands Corner, where there is a choice of refreshment options and superb views over the Down and Weald landscape on a clear day.

The trail then strikes east along a drove road with classic woodland walking. To get to Shere, Surrey's prettiest village, see p86, you need to leave the Way along the bridleway at Hollister Farm, see Map 9, this joins a by-way, crosses the A25 and enters Shere by the car park. The trail emerges at Ranmore Common and passes the Gothic-style church of St Barnabas. This is known as 'the church on the North Downs Way', though it is not the only one on the Way – St Martha's (see box below) bagged the title 'Pilgrims' Church'. However, St Barnabas was built by Sir George Gilbert Scott in 1859 for the Cubit family, then owners of the nearby Denbies Estate. Scott also designed the Albert Memorial and King's Cross St Pancras Station in London. His grandson, Sir Giles, designed Battersea Power Station, Bankside (now the Tate Modern) and the iconic red phone boxes that were once so common all over Britain.

The trail descends through England's largest vineyard on the outskirts of Dorking. A short diversion to the visitor centre and the winery tour are recommended. Dorking has plenty of accommodation options and good transport links.

CHILWORTH [OFF MAP 7]

Chilworth straggles along the A248 but it has a small **grocery store**, a **post office** and **train station** with services to Guildford and Redhill (up to 3/hr). Arriva's **buses** Nos 21, 25 and 32 (Mon-Sat only) stop at the station; see the public transport map and table, pp37-40.

The village also has a good pub, ***The Percy Arms*** (☎ 01483-561765; food Mon-Sat noon-3pm/6-10pm, Sun noon-3pm/6-9pm). Come here to have a 'tailor made' rump steak – you choose your steak from the butcher's counter, it's sized by the inch and is then cooked to order (from £14.95).

❑ St Martha

The church of St Martha (Map 7) stands 525ft atop St Martha's Hill. Some say its name derives from **martyr** as early Christians are reputed to have been killed here. A more mainstream view is that the original Norman church was dedicated to St Martha. It is believed that pilgrims visited the church on the way to Canterbury, so it is often referred to as the Pilgrims' Church, especially when they're fundraising. It's debatable whether there was ever only one route pilgrims followed to Canterbury but it's likely that they found the church a convenient place to stop and rest if not practise their piety.

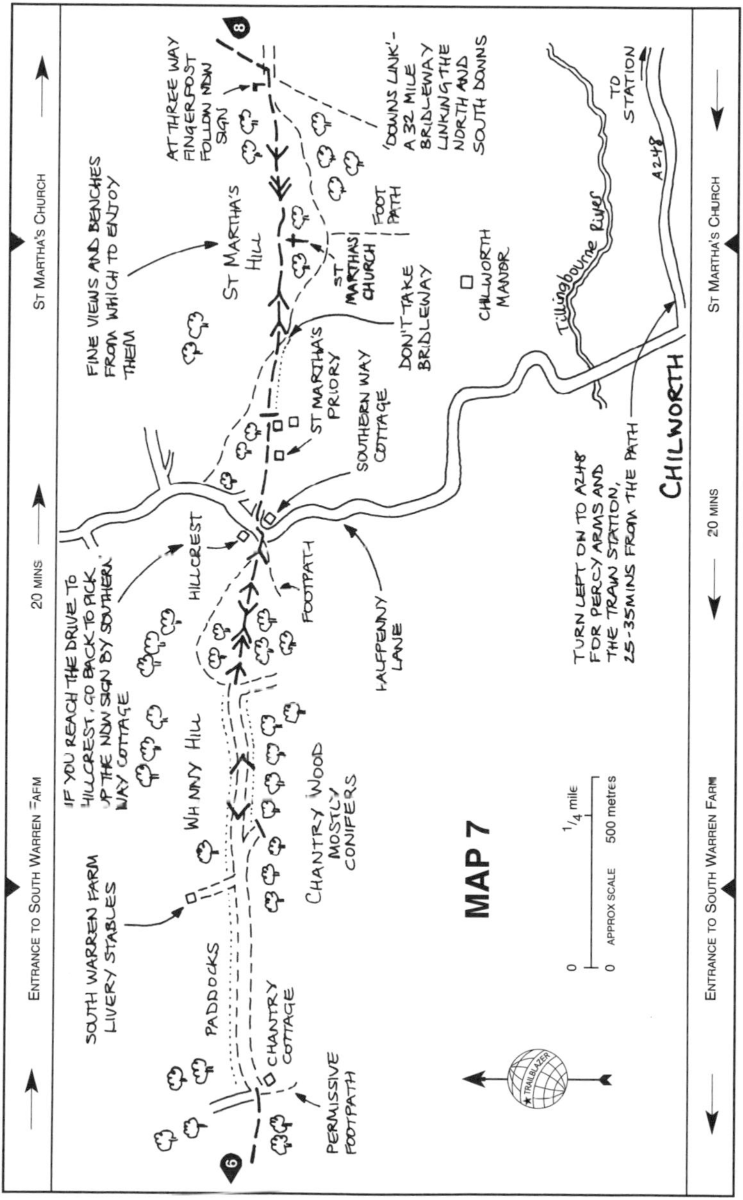
Entrance to South Warren Farm
20 mins
St Martha's Church
South Warren Farm Livery Stables
If you reach the drive to Hillcrest, go back to pick up the NDW sign by Southern Way Cottage
Fine views and benches from which to enjoy them
At three way fingerpost follow NDW sign
Paddocks
Whinny Hill
Hillcrest
St Martha's Hill
Chantry Cottage
Permissive footpath
Chantry Wood mostly conifers
Footpath
Halfpenny Lane
St Martha's Priory
Southern Way Cottage
St Martha's Church
Foot path
Don't take bridleway
'Downs Link' - a 32 mile bridleway linking the North and South Downs
MAP 7
Chilworth Manor
0
1/4 mile
0
Approx scale
500 metres
Turn left on to A248 for Percy Arms and the train station, 25-35mins from the path
Tillingbourne River
To station
A248
Chilworth

ALBURY [OFF MAP 8]

Albury is an estate village belonging to the Duke of Northumberland and buildings owned by the estate are painted in green trim. The village was mentioned in the Domesday Book (see box below) under its original name, Eldeberie.

Well known locally for its highly decorative **Pugin** chimneys, the estate yard also has a restored **dovecote**. Ten minutes east on the A248 is the **Catholic Apostolic Church** (not open) and the **Saxon Old Church, Albury Park** (daily 10am-4pm or dusk) worth a visit for its Pugin mortuary chapel. The building is now managed by the Churches Conservation Trust.

You can get supplies at the **post office shop** (☎ 01483-202123; Mon-Fri 9am-5.30pm, Sat 9am-12.30pm) and at the **Drummond Arms** (☎ 01483-202039; 4D/4T/1F), B&B is £35twn/dbl, £55 single occupancy). Food is served daily – noon-6pm snack menu, full menu noon-3pm/6-10pm and there is a delightful beer garden bordering the Tillingbourne river where you can savour a blue cheese and tomato tartlet (£4.95), or braised lamb shank (£9.95).

Arriva's **buses** Nos 21, 25 and 32 (Mon-Sat only) stop by the Drummond Arms; see the public transport map and table, pp37-40.

❑ Domesday Book

Watch my lips – no new taxes. Not what William the Conqueror's words were when he ordered the compilation of who owned what to back up the King's tax demands. That's why the book brought doom and gloom hence the name *Domesday Book*. Albury is mentioned in it, then called Eldeberie, with one church, one mill, woodland worth 30 hogs and £9 owed in tax.

NEWLANDS CORNER [MAP 8]

The views from here are spectacular on a clear day and this beauty spot was the scene of Agatha Christie's, the mystery writer, ten-day disappearance (see box p86) in December 1926.

The trail passes to the front of the **Surrey Wildlife Trust Countryside Centre** (☎ 01483-401880; open daily 9am to around 4.30pm, depending on the weather, only staffed on Sun), which has an informative display on the flora and fauna of this part of the Downs (see pp45-50). The **snack bar** (open the same hours as the centre) is always crowded, especially at the weekend, with people feasting on the view and egg and bacon rolls (£1.60-2.60). It's a bit of a truck stop really, attracting bikers and people who want the view but can't or won't be bothered to make the effort to walk there.

You may find a quieter berth across the A25 at ***The Barn Restaurant & Coffee Shop*** (☎ 01483-222820; Mon-Fri 8am-5pm, Sat/Sun 9am-5pm), which looks more like a red-brick suburban house than a barn. The portions are generous and the service is friendly; soup and bread is £4.25 and lamb cobbler £7.95.

A short walk down the busy A25 (there is no footpath so use the overgrown grass verge) is ***Carlos Trattoria*** (☎ 01483-224180; Mon-Fri noon-2.30pm/6.30-10pm, Sat 6.30-10.30pm, Sun noon-3pm); Italian food at its best is the claim and veal funghi crema costs £10.20.

If you can go no further after that the ***Manor House Hotel*** (☎ 01483-222624; 50D/T all en suite) has a room rate Mon-Thu of £108/125 excluding breakfast and Fri-Sun £79sgl and from £46dbl including breakfast.

The only **bus** service, and a limited one at that, is the Surrey Hills Explorer **bus** (NT1, Mar/Apr-Oct, weekends and public holidays only); see the public transport map and table, pp37-40.

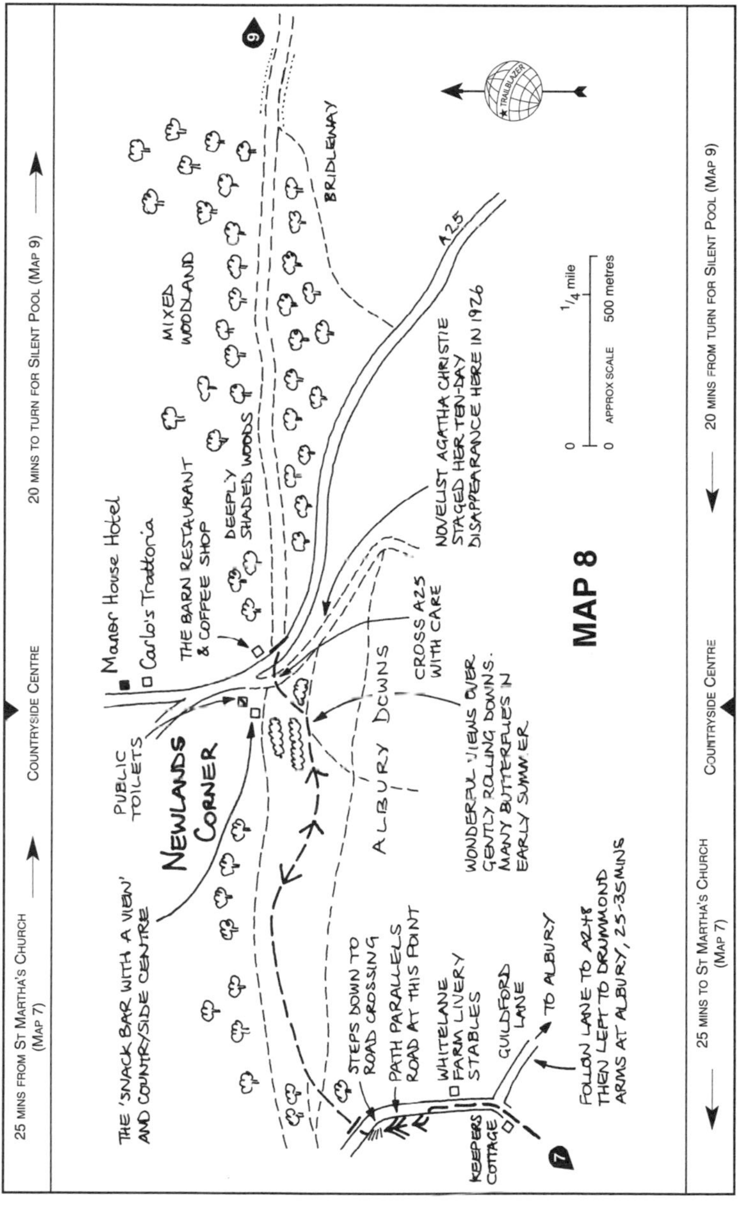
20 MINS TO TURN FOR SILENT POOL (MAP 9)
COUNTRYSIDE CENTRE
25 MINS FROM ST MARTHA'S CHURCH (MAP 7)
9
BRIDLEWAY
MIXED WOODLAND
A25
Manor House Hotel
Carlo's Trattoria
THE BARN RESTAURANT & COFFEE SHOP
DEEPLY SHADED WOODS
NOVELIST AGATHA CHRISTIE STAGED HER TEN-DAY DISAPPEARANCE HERE IN 1926
CROSS A25 WITH CARE
MAP 8
PUBLIC TOILETS
NEWLANDS CORNER
ALBURY DOWNS
WONDERFUL VIEWS OVER GENTLY ROLLING DOWNS. MANY BUTTERFLIES IN EARLY SUMMER
THE 'SNACK BAR WITH A VIEW' AND COUNTRYSIDE CENTRE
STEPS DOWN TO ROAD CROSSING
PATH PARALLELS ROAD AT THIS POINT
WHITELANE FARM LIVERY STABLES
GUILDFORD LANE
TO ALBURY
FOLLOW LANE TO A248 THEN LEFT TO DRUMMOND ARMS AT ALBURY, 25-35MINS
KEEPERS COTTAGE
7
TRAILBLAZER
0
1/4 mile
0
500 metres
APPROX SCALE
20 MINS FROM TURN FOR SILENT POOL (MAP 9)
COUNTRYSIDE CENTRE
25 MINS TO ST MARTHA'S CHURCH (MAP 7)

❑ Agatha Christie and the Mysterious Affair at Newlands Corner

When Agatha Christie disappeared from here in December 1926 she was on the best-seller lists so was well known; thus her disappearance had thousands out searching for her.

She abandoned her car here on a Friday evening. Since it was close to Silent Pool (off Map 9 p87) it prompted fears that she had committed suicide. The pool was dredged but no body was found. It turned out that she had travelled to Harrogate, the Yorkshire spa town.

Did she get there by train and was it from Chilworth, Gomshall or nearby Guildford? We shall never know as she refused to talk about her 'lost days'. She booked into a hotel under the name Neele, her husband's mistress's name, and was eventually found when guests recognized her from newspaper photographs.

On her return the story was put about that she suffered amnesia following her mother's death. But why did she do what she did? Were they the actions of someone unhinged by jealousy or were they pre-planned to embarrass her husband and get away from a bad marriage? Perhaps someone else was in on it and helped her travel from deepest Surrey to Yorkshire? Maybe it's time to call Poirot.

SHERE [MAP 9a]

Described as the prettiest village in Surrey, Shere suffers as a result and may claim the title as one of the busiest. But it's packed with pretty 15th- and 16th-century **timbered buildings** and attractive cottages, and has a stream with ducks. The 12th-century **parish church** of St James is open daily and the lychgate was designed by Sir Edwin Lutyens (see box p88). **Shere Museum** (☎ 01483-203245, 🖳 www.surreymuseums.org.uk), focusing on local history, is open Easter-30th Sep daily except Wed & Sat 1-5pm. It also has useful **services**, a choice of **accommodation** and several **eateries**.

Services

There is a branch of **Lloyds TSB** (Mon-Fri 9.30am-1.30pm, no cash machine) and a **post office** at the **Alldays** store (store hours Mon-Fri 7am-10pm, Sat/Sun 8am-10pm) where you can get baked goods, snacks and drinks. **Crumbs** bakery on Lower St has irregular opening hours.

Arriva's **buses** Nos 21, 25 and 32 (Mon-Sat only) stop near the Village Hall. Both routes of the Surrey Hills Explorer bus stop here; see the public transport map and table, pp37-40.

Where to stay

Cherry Trees (☎ 01483-202288; 1D/2T), a large brick and hung-tile home, does B&B £45sgl occupancy/£30dbl. The ***Prince of Wales*** (☎ 01483-202313; 2S/2T) pub has newly renovated rooms at £35 single occupancy/£32.50twin with a continental breakfast only.

Where to eat

The ***White Horse*** (☎ 01483-202518; Mon-Sat 11am-10pm, Sun noon-9pm) is very popular and takes bookings on the day only

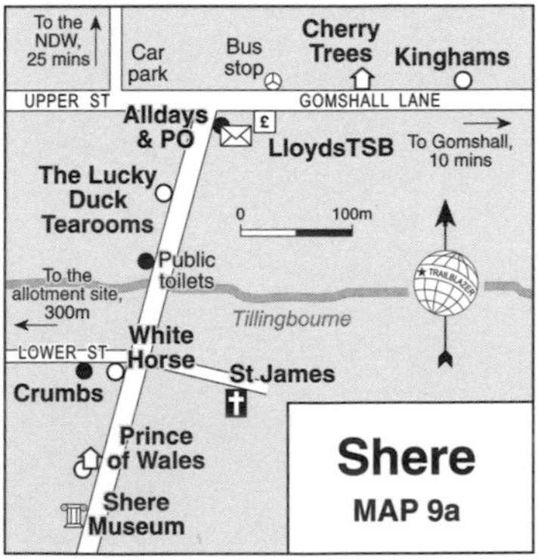

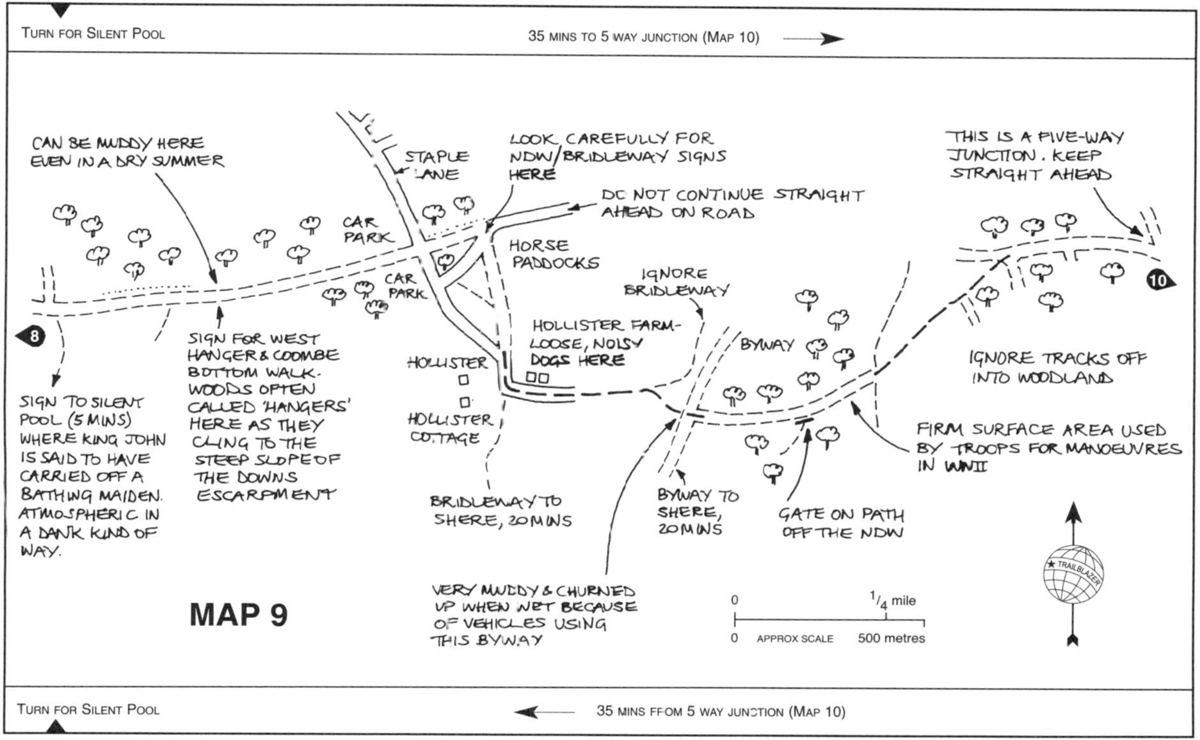

TURN FOR SILENT POOL
35 MINS TO 5 WAY JUNCTION (MAP 10)
CAN BE MUDDY HERE EVEN IN A DRY SUMMER
STAPLE LANE
LOOK CAREFULLY FOR NDW/BRIDLEWAY SIGNS HERE
DO NOT CONTINUE STRAIGHT AHEAD ON ROAD
THIS IS A FIVE-WAY JUNCTION. KEEP STRAIGHT AHEAD
CAR PARK
CAR PARK
HORSE PADDOCKS
IGNORE BRIDLEWAY
10
8
SIGN FOR WEST HANGER & COOMBE BOTTOM WALK. WOODS OFTEN CALLED 'HANGERS' HERE AS THEY CLING TO THE STEEP SLOPE OF THE DOWNS ESCARPMENT
HOLLISTER
HOLLISTER FARM - LOOSE, NOISY DOGS HERE
BYWAY
IGNORE TRACKS OFF INTO WOODLAND
SIGN TO SILENT POOL (5 MINS) WHERE KING JOHN IS SAID TO HAVE CARRIED OFF A BATHING MAIDEN. ATMOSPHERIC IN A DANK KIND OF WAY.
HOLLISTER COTTAGE
FIRM SURFACE AREA USED BY TROOPS FOR MANOEUVRES IN WWII
BRIDLEWAY TO SHERE, 20 MINS
BYWAY TO SHERE, 20 MINS
GATE ON PATH OFF THE NDW
VERY MUDDY & CHURNED UP WHEN WET BECAUSE OF VEHICLES USING THIS BYWAY
MAP 9
0 1/4 mile
0 APPROX SCALE 500 metres
TRAILBLAZER
TURN FOR SILENT POOL
35 MINS FROM 5 WAY JUNCTION (MAP 10)

❑ Sir Edwin Lutyens (1869-1944) and the Surrey Style

Surrey saw a revival in vernacular architecture – the architecture of ordinary buildings – in the late 19th and early 20th century. Lutyens favoured the distinctive Surrey style using materials that would blend in with existing buildings and the surrounding countryside. This was typically oak framing, white plaster infilling, or brick and hanging clay tiles decorating the walls of the first floor. Dormer windows were used and chimneys tended to be large and separately built. His first commission was for the lychgate of **St James's Church** in Shere. His career took off when he met and collaborated with the well-connected doyenne of English garden design, Gertrude Jekyll.

so get there early. It's a lovely beamed pub, with an open fire in the main bar in winter, 25 wines by the glass, and it often has beers from small independent brewers such as Hog's Back brewery. Food portions are generous, there's almost too much on the plate: lamb kofta is £4.25, a mixed grill £10.95 and the Sunday roast turkey or beef is £6.95/7.95.

Kinghams (☎ 01483-202168, 🖳 www.kinghams-restaurant.co.uk; Tue-Sat noon-2pm/7-9pm, Sun noon-3pm) is a more formal experience packed with the good burghers of Surrey and booking is essential. Even if not eating there do walk past the terraced garden dining room in summer – it's glorious. The set lunch is £14.95 and dinner is from £15.95. Expect dishes such as a pillar of smoked chicken and prime Surrey Hills rib steak.

The ***Prince of Wales*** (see p86) also does pub grub Mon-Sat noon-3pm and 6-9pm, Sun noon-3pm. ***The Lucky Duck Tea Room*** (☎ 01483-202445; Mon-Sat 9am-5pm, Sun 9.30am-5pm), where mobiles are banned, has all-day breakfasts for £4.95, sandwiches from £4.95 and ice-cream scoops in summer.

You can walk to Gomshall from Shere, see Map 9a p86, or descend from the North Downs Way ridgeline, see Map 10 opposite.

GOMSHALL [OFF MAP 10]

Pronounced 'gumshull' by the locals, the village is strung out along the main road, the A25. Lacking the prettiness of Shere it is not so overrun and may have rooms if the former does not. It has a **train station** with services to Guildford and Dorking, a **post office shop** (Mon-Sat 7am-9pm, Sun 7am-5pm). There is a **cash machine** outside the Jet garage.

The Compasses Inn (☎ 01483-202506; 2T) charges £49.95 per room including breakfast. A cooked breakfast is served at 9.30am; if you plan on starting early pre-order a continental breakfast. The bar does food noon-9pm, Mon-Sat, Sun noon-6pm. Over the road is ***The Black Horse*** (☎ 01483-202242; food daily noon-3pm, 6-10.30pm). It's best known for its ***Beau Thai*** restaurant (though it also has a curry restaurant) with large multi-dish set meals (£16.95), or choose individual dishes from the menu (£4.95-7.95). ***Bluebeckers*** (☎ 01483-203060; Mon-Fri noon-3pm, Mon-Thur 5.30-10pm, Fri to 10.30pm, Sat noon-10.30pm, Sun noon-9.30pm) is a former mill building and has set menus from £13.50 or burgers from £9.50.

Arriva's **buses** Nos 21 and 25 stop by The Compasses Inn; see the public transport map and table pp37-40.

HOLMBURY ST MARY [OFF MAP 10]

Called Little Switzerland by the Victorians because of the surrounding hills and valleys, dedicated hostellers and campers face an hour's walk off the path to stay at Holmbury St Mary youth hostel, or you could take Arriva **bus** No 21 (see the public

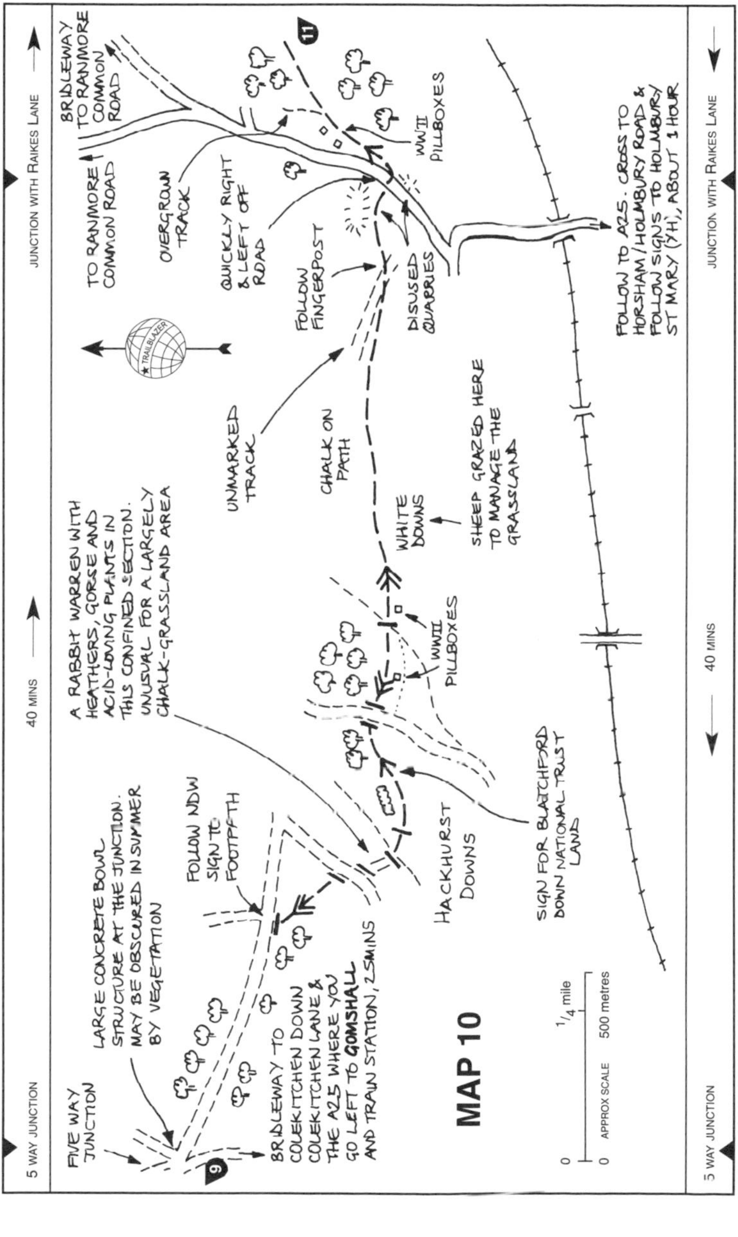
MAP 10
5 WAY JUNCTION
40 MINS
JUNCTION WITH RAIKES LANE
FIVE WAY JUNCTION
LARGE CONCRETE BOWL STRUCTURE AT THE JUNCTION. MAY BE OBSCURED IN SUMMER BY VEGETATION
BRIDLEWAY TO COLEKITCHEN DOWN COLEKITCHEN LANE & THE A25 WHERE YOU GO LEFT TO GOMSHALL AND TRAIN STATION, 25MINS
FOLLOW NDW SIGN TO FOOTPATH
HACKHURST DOWNS
SIGN FOR BLATCHFORD DOWN NATIONAL TRUST LAND
A RABBIT WARREN WITH HEATHERS, GORSE AND ACID-LOVING PLANTS IN THIS CONFINED SECTION. UNUSUAL FOR A LARGELY CHALK-GRASSLAND AREA
WWII PILLBOXES
UNMARKED TRACK
CHALK ON PATH
WHITE DOWNS
SHEEP GRAZED HERE TO MANAGE THE GRASSLAND
TRAILBLAZER
FOLLOW FINGERPOST
DISUSED QUARRIES
QUICKLY RIGHT & LEFT OFF ROAD
OVERGROWN TRACK
TO RANMORE COMMON ROAD
BRIDLEWAY TO RANMORE COMMON ROAD
WWII PILLBOXES
FOLLOW TO A25. CROSS TO HORSHAM/HOLMBURY ROAD & FOLLOW SIGNS TO HOLMBURY ST MARY (YH), ABOUT 1 HOUR
9
11
APPROX SCALE
0 1/4 mile
0 500 metres

transport map and table, pp37-40) from near The Royal Oak pub.

Holmbury St Mary Youth Hostel (☎ 0870-770 5868, 🖳 holmbury@yha.org.uk, 52 beds) charges £11 and reception opens at 5pm. There are 12 tent pitches at £5 per person. The hostel was threatened with closure in 2003 but a £750,000 fundraising campaign is underway to carry out necessary improvements. The ***Royal Oak*** (☎ 01306-730120, 2D en suite) charges £50 per room for B&B and serves pub grub Mon-Sat noon-2.30pm, 6-9pm, Sun 12noon-4pm. Alternatively, the ***King's Head*** (☎ 01306-730282) serves food Tue-Sat 12noon-2pm & 6-9pm, Sun 12noon-2.30pm).

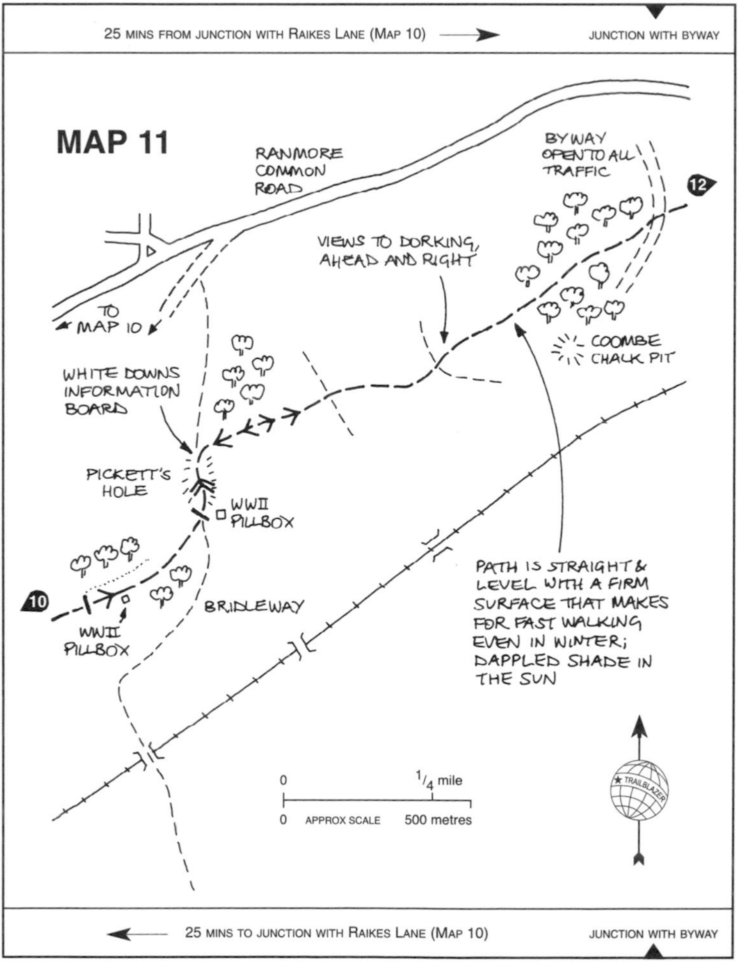

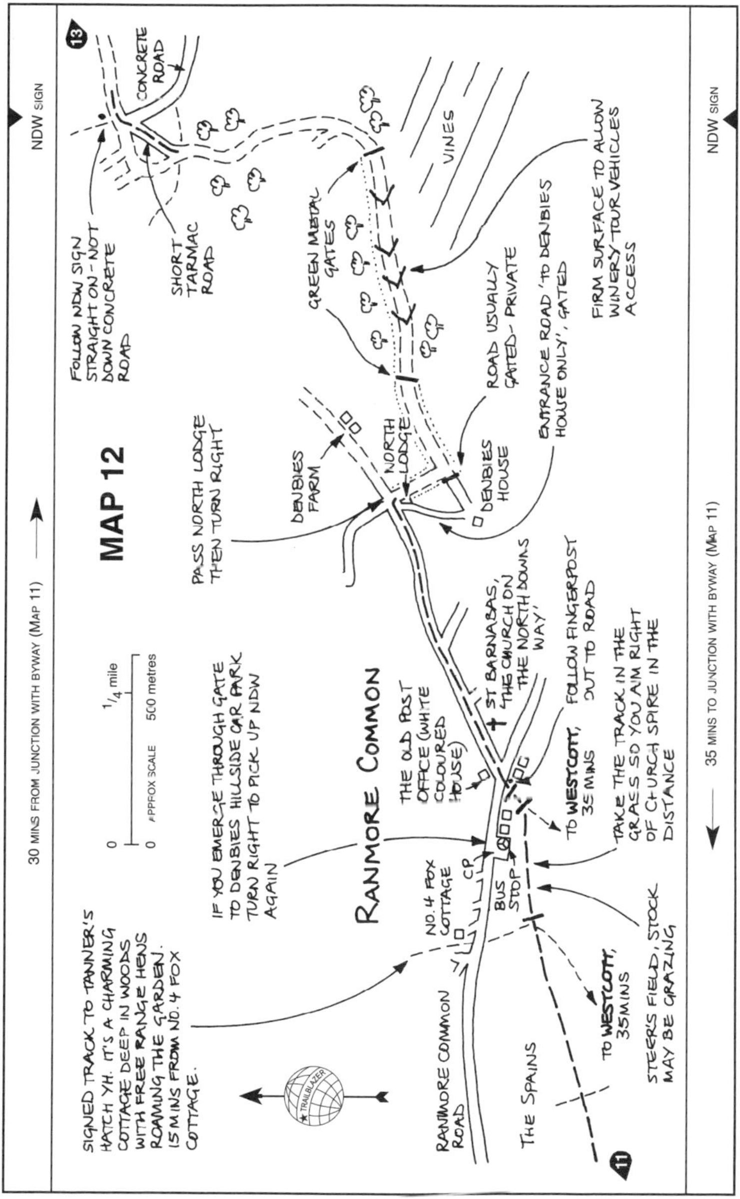
MAP 12
30 MINS FROM JUNCTION WITH BYWAY (MAP 11)
35 MINS TO JUNCTION WITH BYWAY (MAP 11)
NDW SIGN
NDW SIGN
13
11
FOLLOW NDW SIGN STRAIGHT ON - NOT DOWN CONCRETE ROAD
CONCRETE ROAD
SHORT TARMAC ROAD
GREEN METAL GATES
VINES
ROAD USUALLY GATED - PRIVATE
ENTRANCE ROAD 'TO DENBIES HOUSE ONLY', GATED
FIRM SURFACE TO ALLOW WINERY TOUR VEHICLES ACCESS
PASS NORTH LODGE THEN TURN RIGHT
DENBIES FARM
NORTH LODGE
DENBIES HOUSE
0
0
1/4 mile
500 metres
APPROX SCALE
RANMORE COMMON
IF YOU EMERGE THROUGH GATE TO DENBIES HILLSIDE CAR PARK TURN RIGHT TO PICK UP NDW AGAIN
THE OLD POST OFFICE (WHITE COLOURED HOUSE)
ST BARNABAS, 'THE CHURCH ON THE NORTH DOWNS WAY'
FOLLOW FINGERPOST OUT TO ROAD
TO WESTCOTT, 35 MINS
TAKE THE TRACK IN THE GRASS SO YOU AIM RIGHT OF CHURCH SPIRE IN THE DISTANCE
NO. 4 FOX COTTAGE
CP
BUS STOP
SIGNED TRACK TO TANNER'S HATCH YH. IT'S A CHARMING COTTAGE DEEP IN WOODS WITH FREE RANGE HENS ROAMING THE GARDEN. 15 MINS FROM NO. 4 FOX COTTAGE.
RANMORE COMMON ROAD
THE SPAINS
TO WESTCOTT, 35MINS
STEER'S FIELD, STOCK MAY BE GRAZING

RANMORE COMMON [MAP 12]

Tanners Hatch Youth Hostel (☎ 0870-770 6060, 💻 tanners@yha.org.uk; 25 beds at £11.95, 7 tent pitches at £6 per person, supplement £1.50 for non-members), off Ranmore Common Rd and about 20 minutes from the North Downs Way, is a much better option for hostellers and campers than Holmbury St Mary. Once described as 'famously basic', this charming beamed cottage is deep in the woods and has a rambling garden, free-range hens, a small, comfortable lounge with open wood fire, outside toilet and showers.

Ranmore Common Road is a stop on the Heritage Trail route of the Surrey Hills Explorer Bus; see public transport table and map pp37-40.

WESTCOTT [OFF MAP 12]

Alternatively consider going to Westcott by footpath. Plans to turn it into a dormitory town were shelved in the 1940s and it's now a conservation area. Vegetarians get a welcome at ***The Corner House*** (☎ 01306-888798; 1T/1D1F). Mrs Nyman, whose mother does B&B at Cherry Trees (see p86) in Shere, charges £32sgl/21dbl and £18 per person for three sharing. ***Mai Thai*** (☎ 01306-883520; daily noon-3pm/5-11pm) restaurant at ***The Cricketers*** has a range of Thai vegetarian dishes from £3.95. Next door to the Corner House, ***The Prince of Wales*** (☎ 01306-889699; Mon-Sat noon-3pm/6-9.30pm, Sun noon-4pm/6-9pm) does good-value food: fish and chips £5.50, and pizza start at £4.95. ***The Crown Inn*** (☎ 01306-885414; Mon-Sat noon-2.30pm/6-9pm, Sun noon-2.30pm/7-9pm) has filling pub grub. The ***Westcott Bakery*** (Mon-Sat 7am-4pm) has snacks, drinks and sandwiches and there is also a **post office** and a **Londis** (Mon-Fri 8.30am-7pm, Sun 9am-1pm) store.

Arriva's **buses** Nos 21, 22 and 32 (Mon-Sat only) stop on the Green; see the public transport map and table, pp37-40.

DENBIES WINE ESTATE [MAP 13]

With a thirst sharpened along the 13-mile stage it is well worth a detour to the **visitor centre** (☎ 01306-876616, 💻 www.denbiesvineyard.co.uk; Mon-Fri 10am-5pm, Sat to 5.30pm, Sun 11.30am-5.30pm) where a winery tour and tasting costs £7.25.

The stylish ***Gallery Restaurant*** on the third floor has panoramic views of the vineyard. The ground floor ***Servery Restaurant*** has a spacious conservatory area and a wide range of salads and sandwiches from £2.95; hot food is served 12noon-2pm only.

B&B (☎ 01306-876777; 7D all en suite) is offered at the whitewashed farmhouse for £63sgl/42.50dbl. Another option nearby is the luxurious ***Burford Bridge***

❑ Thomas Malthus (1766-1834) – the dismal scientist

The 18th-century political economist Thomas Robert Malthus was born at The Rookery, a country estate near Westcott. In his work *An Essay on the Principle of Population*, Malthus argued that populations inevitably grow quicker than the food supply – population grew at a geometric rate ie 1, 2, 4, 8, 16 and so on while food supply grew at an arithmetic rate ie 1, 2, 3, 4, 5 – until checked by famine and disease. Moral restraint was his prescription, a sort of back to basics for the 18th century. Charles Darwin was inspired by the essay observing that populations tended to produce more offspring than could survive but favourable attributes were passed on by those who did survive; this provided the basis for his theory on the formation of new species.

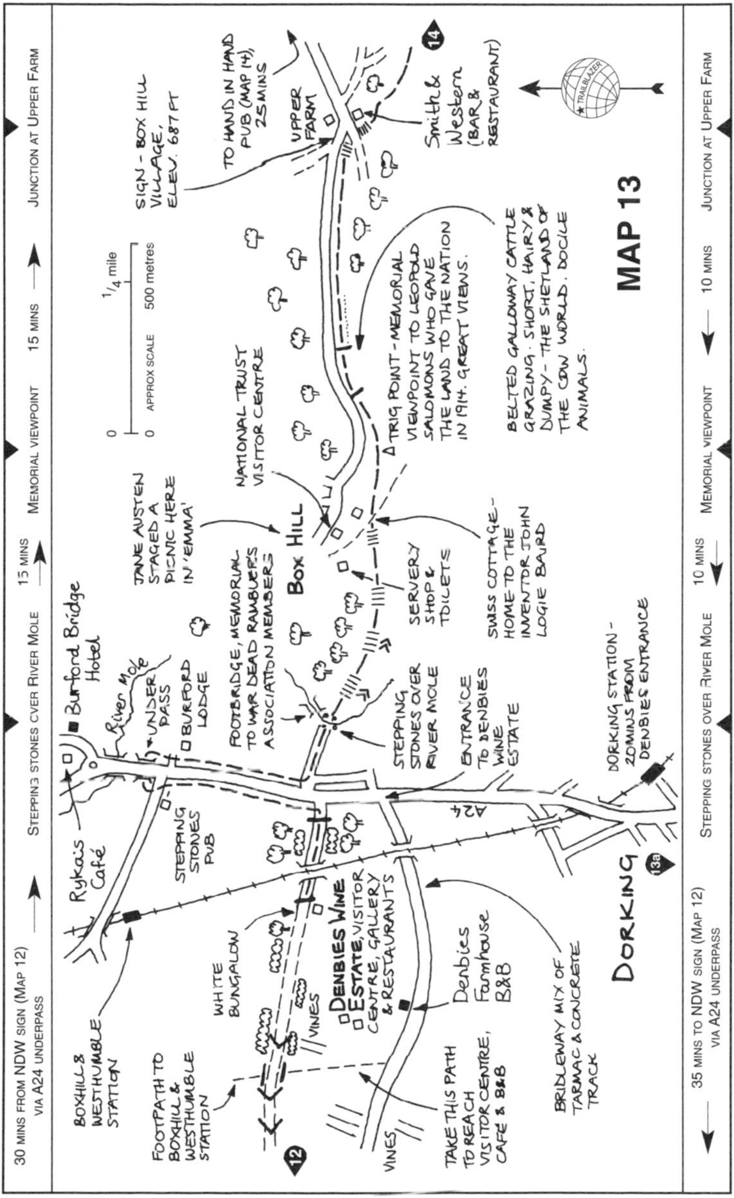
30 MINS FROM NDW SIGN (MAP 12) VIA A24 UNDERPASS
STEPPING STONES OVER RIVER MOLE
15 MINS
MEMORIAL VIEWPOINT
15 MINS
JUNCTION AT UPPER FARM
35 MINS TO NDW SIGN (MAP 12) VIA A24 UNDERPASS
STEPPING STONES OVER RIVER MOLE
10 MINS
MEMORIAL VIEWPOINT
10 MINS
JUNCTION AT UPPER FARM
0 APPROX SCALE 1/4 mile 500 metres
MAP 13
Boxhill & Westhumble Station
Footpath to Boxhill & Westhumble Station
Ryka's Café
Stepping Stones Pub
Burford Bridge Hotel
River Mole
Underpass
Burford Lodge
White Bungalow
Vines
Denbies Wine Estate, visitor centre, gallery & restaurants
Denbies Farmhouse B&B
Take this path to reach visitor centre, café & B&B
Bridleway mix of tarmac & concrete track
Dorking
A24
Dorking Station - 20 mins from Denbies entrance
Entrance to Denbies Wine Estate
Stepping stones over River Mole
Footbridge, memorial to war dead Ramblers' Association members
Jane Austen staged a picnic here in 'Emma'
Box Hill
National Trust Visitor Centre
Servery shop & toilets
Swiss Cottage - home to the inventor John Logie Baird
Trig point - memorial viewpoint to Leopold Salomons who gave the land to the nation in 1914. Great views.
Belted Galloway cattle grazing. Short, hairy & dumpy - the Shetland of the cow world. Docile animals.
Sign - Box Hill Village, elev. 687 ft
To Hand in Hand pub (Map 14), 25 mins
Upper Farm
Smith & Western (bar & restaurant)
12
13a
14
TRAILBLAZER

Hotel (☎ 0870-830 4812, 💻 www.macdonaldhotels.co.uk; 57D all en suite, from £70) where the carpet is so deep it's like walking on spongy moss. Nelson is said to have stayed here before departing for Trafalgar and reputedly Keats completed his poem *Endymion* during a stay. ***The Stepping Stones*** (☎ 01306-889932; food noon-2pm/7-9.30pm, Sun noon-3pm) at Westhumble is walker friendly, even selling plastic boot covers for 20p. A mouthwatering shin of pork is £14.50, and lambs liver and bacon is £8.95. And if you want fast food before tackling Box Hill there is ***Ryka's Café*** (daily 8am-9pm), popular with the burger and biker crowd.

Box Hill & Westhumble station is a couple of minutes' walk away with hourly services to both London Waterloo and Victoria. Both routes of the Surrey Hills Explorer **bus** stop at the Wine Estate and at Burford Bridge Hotel; see public transport map and table, pp37-40.

DORKING [MAP 13a]

Dorking is a thriving town at the foot of the North Downs chalk ridge and Box Hill. The principal streets are High St, West St and South St.

Services

The **tourist information centre** (☎ 01306-879327, 💻 www.visitdorking.com; Mon-Sat 10am-4.30pm, winter to 4pm) is in the attractive Art Deco building **Dorking Halls** to the east of town where **internet access** is charged at £1per half hour. The **sports centre** (☎ 01306-870180) is next door and has a swimming pool. Three **supermarkets** (Marks & Spencer, Sainsbury's and Waitrose) will cater for any lunch needs seven days a week but if you like to buy local visit **Surrey Gourmet** (☎ 01306-884817, 💻 www.surreyproduce.co.uk; Mon-Sat 9am-4.30pm), 61 High St. The pies, wine, beer, cheeses and a host of other produce are from Surrey suppliers. There is also a Boots **chemist** (☎ 01306-882467; Mon-Sat 9am-5.30pm) on the High St.

The outdoor shop **SC Fuller** (☎ 01306-882407; daily 9am-5pm), 28-32 South St, claims to be the oldest in Dorking and there is a **Millets** (☎ 01306-887227; Mon-Sat 9am-5.30pm). There are branches of NatWest and HSBC, both with **cash machines**, on West St and High St. The main **post office** (Mon-Fri 9am-5.30pm, Sat 9am-12.30pm) is on High St.

There are three **train stations**: Dorking (sometimes referred to as Dorking North) with up to three services an hour to London Victoria/Waterloo and services to Horsham, Chichester and Portsmouth; Dorking West and Dorking Deepdene have at least two services an hour to Redhill (and Gatwick Airport). From Redhill there are up to four services an hour to Gatwick Airport on the First Great Western Link. There is a **taxi rank** in front of the station.

The **National Trust Surrey Hills Explorer bus** starts and ends in Dorking. Arriva's **buses** Nos 21 and 32 and Surrey Connect bus No 516 (all Mon-Sat only) stop by the White Horse (see below) and at the railway station. The No 516 serves Box Hill, about a 20-minute journey; see the public transport map and table, pp37-40.

Where to stay

Coming into town off the A24 is ***Travelodge*** (☎ 0870-191 1526, 💻 www.travelodge.co.uk; 55D en suite). Each room has an extra double sofa bed so it can sleep up to four walkers. Room prices are from £52 Fri-Sun, £63 Mon-Thu. What it lacks in character is more than made up for by its consistent quality and good value even if breakfast is not included. Just off the High St on Moores Rd is ***Fairdene*** (☎ 01306-888337; 7D, 2 en suite) charging £40sgl/£25dbl, and £65sgl/27.50dbl for the two en suite rooms and serving a light breakfast of cereal, toast and juice.

Centrally located on the High St is the ***White Horse Hotel*** (☎ 01306-881138, 💻 www.macdonaldwhitehorsehotel.co.uk; 47D/10T all en suite), an historic coaching inn charging £50dbl/70sgl.

By South St on Rose Hill is ***Claremont Cottage*** (☎ 01306-885487; 1T/2D), an attractive modern house with all rooms en suite: rates are £45sgl/32.50dbl. Access is down the gravel drive by the retirement home. Further up on Rose Hill is the ***Waltons*** (☎ 01306-883127, 💻 www.a1tourism.com/uk/walt/html; 1D/1T/2F), charging £40sgl/30dbl, twin or fml, including a continental breakfast.

Coming from Dorking West station the closest B&B is the no-nonsense ***Pilgrim*** pub (☎ 01306-889951; 1D/3T/1F), Station Rd, charging £25 per person without breakfast, £30 with.

If your legs just won't carry you any further coming into town along the A24 from the trail there is always ***The Lincoln Arms Hotel*** (☎ 01306-882820; 5S/4D/9T/3F) next to Dorking Station. It's seen a few incarnations but has always been a station hotel. Rates are £30sgl/35dbl or twin/£40fml including a continental breakfast; a hot breakfast costs extra.

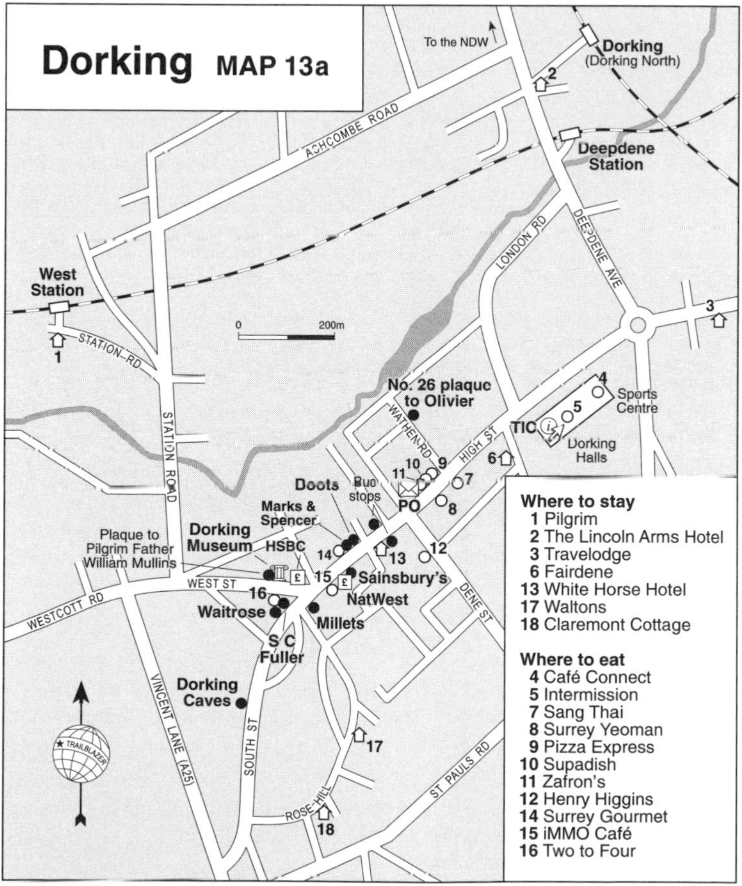

Where to eat

The High St has numerous good-value food options. ***Pizza Express*** (☎ 01306-888236; Mon-Thu noon-11pm, Fri & Sat noon-midnight, Sun noon-11pm) consistently serves up affordable pizza from £4.95 and ***iMMO Café*** (☎ 01306-644998; Mon-Sat noon-11pm, Sun to 10pm) is a busy Italian restaurant set in a former bank. The dining area is a light and airy atrium with pizza from £5.45 and bowls of pasta from £5.95. Also popular is ***Sang Thai*** (☎ 01306-889053; daily noon-2pm/6-11pm) where tofu fried with ginger (£4.50) features in the vegetarian specials. ***Zafron's*** (☎ 01306-876296; daily noon-2.30pm/6.30-11pm, Fri & Sat to midnight) is a snazzy offering from the sub-continent where you can satisfy a curry craving for £5.35.

Fans of the all-day breakfast will like ***Supadish*** (daily 8am-11pm, Sat to 9pm), and ***Henry Higgins*** (☎ 01306-889672; Mon-Sat 11.30am-2pm, Mon-Wed 4.30-9pm, Thu-Sat 4.30-10pm), on Dene St, has been dishing out fish and chips since 1914. Lunchtime pub grub is available at the ***Surrey Yeoman*** (☎ 01306-741492; food served daily noon-3pm).

Intermission is a pleasant coffee bar in the Dorking Halls (see p94) and if a toasted marmite sandwich (£1.50) appeals, head for ***Café Connect*** (Mon-Fri 9am-7pm, Sat & Sun 9am-6pm) at the sports centre (see p94).

For stylish and contemporary dining ***Two to Four*** (☎ 01306-889923, Tue-Sat noon-2.30pm, 6.30-10.30pm), on West St, fits the bill with prices to match. A short but appealing menu includes scallops and carrot fritters for £7.50 and seared seabass with crushed artichokes, braised peas and smoked bacon for £17.

What to see and do

Dorking Museum (☎ 01306-876591; Wed & Thu 2-5pm, Sat 10am-4pm) has exhibits of the town's history and there is memorabilia of composer **Ralph Vaughan Williams** who lived locally. There is now a statue of him outside the Dorking Halls (see p94). At 26 Wathen Rd a blue plaque commemorates **Sir Lawrence Olivier** who was born there. **West Street** is the centre of the antique trade and by the sign to the museum notice the plaque above the former home of **William Mullins** (at No 58), a shoemaker who joined the Pilgrim Fathers and sailed on the *Mayflower* to America in 1620. You need to book visits to **Dorking Caves** through the tourist information centre (see p94). There are four guided tours (£4) on the second Sunday of each month. The maze of passages under South St have been used as warehouses, smugglers' dens and for illegal cock fighting in the past.

On the second and fifth Saturday of every month there is a farmers' market on St Martin's Walk, off the High St.

DORKING TO MERSTHAM [MAPS 13-17]

Shortly into this **10mile/16km** stage after crossing the River Mole by stepping stones there is a calf-crunching climb to the top of Box Hill where there are extensive views on a clear day. Crossing National Trust land, acquired between 1915 and 1952, the trail runs through dense woods with occasional views over former lime quarries, climbing short but steep hills to Juniper Hill and Colley Hill then following the ridgeline to Reigate Hill. Chalk is the prominent rock type which can get very slippery when wet and combined with the elevation gains it makes for a good work out.

(Opposite) Top left: The National Trust's Shalford Mill (p76) has a woodframe construction. (Photo © Jennifer Ullman). **Top right**: Box Hill (see p98). (Photo © John Curtin). **Bottom**: The secluded and popular Tanners Hatch Youth Hostel (see p92) nestles in the woods near Ranmore Common. (Photo © Jennifer Ullman).

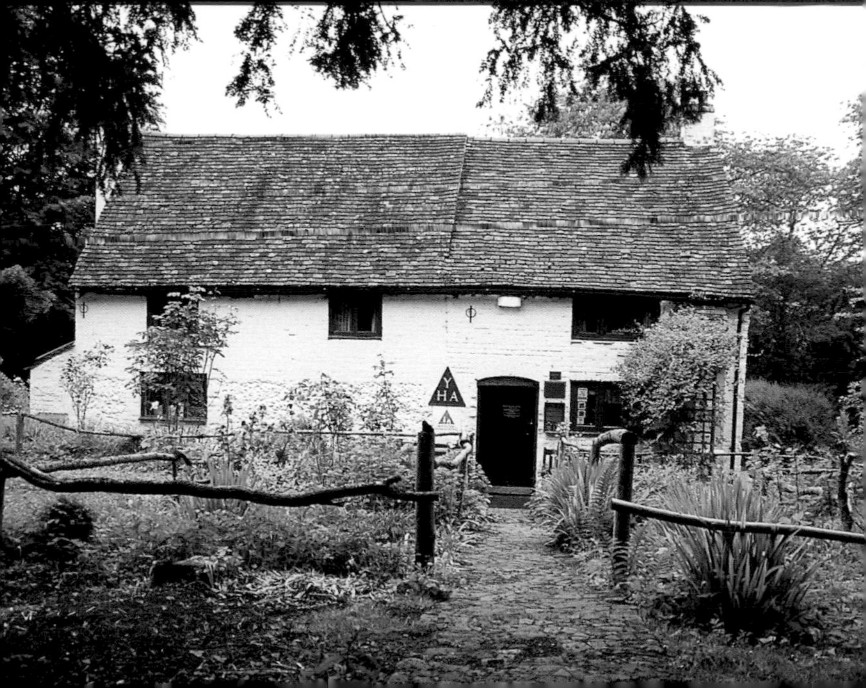
YHA

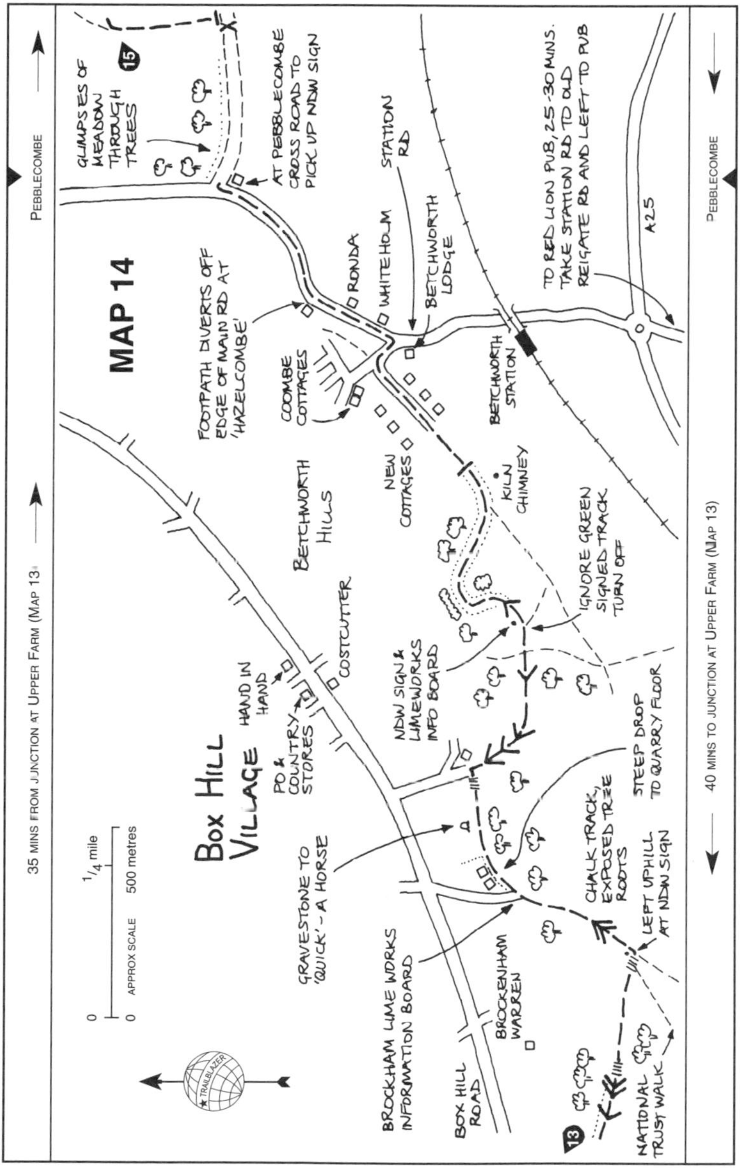
MAP 14
35 MINS FROM JUNCTION AT UPPER FARM (MAP 13)
PEBBLECOMBE
40 MINS TO JUNCTION AT UPPER FARM (MAP 13)
PEBBLECOMBE
0
1/4 mile
0
APPROX SCALE
500 metres
15
GLIMPSES OF MEADOW THROUGH TREES
AT PEBBLECOMBE CROSS ROAD TO PICK UP NDW SIGN
STATION RD
TO RED LION PUB, 25-30 MINS. TAKE STATION RD TO OLD REIGATE RD AND LEFT TO PUB
A25
FOOTPATH DIVERTS OFF EDGE OF MAIN RD AT 'HAZELCOMBE'
RONDA
WHITEHOLM
BETCHWORTH LODGE
COOMBE COTTAGES
BETCHWORTH STATION
NEW COTTAGES
BETCHWORTH HILLS
KILN CHIMNEY
IGNORE GREEN SIGNED TRACK TURN OFF
COSTCUTTER
HAND IN HAND
NDW SIGN & LIMEWORKS INFO BOARD
BOX HILL VILLAGE
PO & COUNTRY STORES
STEEP DROP TO QUARRY FLOOR
CHALK TRACK, EXPOSED TREE ROOTS
GRAVESTONE TO 'QUICK' - A HORSE
LEFT UPHILL AT NDW SIGN
BROCKHAM LIME WORKS INFORMATION BOARD
BROCKENHAM WARREN
BOX HILL ROAD
NATIONAL TRUST WALK
13
TRAILBLAZER

(Opposite) Top: Kit's Coty (see p138). **Bottom**: WWII pillbox (see p100). (© J Curtin).

It has to be said that this is not the quietest of stages and a feature of the day's walk is the hum of traffic noise building up as you approach Reigate Hill. Despite the presence of the M25 the day ends with a pleasant stroll across Reigate Hill Golf Club where you're likely to find skylarks pouring out their song as they spiral skyward from the rough. It's best to provision snacks and water before setting out as there is no convenient opportunity to do so until near the end of the day at Reigate Hill.

BOX HILL [MAP 13]

Managed by the National Trust, Box Hill is a Site of Special Scientific Interest (SSSI) with a variety of habitats and many trees including box but also juniper and yew.

The smell of cat's pee as you climb through the box woods is characteristic of the species. Two-thirds of Britain's butterfly species have been recorded on Box Hill and it's home to important chalk grassland plants, see pp47-9.

The ***servery*** (☎ 01306-888793; daily 9am-5pm in summer; 11am-4pm in good weather the rest of the year) offers a £1 discount on purchases over £2.50 if you arrived by public transport (see pp37-40) – show your ticket. A cheese and bacon muffin is £2.50 and tea £1.20. There is also a popular **visitor centre** and **gift shop.**

Further on, and opposite Upper Farm – but possibly hidden by trees in full leaf in summer – is ***Smith & Western*** (☎ 01737-841666; daily noon-9pm, weekends to 10.30pm) an American themed diner (£8.95 for a club sandwich with fries and coleslaw, steaks £14.95) where the portions are huge plus you get a lollipop with your bill.

Surrey Connect **bus** No 516 (Mon-Sat only) stops at the National Trust Visitor Centre and at Upper Farm; see the public transport map and table, pp37-40.

BOX HILL VILLAGE [MAP 14]

A mile down Box Hill Rd there is a **Costcutter** (daily, 7am-7pm) and across the road a **post office** and **Boxhill Village Country Stores** (Mon-Fri, 7am-6.15pm, Sat to 6.30pm, Sun to 1pm).

Further on is the ***Hand in Hand*** (☎ 01737-843352; Mon-Sat 11am-3pm/5.30-11pm, Sun to 10.30pm), which serves drinks only.

BETCHWORTH [OFF MAP 14]

The Red Lion (☎ 01737-843336; 4D/1S all en suite) charges £37.50dbl/65sgl for B&B and food is served noon-3pm/6-9.30pm. There is a cricket pitch behind the put.

Arriva **bus** No 32 (Mon-Sat only) stops by the post office. **Trains** run approximately hourly to London Victoria; this may require changing at Dorking, Dorking Deepdene, Clapham Junction or going via Redhill; see the public transport map and table, pp37-40.

After climbing both Juniper Hill and Colley Hill don't be put off by the short detour to Pilgrims Holt (Map 16), a modern house with a stained-glass window depicting the Last Supper. It's then a straight shot along the ridgeline passing Reigate Fort to arrive at Reigate Hill.

REIGATE HILL [MAP 16]

The path passes above and behind ***The Bridge House Hotel*** (☎ 01737-246801; 39D en suite). B&B is £69sgl/55dbl with the attached ***Lanni's*** restaurant (☎ 01737-244821, Sun-Fri 12.30-2pm, Mon-Thur 7-9.30pm, Fri & Sat 7.30-10pm, Sun to 9pm) offering a £15 three-course menu and á la carte options. To reach the hotel you need to cross the footbridge over the A217 to the snack bar and car park, and then cross the

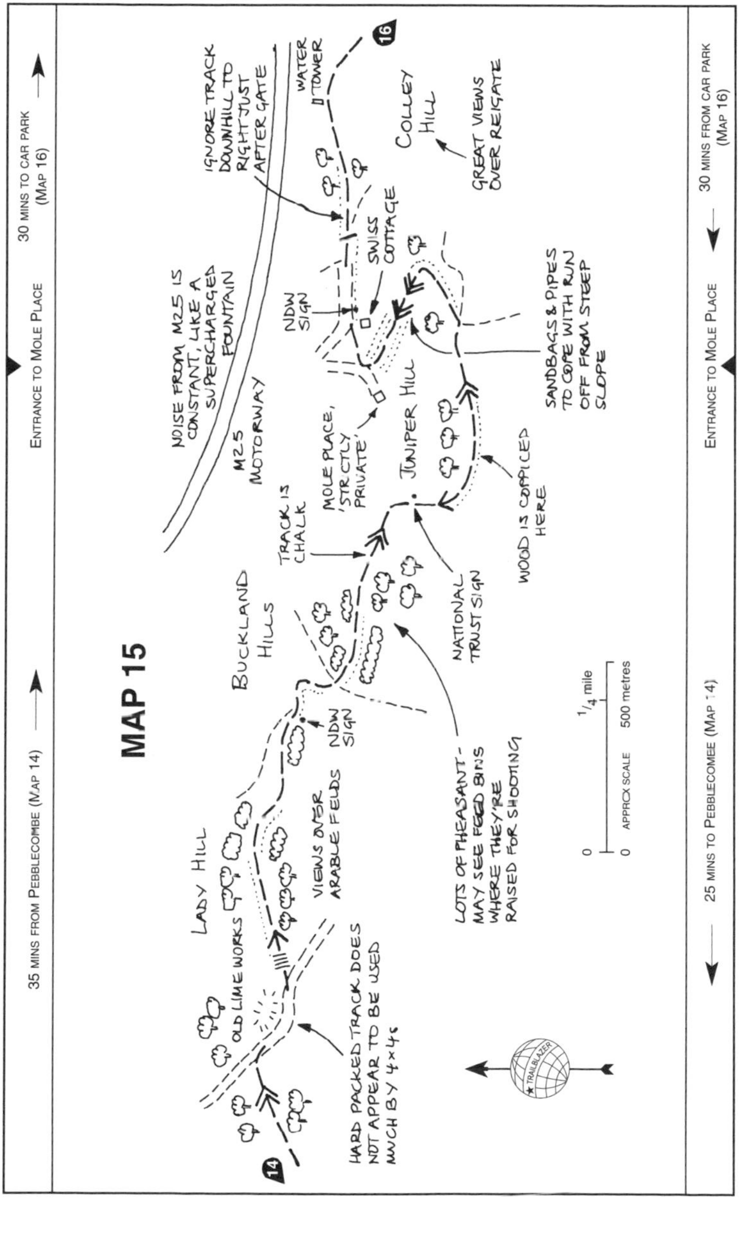
MAP 15
35 MINS FROM PEBBLECOMBE (MAP 14)
ENTRANCE TO MOLE PLACE
30 MINS TO CAR PARK (MAP 16)
25 MINS TO PEBBLECOMEE (MAP 14)
30 MINS FROM CAR PARK (MAP 16)
14
16
HARD PACKED TRACK DOES NOT APPEAR TO BE USED MUCH BY 4×4s
OLD LIME WORKS
LADY HILL
VIEWS OVER ARABLE FIELDS
NDW SIGN
BUCKLAND HILLS
LOTS OF PHEASANT - MAY SEE FEED BINS WHERE THEY'RE RAISED FOR SHOOTING
NATIONAL TRUST SIGN
TRACK IS CHALK
M25 MOTORWAY
MOLE PLACE, 'STRICTLY PRIVATE'
JUNIPER HILL
WOOD IS COPPICED HERE
NOISE FROM M25 IS CONSTANT, LIKE A SUPERCHARGED FOUNTAIN
NDW SIGN
SWISS COTTAGE
SANDBAGS & PIPES TO COPE WITH RUN OFF FROM STEEP SLOPE
IGNORE TRACK DOWNHILL TO RIGHT JUST AFTER GATE
WATER TOWER
COLLEY HILL
GREAT VIEWS OVER REIGATE
1/4 mile
500 metres
0
APPROX SCALE
TRAILBLAZER

A217 itself. The ***snack bar*** (daily, 9am-4pm) is run by a friendly mother and daughter team, and is conveniently situated at the top of Reigate Hill. If the footbridge is being repaired (a possibility) there will be diversion signs in place. Below the car park is Wray Lane leading to Redhill.

❑ Wartime defences – Surrey's Maginot Line

Reigate Fort (see Map 16) was built in 1890 as one of 13 installations forming a defence chain over 70 miles of the Downs escarpment to protect London from invasion from the south and east. At the time the victory over Napoleon was recent and France was considered the greatest potential threat.

The structures were not forts in the ordinary sense but large gun encampments. At the time they were cutting-edge military tactics – a static defence line facing the enemy along the ridge of the North Downs. The same methods were adopted in WWII with pillboxes creating a Surrey Maginot Line – Maginot was the French General who devised the tactic.

The tank traps and pill-boxes seen along the trail (see Map 6 p77, Map 10 p89, and Map 11 p90) are remnants of defence thinking in the inter-war years. The concrete boxes, complete with machine gun slits and 17-inch thick walls, dotting the route in Surrey were part of a three-tier system of national defence – coastal defences on beaches, stop lines inland and finally a fixed line of tank traps and pillboxes 50 miles behind the south and east coasts.

REDHILL [MAP 16a]

A commuter town with five roundabouts shows how much it has given over to the car but it has useful services and good transport links and for this reason alone walkers may want to come here. The central area around High St, Station Rd, and the Harlequin Centre is pedestrianized.

Services

There is **free internet access** at the **public library** (☎ 01737-763332; Mon/Wed/Fri 9am-6pm, Tue/Thu 9am-8pm, Sat 9am-4pm) on Warwick Quadrant. There is an **outdoor shop**, Millets (☎ 01737-765177; Mon–Sat 9am-5.30pm, Sun 10am-4pm), on the High St and the **Harlequin Cinema** (☎ 01737-765547) if you want to rest up at a film. Footsore walkers will find relief at **Alliance Pharmacy** (☎ 01737-762776; Mon-Fri 9am-6pm, Sat to 5pm) and **Road Runners taxi** (☎ 01737-760076) can always drop you back on the trail.

There are several banks with **cash machines** on Station Rd and a **post office** (Mon-Fri 9am-6pm, Sat to 5pm) in the **Belfry Centre.** The Sainsbury's **supermarket** north of the Harlequin Centre is open daily. The town centre is host to a **farmers' market** on the second Friday of every month.

The main **bus** services are Arriva No 32 (Mon-Sat only) to Guildford and Metrobus No 405 to West Croydon, No 410 (Westerham via Oxted, Mon-Sat, hourly), No 411 (Oxted only, Mon-Fri mornings only) and No 435 (Merstham, Mon-Sat 2/hr, Sun 1/hr); all leave from the bus station.

The **train station** has services to a number of destinations including London Victoria and London Bridge (both 2/hr), Gatwick (4/hr) and Brighton (hourly); see the public transport map and table, pp37-40.

Where to stay

Convenient to the station is ***The Innkeepers' Lodge*** (☎ 01737-768434, 🖳 www.innkeeperslodge.com; 37D all en suite), which has rooms from £45sgl/22.50dbl Fri-Sat and from £69.95sgl/35dbl Sun-Thu including breakfast. There's not much by way of character but you get consistently clean, comfortable rooms, four white towels and

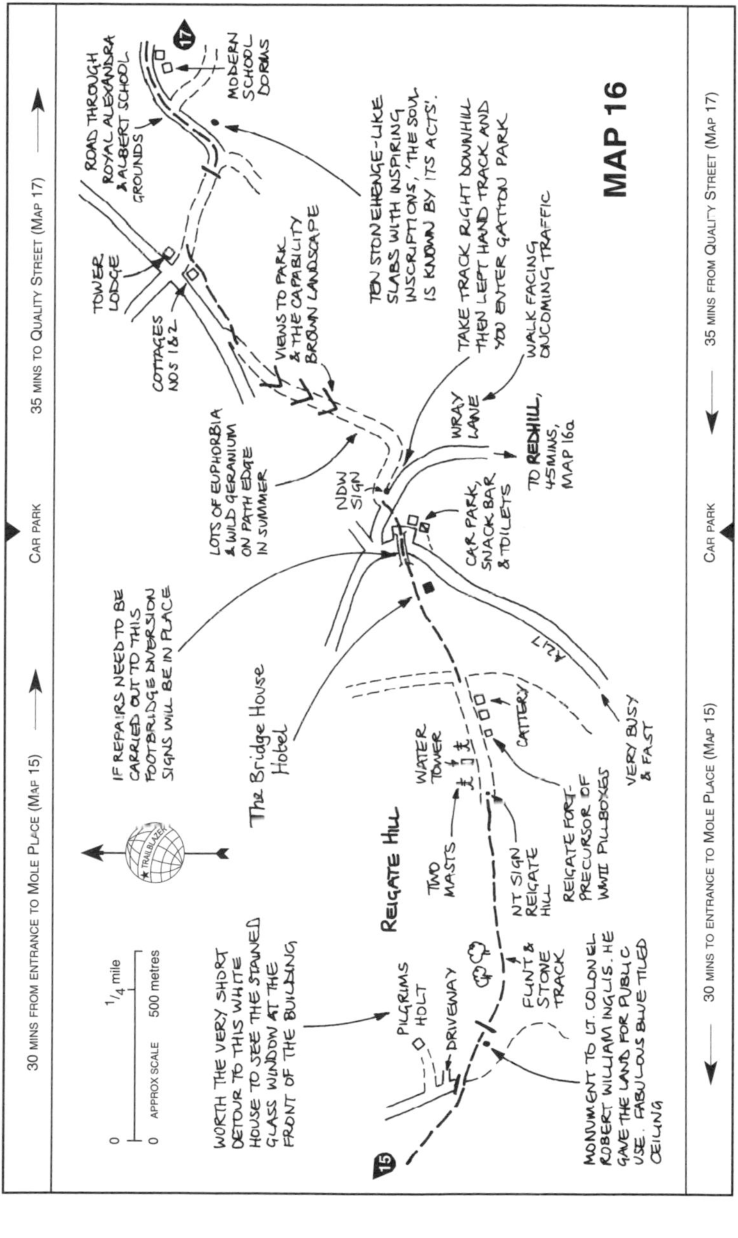
30 MINS FROM ENTRANCE TO MOLE PLACE (MAP 15)
CAR PARK
35 MINS TO QUALITY STREET (MAP 17)
30 MINS TO ENTRANCE TO MOLE PLACE (MAP 15)
CAR PARK
35 MINS FROM QUALITY STREET (MAP 17)
MAP 16
0
1/4 mile
0
APPROX SCALE
500 metres
TRAILBLAZER
15
17
WORTH THE VERY SHORT DETOUR TO THIS WHITE HOUSE TO SEE THE STAINED GLASS WINDOW AT THE FRONT OF THE BUILDING
PILGRIMS HOLT
DRIVEWAY
REIGATE HILL
TWO MASTS
WATER TOWER
NT SIGN REIGATE HILL
FLINT & STONE TRACK
MONUMENT TO LT. COLONEL ROBERT WILLIAM INGLIS. HE GAVE THE LAND FOR PUBLIC USE. FABULOUS BLUE TILED CEILING
REIGATE FORT - PRECURSOR OF WWII PILLBOXES
CATTERY
VERY BUSY & FAST
A217
The Bridge House Hotel
IF REPAIRS NEED TO BE CARRIED OUT TO THIS FOOTBRIDGE DIVERSION SIGNS WILL BE IN PLACE
LOTS OF EUPHORBIA & WILD GERANIUM ON PATH EDGE IN SUMMER
NDW SIGN
CAR PARK, SNACK BAR & TOILETS
TO REDHILL, 45MINS, MAP 16a
WRAY LANE
WALK FACING ONCOMING TRAFFIC
TAKE TRACK RIGHT DOWNHILL THEN LEFT HAND TRACK AND YOU ENTER GATTON PARK
TEN STONEHENGE-LIKE SLABS WITH INSPIRING INSCRIPTIONS, 'THE SOUL IS KNOWN BY ITS ACTS'.
VIEWS TO PARK & THE CAPABILITY BROWN LANDSCAPE
COTTAGES NOS 1&2
TOWER LODGE
ROAD THROUGH ROYAL ALEXANDRA & ALBERT SCHOOL GROUNDS
MODERN SCHOOL DORMS

SKY TV to indulge in some channel hopping. Close by is ***Brompton Guest House*** (☎ 01737-765613, 🖳 www.bromptonguesthouse.com; 1S/3D/2F), a comfortable Edwardian house about five minutes from the station charging from £35sgl/25dbl/£70fml plus VAT. The single has a private bathroom; the other rooms are en suite.

Also a quarter of a mile (500 metres) away is ***Lynwood Guest House*** (☎ 01737-766894, 🖳 www.lynwoodguesthouse.co.uk; 2S/1D/2T/4F), on the corner of Lynwood Rd and London Rd. B&B is from £32sgl/26dbl or twin. A family room costs £62 for three people. The double and two family rooms are en suite. ***Parklands House*** (☎ 01737-765026, 🖳 www.parklandsguesthouse.co.uk; 1S/3D/1F), a large Victorian house at 10 Lynwood Rd, has B&B from £34sgl/26dbl; the family room costs £66 for three people.

Where to eat

The best of the bunch is ***Prezzo*** (☎ 01737-779927; Mon-Sat noon-11pm, Sun noon-10pm), at 33 London Rd, close to Lynwood and Parklands guesthouses. It's in a converted post office; pizza starts at £5.45 and the grilled chicken in £8.50.

The ***Toby Carvery*** (☎ 01737-768434; daily noon-10pm) next to the Innkeepers' Lodge (see p100) dishes up its 'famous'

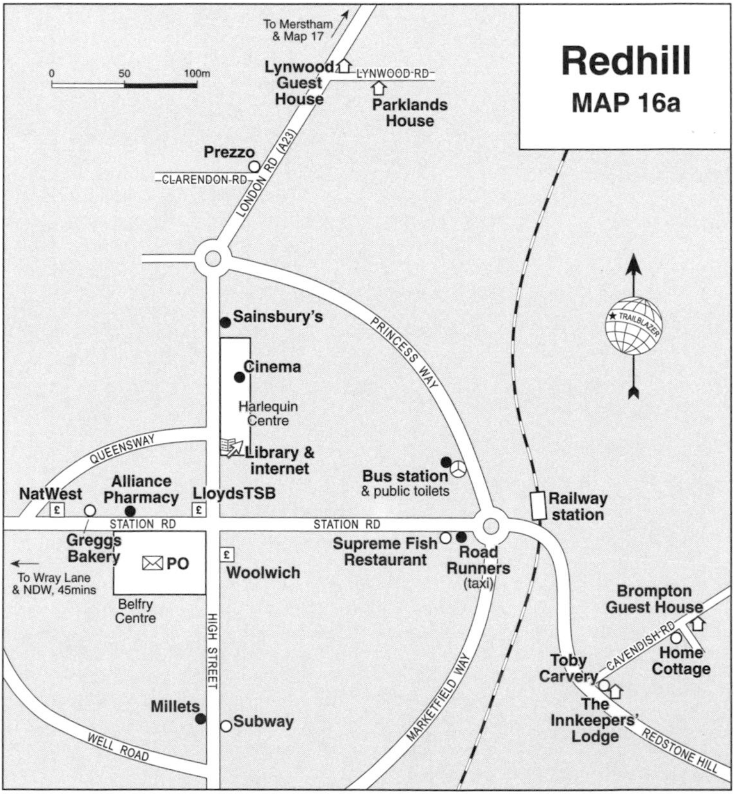

carvery for £6.99; choose from gammon, turkey or beef with eat-as-much-as-you-can trimmings. Good pub grub can be had at ***Home Cottage*** (☎ 01737-762771; Mon-Fri noon-2.45pm/6-8.45pm, Sat & Sun noon-3.45pm), a Victorian pub serving Young's and which is just around the corner from Brompton Guest House (see opposite). Steak and kidney pie is £5.95. The spotless ***Supreme Fish Restaurant*** (Mon-Sat 11am 2.30pm/4.30-9.30pm), on Station Rd, is licensed. Large cod and chips is £6.40 and cod roe is £3.20. There are several **coffee shops** in the Belfry Centre (Mon-Sat 9am-6pm, Sun 11am-4.30pm). For an instant sugar hit ***Greggs Bakery***, on Station Rd, does four glazed doughnut rings for £1.10 and you can also stock up on pies and pasties for the walk. Alternatively try ***Subway*** (Mon-Sat 7.30am-10.30pm, Sun 10am-6pm) on the High St. Subway serves a large variety of American-style submarine sandwiches (6" and 12") as well as salads, cookies and muffins.

The North Downs Way enters Merstham by the quaintly named Quality St below the M23/M25 interchange yet it's surprisingly quiet.

MERSTHAM [MAP 17]

The ***Q8*** petrol station shop is open 24 hours a day and below this the ***Railway Arms*** (☎ 01737-642289) does pub grub at lunch only (Mon-Sat 12noon-2.15pm, Sun 12noon-2pm). Across from Q8 is ***The Feathers*** (☎ 01737-645643; food Mon-Fri noon-3pm/6-10pm, Sat/Sun noon-10pm), with a diverse menu offering veggie sandwiches (£4.70) to lamb rump with mint gravy (£7.90).

By Station Rd North is ***Hunger's End*** (☎ 01737-642291; Mon-Fri 8am-3pm, Sat 9am-2pm) which does filling warm baguettes and sandwiches from £3.70. ***Merstham Café***, Station Rd South, is a cabbies' hang out serving huge portions of bubble and squeak (90p) and greasy-spoon standards such as Spanish omelette, chips, beans and tea for £4.90.

There is also a **newsagent** (open daily, 5.30am-5.30pm), and Station Cars **taxi** (☎ 01737-645588), who are based at the station.

Train services operate to a number of destinations including London Victoria and London Bridge (Mon-Sat 2/hr, Sun 1/hr) and Redhill (daily 2/hr). **Bus** (Metrobus) Nos 430 (Mon-Sat 3-4/hr) and 435 (Sun No 435 only, 1/hr) stop on Delabole Rd and serve Redhill Station; No 405 goes to West Croydon and Redhill Station (daily, 2-3/hr) from by The Feathers pub; see the public transport map and table, pp37-40.

Accommodation is available at ***Boors Green Farmhouse*** (☎ 01737-643903; 1S/2D) where B&B is £30, but advance booking is essential as they have a regular business clientele. The owners, avid cross-country runners, are happy to collect you from Merstham, thus saving the walk up the A23 to Harps Oak Lane, and they'll do a light supper for £7.50 if pre-arranged. If you were up to it you could walk back down to ***Vojan*** (☎ 01737-644171; daily noon-2.30pm/6-11.30pm), 229 London Rd North, on the A23, for a duck tikka biryani (£7.50). Alternatively take the twice-hourly train back to Redhill (less than ten minutes) for a greater choice of accommodation and food.

MERSTHAM TO OXTED (CHALK PIT LANE) [MAPS 17-21]

The Way leaves Merstham, at the start of this **8mile/12.8km** stage by Quality St with its diverse collection of houses dating from the 1700s. Crossing the M25 and M23 in quick succession the path climbs steadily to the ridgeline where the traffic noise recedes. The level track continues past Quarry Hangers Nature Reserve (see Map 18), a chalk grassland habitat. *(cont'd on p106)*

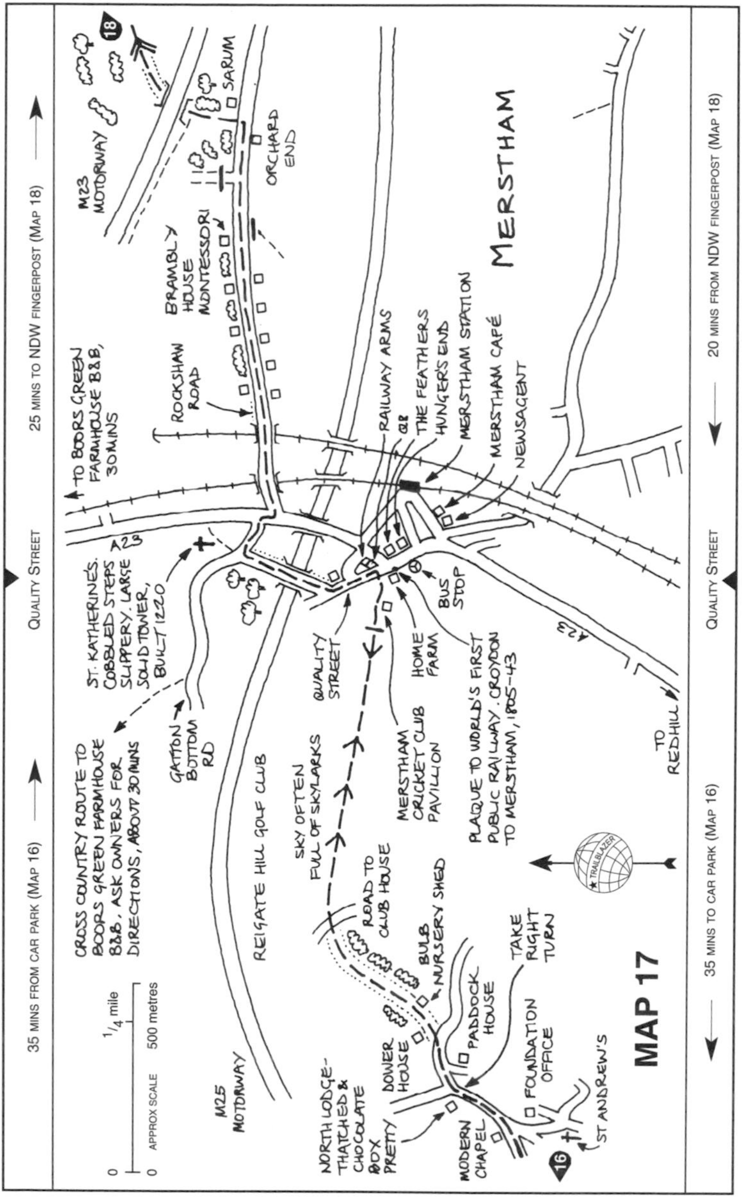
MAP 17
35 MINS FROM CAR PARK (MAP 16)
QUALITY STREET
25 MINS TO NDW FINGERPOST (MAP 18)
35 MINS TO CAR PARK (MAP 16)
QUALITY STREET
20 MINS FROM NDW FINGERPOST (MAP 18)
0 1/4 mile
0 APPROX SCALE 500 metres
M25 MOTORWAY
CROSS COUNTRY ROUTE TO BOORS GREEN FARMHOUSE B&B. ASK OWNERS FOR DIRECTIONS, ABOUT 30 MINS
REIGATE HILL GOLF CLUB
GATTON BOTTOM RD
ST. KATHERINE'S. COBBLED STEPS SLIPPERY. LARGE SOLID TOWER, BUILT 1220
A23
TO BOORS GREEN FARMHOUSE B&B, 30 MINS
ROCKSHAW ROAD
BRAMBLY HOUSE MONTESSORI
M23 MOTORWAY
SARUM
ORCHARD END
MERSTHAM
RAILWAY ARMS
Q8
THE FEATHERS
HUNGER'S END
MERSTHAM STATION
MERSTHAM CAFÉ
NEWSAGENT
BUS STOP
HOME FARM
QUALITY STREET
MERSTHAM CRICKET CLUB PAVILION
PLAQUE TO WORLD'S FIRST PUBLIC RAILWAY, CROYDON TO MERSTHAM, 1805-43
TO REDHILL
SKY OFTEN FULL OF SKYLARKS
ROAD TO CLUB HOUSE
BULB NURSERY SHED
TAKE RIGHT TURN
PADDOCK HOUSE
DOWER HOUSE
NORTH LODGE - THATCHED & CHOCOLATE BOX PRETTY
MODERN CHAPEL
FOUNDATION OFFICE
ST ANDREW'S
TRAILBLAZER
16
18

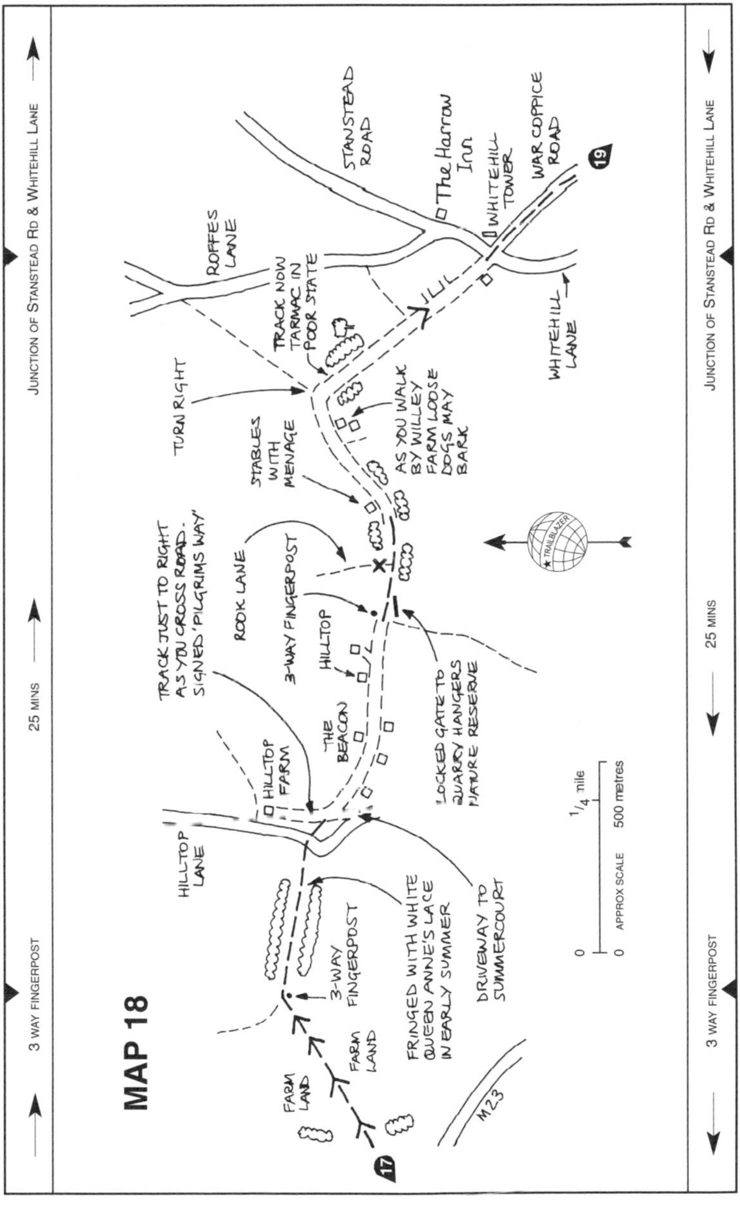
MAP 18
3 WAY FINGERPOST
25 MINS
JUNCTION OF STANSTEAD RD & WHITEHILL LANE
17
FARM LAND
FARM LAND
3-WAY FINGERPOST
FRINGED WITH WHITE QUEEN ANNE'S LACE IN EARLY SUMMER
DRIVEWAY TO SUMMERCOURT
M23
HILLTOP LANE
HILLTOP FARM
TRACK JUST TO RIGHT AS YOU CROSS ROAD. SIGNED 'PILGRIMS WAY'
THE BEACON
HILLTOP
3-WAY FINGERPOST
ROOK LANE
LOCKED GATE TO QUARRY HANGERS NATURE RESERVE
STABLES WITH MENAGE
AS YOU WALK BY WILLEY FARM LOOSE DOGS MAY BARK
TURN RIGHT
TRACK NOW TARMAC IN POOR STATE
ROFFES LANE
STANSTEAD ROAD
The Harrow Inn
WHITEHILL TOWER
WAR COPPICE ROAD
19
WHITEHILL LANE
TRAILBLAZER
0 1/4 mile
0 500 metres
APPROX SCALE

ROUTE GUIDE AND MAPS

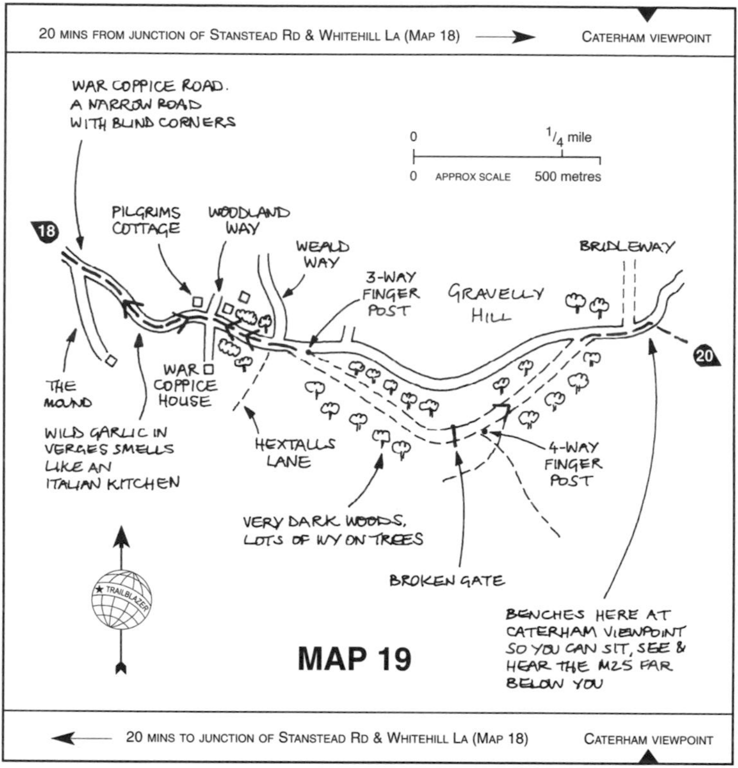

(cont'd from p103) Surrey Wildlife Trust (see box p44) manage the reserve and keep the gate locked to prevent vehicle access but pedestrians can climb the gate to see the reserve. The track then leads to Whitehill Tower (see box below), a folly. From the folly it is a short walk to ***The Harrow Inn*** (☎ 01883-343260;

❑ Whitehill Tower

Follies, bizarre and quirky buildings with no apparent practical use or purpose, were built by the grieving, the eccentric, and the out and out bonkers. Whitehill Tower (Map 18) is also known as Whitehill Folly Tower and the Sight Tower. Built in 1862 by Jeremiah Long after his son was killed at sea, you are able, supposedly, to see the sea from the top. A fourth floor was reputedly added after the trees around the tower grew.

The bible on follies is *Follies, Grottoes and Garden Buildings*, Headley & Meulenkamp, Aurum Press, or visit 🖳 www.follies.org.uk.

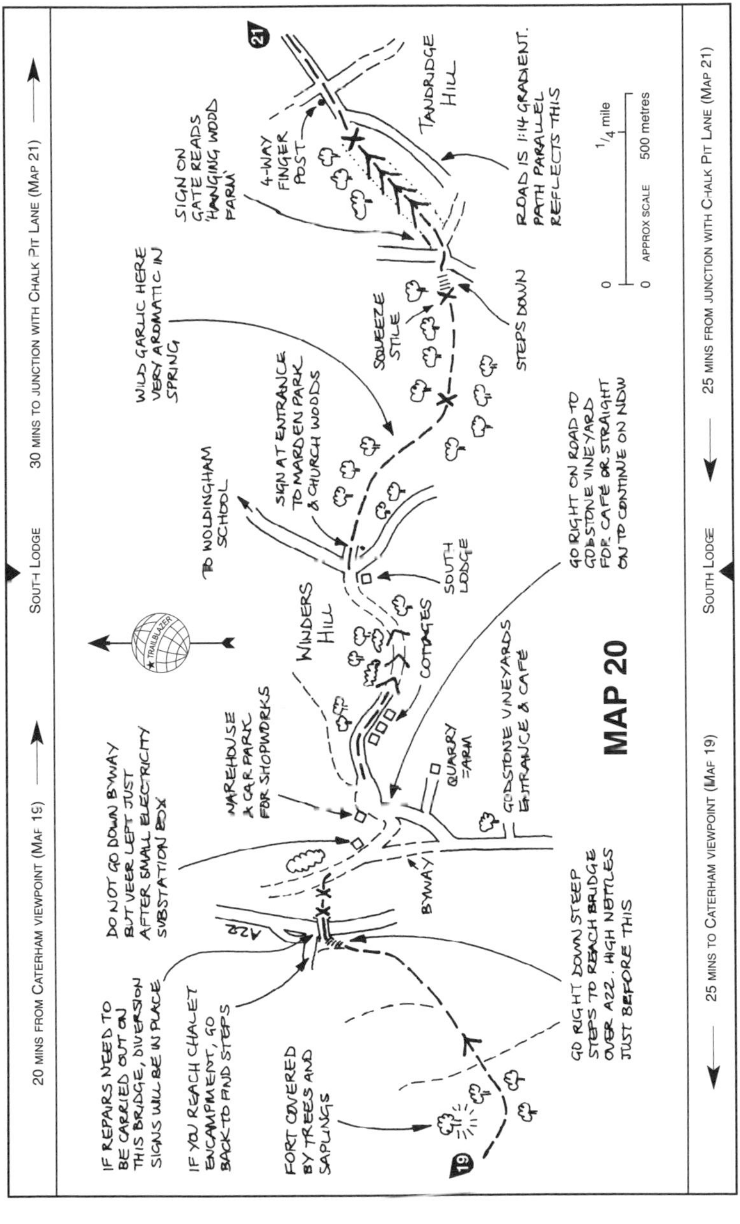
20 MINS FROM CATERHAM VIEWPOINT (MAP 19) →
SOUTH LODGE
30 MINS TO JUNCTION WITH CHALK PIT LANE (MAP 21) →
IF REPAIRS NEED TO BE CARRIED OUT ON THIS BRIDGE, DIVERSION SIGNS WILL BE IN PLACE
IF YOU REACH CHALET ENCAMPMENT, GO BACK TO FIND STEPS
FORT COVERED BY TREES AND SAPLINGS
19
A22
DO NOT GO DOWN BYWAY BUT VEER LEFT JUST AFTER SMALL ELECTRICITY SUBSTATION BOX
WAREHOUSE & CAR PARK FOR SHOPWORKS
WINDERS HILL
TRAILBLAZER
TO WOLDINGHAM SCHOOL
SIGN AT ENTRANCE TO MARDEN PARK & CHURCH WOODS
WILD GARLIC HERE VERY AROMATIC IN SPRING
SIGN ON GATE READS 'HANGING WOOD FARM'
4-WAY FINGER POST
21
TANDRIDGE HILL
SQUEEZE STILE
STEPS DOWN
ROAD IS 1:14 GRADIENT. PATH PARALLEL REFLECTS THIS
SOUTH LODGE
COTTAGES
QUARRY FARM
GODSTONE VINEYARDS ENTRANCE & CAFE
BYWAY
MAP 20
GO RIGHT DOWN STEEP STEPS TO REACH BRIDGE OVER A22. HIGH NETTLES JUST BEFORE THIS
GO RIGHT ON ROAD TO GODSTONE VINEYARD FOR CAFE OR STRAIGHT ON TO CONTINUE ON NDW
0 1/4 mile
0 500 metres
APPROX SCALE
← 25 MINS TO CATERHAM VIEWPOINT (MAP 19)
SOUTH LODGE
← 25 MINS FROM JUNCTION WITH CHALK PIT LANE (MAP 21)

food daily noon-3pm/6-9pm). The menu includes grilled trout with horseradish mash (£7.95), 'posh bangers and mash' (£7.50), or you can settle for a crispy bacon, brie and redcurrant baguette (£4.25). The only other refreshment possibility on this short section is just off the trail at Godstone Vineyards (see below).

After a short section of road walking the trail returns to dense woodland emerging briefly at Caterham viewpoint then returning once more to woodland before crossing over the A22. If the footbridge is being repaired diversion signs will be in place.

To get to ***Godstone Vineyards*** (see Map 20; ☎ 01883-744590, 🖳 www.godstonevineyards.com; May-Sep weekdays 10.30am-4.30pm, weekends 10am-5.30pm; Oct-Apr weekdays 11am-4pm, weekends 11am-4.30pm) leave the Way opposite Shopworks Car Park and turn right onto the road following it downhill to the entrance. Their mini cream tea at £2.95 is a good energy booster which you'll appreciate on the 1:14 gradient that follows.

Having reached the top of Tandridge Hill you descend sharply by wooden steps to Oxted Downs, a chalk grassland habitat and site of special scientific interest (SSSI) packed with wildflowers in spring and such a counterpoint to the M25 running below it. Cattle are grazed to conserve the downland habitat and prevent trees taking over. The trail then cuts across the grassland to Chalk Pit Lane from where it's a 25-minute or so walk to Oxted. Call Oxted Station **Taxis** (☎ 01883-722999) if you prefer the thought of a lift.

OXTED [MAP 21a]

Oxted is separated from Old Oxted by the A25 and divided east and west by the railway line with a parade of shops either side of the station.

Services

Getting cash should not be a problem as there are four banks with **cash machines** and two **post offices** (Mon-Fri 9am-5.30pm, Sat 2.30pm). The **cinema** (☎ 01883-722288) is behind a mock Tudor facade and the **leisure centre** (☎ 01883-716717, 🖳 www.tandridgeleisure.co.uk) has a swimming pool to relax in.

Morrisons **supermarket** (Mon-Sat 8am-10pm, Sun 10am-4pm) will fill a lunch box and should you need a **chemist** there is a Boots (Mon-Sat 8.30am-5.30pm) on Station Rd East.

Free internet access is available at the **library** (☎ 01883-714225; Tue/Fri 9.30am-8pm, Wed 9.30am-1pm, Thu 9.30am-5pm, Sat 9.30am-4pm).

There is a **train station** with daily services to London (Victoria, Charing Cross, London Bridge and Waterloo, 1-3hr).

Bus services (Metrobus) include: No 410 which operates between Redhill and Westerham and stops at the George (Old Oxted) and on Station Rd East (Oxted); No 411 to Redhill; and Buses 4U's No 510, a Sunday Rambler service leaving from Station Rd East; see the public transport map and table, pp37-40.

Where to stay

Meads (☎ 01883-730115; 1T en suite/2D with shared bathroom), 23 Granville Rd, is a substantial 1920s Tudor-style house where B&B is £40sgl/35twin/30dbl; they also have a one-bed flat for £85 per night, minimum two nights.

Pinehurst Grange Guesthouse (☎ 01883-716413; 1S/1D/1T) is convenient for the pubs in Old Oxted and does B&B for £35sgl/27.50dbl.

Slightly further out, on leafy Quarry Rd, is ***The Croft*** (☎ 01883-713605, 🖳 www.thecroftbedandbreakfast.co.uk; 1S/2D/2F), charging £45sgl/32.50dbl, £37.50 for an en suite double. Three sharing a family room costs £32 per person and four sharing is £31.

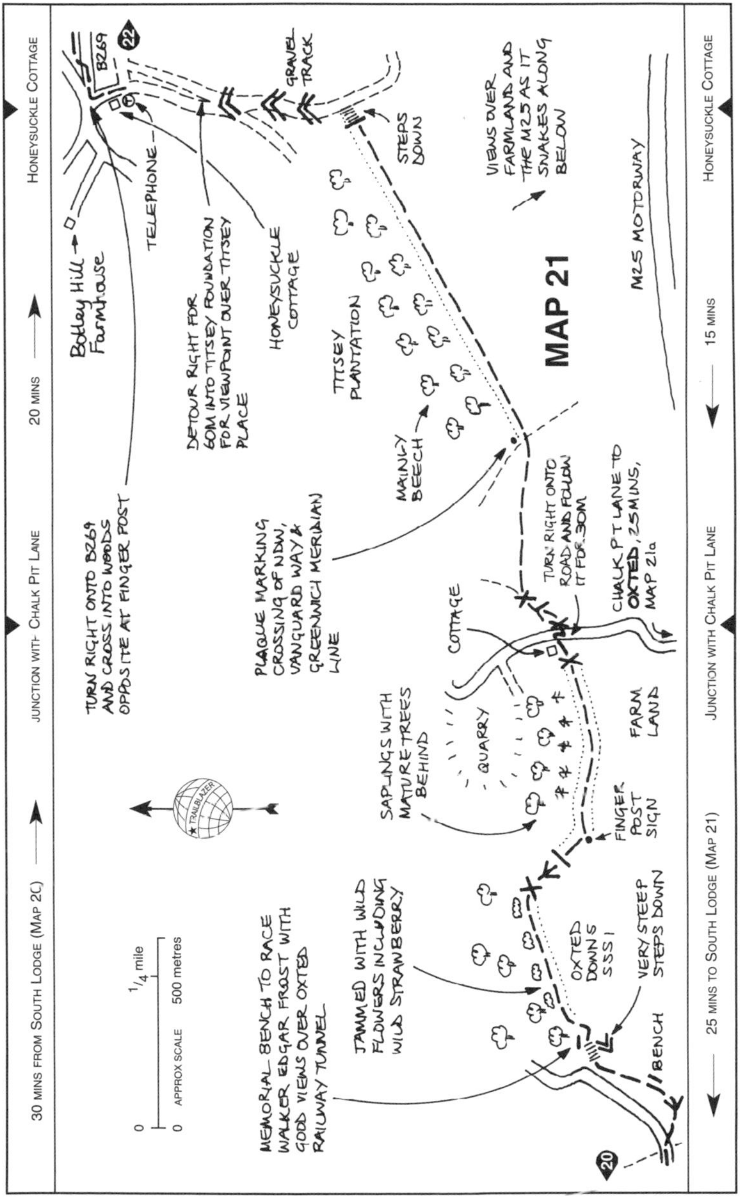
30 MINS FROM SOUTH LODGE (MAP 20)
20 MINS
JUNCTION WITH CHALK PIT LANE
HONEYSUCKLE COTTAGE
25 MINS TO SOUTH LODGE (MAP 21)
JUNCTION WITH CHALK PIT LANE
15 MINS
HONEYSUCKLE COTTAGE
MAP 21
APPROX SCALE
0
1/4 mile
0
500 metres
TRAILBLAZER
B269
22
GRAVEL TRACK
Botley Hill Farmhouse
TELEPHONE
STEPS DOWN
VIEWS OVER FARMLAND AND THE M25 AS IT SNAKES ALONG BELOW
DETOUR RIGHT FOR 60M INTO TITSEY FOUNDATION FOR VIEWPOINT OVER TITSEY PLACE
HONEYSUCKLE COTTAGE
TITSEY PLANTATION
M25 MOTORWAY
TURN RIGHT ONTO B269 AND CROSS INTO WOODS OPPOSITE AT FINGER POST
MAINLY BEECH
PLAQUE MARKING CROSSING OF NDW, VANGUARD WAY & GREENWICH MERIDIAN LINE
TURN RIGHT ONTO ROAD AND FOLLOW IT FOR 30M
CHALK PIT LANE TO OXTED, 25 MINS, MAP 21a
COTTAGE
SAPLINGS WITH MATURE TREES BEHIND
QUARRY
FARM LAND
FINGER POST SIGN
JAMMED WITH WILD FLOWERS INCLUDING WILD STRAWBERRY
OXTED DOWNS SSSI
VERY STEEP STEPS DOWN
MEMORIAL BENCH TO RACE WALKER EDGAR FROST WITH GOOD VIEWS OVER OXTED RAILWAY TUNNEL
BENCH
20

Where to eat

The Gurkha Kitchen (☎ 01883-722621; Mon-Sat noon-2pm/6-11pm, Sun 6-10pm) is a stylish Nepalese restaurant on Station Rd East just as you leave the station. Sherpa lamb is £6.95 and *asala macha* (salmon in yoghurt) is £8.95.

Enticing wafts of garlic escape from the glass-fronted ***Pizza Express*** (☎ 01883-723142, 💻 www.pizzaexpress.com; Mon-Sat 11.30am-10.30pm, Sun to 10pm) with pizzas from £4.95.

The award for longest opening hours goes to ***Plaxtol Bakery*** (Mon-Sat 5.30am-5pm). Next door to HSBC is ***Kim's Café*** (Mon-Sat 8.30am-3pm) where a fragrant and filling onion and parsnip soup is £4.95. ***Nonna Cappuchino*** (Mon-Sat 8am-5pm) has a very popular summer outdoor seating area for the latte crowd and a roasted pepper, courgette and robiola cheese sandwich is £4.

Fishers (Mon 8am-6pm, Tue-Thu 8am-8pm, Fri 8am-9pm), 7 Station Rd East, does fish and chips. Takeaway hours are Mon-Sat 11.30am-10pm.

Behind yet another mock Tudor façade is ***The Rainbow*** (☎ 01883-713988; daily 11am-2pm/5.45pm-11pm, Fri & Sat to

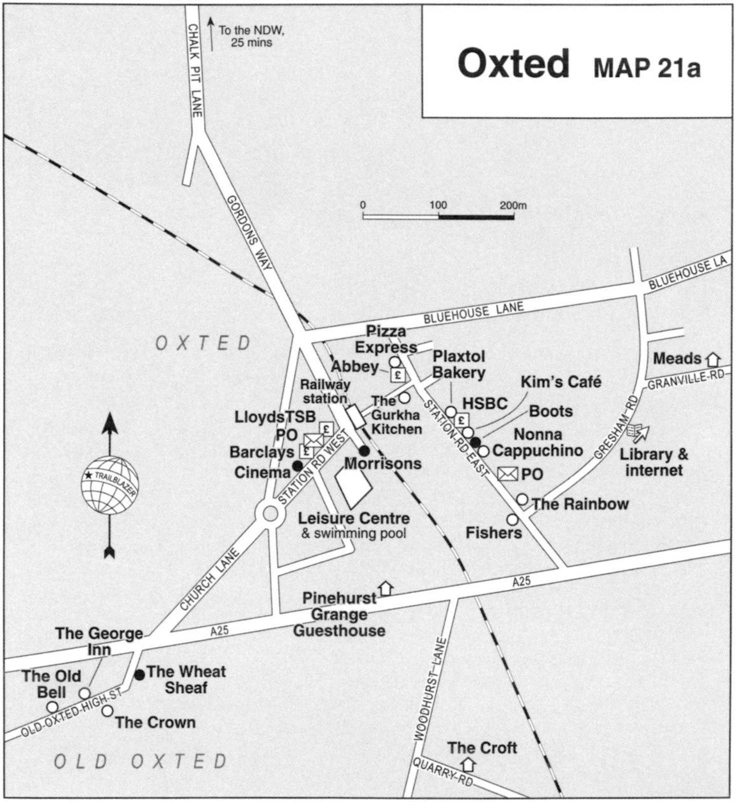

11.30pm), with keenly priced Szechuan and Peking cuisine.

On the High St, in **Old Oxted**, the pick of the pubs is ***The George Inn*** (☎ 01883-713453, 🖳 www.thegeorge-inn.com; Mon-Thur 11am-3pm, 6-9pm, to 10pm Wed & Thur, Fri & Sat 11am-10pm, Sun noon-7.45pm) which dishes out hearty tapas at £2.95 a plate during the week. Main courses include roast duckling (£13) and lamb shank (£13.50). ***The Old Bell*** (☎ 01883-712181; food served Mon-Sat noon-10pm, Sun noon-9.30pm) packs them in for a roast on Sundays.

The Crown (☎ 01883-717853; food Mon-Fri noon-2.30pm/7-9.30pm, Sat/Sun noon-9.30pm) has a pleasant beer garden and big plates of pub grub; liver and bacon is £9.50. Or, if you just want a pint, you could try the ***Wheatsheaf***.

OXTED (CHALK PIT LANE) TO OTFORD [MAPS 21-26]

Let's just say this **12mile/19.2km** section isn't a wilderness experience. Greater London is only a few miles away at times and the visual spoil and sound of motorways intrudes. After leaving Chalk Pit Lane the trail climbs through the extensive beech woods of Titsey Plantation and on the way passes the point marking the crossing of the Greenwich Meridian Line.

A short detour off the Way at Botley Hill is ***Botley Hill Farmhouse*** (Map 21; ☎ 01959-577154; food Mon-Sat noon-3pm/6.30-9.30pm, Sun noon-9.30pm) a pub-restaurant whose previous incarnation was a tea room. It's very popular especially on Sundays when there is a set menu of roast beef, lamb or turkey with all the trimmings for £9.95.

After crossing the B269 the trail continues through woods to emerge at Church Hill below St Mary's church (see Map 22), which is a short way off the trail. Volunteers usually sell tea, cake and scones in the church hall for the bargain price of £1.50 on Sundays, 3-5pm, March-September. Fortified by this it's a quick walk to the A233 (see Map 23) where you can detour to Westerham.

❑ Westerham's historic connections

The childhood home of General James Wolfe, who captured Quebec in the French Indian war in 1759 only to die a few days later of gunshot wounds, **Quebec House** (☎ 01959-562206) is open to visitors (Apr-Oct Wed-Sun and Bank Holiday Mondays 1-5pm). The house contains Georgian memorabilia as well as a Battle of Quebec exhibition and is run by the National Trust.

Chartwell (☎ 01732-866368), Sir Winston Churchill's former home, is also run by the National Trust and is one of its most popular properties. Winston Churchill lived here from 1924 till the end of his life and the house is still much as he left it. Parts of the garden were created by him and his wife. The house and garden are open Mar-Oct Wed-Sun 11am-5pm and on Bank Holiday Mondays; from July to September it is also open on Tuesdays. Timed tickets are issued on arrival (they cannot be prebooked) so it could be a while before you get in.

Chartwell is about three miles south of the trail; Metrobus's **bus** No 246 runs hourly, on Sundays and public holidays, from Bromley North, and the No 401 runs from Tunbridge Wells. The No 236 from Westerham to East Grinstead operates Mon-Fri and stops within half a mile of the property. See also pp37-40.

For more information on both properties visit 🖳 www.nationaltrust.org.

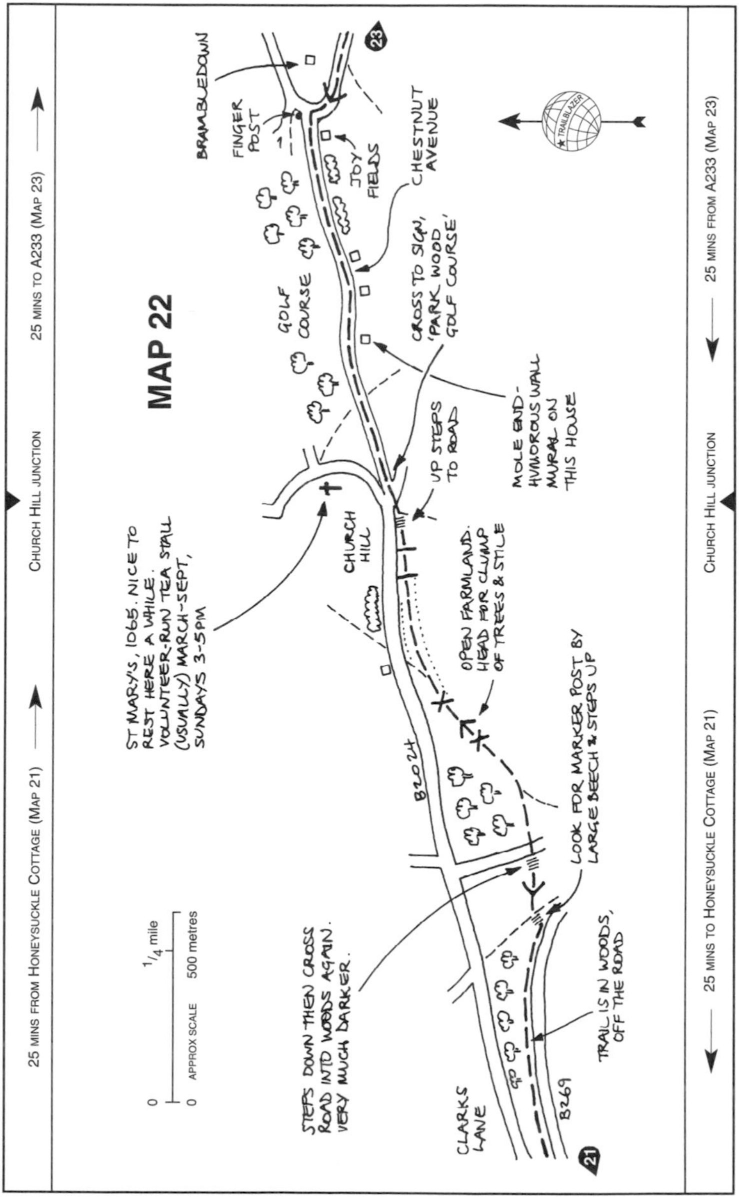
MAP 22
25 MINS FROM HONEYSUCKLE COTTAGE (MAP 21)
CHURCH HILL JUNCTION
25 MINS TO A233 (MAP 23)
25 MINS TO HONEYSUCKLE COTTAGE (MAP 21)
CHURCH HILL JUNCTION
25 MINS FROM A233 (MAP 23)
0 1/4 mile
0 APPROX SCALE 500 metres
ST MARY'S, 1065. NICE TO REST HERE A WHILE. VOLUNTEER-RUN TEA STALL (USUALLY) MARCH-SEPT, SUNDAYS 3-5PM
CHURCH HILL
UP STEPS TO ROAD
OPEN FARMLAND. HEAD FOR CLUMP OF TREES & STILE
LOOK FOR MARKER POST BY LARGE BEECH & STEPS UP
STEPS DOWN THEN CROSS ROAD INTO WOODS AGAIN. VERY MUCH DARKER.
TRAIL IS IN WOODS, OFF THE ROAD
CLARKS LANE
B269
B2024
GOLF COURSE
CROSS TO SIGN, 'PARK WOOD GOLF COURSE'
MOLE END-HUMOROUS WALL MURAL ON THIS HOUSE
CHESTNUT AVENUE
JOY FIELDS
FINGER POST
BRAMBLEDOWN
TRAILBLAZER
21
23

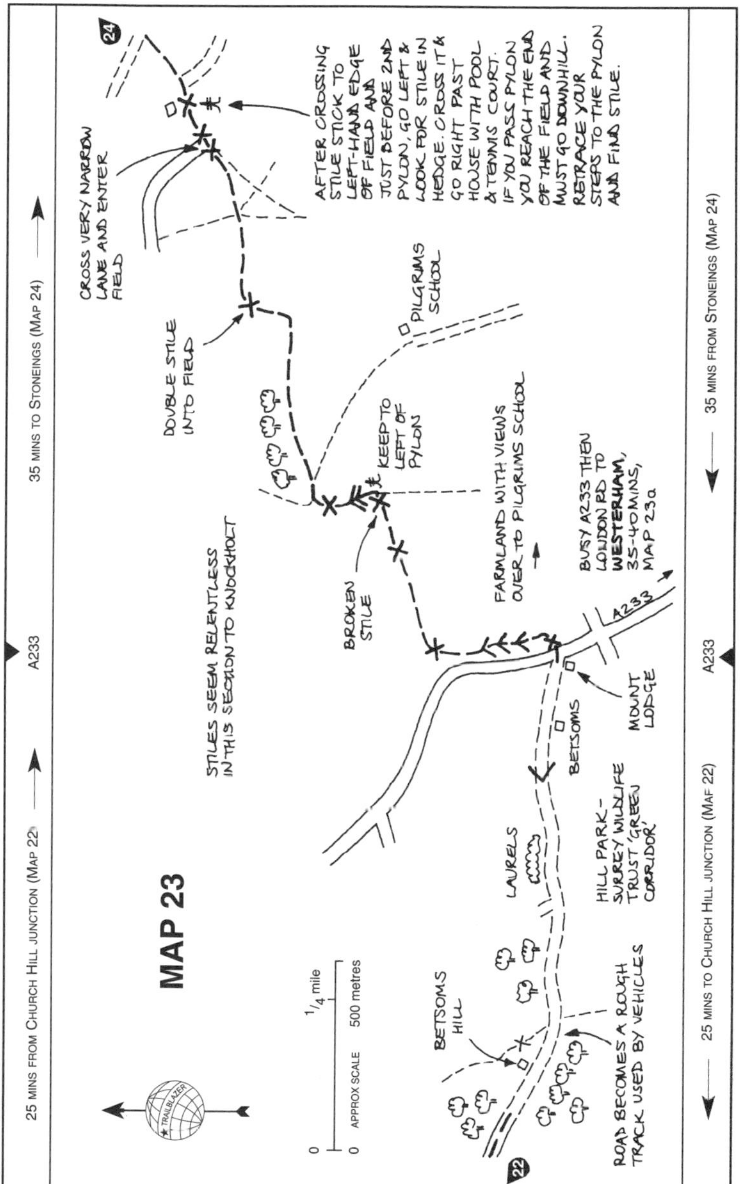
25 MINS FROM CHURCH HILL JUNCTION (MAP 22)
A233
35 MINS TO STONEINGS (MAP 24)
25 MINS TO CHURCH HILL JUNCTION (MAF 22)
A233
35 MINS FROM STONEINGS (MAP 24)
MAP 23
TRAILBLAZER
0
1/4 mile
0
500 metres
APPROX SCALE
22
24
BETSOMS HILL
ROAD BECOMES A ROUGH TRACK USED BY VEHICLES
LAURELS
HILL PARK– SURREY WILDLIFE TRUST 'GREEN CORRIDOR'
BETSOMS
MOUNT LODGE
STILES SEEM RELENTLESS IN THIS SECTION TO KNOCKHOLT
BROKEN STILE
A233
FARMLAND WITH VIEWS OVER TO PILGRIMS SCHOOL
BUSY A233 THEN LONDON RD TO WESTERHAM, 35-40 MINS, MAP 23a
KEEP TO LEFT OF PYLON
DOUBLE STILE INTO FIELD
PILGRIMS SCHOOL
CROSS VERY NARROW LANE AND ENTER FIELD
AFTER CROSSING STILE STICK TO LEFT-HAND EDGE OF FIELD AND JUST BEFORE 2ND PYLON, GO LEFT & LOOK FOR STILE IN HEDGE. CROSS IT & GO RIGHT PAST HOUSE WITH POOL & TENNIS COURT. IF YOU PASS PYLON YOU REACH THE END OF THE FIELD AND MUST GO DOWNHILL. RETRACE YOUR STEPS TO THE PYLON AND FIND STILE.

WESTERHAM **[MAP 23a]**

Westerham lies on the A25 but it remains an attractive town with historic connections (see box p111). The **library** (☎ 01959-562326; open Tue-Fri 9am-1pm, Tue 2-6pm, Thu & Fri 2-5pm, Sat 9am-12.30pm) offers **free internet access**.

There are banks with **cash machines** on Market Square. Services include a **Co-op** (daily 7am-10pm) and a **Spar** convenience store, a newsagent with a **post office** and a **pharmacy** (☎ 01959-563130; Mon-Fri 9am-6pm, Sat 9am-5pm).

Bus (Metrobus) No 410 stops by the King's Arms and serves Redhill Station (Mon-Sat only, 12/day); see the box p111 and the public transport map and table, pp37-40.

King's Arms Hotel (☎ 01959-562990; 1S/3T/11D/4F all en suite), on Market Sq, charges £90sgl/57.50dbl/35fml. On the western edge of the village is ***Worples Field*** (☎ 01959-562869; 1S/2D) which does B&B for £40sgl with shared bathroom and £30dbl with private bathroom but there is a minimum stay of two nights at the weekend.

There's a good choice of eateries. The upmarket ***Kinara*** (☎ 01959-562125; Thu, Fri, Sun 12.30-3pm and daily 5.30-11.30pm), an Indian restaurant, is located in Pitt's Cottage; a 12th-century cottage used by William Pitt (1754-1806) as a country retreat. (William Pitt the Younger was, at age 24, and still is the youngest politician to become prime minister in the UK.) Seafood prices are not cheap – king prawn jalfrezi is £12.95.

To the east is ***Tulsi*** (☎ 01959-563397), another Indian restaurant serving staples such as lamb korma for £5.75.

Montien (☎ 01959-565833) serves good-value noodle dishes: pad thai is £6.20.

The Grasshopper (☎ 01959-562926; food Mon 11am-8pm, Tue 11am-3.30pm Wed-Sat 11am-9pm, Sun noon-6pm) is an old coaching inn with a non-smoking restaurant serving down-to-earth sausage and mash for £7.95 or a lighter feta salad, £6.50. Ribeye steak is £13.95. There is also pub grub at the ***General Wolfe*** (☎ 01959-562104, food daily noon-8pm).

For takeaway ***Fish & Chips*** (☎ 01959-562462; Tue-Sat 11.45am-2pm, Mon-Sat 5-10pm) leaves you in no doubt what it does and the ***Sultan Kebab House*** is next door.

Food For Thought (☎ 01959-569888, Mon-Sat 9am-5.30pm, Sun 9am-6pm; bookings required for Sunday lunch) overlooking the village green is a nice spot for a cream tea; coffee lovers will like ***The Coffee Garden*** (☎ 01959-561706; Mon-Fri 8.30am-4pm, Sat 9.30am-4pm). For a fill-

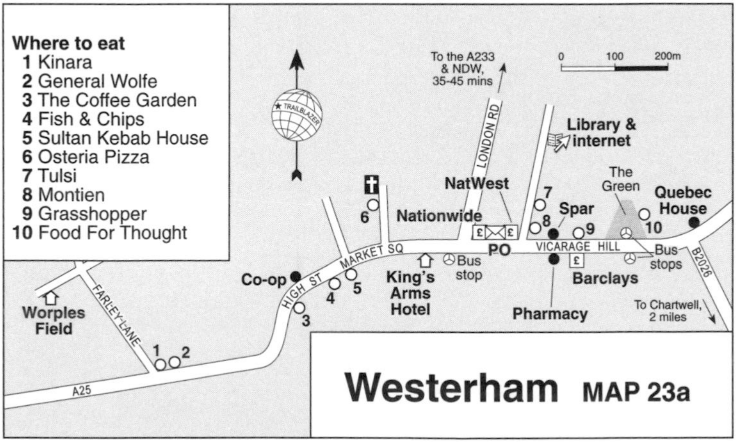

ing Italian meal try ***Osteria Pizzeria*** (☎ 01959-561688; Tue-Sat noon-3pm/6-11pm, Sun 7-10.30pm) with pizza from £5.90 and bowls of pasta from £6.50.

A 15-minute walk down **Stoneings Lane** leads to ***Tally Ho*** (Map 24; ☎ 01959-533602; food Tue-Fri noon-2pm/6.30-9pm, Sun/Mon noon-2.30pm), a walker-friendly pub attracting locals for a lunchtime pint. Hunting horns hang from the dark panelling and a tasty thick-cut ham ploughmans is £5.50.

You cross a total of 32 stiles in various states of repair on the section from Titsey Plantation to Knockholt; you many want to take to the country lanes to avoid some of them. To avoid yet more stiles after Stoneings Lane you may want to walk along Brasted Lane (see Map 24).

KNOCKHOLT [MAP 24]

Not actually on the North Downs Way but if you're comparing local pubs take the signed footpath before Sundridge Lane to reach the ***Crown Inn*** (☎ 01959-532142; food Tue-Sun noon-2pm, Sat 7-9pm) at Knockholt.

KNOCKHOLT POUND [OFF MAP 25]

For a more popular pub continue on to reach ***The Three Horseshoes*** (☎ 01959-532102; food Mon-Sat noon-2pm/6.30-9.30pm, Mon & Tue to 8.30pm, Sun noon-2.30pm) where a stilton and bacon salad is £7.95 and trout with garlic butter and prawns is £8.95. There are classic car meets here on Sundays, June-September and the welcoming bar is decorated with vintage-car memorabilia. The pub is about 15 minutes down Chevening Lane.

Up the road is ***The Harrow Inn*** (☎ 01959 532168; food Mon-Sat noon-2pm/7-9pm, no food Sun/Mon evening) serving a range of baguettes for £4.25 or for something hot try the minted lamb for £7.95.

The North Downs Way skirts the mixed woodland of the grounds of Chevening House, the Foreign Secretary's country house, and descends quickly with views over to the M25/M26 interchange.

Chevening is not on the trail and as the house isn't open to the public and the church is often locked there's not much reason to go there; even though the estate cottages by the church are very attractive they hardly merit the wear and tear on your feet. But there is accommodation (about 25 minutes away) at the 18th-century ***Crossways House*** (☎ 01732-456334; 3D one private bathroom, remainder en suite) for £30sgl/25dbl. ***Windmill Farm*** (☎ 01732-452054; 2D) has a self-contained flat attached to the house and charges £30sgl/dbl.

The trail crosses over the M25 after Morants Court Farm (Map 25) and heads towards Dunton Green and the ***Rose & Crown*** (☎ 01732-462343; food Mon-Sat noon-2.30pm/6.30-9.30pm, Sun noon-8pm). Friday is fish and chips night (£8.90).

DUNTON GREEN [OFF MAP 26]

The **train station**, about half a mile off the path on the London Rd over the M26, has an hourly service to London Victoria, Charing Cross and Waterloo and twice an hour to Tonbridge with onward connections to Hastings. Arriva's **bus** Nos 431 and 432 stop by The Dukes Head and operate the same route to and from *(cont'd on p118)*

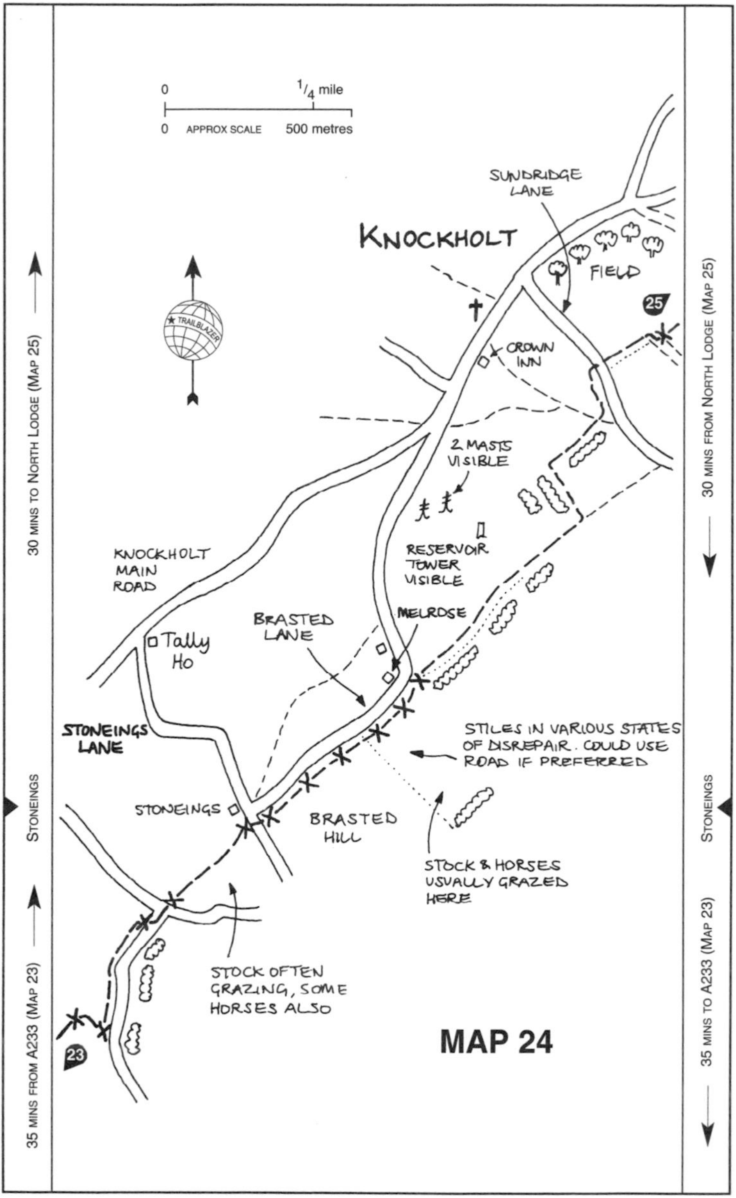
30 mins to North Lodge (Map 25)
Stoneings
35 mins from A233 (Map 23)
30 mins from North Lodge (Map 25)
Stoneings
35 mins to A233 (Map 23)
0 1/4 mile
0 APPROX SCALE 500 metres
TRAILBLAZER
SUNDRIDGE LANE
KNOCKHOLT
FIELD
25
CROWN INN
2 MASTS VISIBLE
RESERVOIR TOWER VISIBLE
KNOCKHOLT MAIN ROAD
BRASTED LANE
MELROSE
Tally Ho
STONEINGS LANE
STILES IN VARIOUS STATES OF DISREPAIR. COULD USE ROAD IF PREFERRED
STONEINGS
BRASTED HILL
STOCK & HORSES USUALLY GRAZED HERE
STOCK OFTEN GRAZING, SOME HORSES ALSO
23
MAP 24

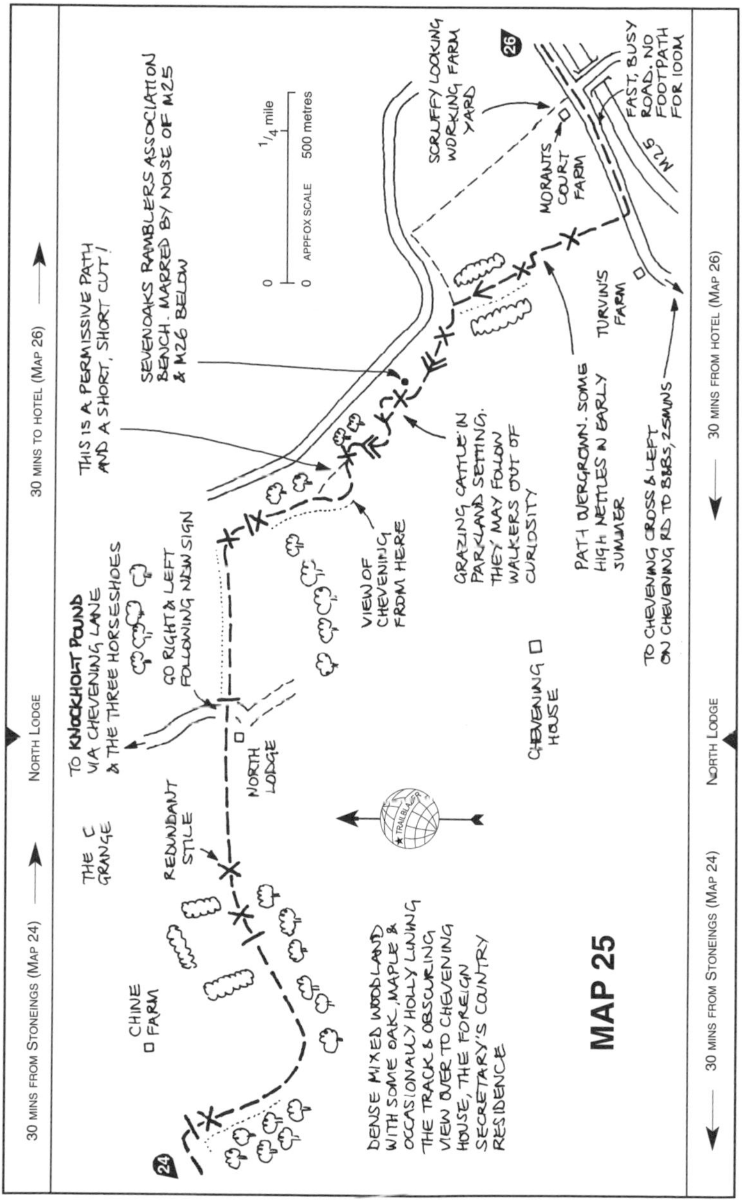
30 MINS FROM STONEINGS (MAP 24)
NORTH LODGE
30 MINS TO HOTEL (MAP 26)
24
CHINE FARM
THE GRANGE
REDUNDANT STILE
NORTH LODGE
TO KNOCKHOLT POUND VIA CHEVENING LANE & THE THREE HORSESHOES
GO RIGHT & LEFT FOLLOWING NEW SIGN
VIEW OF CHEVENING FROM HERE
THIS IS A PERMISSIVE PATH AND A SHORT, SHORT CUT!
SEVENOAKS RAMBLERS ASSOCIATION BENCH. MARRED BY NOISE OF M25 & M26 BELOW
0 1/4 mile
0 APPFOX SCALE 500 metres
SCRUFFY LOOKING WORKING FARM YARD
26
FAST, BUSY ROAD. NO FOOTPATH FOR 100M
M25
MORANTS COURT FARM
TURVIN'S FARM
GRAZING CATTLE IN PARKLAND SETTING. THEY MAY FOLLOW WALKERS OUT OF CURIOSITY
PATH OVERGROWN. SOME HIGH NETTLES IN EARLY SUMMER
TO CHEVENING CROSS & LEFT ON CHEVENING RD TO B&BS, 25MINS
CHEVENING HOUSE
TRAILBLAZER
DENSE MIXED WOODLAND WITH SOME OAK, MAPLE & OCCASIONALLY HOLLY LINING THE TRACK & OBSCURING VIEW OVER TO CHEVENING HOUSE, THE FOREIGN SECRETARY'S COUNTRY RESIDENCE
MAP 25
30 MINS FROM STONEINGS (MAP 24)
NORTH LODGE
30 MINS FROM HOTEL (MAP 26)

(cont'd from p115) Sevenoaks via Otford (Mon-Sat, 3-4/day) but in the opposite direction; see the public transport map and table, pp37-40.

There is a clutch of shops nearby, a **newsagent** (Mon/Tue 6.30am-6.30pm, Wed-Fri 7am-6.30pm, Sat 7am-7pm, Sun 7am-1pm) which does **snacks** and a pub, ***The Dukes Head*** (☎ 01732-456123), which may cobble together some basic food but is struggling to survive. There is a Tesco **supermarket** a quarter of a mile due south at the roundabout. ***Taj Tandoori*** (☎ 01732-462277; daily noon-2.30pm/6-11pm) optimistically rises above the ordinariness of the area with curries starting at £4.55.

There is also accommodation at the ***Donnington Manor Hotel*** (☎ 01732-462681; 26T/33D/2F). All rooms are en suite in this Best Western hotel charging £110sgl/60dbl or twin/40 for a family room (two adults, two children).

From here it is a pleasant walk through fields, then along a hard track through a lavender nursery before a long section pounding the tarmac, then crossing the river Darent and arriving at Otford's picturesque duck pond.

OTFORD [MAP 26a]

Called Otta's Ford by the Anglo-Saxons, you cross the river Darent to arrive at Otford's picturesque duck pond.

There are also the **ruins** of an archbishop's palace, which went into decay following its surrender to Henry VIII, and the world's largest scale **model of the solar system** (see box p120).

On a more practical level there is a **library** (☎ 01959-522488; Mon-Fri 9.30am-5pm, Tue to 7pm, Sat 9.30am-12.30pm) with **free internet access** after joining the library system; just sign up and present two pieces of identification.

The **pharmacy** (☎ 01959-522072; Mon-Fri 8.35am-6.30pm, Sat 9am-5pm,

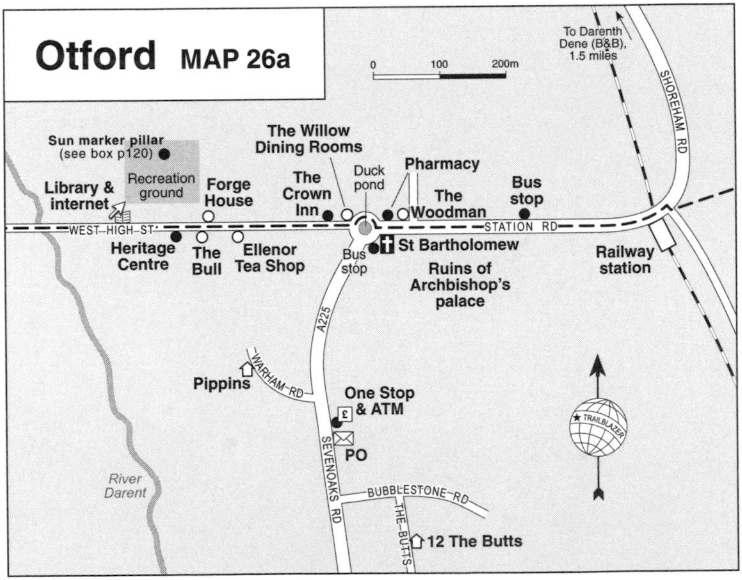

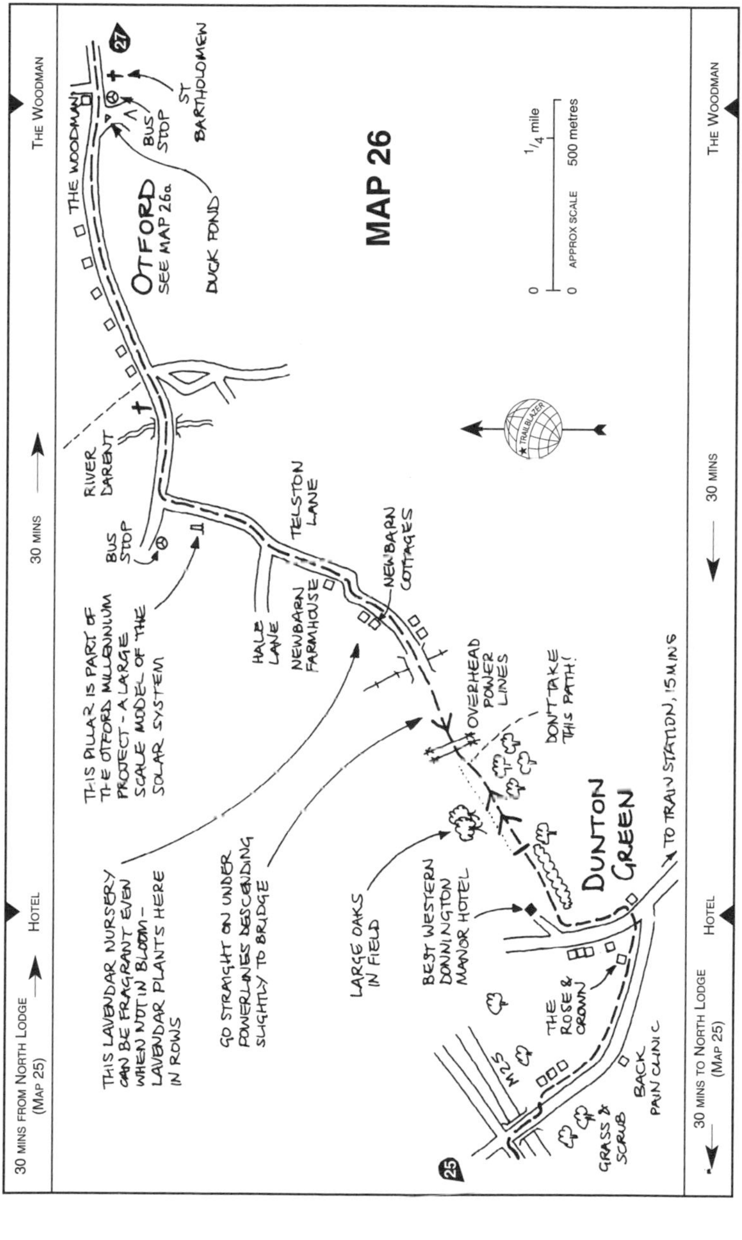
MAP 26
30 MINS FROM NORTH LODGE (MAP 25)
HOTEL
30 MINS
THE WOODMAN
THIS LAVENDAR NURSERY CAN BE FRAGRANT EVEN WHEN NOT IN BLOOM – LAVENDAR PLANTS HERE IN ROWS
GO STRAIGHT ON UNDER POWERLINES DESCENDING SLIGHTLY TO BRIDGE
THIS PILLAR IS PART OF THE OTFORD MILLENNIUM PROJECT - A LARGE SCALE MODEL OF THE SOLAR SYSTEM
BUS STOP
RIVER DARENT
OTFORD
SEE MAP 26a
DUCK POND
BUS STOP
ST BARTHOLOMEW
THE WOODMAN
27
TELSTON LANE
HALE LANE
NEWBARN FARMHOUSE
NEWBARN COTTAGES
OVERHEAD POWER LINES
DON'T TAKE THIS PATH!
LARGE OAKS IN FIELD
BEST WESTERN DONNINGTON MANOR HOTEL
DUNTON GREEN
TO TRAIN STATION, 15 MINS
THE ROSE & CROWN
M25
BACK PAIN CLINIC
GRASS & SCRUB
25
TRAILBLAZER
0
1/4 mile
0
500 metres
APPROX SCALE
30 MINS TO NORTH LODGE (MAP 25)
HOTEL
30 MINS
THE WOODMAN

❑ Otford's Solar System Model
As part of Otford Parish Council's Millennium celebrations the world's largest scale model of the solar system was built in Otford. Starting at the recreation ground, pillars mark the position of the planets at midnight on 1 January 2000. Pick up a leaflet map from the Heritage Centre and 'walk' the solar system if you have time.

closed 1-2.15pm, Bank Holidays 10am-1pm) does not accept credit or debit cards.

There is a **cash machine** outside the **One Stop** (daily 7am-10pm) convenience store and the **post office** is down the road from that.

The **Heritage Centre** (☎ 01959-524808; Mon-Fri 9am-noon, Sat & Sun 2.30-4.30pm) has local history displays.

The **train** station has services to London Victoria (daily, 2/hr) and Maidstone East (Mon-Sat 3/hr, Sun 1/hr).

Arriva's **buses** Nos 431 and 432 stop by the pond and operate the same route to and from Sevenoaks via Dunton Green but in the opposite direction; No 434 runs between Sevenoaks and Shoreham; both the No 433 (Arriva) and the 421 (Metrobus) go from the train station to Sevenoaks; see the public transport map and table, pp37-40.

Where to stay

Pippins (☎ 01959-523596; 1S/1D/1T), on Warham Rd, is a very well-kept house with a friendly collie dog and is very close to all the pubs and the North Downs Way; Mrs Smith charges £25 per person. Mrs Reynolds at ***12 The Butts*** (☎ 01959-523107; 1D/1T) also charges £25 per person.

The other option is to walk, over a mile and a half on the Shoreham Rd, a road with no pavement, to ***Darenth Dene*** (☎ 01959-522293; 1T/2D), the last house on the left before Fackenden Rd. Mrs Reid can lodge up to six people and charges £30 per person. The twin room is en suite.

Where to eat

The Bull (☎ 01959-523198; food Mon-Sat 111m-10pm, Sun noon-9pm) is very popular and several fish dishes feature on the menu. A starter of Bantry Bay mussels is £7.65 and a main course of blackened Cajun salmon fillet is £8.95 at this Chef & Brewer outfit. The pub's fireplace is reputedly 16th century and said to have come from the ruined archbishop's palace.

The Woodman (☎ 01959-522195) does bar food and at the upmarket end there is the ***Forge House*** (☎ 01959-522463; Mon-Sat noon-2.30pm/6.30-10.30pm, Sun noon-3.30pm) with mains from a French-inspired menu, duck (£12.95) or medallions of monkfish (£14.95).

The Willow Dining Rooms will appeal to those seeking the cafeteria experience. To salve your conscience, profits from the charming ***Ellenor Tea Shop*** (Mon-Fri 10am-5pm, Nov-Mar until 4pm, Sat 10am-5pm all year) at the rear of the antiques centre go to the Hospice of Hope, a Romanian Christian-based charity. A pot of tea and a toasted tea cake, slathered with butter if you want, is £1.85 while sandwiches start at £3.25.

The ***Crown Inn*** (☎ 01959-522847) does pub grub daily at lunch (Mon-Sat noon-3pm, Sun noon-4pm).

OTFORD TO ROCHESTER [MAPS 27-36a]

This **17½mile/28km** stage climbs out of Otford to meadow and woodland above Kemsing, which is an important chalk grassland habitat, and across pleasant farmland, much of it now given over to horse paddocks.

Following a rutted byway the North Downs Way emerges to cross alongside arable land to Wrotham where there are the remains of another arch-

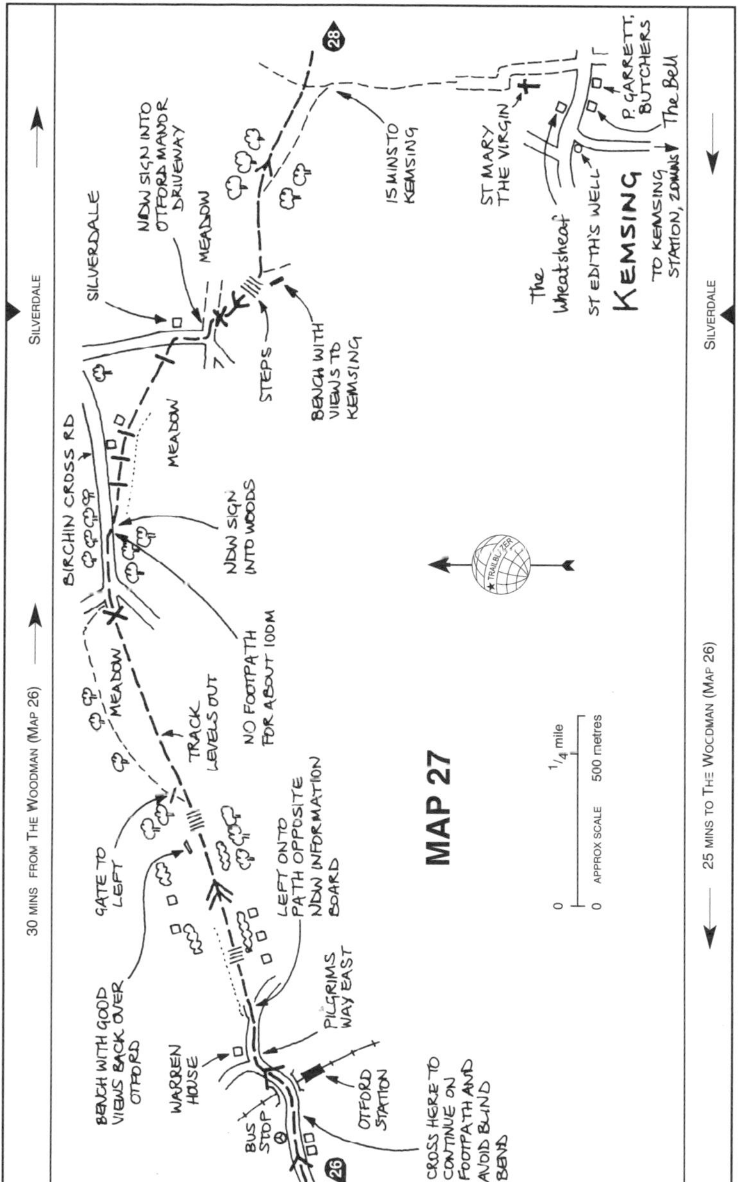
30 MINS FROM THE WOODMAN (MAP 26)
SILVERDALE
25 MINS TO THE WOODMAN (MAP 26)
SILVERDALE
MAP 27
APPROX SCALE
0
1/4 mile
0
500 metres
TRAILBLAZER
CROSS HERE TO CONTINUE ON FOOTPATH AND AVOID BLIND BEND
BUS STOP
OTFORD STATION
WARREN HOUSE
PILGRIMS WAY EAST
BENCH WITH GOOD VIEWS BACK OVER OTFORD
LEFT ONTO PATH OPPOSITE NDW INFORMATION BOARD
GATE TO LEFT
TRACK LEVELS OUT
MEADOW
NO FOOTPATH FOR ABOUT 100M
BIRCHIN CROSS RD
NDW SIGN INTO WOODS
MEADOW
SILVERDALE
STEPS
BENCH WITH VIEWS TO KEMSING
NDW SIGN INTO OTFORD MANOR DRIVEWAY
MEADOW
15 MINS TO KEMSING
ST MARY THE VIRGIN
The Wheatsheaf
ST EDITH'S WELL
KEMSING
TO KEMSING STATION, 20 MINS
P. GARRETT, BUTCHERS
The Bell
26
28

bishop's palace east of the church. There are refreshment opportunities on the trail at Wrotham and Trosley Country Park and then nothing for about seven miles until reaching Cuxton on the outskirts of Rochester.

KEMSING [MAP 27]

Kemsing Youth Hostel has just closed, to be sold as part of the YHA's reorganization plans. As a result, fewer walkers now descend the Downs here unless interested in visiting the church of **St Mary the Virgin** and its decorative choir stall. There is also a collection of stained-glass windows from the 14th to 20th centuries. St Edith's Well, a **healing spring** (reputedly good for sore eyes), is bordered by timber and tile-hung houses.

The **train station**, about 20 minutes to the south of the village, has services to London Victoria (Mon-Sat only, 1-2/hr) and to Maidstone East (Mon-Sat, 1/hr) with onward connections to Folkestone and Dover. Arriva's **buses** Nos 425 and 433 serve Sevenoaks and both stop by St Mary's Church; see the public transport map and table, pp37-40.

The Bell (☎ 01732-761550; food Mon-Sat noon-2.30pm, Sun noon-5pm, Tue-Sat 7-9.30pm) serves soup (£2.50) and filling pies (£6.75). There is also ***The Wheatsheaf*** opposite to slake your thirst. The butcher, ***P Garrett & Son*** (Mon-Fri 8.30am-5pm, half day closing 12.30pm Tue & Sat), sells bread, milk, pies, sandwich meats and fruit.

WROTHAM [MAP 29]

Pronounced 'root ham' the village lies relatively unspoilt below the M20/A20 interchange and above the M26. There is a good range of accommodation and services.

Wrotham Village Stores (Mon-Fri 7.30am-8pm, Sat 8am-8pm, Sun 9am-6pm) has a **cash machine** and sells all the lunch supplies you'd need. **P & H Newsagents** (Mon-Fri 6am-5.30pm, Sat 8am-5.30pm, Sun 8am-12.15pm) opens earlier most days and has snacks and drinks.

Arriva's **bus** No 308 (Mon-Sat only) stops in the Square and will take you to Borough Green, to Bluewater (in case you have a need for some retail therapy), and to Sevenoaks; New Enterprise's No 222 (Mon-Sat only, 2/day) also stops in the Square and goes to Tonbridge via Borough Green; see the public transport map and table, pp37-40.

The closest B&B to the trail is ***Hillside House*** (☎ 01732-822564; 1S/1D/1T all en suite) which charges £22sgl/22.50dbl and it's only five minutes to the village.

The ***George & Dragon*** (☎ 01732-884298; 3D/1T) on the High St charges £40sgl/30dbl for B&B; it also has **internet access**. Food is available Mon-Fri noon-2pm/6-8pm, Sat/Sun noon-2pm, Sat 6-9pm. Rooms are available at the ***Rose & Crown*** (☎ 01732-882409; 1T/1D) £35sgl/20dbl with breakfast served from 8am, lunch daily, food in the evening (7-9pm) on Fri & Sat only. ***The Bull Hotel*** (☎ 01732-789800, 💻 www.thebullhotel.com; 2S/4D/5T all en suite) is an upmarket choice with attention to detail and décor appropriate to the historic inn. B&B is £55sgl/32.50dbl. The restaurant has a tempting seared scallops and monkfish starter for £5.65 and honey-glazed loin of ham with peach and rocket salad for £10.95.

Walkers get a welcome at ***The Three Post Boys*** (☎ 01732-780167; food daily noon-2pm, Thu-Sat 6.30-9pm). It's close to the trail as well and has a rib-sticking steak and ale pie for £8.25.

Dedicated campers (with their own tents) will find pitches at ***Gate House Wood Touring Park*** (Map 30; ☎ 01732-843062) for £6.50-7.50 with use of showers, laundry and a year-round brick-built BBQ. It's really in Wrotham Heath. The owners are friendly and as it's about a 40-minute walk they say they'll 'come and rescue walkers from the trail'.

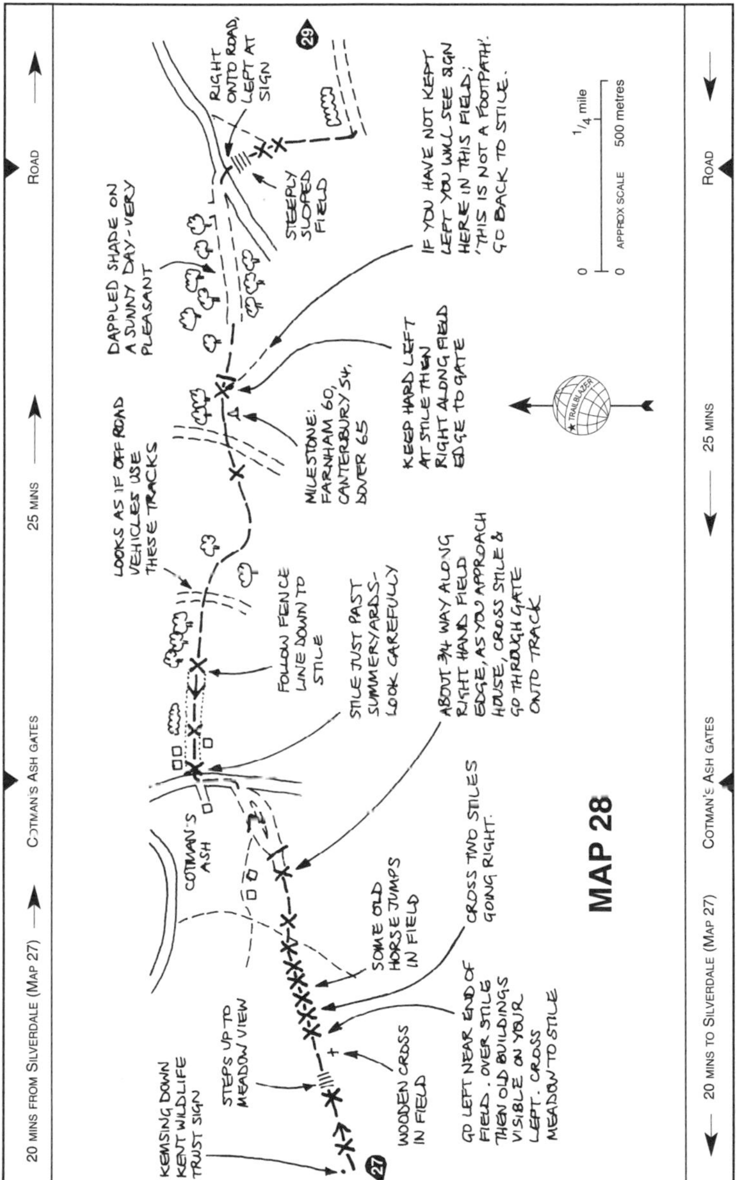
20 mins from Silverdale (Map 27)
Cotman's Ash gates
25 mins
Road
20 mins to Silverdale (Map 27)
Cotman's Ash gates
25 mins
Road
MAP 28
Kemsing Down Kent Wildlife Trust sign
Steps up to meadow view
Wooden cross in field
Go left near end of field. Over stile then old buildings visible on your left. Cross meadow to stile
Cross two stiles going right.
Some old horse jumps in field
Cotman's Ash
About 3/4 way along right hand field edge, as you approach house, cross stile & go through gate onto track
Stile just past summeryards. Look carefully
Follow fence line down to stile
Looks as if off road vehicles use these tracks
Milestone: Farnham 60, Canterbury 54, Dover 65
Keep hard left at stile then right along field edge to gate
Dappled shade on a sunny day - very pleasant
If you have not kept left you will see sign here in this field; 'This is not a footpath'. Go back to stile.
Steeply sloped field
Right onto road, left at sign
27
29
Approx scale
0
1/4 mile
0
500 metres
Trailblazer

❑ Allotments – a very British thing

Having laboured under a flat-cap image for many years allotments are experiencing a renaissance with more and more people experiencing the life-enhancing pleasure of growing their own vegetables. Food scares, lack of variety in the shops, and expense have rekindled people's interest. Shere (off Map 9a, p86) has the most attractive site near the trail. Bordered by the Tillingbourne on one side, surrounded by a low mellow brick wall and flanked by 16th- and 17th-century cottages, it's brilliantly tended by committed growers. The allotment gardens on the edge of Wrotham (Map 29 opposite) are well tended and there is a large and impressive site on the outskirts of Canterbury (Map 56, p167).

Allotments date back to the 18th century and the Enclosure Acts which basically privatized common land leaving the poorest without any land to cultivate. As towns and factories grew and food was scarce and expensive there was a need to feed factory workers so allotments were created – each worker was allotted a piece of land to cultivate. Out of fashion by the late 20th century, more than half of all Britain's allotments have been lost in the last 40 years, many sold off for housing developments. The standard-size allotment is about 100 sq metres and most are managed by local authorities.

Rents range from £12 to £80 a year and I'm told there is a thriving, illicit, market in sub-letting plots for up to £300 in some London boroughs, so keen are people to get growing their own fresh veggies. Cultivating an allotment organically is high up on the scale of green activities as the labour is local and there's usually little transport involved.

BOROUGH GREEN [OFF MAP 29]

The nearest **train station** to Wrotham is at Borough Green with services to London Victoria (daily 1-2/hr) and to Maidstone East (daily 1-2/hr). Arriva's **bus** No 308 (to Sevenoaks) stops here as do the No 70, which goes to Maidstone, and Nu Venture's No 222, to Tonbridge; see also the public transport map and table, pp37-40.

There is a **Co-op** (Mon-Sat 7am-10pm, Sun 8am-8pm) next to the station with a **cash machine** outside. A **taxi** to/from Wrotham is £3 and saves an unremarkable 20-minute walk; Borough Green Taxis (☎ 01732-882020/780090) have an office at the station. ***The Snicket*** (☎ 01732-883620; 1D/1S), 14 The Avenue, on the left before the railway bridge if approaching the station from Wrotham, is a modest house in a post-war estate and may have rooms if they're not let to student lodgers. B&B is £24 per person.

The Geographers' A-Z Map Company is based in Borough Green. It was founded by the intrepid Phyllis Pearsall MBE whose daily involvement with the company continued until her death in 1996 at the age of 89.

The rush of the A20 and M20 is soon left behind as the trail leaves Wrotham and climbs through the woods to the ***Vigo Inn*** (see Map 31) whose landlord may or may not open during the usual pub hours (Mon-Sat 11am-11pm, Sun noon-10.30pm) but there are pubs and accommodation in Trottiscliffe.

TROTTISCLIFFE [OFF MAPS 30 & 31]

A 25-minute walk down Taylor's Lane brings you first to ***The Plough*** (☎ 01732-822233; food Mon noon-2pm, Tue-Sat noon-2pm/6.30-9pm, Sun noon-2.30pm). It's popular at lunchtime with OAP specials midweek and Sunday roasts for £7.

Further down the lane is ***The George*** (☎ 01732-822462; food served Mon-Fri

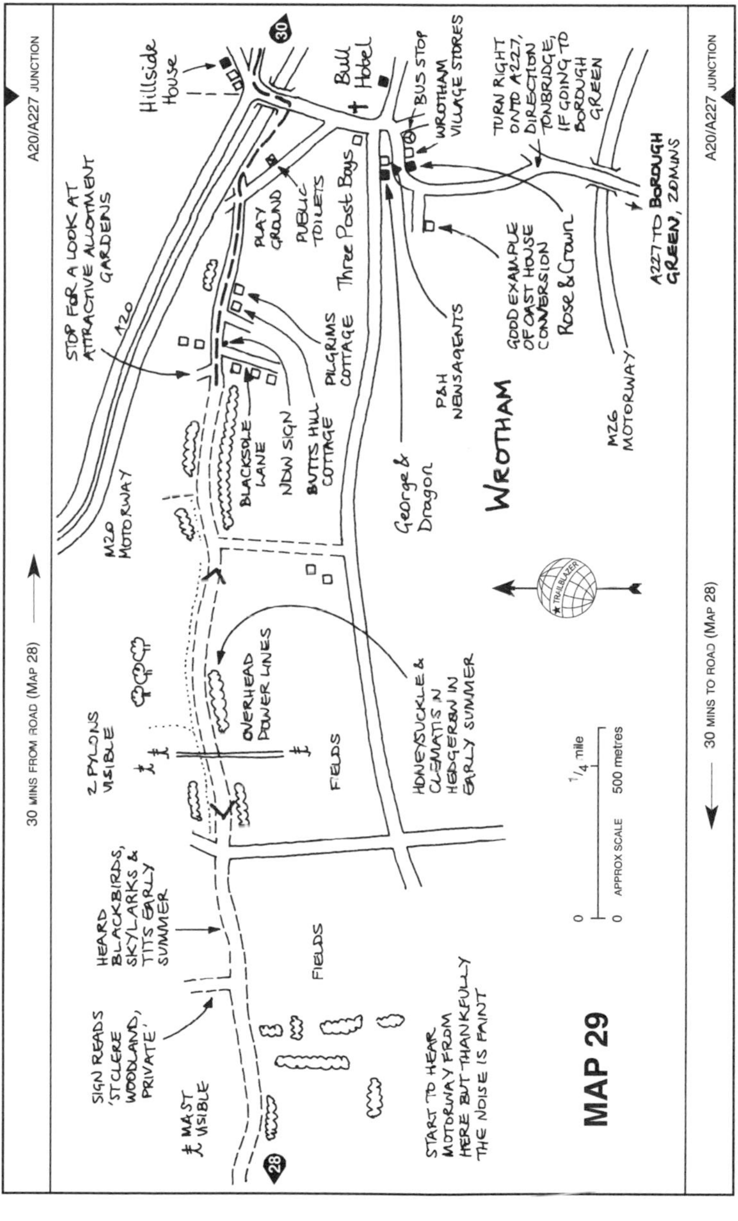
A20/A227 JUNCTION
30 MINS FROM ROAD (MAP 28)
30 MINS TO ROAD (MAP 28)
A20/A227 JUNCTION
30
28
Hillside House
Bull Hotel
BUS STOP
WROTHAM VILLAGE STORES
TURN RIGHT ONTO A227, DIRECTION TONBRIDGE, IF GOING TO BOROUGH GREEN
A227 TO BOROUGH GREEN, 20MINS
STOP FOR A LOOK AT ATTRACTIVE ALLOTMENT GARDENS
A20
PLAY GROUND
PUBLIC TOILETS
Three Post Boys
PILGRIMS COTTAGE
GOOD EXAMPLE OF OAST HOUSE CONVERSION
Rose & Crown
P&H NEWSAGENTS
NDW SIGN
BUTTS HILL COTTAGE
BLACKSOLE LANE
M20 MOTORWAY
George & Dragon
WROTHAM
M26 MOTORWAY
TRAILBLAZER
OVERHEAD POWER LINES
HONEYSUCKLE & CLEMATIS IN HEDGEROW IN EARLY SUMMER
2 PYLONS VISIBLE
FIELDS
FIELDS
0
1/4 mile
0
500 metres
APPROX SCALE
HEARD BLACKBIRDS, SKYLARKS & TITS EARLY SUMMER
SIGN READS 'ST CLERE WOODLAND, PRIVATE'
MAST VISIBLE
START TO HEAR MOTORWAY FROM HERE BUT THANKFULLY THE NOISE IS FAINT
MAP 29

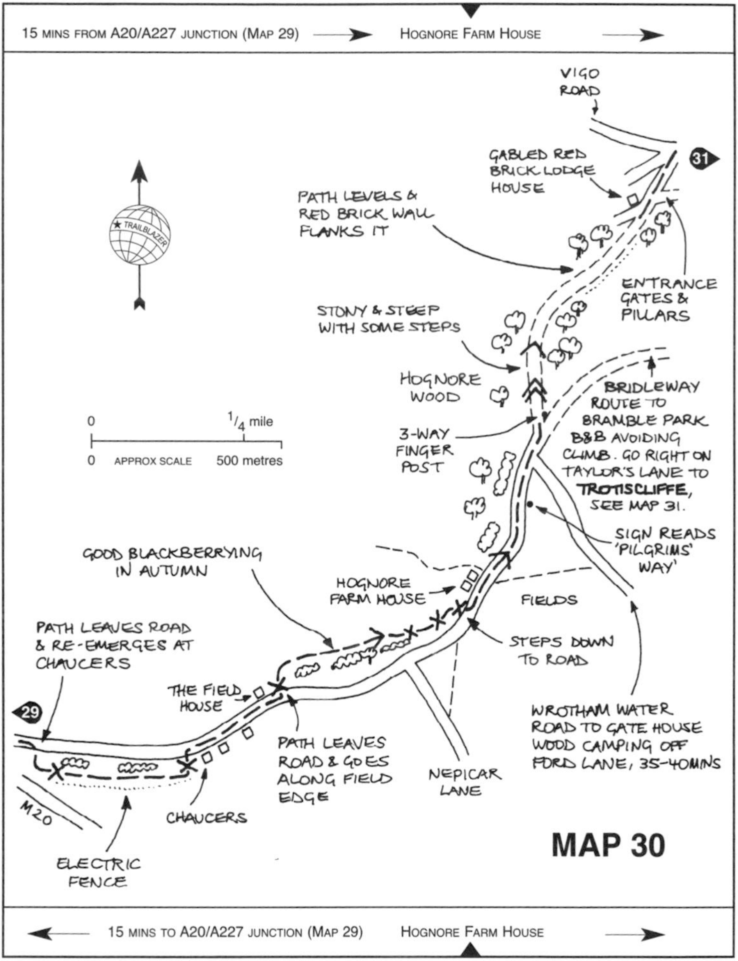

noon-2.30pm, Sat & Sun noon-3pm), a lovely oak-beamed pub with lots of nooks and crannies. The menu is extensive from soup of the day (£3.20) and good-value sandwiches, (£2.75) to pub staples such as fish pie (£9.50). ***Bramble Park B&B*** (☎ 01732-822397; 1S/6D/1F) is a former rectory dating from the 1850s. Cigar-smoking proprietor Michael Towler, known locally for his pet foxes, charges £25 per person.

Nu-Venture's **bus** No 58 stops by The George; see the public transport map and table pp37-40.

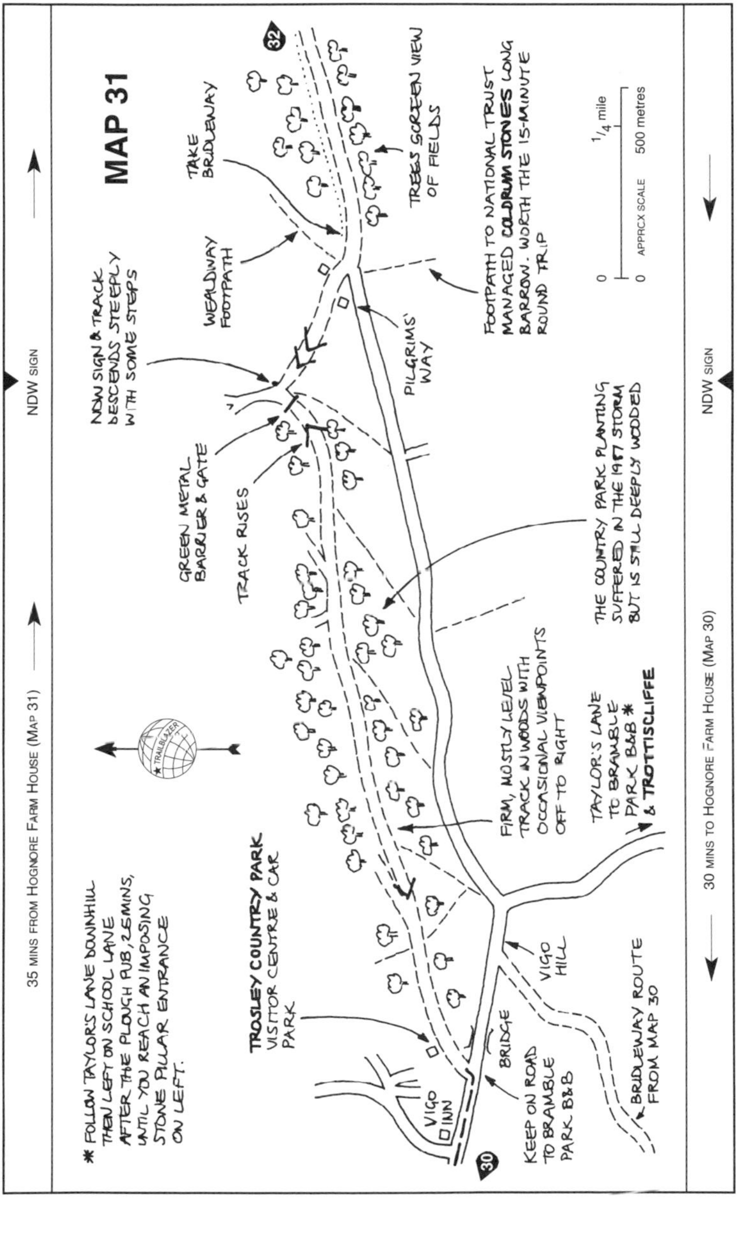
MAP 31
35 MINS FROM HOGNORE FARM HOUSE (MAP 31)
30 MINS TO HOGNORE FARM HOUSE (MAP 30)
NDW SIGN
NDW SIGN
TRAILBLAZER
32
30
TAKE BRIDLEWAY
WEALDWAY FOOTPATH
TREES SCREEN VIEW OF FIELDS
FOOTPATH TO NATIONAL TRUST MANAGED COLDRUM STONES LONG BARROW. WORTH THE 15-MINUTE ROUND TRIP
0 1/4 mile
0 500 metres
APPROX SCALE
NDW SIGN & TRACK DESCENDS STEEPLY WITH SOME STEPS
PILGRIMS' WAY
GREEN METAL BARRIER & GATE
TRACK RISES
THE COUNTRY PARK PLANTING SUFFERED IN THE 1987 STORM BUT IS STILL DEEPLY WOODED
FIRM, MOSTLY LEVEL TRACK IN WOODS WITH OCCASIONAL VIEWPOINTS OFF TO RIGHT
TAYLOR'S LANE TO BRAMBLE PARK B&B * & TROTTISCLIFFE
* FOLLOW TAYLOR'S LANE DOWNHILL THEN LEFT ON SCHOOL LANE AFTER THE PLOUGH PUB, 25 MINS, UNTIL YOU REACH AN IMPOSING STONE PILLAR ENTRANCE ON LEFT.
TROSLEY COUNTRY PARK VISITOR CENTRE & CAR PARK
VIGO HILL
VIGO INN
BRIDGE
KEEP ON ROAD TO BRAMBLE PARK B&B
BRIDLEWAY ROUTE FROM MAP 30

Coldrum Stones

This Neolithic site (see photo opposite) is managed by the National Trust and is a largely intact long barrow burial site or tomb despite the efforts of Victorian trophy collectors. Some of the kerb or **peristaliths** surrounding the chamber survive and the structure dates from around 3000 years ago when agriculture was developing in Europe, stone tools were used and metal ones had yet to be invented. In the 1900s the bones of 22 people were excavated. Some pagans and druids camp out by the stones attributing spiritual powers to the place and it's said that the name derives from the old Cornish word *Galdrum* or 'place of enchantments'. It's certainly a pretty location at the foot of the Downs overlooking farmland toward Blue Bell Hill and east to the Medway valley.

The North Downs Way enters **Trosley Country Park** (Map 31; ☎ 01732-823570; refreshment kiosk daily 10am-around 4pm, weekends only in winter) off Vigo Hill. Arriva's **bus** No 308 stops at Trosley Country Park; see the public transport map and table pp37-40. The firm track in the woods makes for fast walking eventually descending sharply to meet the Pilgrims' Way where a short detour to **Coldrum Stones** (off Map 31) is recommended. The North Downs Way continues up Holly Hill and once more into woodland above **Ryarsh**.

RYARSH [OFF MAP 32]

You probably wouldn't come here unless staying at ***Heavers House Farm*** (☎ 01732-842074, 💻 www.kentbedandbreakfast.co.uk; 1S/2D), £30 per person. There is a magnificent topiary hedge in front of this solid-brick farmhouse. But call in advance to see what is available as B&B is run as a sideline. The ***Duke of Wellington*** (☎ 01732-842318; food Mon-Sat noon-2pm/7-9pm, Sun noon-9pm) pub has polished wood floors and cosy snugs. A kilo of mussels is £13.95 or a tasty snack of potatoes and chorizo is £3.95.

Nu-Venture's **bus** No 58 (Mon-Sat only) stops opposite the Duke of Wellington; see public transport info, pp37-40.

It feels wonderfully isolated and peaceful along this section even though the industrial towns of the Medway valley are only a couple of miles away. You get little sense of that as the trail eventually drops down through a series of undulating arable fields, through the attractive hamlet of Upper Bush to arrive at Cuxton.

CUXTON [MAPS 34 & 35]

There is a **train station** with services to Rochester (Mon-Fri 4/hr, Sat 2/hr, Sun 1/hr) where you need to change for trains to London. Arriva's **bus** No 151 stops by the White Hart and operates to Rochester (Mon-Sat 1/hr, Sun 5/day); see the public transport map and table, pp37-40.

On Bush Rd there is a **mini-market** (Mon-Sat 5am-7.30pm, Sun 5am-1.30pm) so you could stock up for lunch if you got an incredibly early start. There is a **post office** next door sharing room in the butcher's.

Unless you intend staying in Rochester, which would be worth it, your accommodation options are the luxurious ***North Downs Barn*** (☎ 01634-296829, 💻 www.northdownbarn.co.uk; 1S/1D/1T/1D or F), a sympathetic barn conversion. *(cont'd on p134)*

(Opposite) Top: With much of the route on the crest of the Downs there are numerous panoramic views such as this from Blue Bell Hill picnic site over the Medway Valley. **Bottom**: The Coldrum Stones and the view east. (Photos © John Curtin).

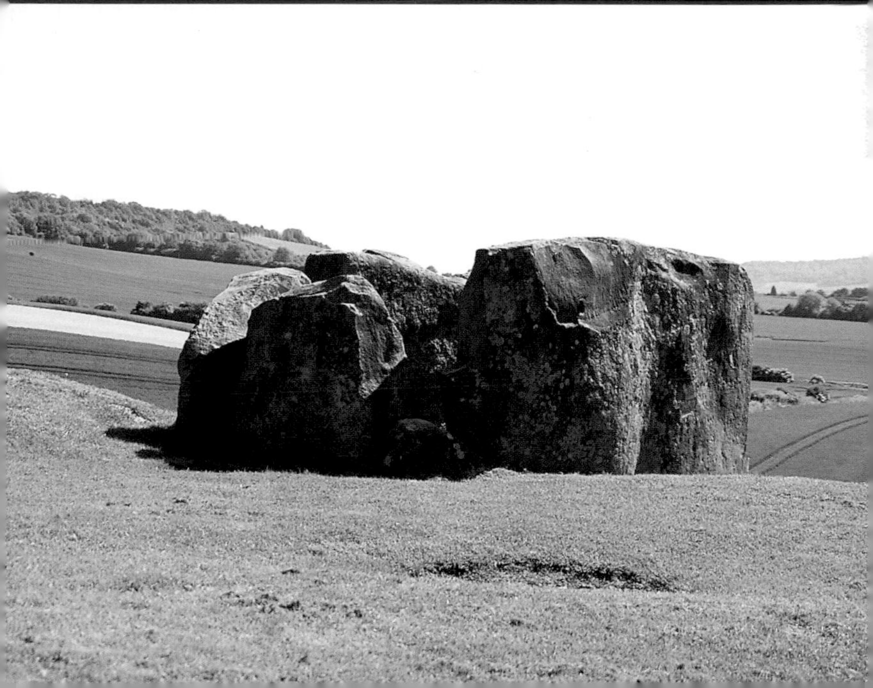

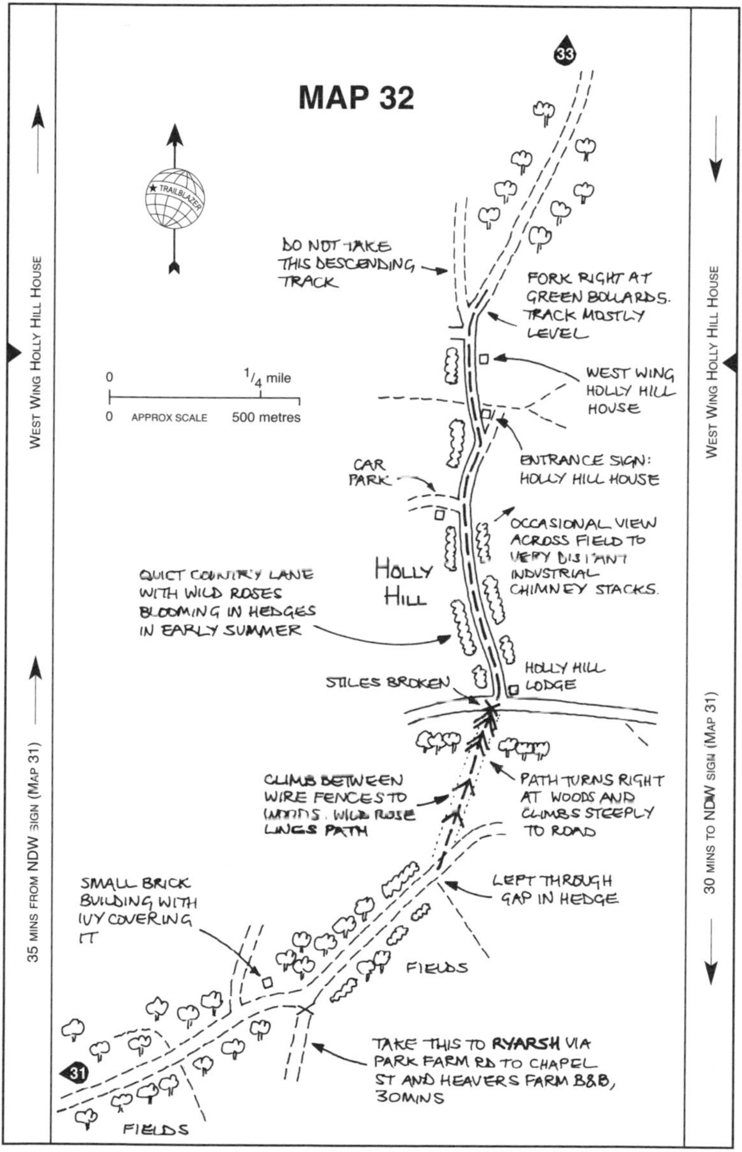

(Opposite) Keeper's Lodge (see Map 37, p137) is a fine example of late Victorian Surrey style architecture. (Photo © Jennifer Ullman).

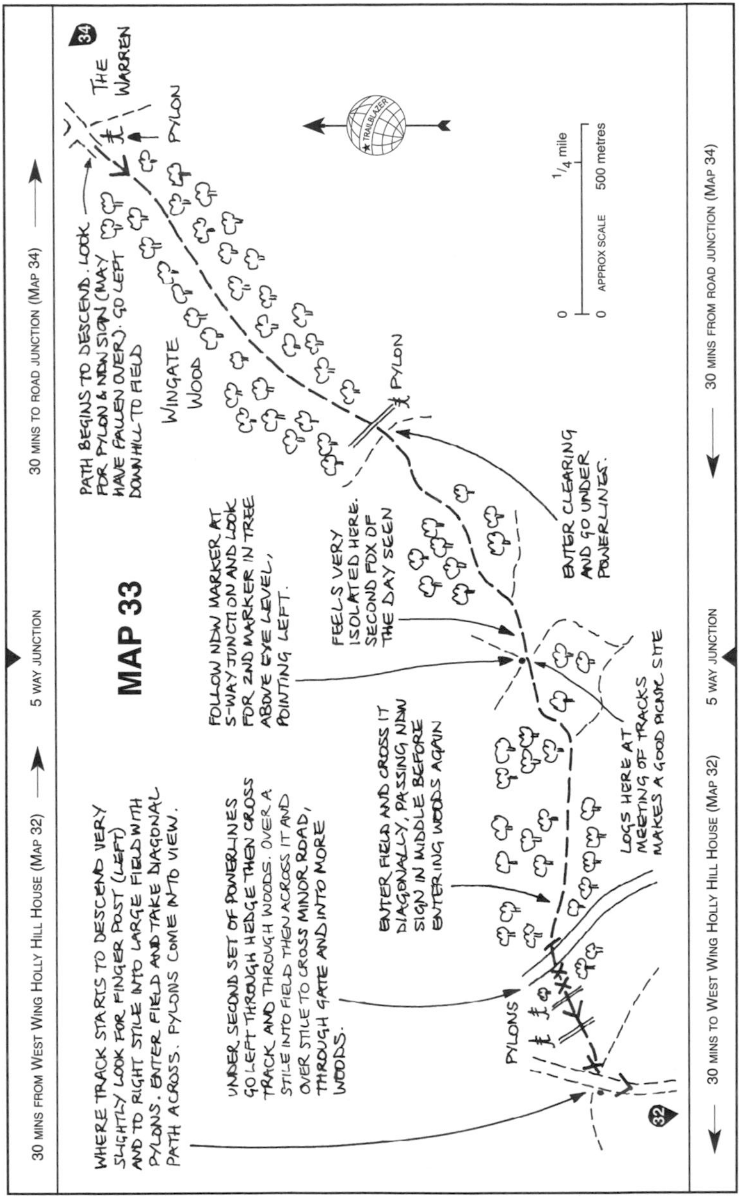
30 MINS FROM WEST WING HOLLY HILL HOUSE (MAP 32) →
5 WAY JUNCTION
30 MINS TO ROAD JUNCTION (MAP 34) →
MAP 33
34
THE WARREN
PYLON
WHERE TRACK STARTS TO DESCEND VERY SLIGHTLY LOOK FOR FINGER POST (LEFT) AND TO RIGHT STILE INTO LARGE FIELD WITH PYLONS. ENTER FIELD AND TAKE DIAGONAL PATH ACROSS. PYLONS COME INTO VIEW.
UNDER SECOND SET OF POWERLINES GO LEFT THROUGH HEDGE THEN CROSS TRACK AND THROUGH WOODS. OVER A STILE INTO FIELD THEN ACROSS IT AND OVER STILE TO CROSS MINOR ROAD, THROUGH GATE AND INTO MORE WOODS.
FOLLOW NDW MARKER AT 5-WAY JUNCTION AND LOOK FOR 2ND MARKER IN TREE ABOVE EYE LEVEL, POINTING LEFT.
PATH BEGINS TO DESCEND. LOOK FOR PYLON & NDW SIGN (MAY HAVE FALLEN OVER). GO LEFT DOWNHILL TO FIELD
WINGATE WOOD
PYLON
TRAILBLAZER
ENTER FIELD AND CROSS IT DIAGONALLY, PASSING NDW SIGN IN MIDDLE BEFORE ENTERING WOODS AGAIN
FEELS VERY ISOLATED HERE. SECOND FOX OF THE DAY SEEN
ENTER CLEARING AND GO UNDER POWERLINES.
LOGS HERE AT MEETING OF TRACKS MAKES A GOOD PICNIC SITE
PYLONS
32
0
1/4 mile
0
APPROX SCALE
500 metres
← 30 MINS TO WEST WING HOLLY HILL HOUSE (MAP 32)
5 WAY JUNCTION
← 30 MINS FROM ROAD JUNCTION (MAP 34)

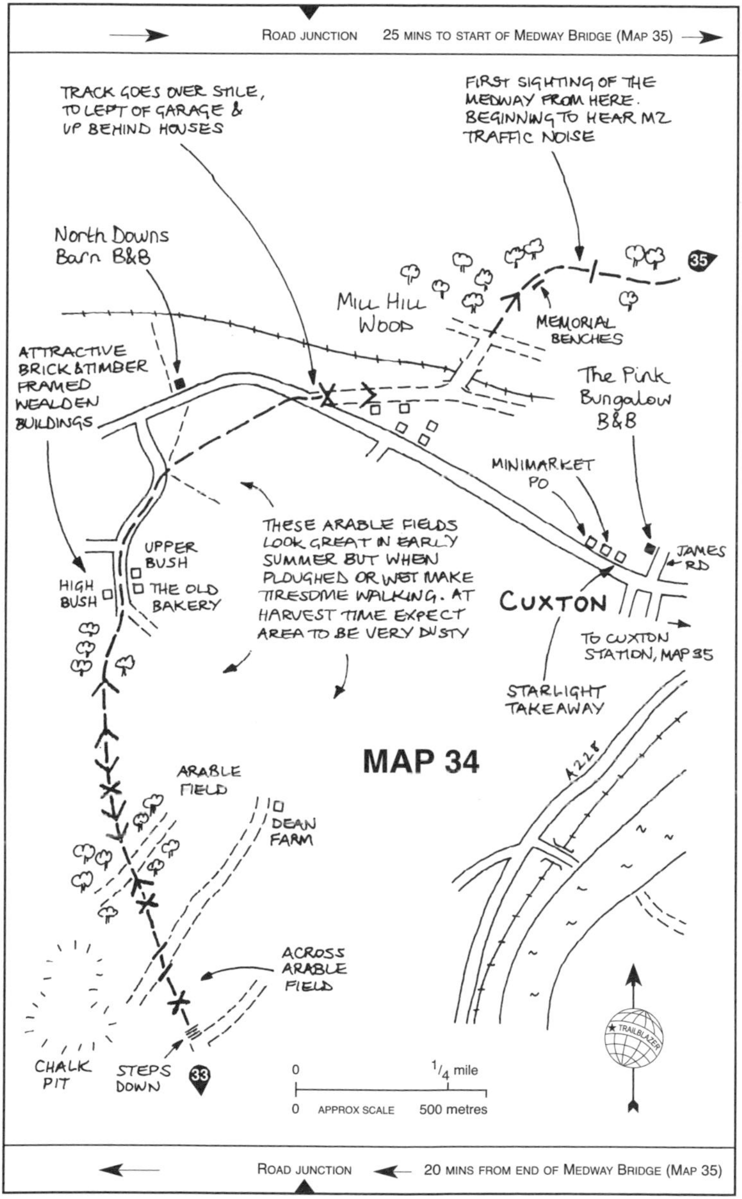
Road junction
25 mins to start of Medway Bridge (Map 35)
TRACK GOES OVER STILE, TO LEFT OF GARAGE & UP BEHIND HOUSES
FIRST SIGHTING OF THE MEDWAY FROM HERE. BEGINNING TO HEAR M2 TRAFFIC NOISE
North Downs Barn B&B
35
MILL HILL WOOD
MEMORIAL BENCHES
ATTRACTIVE BRICK & TIMBER FRAMED WEALDEN BUILDINGS
The Pink Bungalow B&B
MINIMARKET
PO
UPPER BUSH
HIGH BUSH
THE OLD BAKERY
THESE ARABLE FIELDS LOOK GREAT IN EARLY SUMMER BUT WHEN PLOUGHED OR WET MAKE TIRESOME WALKING. AT HARVEST TIME EXPECT AREA TO BE VERY DUSTY
JAMES RD
CUXTON
TO CUXTON STATION, MAP 35
STARLIGHT TAKEAWAY
A228
MAP 34
ARABLE FIELD
DEAN FARM
ACROSS ARABLE FIELD
CHALK PIT
STEPS DOWN
33
0
1/4 mile
0
APPROX SCALE
500 metres
TRAILBLAZER
Road junction
20 mins from end of Medway Bridge (Map 35)

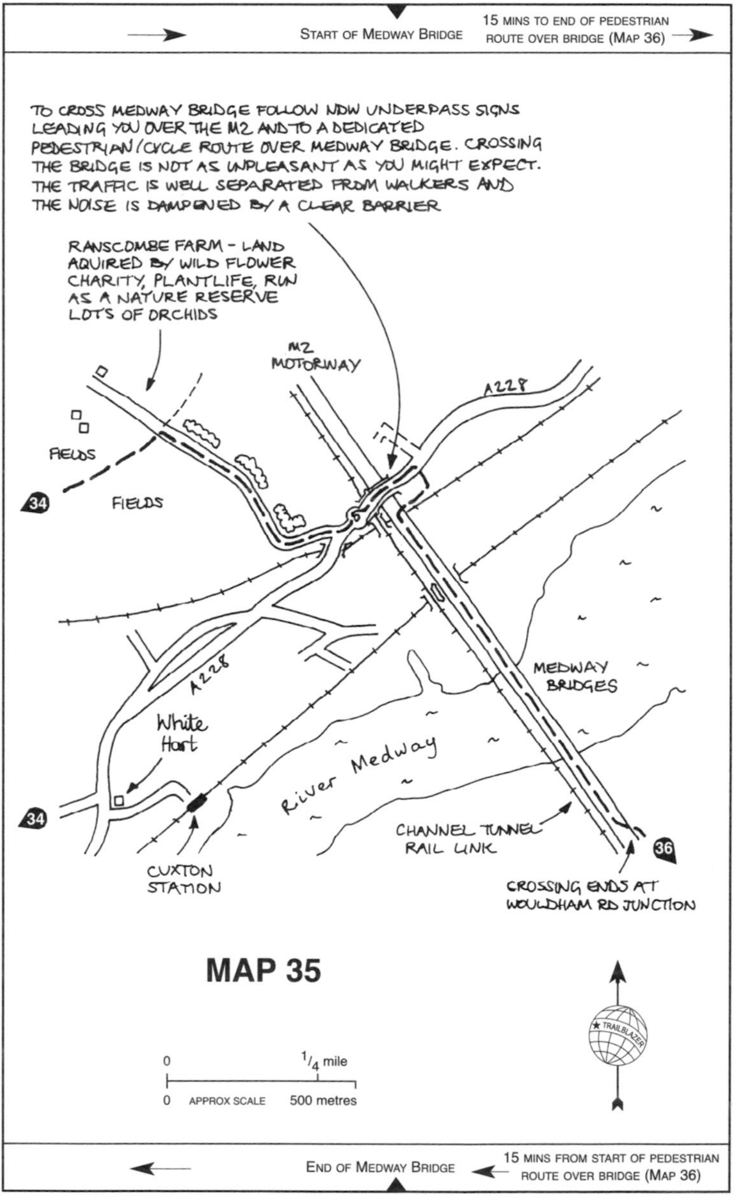
START OF MEDWAY BRIDGE
15 MINS TO END OF PEDESTRIAN ROUTE OVER BRIDGE (MAP 36)
TO CROSS MEDWAY BRIDGE FOLLOW NDW UNDERPASS SIGNS LEADING YOU OVER THE M2 AND TO A DEDICATED PEDESTRIAN/CYCLE ROUTE OVER MEDWAY BRIDGE. CROSSING THE BRIDGE IS NOT AS UNPLEASANT AS YOU MIGHT EXPECT. THE TRAFFIC IS WELL SEPARATED FROM WALKERS AND THE NOISE IS DAMPENED BY A CLEAR BARRIER
RANSCOMBE FARM – LAND AQUIRED BY WILD FLOWER CHARITY, PLANTLIFE, RUN AS A NATURE RESERVE LOTS OF ORCHIDS
M2 MOTORWAY
A228
FIELDS
34
FIELDS
A228
MEDWAY BRIDGES
White Hart
River Medway
34
CHANNEL TUNNEL RAIL LINK
36
CUXTON STATION
CROSSING ENDS AT WOULDHAM RD JUNCTION
MAP 35
0
1/4 mile
0
APPROX SCALE
500 metres
TRAILBLAZER
END OF MEDWAY BRIDGE
15 MINS FROM START OF PEDESTRIAN ROUTE OVER BRIDGE (MAP 36)

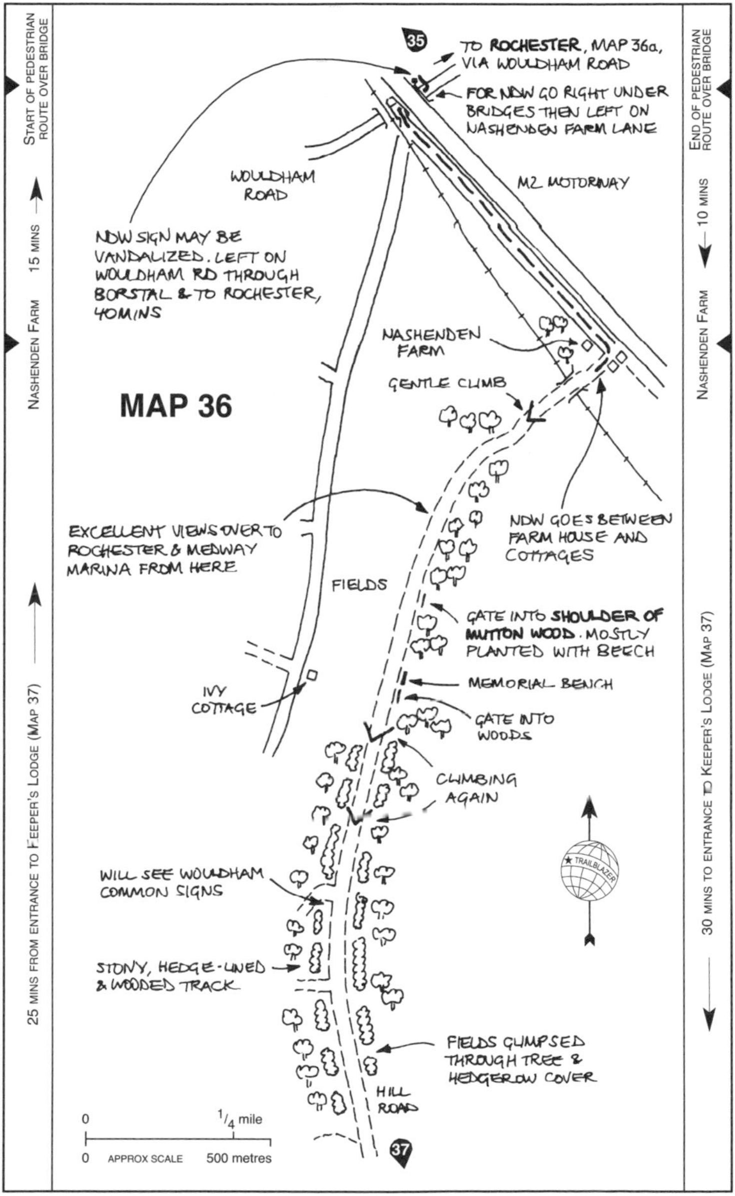
MAP 36
35
TO ROCHESTER, MAP 36a, VIA WOULDHAM ROAD
FOR NDW GO RIGHT UNDER BRIDGES THEN LEFT ON NASHENDEN FARM LANE
WOULDHAM ROAD
M2 MOTORWAY
NDW SIGN MAY BE VANDALIZED. LEFT ON WOULDHAM RD THROUGH BORSTAL & TO ROCHESTER, 40MINS
NASHENDEN FARM
GENTLE CLIMB
NDW GOES BETWEEN FARM HOUSE AND COTTAGES
EXCELLENT VIEWS OVER TO ROCHESTER & MEDWAY MARINA FROM HERE
FIELDS
GATE INTO SHOULDER OF MUTTON WOOD. MOSTLY PLANTED WITH BEECH
MEMORIAL BENCH
IVY COTTAGE
GATE INTO WOODS
CLIMBING AGAIN
TRAILBLAZER
WILL SEE WOULDHAM COMMON SIGNS
STONY, HEDGE-LINED & WOODED TRACK
FIELDS GLIMPSED THROUGH TREE & HEDGEROW COVER
HILL ROAD
0 1/4 mile
0 APPROX SCALE 500 metres
37
START OF PEDESTRIAN ROUTE OVER BRIDGE
15 MINS
NASHENDEN FARM
25 MINS FROM ENTRANCE TO KEEPER'S LODGE (MAP 37)
END OF PEDESTRIAN ROUTE OVER BRIDGE
10 MINS
NASHENDEN FARM
30 MINS TO ENTRANCE TO KEEPER'S LODGE (MAP 37)

(cont'd from p128). North Downs Barn is just off the North Downs Way. B&B is £30 per person. ***The Pink Bungalow*** (☎ 01634-715154; 1S/2D) is just that, in a road of modest houses, charging £25 per person and is closer to Cuxton's limited food options. The ***Starlight*** (☎ 01634-296888; Mon-Thurs 5-10pm, Fri/Sat noon-2pm/5-10pm) Chinese takeaway also does fish and chips. The ***White Hart*** (Map 35; ☎ 01634-711857; food daily noon-3pm, Wed-Sat 6-9pm) does filling pub grub.

Climbing behind Cuxton with views over the Medway, the trail emerges to cross the Medway Bridge. There are in fact two – a road bridge carrying the M2 and another carrying the Channel Tunnel rail link. There is a dedicated pedestrian and cycle crossing.

> **❑ Kentish Men or Men of Kent**
> The Medway divides Kent in two at Rochester. People to the east were known as Men of Kent and those to the west including Canterbury were known as Kentish Men.

ROCHESTER [MAP 36a]

As you've just passed the halfway point it's a good excuse to come here, a 40-minute walk off the path, and perhaps celebrate with a day off and a good meal. Sometimes referred to as the city of Great Expectations, the great Victorian novelist, **Charles Dickens**, is to Rochester what Mickey Mouse is to Disney. Growing up in nearby Chatham, he used local settings in his novels. With two Dickens' festivals a year, one in July and one in December, accommodation goes fast. But this commercialism aside there's plenty to see including a **Norman castle**, England's second oldest **cathedral**, a wonderful **Restoration house** and a fascinating **almshouse** for poor travellers 'not being rogues or proctors'.

Services

The **train station** has services to London Victoria and Charing Cross (Mon-Sat 3/hr, Sun 2/hr), and to Canterbury East and Dover Priory (Mon-Sat 2/hr, Sun 1/hr). Arriva's **bus** No 155 (Mon-Sat only) connects Rochester (Star Hill) with Chatham, Aylesford and Maidstone; the No 135 operates a similar route but on Sunday only and it stops at the railway station; Nos 142 and 151 also serve Chatham; see the public transport map and table pp37-40. There is a **taxi rank** (☎ 01634-848848) in front of the station; the fare to Medway Bridge is £4.50.

The **tourist information centre** (☎ 01634-843666; Mon-Fri 9am-5pm, Sat 10am-5pm, Sun 10.30am-5pm) is at 95 High St. It has a 24-hour interactive screen for information and there's an art gallery upstairs. There are two **cash machines** nearby; the Lloyds TSB machine is at the site of the **Abdication House** where King James stayed before leaving for France in 1688. **DOT Café** (Mon, Tue & Sat 9am-5pm, Wed-Fri 9am-10pm, Sun 9.30am-3.30pm) has **internet access**, 25p a minute, no minimum charge, and for any ailments there is **Paydens Chemists** (☎ 01634-842838; Mon-Sat 9am-5.30pm, no prescriptions 1-2.15pm) which also has a **post office** counter. **Castle Food & Wine** (☎ 01634-815255; daily 8am-8pm) sells snacks, food and drinks. Rochester Castle moat hosts the monthly **Farmers' Market**, on the third Sunday of each month.

Where to stay

Very close to the station and having welcomed generations of walkers to her tall town house, decorated with hanging baskets, is the talkative Erica Thomas (☎ 01634-842737; 1S/2D), ***255 High St***, £20sgl/£15dbl. One double has an en suite shower.

If you come in from the Medway Bridge there are several choices on Borstal Rd, about 15 minutes from the centre. ***St Martin*** (☎ 01634-848192; 2T/1D), 104 Borstal Rd, a comfortable family home, is one of six steeply gabled Victorian houses all named by the builder after coastal bays in Guernsey and Jersey. Dogs are welcome and there are great views from the rear garden down to the Medway. B&B is £20sgl/19dbl. Up from this is ***Riverview Lodge*** (☎ 01634-842241; 2S/7D en suite), 88 Borstal Rd, a utilitarian set up with continental breakfast; B&B is £27sgl/22.50dbl.

Borstal Rd meets St Margaret's St about five minutes from the Cathedral where ***Grayling House*** (☎ 01634-826593; 3S/6T), 54 St Margaret's St, offers B&B at £30sgl/27.50dbl per person. With two rooms en suite, another has its own shower and the rest have shared facilities.

If you fancy following in the footsteps of Dickens stay at the ***Royal Victoria and Bull Hotel*** (☎ 01634-846266; 2S/9D/5T/3F en suite, 3S private bathrooms). A top floor room will have you wandering the twisting corridors in search of your billet. Rates in the en suite rooms are £57.50sgl/36.25 dbl or twin/26.50fml; the other singles are £52.50. If you have a room facing the High St you may hear the early morning trains.

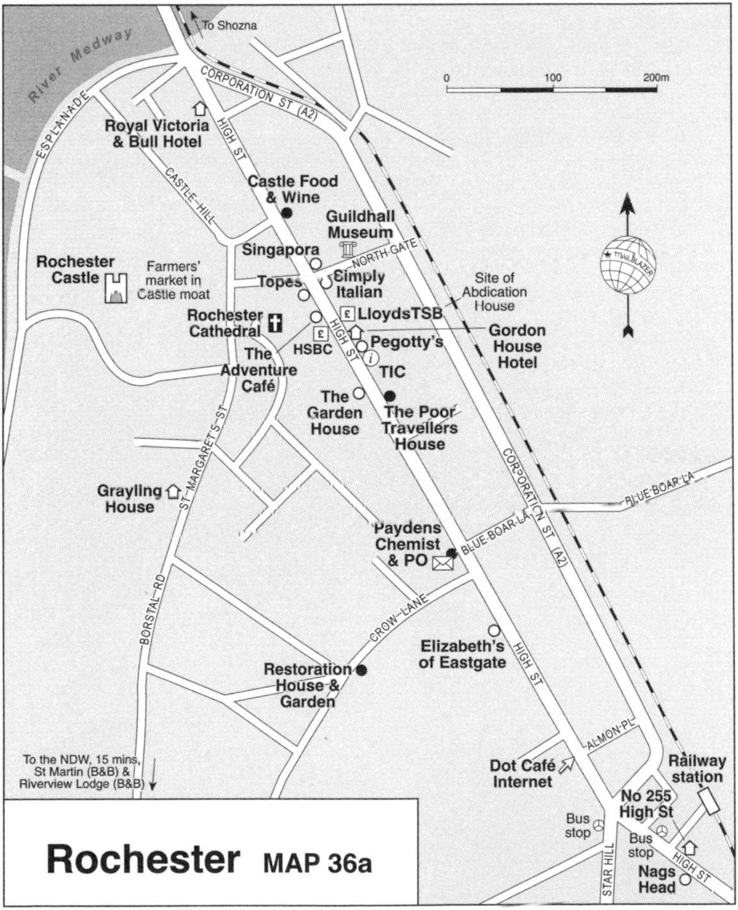

Rochester MAP 36a

Dickens called this The Bull in his *Pickwick Papers* and The Blue Boar in *Great Expectations*. Another hotel is ***Gordon House Hotel*** (☎ 01634-831000, 💻 www.gordonhousehotel.net; 5S/5D/3F). Rates are £60sgl/35dbl/28 three sharing, all en suite.

Where to eat

For a budget bite the ***Nags Head*** (☎ 01634-843150; food Mon-Fri noon-2.30pm/5-8.30pm, Sat-Sun noon-8pm) opposite No 255 High St (see p134) is hard to beat with most dishes under a fiver and generously sized. Chicken kiev is £4.50 as are bangers and mash. You can soak up the beer with a chip butty for £1.50. ***Singapora*** (☎ 01634-842178; Mon-Sat noon-3pm/6pm-12midnight, Sun noon-10.30pm), 51 High St, attracts a crowd offering a fusion of Malaysian, Thai, and Japanese cuisine. A spicy pork *phad prik* is £4.80. And ***Simply Italian*** (☎ 01634-408077; Mon-Sat noon-10.30pm, Sun noon-10pm) does bowls of pasta and plates of pizza for under a fiver.

Two chefs, 'DFLs' or down from London as the locals call them, run ***The Garden House*** (☎ 01634-842460; Mon-Fri 10am-6pm, Sat 10.30am-6pm, Sun 11.30am-5pm). A fine cafetière of coffee (£1.50) and their quiche (£4.50) is a big seller. Try the traditional ***Pegotty's Parlour*** (Mon-Sat 9.30am-5pm, Sun 11am-5pm) for a toasted tea cake.

Travel-shop-cum-café ***The Adventure Café*** (☎ 01634-404400, 💻 www.adventure-cafe.com or www.adventure-fitness.com; Mon-Sat 9.30am-5.30pm) is well worth a visit. It's the place to swap tales and plan your next trip whether it's here or abroad. And they serve excellent lattes.

A short walk across Rochester Bridge leads to ***Shozna*** (☎ 01634-710701, daily 5.30-11pm), 18 High St, Strood; it is worth the effort. They cook a richly flavoured six-dish mixed thali to order (£12). Expect to wait a while but amuse yourself with a large bottle of ice cold Kingfisher (£3.50).

Elizabeth's of Eastgate (☎ 01634-843472; Tue-Sun noon-2pm and Tue-Sat 6.45-9.45pm) has a cozy feel to it with a twist of Spanish in the menu. Roasted *piquillo* peppers in a stilton sauce is £16. There are plenty of fish dishes and the 16th-century building was the setting for the home of Uncle Pumblechuck in Dickens's *Great Expectations*. ***Topes*** (☎ 01634-845270, 💻 www.topesrestaurant.com; Tue-Sun noon-3pm/Tue-Sat 6.30-10pm), 60 High St, offers British cuisine in a restaurant combining the exposed brick-and-beam look with crisp linen tablecloths. Pan-fried guinea fowl is £12.60.

What to see and do

Rochester Cathedral (☎ 01634-843366, 💻 www.rochester.cathedral.org; daily 7.30am-6.30pm) celebrated its 1400th year in 2004 and is the second oldest cathedral in England; Canterbury Cathedral claims the title as the oldest). Admission is free but a donation of £3 is suggested. **Rochester Castle** (☎ 01634-402276; daily 10am-6pm, 10am-4pm 1 Oct-31 Mar) is the other obvious site and reckoned to be one of the country's best-preserved Norman castles. Admission is £4, free to English Heritage members. Started in the 11th century by Bishop Gundolf there are excellent views from the top of the 113ft tower over the Medway and the cathedral. The **Guildhall Museum** (☎ 01634-848717, 💻 www.medway.gov.uk; daily 10am-4.30pm) is strong on local Medway history and it's free. Well-worth seeing is the **Restoration House & Gardens** (☎ 01634-848520, 💻 www.restorationhouse.co.uk; Thu & Fri Jun-Sep only). The house, a 17th-century mansion house, takes its name from King Charles II's stay there on the eve of the Restoration. It's privately owned and superbly maintained, filled with period furniture and a good collection of English portraits. It is said to have been Dickens' inspiration for Satis House in *Great Expectations*. In a different class, the other delight is **The Poor Travellers House** (☎ 01634-845609; Mar-Oct, Tue-Sat 2-5pm), taking its name from the poor travellers 'not being rogues or proctors' who were given one night's lodging in the six bedrooms at the rear of the 16th-century almshouse. They were also provided with a supper of meat, bread and a pint of ale, a pretty generous allowance even by today's standards.

❑ Borstal – what's in a name?
Borstal was the name given to young offender institutions after the prison of the same name in Rochester where imprisoned men were first separated from young boys. Troublesome youths were sent to borstal to benefit from military-style discipline and learn a workshop trade. Sounds familiar? Brendan Behan's novel, *Borstal Boy*, 1958, subsequently dramatized, is based on his experience of a spell in borstal during WWII.

ROCHESTER TO HOLLINGBOURNE [MAPS 36-42]

There's a lot of interest on this **14¼mile/22.8km** section including a Neolithic burial site, Kent's oldest village and smallest pub, the chance to stay with monks at Aylesford Friary, and visit the ruins of Thurnham Castle.

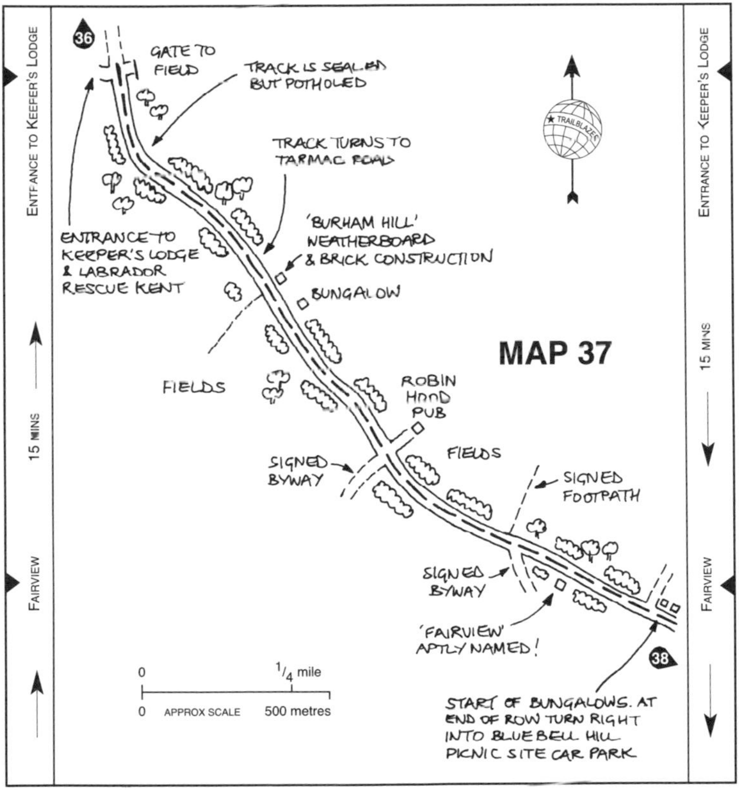

❑ Medway burial tombs

Kit's Coty is a Neolithic burial site built between 3500BC and 2500BC near Aylesford consisting of three upright stones and a capstone across the top standing about 15ft high. The structure is thought to have been at the entrance to a long barrow burial chamber about 200ft long running east to west. The site is now railed off and managed by English Heritage. The White Horse Stone (see Map 38) is also thought to be a Neolithic burial site.

The day begins with a climb along the edge of Shoulder of Mutton wood eventually emerging on a tarmac road to pass within view of the ***Robin Hood*** pub (☎ 01634-861500; food served Mon-Sat noon-2pm, 6-9pm, Sun noon-2pm) and on to reach **Blue Bell Hill** picnic site from where you drop down along a surfaced bridleway to pass **Kit's Coty** (see box above). From there the trail crosses the A229 by an underpass. However, this is prone to **flooding**, year-round, and diversion signs may be in place at Blue Bell Hill; see the advisory on Map 38 opposite. Arriva's bus No 142 (Mon-Sat 4/day) operates from Chatham to Kit's Coty via Rochester and Blue Bell Hill Village; see the public transport map and table pp37-40.

The only refreshments directly on the trail are at the petrol station shop by the A229 and then at Detling nearly nine miles into the day.

After Kit's Coty walkers can detour to Aylesford along the Rochester Rd or continue along the Pilgrims' Way to the underpass and the A229 crossing, if not flooded.

AYLESFORD [MAP 38a]

Pronounced 'ales ford' and reputedly one of the oldest villages in Kent, the buildings along the narrow High St are stacked tightly together above the River Medway.

The **train station** has services to London Victoria (Mon-Sat 1-2/hr, Sun 1/hr) change at Strood and Rochester, and to Maidstone Barracks (similar frequency). Arriva's **buses** Nos 155 (Mon-Sat) and No 135 (Sun only) serve Chatham, Maidstone and Rochester; see the public transport map and table pp37-40.

There is a HSBC **cash machine** and also a **post office** (Mon-Fri 9am-5.30pm,

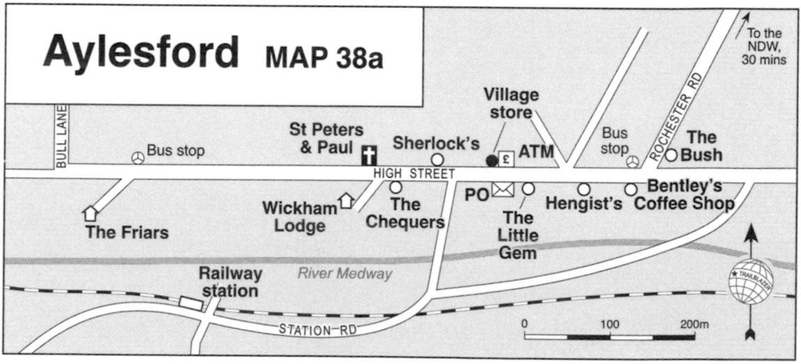

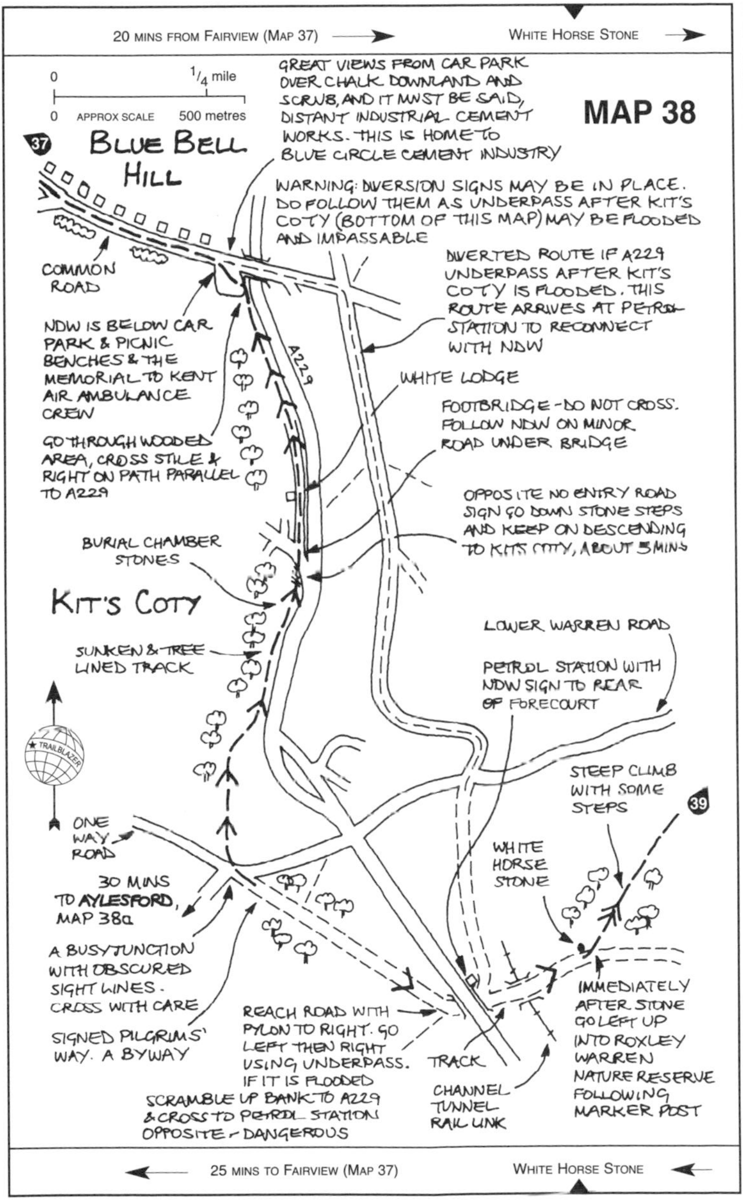
20 MINS FROM FAIRVIEW (MAP 37)
WHITE HORSE STONE
0 1/4 mile
0 APPROX SCALE 500 metres
MAP 38
37
BLUE BELL HILL
GREAT VIEWS FROM CAR PARK OVER CHALK DOWNLAND AND SCRUB, AND IT MUST BE SAID, DISTANT INDUSTRIAL CEMENT WORKS. THIS IS HOME TO BLUE CIRCLE CEMENT INDUSTRY
WARNING: DIVERSION SIGNS MAY BE IN PLACE. DO FOLLOW THEM AS UNDERPASS AFTER KIT'S COTY (BOTTOM OF THIS MAP) MAY BE FLOODED AND IMPASSABLE
COMMON ROAD
DIVERTED ROUTE IF A229 UNDERPASS AFTER KIT'S COTY IS FLOODED. THIS ROUTE ARRIVES AT PETROL STATION TO RECONNECT WITH NDW
NDW IS BELOW CAR PARK & PICNIC BENCHES & THE MEMORIAL TO KENT AIR AMBULANCE CREW
A229
WHITE LODGE
FOOTBRIDGE - DO NOT CROSS. FOLLOW NDW ON MINOR ROAD UNDER BRIDGE
GO THROUGH WOODED AREA, CROSS STILE & RIGHT ON PATH PARALLEL TO A229
OPPOSITE NO ENTRY ROAD SIGN GO DOWN STONE STEPS AND KEEP ON DESCENDING TO KITS COTY, ABOUT 5 MINS
BURIAL CHAMBER STONES
KIT'S COTY
LOWER WARREN ROAD
SUNKEN & TREE LINED TRACK
PETROL STATION WITH NDW SIGN TO REAR OF FORECOURT
TRAILBLAZER
STEEP CLIMB WITH SOME STEPS
39
ONE WAY ROAD
WHITE HORSE STONE
30 MINS TO AYLESFORD, MAP 38a
A BUSY JUNCTION WITH OBSCURED SIGHT LINES. CROSS WITH CARE
IMMEDIATELY AFTER STONE GO LEFT UP INTO ROXLEY WARREN NATURE RESERVE FOLLOWING MARKER POST
REACH ROAD WITH PYLON TO RIGHT. GO LEFT THEN RIGHT USING UNDERPASS. IF IT IS FLOODED SCRAMBLE UP BANK TO A229 & CROSS TO PETROL STATION OPPOSITE - DANGEROUS
SIGNED PILGRIMS' WAY. A BYWAY
TRACK
CHANNEL TUNNEL RAIL LINK
25 MINS TO FAIRVIEW (MAP 37)
WHITE HORSE STONE

Sat 9am-12.30pm). The **village store** (Mon-Fri 6.30am-6pm, Sat 7am-6pm, Sun 7am-noon) has a range of snacks, drinks and groceries.

Where to stay

The Carmelite Friary at Aylesford was founded in 1242, subsequently dissolved by Henry VIII and then re-established in 1949. ***The Friars*** (☎ 01622-717272, 🖳 www.thefriars.org.uk; 80S/T) offer a great welcome with simple rooms and communal facilities. Rates are £22sgl/21dbl including breakfast; spiritual sustenance is free. It's a large and busy complex complete with tea room, chapels and shrines. Judging by the calendar of events they've cornered the market in retreats and pilgrimage. At the time of writing the monks were fundraising to restore a 17th-century barn in the grounds. The monks are also called Whitefriars because of the colour of their robes.

Wickham Lodge (☎ 01622-717267, 🖳 www.wickhamlodge.co.uk; 1S/1D/1T) is a Georgian-looking house with Tudor origins. It's just off the High St on the quay above the Medway. With well-tended gardens and clipped standard box trees framing the entrance, B&B is £40sgl/35dbl and £50 for single occupancy of a double or twin room. All rooms are en-suite. Breakfast is a continental-style buffet.

Where to eat

Filling pub grub is available at ***The Chequers*** (☎ 01622-717286; food Mon-Sat noon-3pm/6-9pm, Sun noon-4pm) and the popular Sunday roast is £6.95. Reputedly the smallest pub in Kent, ***The Little Gem*** (☎ 01622-717510; food Tue-Sun noon-2.30pm) is a treat. The pub only has six tables and a tiny minstrel gallery above the bar; they have guest beers (from independent breweries) and always have Adnams Broadside and Harveys Sussex Bitter. ***The Bush*** (☎ 01622-717446; food Mon/Tue noon-3pm/6-9pm, Wed-Sat noon-9pm, Sun noon-4pm) also does bar food.

The themed restaurant ***Sherlock's*** (☎ 01622-710649; Thu-Sat 7-10pm) eliminated the impossible and is left with the improbable to paraphrase the great sleuth. Paté de foie gras 'inspired by Mycroft's travels' is £5.80 and 'Sherlock' beef steak is £13.55. For upmarket modern French cuisine there is ***Hengist's*** (☎ 01622-719273, Tue-Sun noon-2.30pm, Tue-Sat 6-11pm) but unless you carry stylish glad rags in your pack you'll probably feel out of place at this elegant restaurant. A starter of foie gras here is £9.50 and steamed halibut is £15.25.

If it's just a coffee you're after there is ***Bentley's Coffee Shop*** (Mon-Sat 9.30am-4pm).

After crossing the A229, whether by the underpass or the flood diversion route, the trail passes the petrol station **shop** with snacks and drinks, and climbs by the insignificant looking **White Horse Stone** (easily missed) and into **Roxley Warren Nature Reserve** remaining substantially in woodland until emerging above Detling.

DETLING [MAP 40]

It's well-worth stopping for lunch at the ***Cock Horse Inn*** (☎ 01622-737092; food noon-10pm, non-smoking throughout) and it's on the trail; a substantial chicken Caesar sandwich on wedges of granary bread, accompanied by a salad garnish, drizzled with a delicate oil and vinegar dressing, is £3.95. For something more substantial there is pan-fried John Dory for £7.95.

The **post office** (Mon-Fri 9am-5.30pm, closed 1-2pm and Sat 9am-12.30pm) shares space with **Detling Stores** (Mon-Fri 7am-5.30pm, also closed for lunch, Sat 7am-12.30pm, Sun 9-11am).

Arriva's **bus** services No 333 (Maidstone to Faversham, Mon-Sat only) and No 335 (Maidstone to Canterbury, Sundays only) stop near Cock Horse Inn.

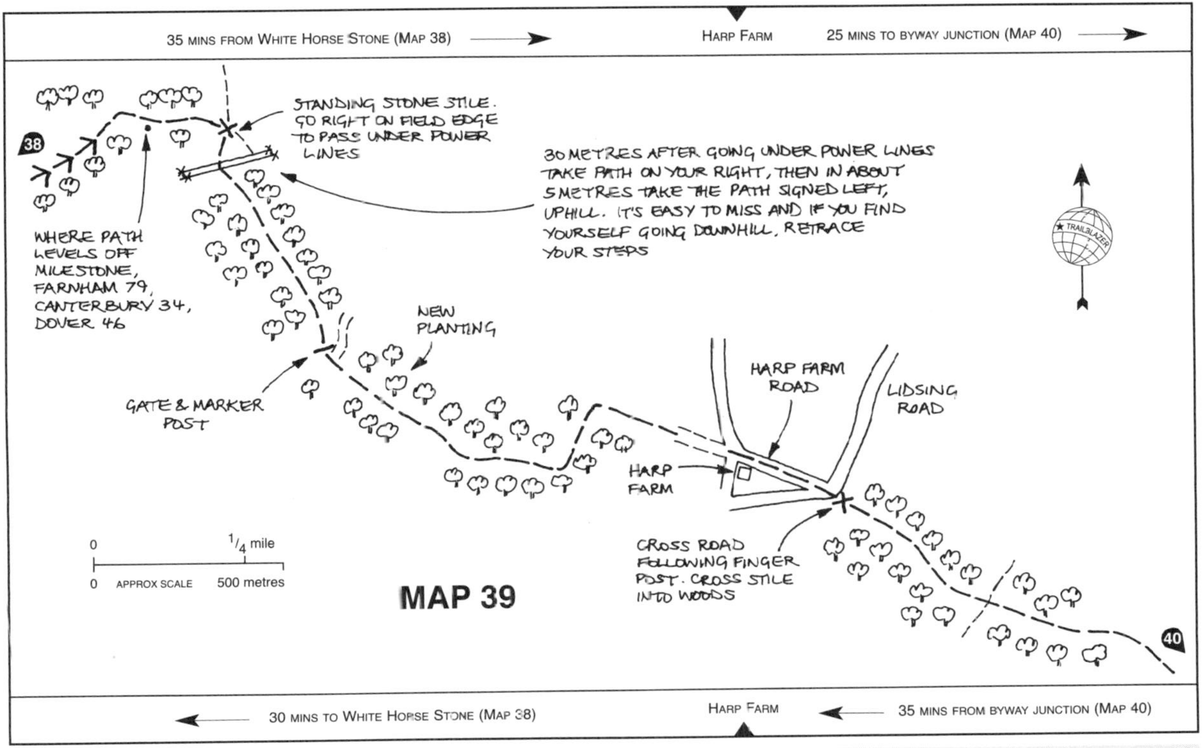
35 MINS FROM WHITE HORSE STONE (MAP 38)
HARP FARM
25 MINS TO BYWAY JUNCTION (MAP 40)
38
STANDING STONE STILE. GO RIGHT ON FIELD EDGE TO PASS UNDER POWER LINES
30 METRES AFTER GOING UNDER POWER LINES TAKE PATH ON YOUR RIGHT, THEN IN ABOUT 5 METRES TAKE THE PATH SIGNED LEFT, UPHILL. IT'S EASY TO MISS AND IF YOU FIND YOURSELF GOING DOWNHILL, RETRACE YOUR STEPS
TRAILBLAZER
WHERE PATH LEVELS OFF MILESTONE, FARNHAM 79, CANTERBURY 34, DOVER 46
NEW PLANTING
GATE & MARKER POST
HARP FARM ROAD
LIDSING ROAD
HARP FARM
CROSS ROAD FOLLOWING FINGER POST. CROSS STILE INTO WOODS
0
1/4 mile
0
APPROX SCALE
500 metres
MAP 39
40
30 MINS TO WHITE HORSE STONE (MAP 38)
HARP FARM
35 MINS FROM BYWAY JUNCTION (MAP 40)

Regaining the ridgeline the trail strikes out for the overgrown ruins of Thurnham Castle. It's known as a 'motte and bailey' fortification, basically a mound surrounded by an enclosure, and dates from the Norman period. Souvenir hunters pilfered most of the stone work and quarrying damaged what remains but it was a large garrison – about 70 metres in diameter.

THURNHAM [MAP 40]

Accommodation is available at ***The Black Horse Inn*** (☎ 01622-737185, 🖳 www.wellieboot.net; food noon-10pm, 4D/1T/1F), a very attractive dark-beamed candle-strewn country pub just off the trail. Rates are £60sgl/37.50dbl/26fml. Priding itself as a 'gastro inn', sweet potato risotto is £9.95 and roast duck £14.95.

If you feel like really spoiling yourself ***Thurnham Keep*** (☎ 01622-734149, 🖳 www.thurnhamkeep.co.uk; 3D all en suite) is a luxury B&B also just off the trail. The Edwardian country house is set in seven acres and rates are £50 weekdays and £60 weekends.

Following the fence line up through fields the trail crosses Coldblow Lane from where it is a 15-minute walk uphill to camping and bunk barn accommodation at ***Coldblow Farm*** (Map 41; ☎ 0870-770 8868, 🖳 www.yha.org.uk). It's so named after the Saxon for 'crossing of the ways' though it's hard not to credit the sometimes chill wind whipping across the Downs ridge for the name. Booking is through the YHA and is essential at any time; the rates below are for individual bookings on weekdays only, sole-use bookings only are permitted at the weekend (two-night minimum). The camping barn sleeps up to 18 and costs £7 per person. The Old Bunk Barn sleeps ten and costs £11 and the New Bunk Barn sleeps 32 and costs £11 per person per night. There is a kitchen and there are showers on meter. Tent pitches cost £10 for two people.

After crossing mostly open fields on a well-defined track the Way drops down to Hollingbourne. The path passes the wonderfully named ***Dirty Habit*** (Map 42; ☎ 01622-880880; food Tue-Fri noon-2.30pm/6-9.30pm, Sat/Sun noon-9.30pm, Mon 6-9.30pm) pub, which has a store cupboard drawing on four corners of the world offering Indian, Thai and Italian dishes along with traditional English bar food. This is the most convenient eating place for the path, but not the only one in the village (see below).

HOLLINGBOURNE [MAP 42]

Accommodation options are limited as several B&Bs have closed over the past few years. There is camping at ***Pine Lodge Touring Park*** (☎ 01622-730018; pitches from £10) but it's a long slog along the A20. Getting there you'll pass the ***Ramada Hotel*** (☎ 0845-730 3040, 🖳 www.ramadajarvis.co.uk; 78D/41T), a conference hotel charging £77sgl/49.50dbl, and brown and white signs to **Leeds Castle** (☎ 01622-765400, 🖳 www.leeds-castle.com; Apr-Oct 10am-5pm, Nov-Mar 10am-3.30pm) called the 'loveliest castle in the world'. Admission is £13.50 (£8 child/£11 senior citizen) but £10.50 if only visiting the grounds, aviary and dog collar museum – not perhaps the greatest bargain you'll find.

Beyond the train station are ***The Sugar Loaves*** (☎ 01622-880220; food daily noon-2.30pm/7-9pm, Sun noon-2.30pm only) pub and ***The Windmill*** (☎ 01622-880280; food Mon-Fri noon-2.30pm/6-10pm, Sat noon-10pm, Sun noon-9.30pm). **Christopher's** (☎ 01622-880338), the vil-

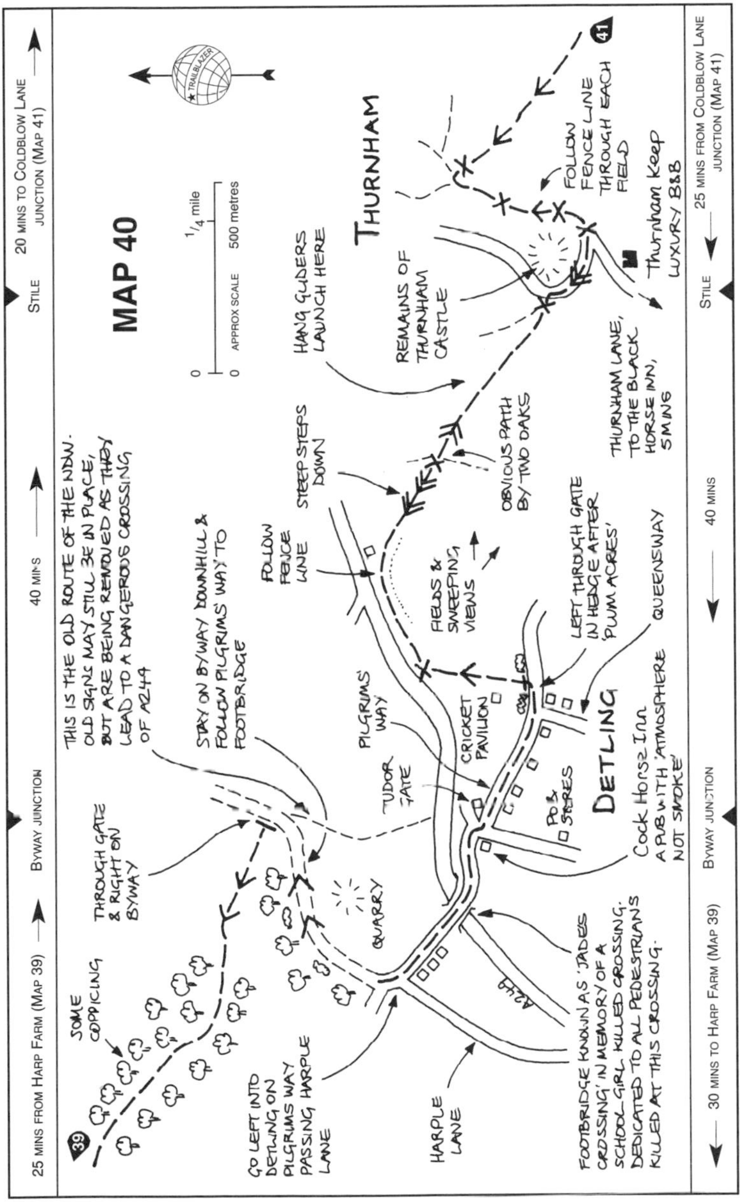
MAP 40
25 MINS FROM HARP FARM (MAP 39)
BYWAY JUNCTION
40 MINS
STILE
20 MINS TO COLDBLOW LANE JUNCTION (MAP 41)
TRAILBLAZER
0
1/4 mile
0
APPROX SCALE
500 metres
39
SOME COPPICING
THROUGH GATE & RIGHT ON BYWAY
THIS IS THE OLD ROUTE OF THE NDW. OLD SIGNS MAY STILL BE IN PLACE, BUT ARE BEING REMOVED AS THEY LEAD TO A DANGEROUS CROSSING OF A249
STAY ON BYWAY DOWNHILL & FOLLOW PILGRIMS' WAY TO FOOTBRIDGE
QUARRY
GO LEFT INTO DETLING ON PILGRIMS WAY PASSING HARPLE LANE
TUDOR GATE
PILGRIMS' WAY
FOLLOW FENCE LINE
STEEP STEPS DOWN
HANG GLIDERS LAUNCH HERE
THURNHAM
REMAINS OF THURNHAM CASTLE
FOLLOW FENCE LINE THROUGH EACH FIELD
41
Thurnham Keep LUXURY B&B
CRICKET PAVILION
FIELDS & SWEEPING VIEWS
OBVIOUS PATH BY TWO OAKS
PO & STORES
DETLING
LEFT THROUGH GATE IN HEDGE AFTER 'PLUM ACRES'
QUEENSWAY
THURNHAM LANE, TO THE BLACK HORSE INN, 5 MINS
Cock Horse Inn A PUB WITH 'ATMOSPHERE' NOT SMOKE
A249
HARPLE LANE
FOOTBRIDGE KNOWN AS 'JADES CROSSING' IN MEMORY OF A SCHOOL GIRL KILLED CROSSING. DEDICATED TO ALL PEDESTRIANS KILLED AT THIS CROSSING.
30 MINS TO HARP FARM (MAP 39)
BYWAY JUNCTION
40 MINS
STILE
25 MINS FROM COLDBLOW LANE JUNCTION (MAP 41)

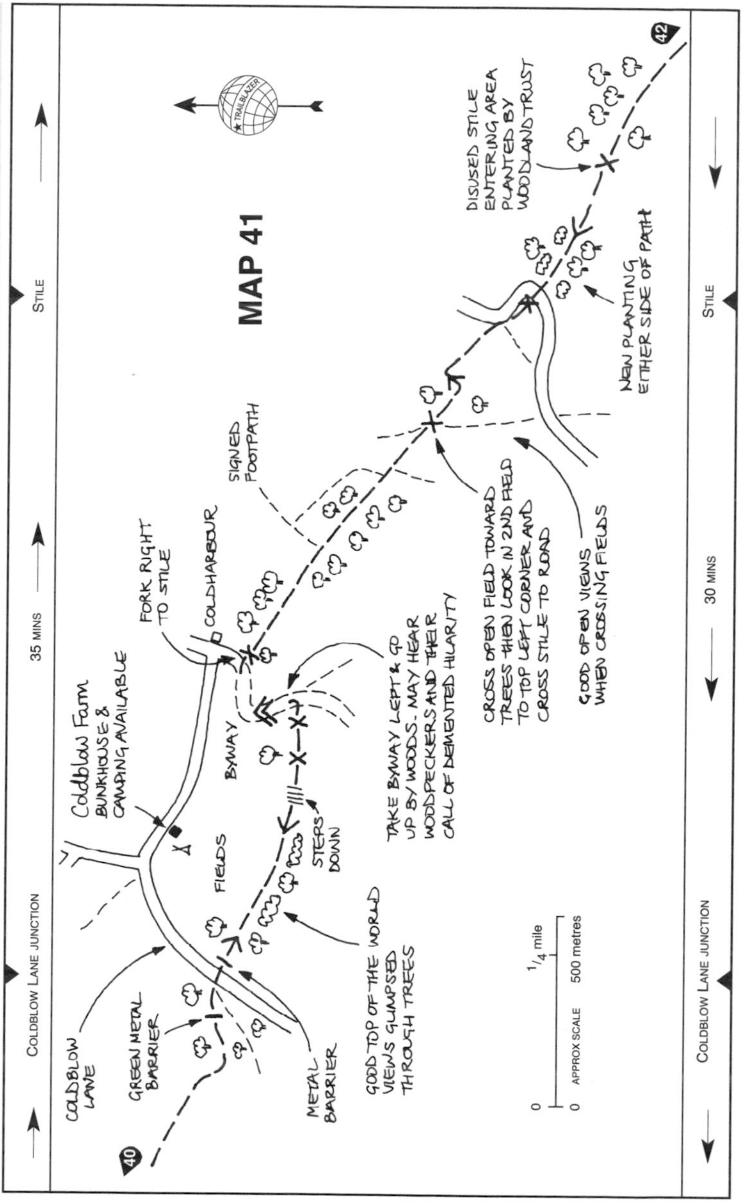
MAP 41
STILE
35 MINS
COLDBLOW LANE JUNCTION
COLDBLOW LANE
GREEN METAL BARRIER
METAL BARRIER
GOOD TOP OF THE WORLD VIEWS GLIMPSED THROUGH TREES
FIELDS
STEPS DOWN
Coldblow Farm
BUNKHOUSE & CAMPING AVAILABLE
BYWAY
TAKE BYWAY LEFT & GO UP BY WOODS. MAY HEAR WOODPECKERS AND THEIR CALL OF DEMENTED HILARITY
FORK RIGHT TO STILE
COLDHARBOUR
SIGNED FOOTPATH
CROSS OPEN FIELD TOWARD TREES THEN LOOK IN 2ND FIELD TO TOP LEFT CORNER AND CROSS STILE TO ROAD
GOOD OPEN VIEWS WHEN CROSSING FIELDS
NEW PLANTING EITHER SIDE OF PATH
DISUSED STILE ENTERING AREA PLANTED BY WOODLAND TRUST
TRAILBLAZER
40
42
30 MINS
STILE
COLDBLOW LANE JUNCTION
APPROX SCALE
0
1/4 mile
0
500 metres

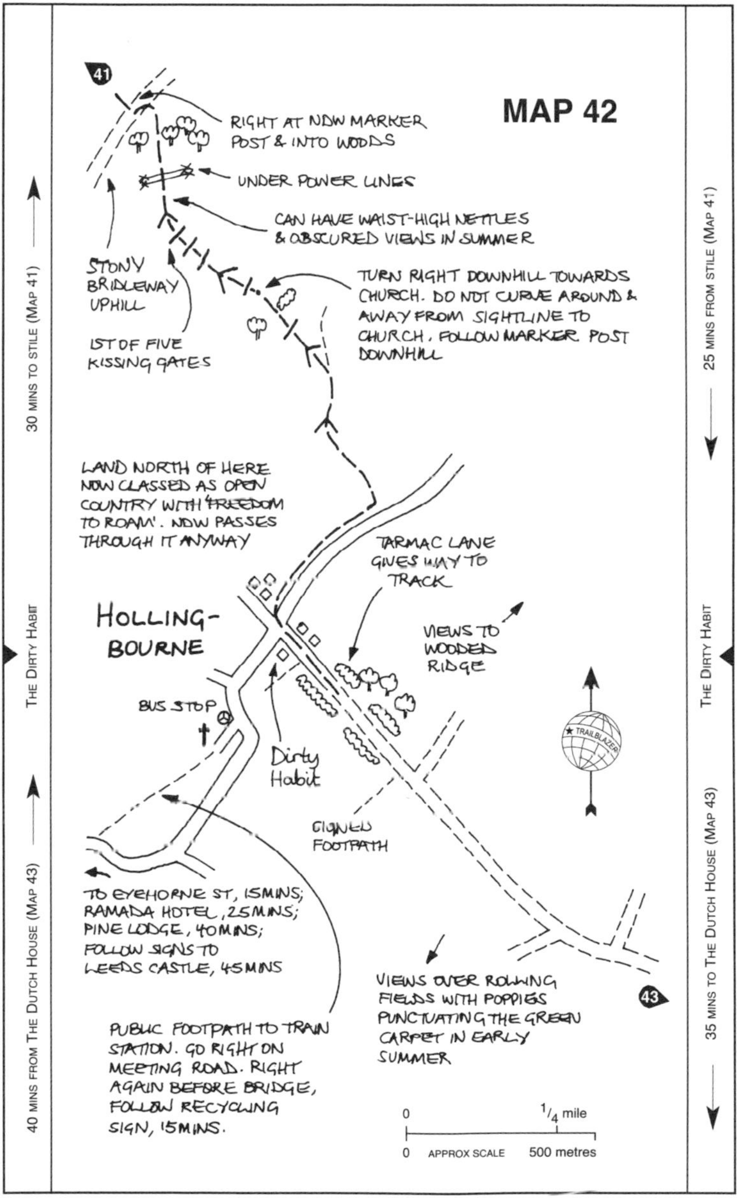
MAP 42
41
RIGHT AT NDW MARKER POST & INTO WOODS
UNDER POWER LINES
CAN HAVE WAIST-HIGH NETTLES & OBSCURED VIEWS IN SUMMER
STONY BRIDLEWAY UPHILL
1ST OF FIVE KISSING GATES
TURN RIGHT DOWNHILL TOWARDS CHURCH. DO NOT CURVE AROUND & AWAY FROM SIGHTLINE TO CHURCH. FOLLOW MARKER POST DOWNHILL
LAND NORTH OF HERE NOW CLASSED AS OPEN COUNTRY WITH 'FREEDOM TO ROAM'. NDW PASSES THROUGH IT ANYWAY
TARMAC LANE GIVES WAY TO TRACK
HOLLING-BOURNE
VIEWS TO WOODED RIDGE
BUS STOP
Dirty Habit
SIGNED FOOTPATH
TO EYEHORNE ST, 15MINS; RAMADA HOTEL, 25MINS; PINE LODGE, 40MINS; FOLLOW SIGNS TO LEEDS CASTLE, 45MINS
VIEWS OVER ROLLING FIELDS WITH POPPIES PUNCTUATING THE GREEN CARPET IN EARLY SUMMER
43
PUBLIC FOOTPATH TO TRAIN STATION. GO RIGHT ON MEETING ROAD. RIGHT AGAIN BEFORE BRIDGE, FOLLOW RECYCLING SIGN, 15MINS.
0 1/4 mile
0 APPROX SCALE 500 metres
30 MINS TO STILE (MAP 41)
THE DIRTY HABIT
40 MINS FROM THE DUTCH HOUSE (MAP 43)
25 MINS FROM STILE (MAP 41)
THE DIRTY HABIT
35 MINS TO THE DUTCH HOUSE (MAP 43)

lage store (Mon-Fri 7am-6pm, Sat 7am-1pm, Sun 7am-noon), also houses the **post office**.

The **train station**, on Eyhorne St, has services (daily, hourly) to London Victoria, Ashford International (change for Canterbury) and Dover Priory. Nu-Venture's **bus** No 13 (Mon-Sat only, 4-5/day) departs from the church and is a useful service stopping at Eyhorne post office and Leeds Castle main entrance. Stagecoach's bus No 510 stops by the Great Danes pub; see the public transport map and table pp37-40.

HOLLINGBOURNE TO CHARING [MAPS 42-46]

After Hollingbourne the route follows the so-called Pilgrims' Way (see p165) for much of its length on this **8³/₄mile/14km** section. It's a fairly straight and level track bordered by hedges with occasional views over vast arable fields. This makes for fast walking on a mostly firm track below the ridge line and at times it's all too easy to drift into a trance-like state as the miles slip by.

HARRRIETSHAM [OFF MAP 43]

The village struggles to offer the walker much other than a **train station** with services (daily, hourly) to London Victoria, Ashford International (change for Canterbury) and Dover Priory. Stagecoach's **bus** No 510 stops by the Roebuck en route between Maidstone, Ashford International, Charing and Lenham; see the public transport map and table pp37-40.

The **Mace Express** (Mon-Sat 7am-8pm, Sun 8am-3pm) grocery store offers cashback up to £30 for which there is a charge of £1.50. The postmistress at the **post office** lamented the village's decline from having five B&Bs and four pubs to only one of each. 'Most ordinary folk go to the Working Man's Club for cheap drink – or so they tell me as I've never been', she confessed. ***The Roebuck*** (☎ 01622-858388) pub is a music-and-karaoke-type joint trying to get the punters in but locals speak well of the accommodation at ***Homestay*** (☎ 01622-858698, 🖳 www.kent-homestay.info; 2T), 14 Chippendale Drive, a proudly kept house in a small cul-de-sac estate charging £30sgl/24.50dbl.

There's more choice if you push on to **Lenham** where the focus of the village is the square.

LENHAM [MAP 44a]

There are services (daily, hourly) to London Victoria, Ashford International (change for Canterbury) and Dover Priory from the **train station**. Stagecoach's **bus** No 510 stops by the Square en route between Maidstone, Ashford International, Charing and Harrietsham; see the public transport map and table, pp37-40.

The **library** (☎ 01622-859140; Tue 9.30am-12.30pm/2-5pm & 5.30-7.30pm, Thu 9.30am-12.30pm/2-5pm, Fri 2-5pm, Sat 9.30am-12.30pm) has free **internet access** and there is a **pharmacy** (☎ 01622-858287; Mon-Fri 9am-5.30pm, Sat 9am-1pm). You can stock up for lunch on the go at the **Spar** (Mon-Sat 8.30am-9.30pm, Sun 10am-9pm) and send a post card at the **post office** (Mon-Fri 9am-5.30pm, Wed 9am-5.15pm, Sat 9am-noon). **Cashback** is available from The Red Lion (see p148) though they charge 50p. A **farmers' market** is held in the square on the second Sunday of each month.

Where to stay

The Dog and Bear Hotel (☎ 01622-858219, 🖳 www.dogandbearlenham.co.uk; 3S/13D/5T/1F), part of the Shepherd

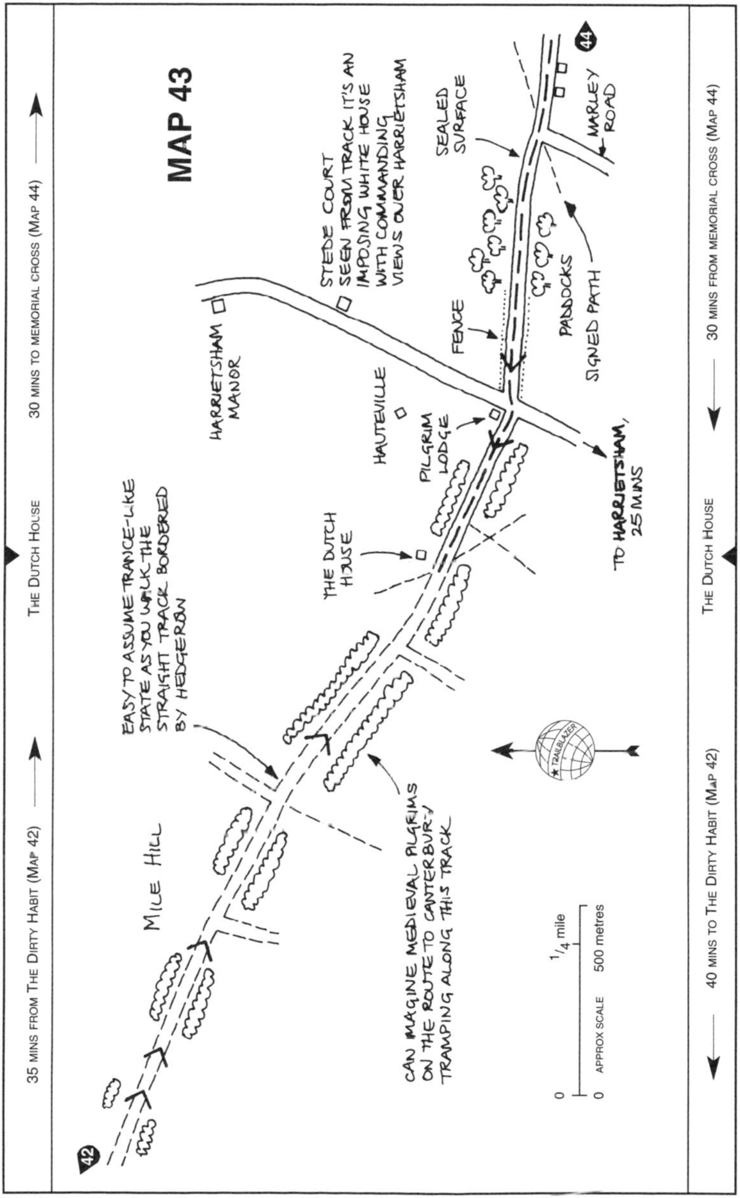
MAP 43
35 MINS FROM THE DIRTY HABIT (MAP 42)
THE DUTCH HOUSE
30 MINS TO MEMORIAL CROSS (MAP 44)
40 MINS TO THE DIRTY HABIT (MAP 42)
THE DUTCH HOUSE
30 MINS FROM MEMORIAL CROSS (MAP 44)
42
44
MILE HILL
EASY TO ASSUME TRANCE-LIKE STATE AS YOU WALK THE STRAIGHT TRACK BORDERED BY HEDGEROW
CAN IMAGINE MEDIEVAL PILGRIMS ON THE ROUTE TO CANTERBURY TRAMPING ALONG THIS TRACK
THE DUTCH HOUSE
PILGRIM LODGE
HAUTEVILLE
HARRIETSHAM MANOR
STEDE COURT SEEN FROM TRACK IT'S AN IMPOSING WHITE HOUSE WITH COMMANDING VIEWS OVER HARRIETSHAM
FENCE
PADDOCKS
SIGNED PATH
SEALED SURFACE
MARLEY ROAD
TO HARRIETSHAM, 25 MINS
TRAILBLAZER
1/4 mile
500 metres
APPROX SCALE
0
0

Neame brewery group, started life as a 15th-century coaching inn. B&B is £60sgl/ £40dbl/30fml in this friendly establishment. All rooms are en suite. The style-conscious ***Lime Tree Restaurant & Hotel*** (☎ 01622-859509, 🖳 www.limetreerestaurant.co.uk; 8D/1T/1F all en suite) does B&B Mon-Thurs from £25 and Fri-Sun from £37.50.

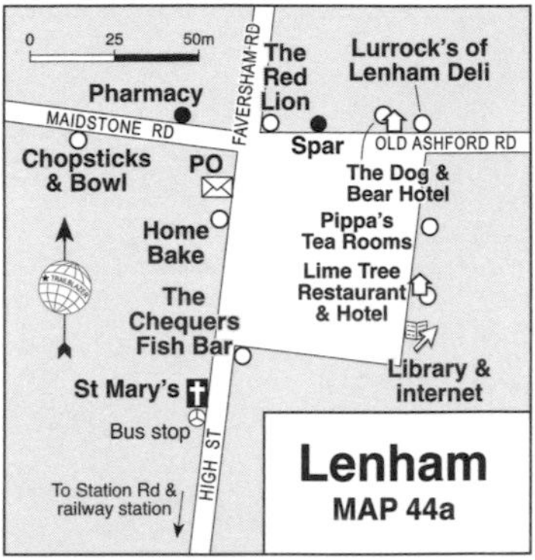

Where to eat

There are tasty fish and chips (£4.25) at ***The Chequers Fish Bar*** (☎ 01622-859878; Mon-Fri 8.30am-2.30pm/4.00-10.30pm, Sat 8.30am-10.30pm, Sun 11am-9pm). ***Home Bake*** (Mon-Fri 8am-5pm, Sat 8am-1pm) has nice baked goods and ***Lurrocks of Lenham Deli*** (Mon-Fri 9am-5.30pm, Wed 9am-5pm, Sat 9am-3pm) has cheese rolls for £1.60 and baked potatoes for £2.80. A little pricier but with a fancy eat-in area is ***Pippa's Tea Rooms*** (☎ 01622-851360; Mon-Sat 10am-5pm, Sun 11am-4pm) where a cream tea is £3.95. Take-away Chinese food from ***Chopsticks & Bowl*** (☎ 01622-858416; Mon-Thu noon-2pm/5-11.30pm, Fri & Sat noon-2.30pm/5-11.45pm, Sun noon-2.30pm/5-11pm) is good value; a portion of Singapore Special Fried Noodles is £3.40.

The fanciest eating in town is at the ***Lime Tree Restaurant and Hotel*** (see column opposite; Tue-Sat & Sun lunch only) where an assiette of charcuterie is £5.50 and foccacia fillet steak is £10.95. And for good pub grub try ***The Red Lion*** (☎ 01622-858531; food Mon-Sat noon-2.30pm/6-9pm, Sun noon-4pm) where the steak pie is £7.50. At the ***Dog and Bear*** (see p146; Mon-Sat noon-2.30pm/6.30-9.30pm, Sun noon-7pm) vegetarians may be tempted by the aubergine and courgette tempura (£8.75).

If all the accommodation in Lenham is booked up ***The Harrow Hill Hotel*** (☎ 01622-858727; 5T/6D/1F all en suite) is 20 minutes off the trail (see Map 45). It's a jazzed-up country pub and rates are £25dbl/twin and £35 per person for a family room. Food is served noon-2.30pm and 7-9pm; the bar is closed 3-6pm.

After Lenham the North Downs Way follows a byway with little evidence of much vehicle use. With views over large arable fields the trail passes through woodland and descends to the A252 and Charing a short distance away.

CHARING [MAP 46]

The village is quite charming and the long High St continues into Station Rd. Many of the buildings are half timbered and the **church** has a fine tower. Right next to it and just off the High St the **ruins** of a former archbishop's palace are worth a look.

There are services (daily, hourly) to London Victoria, Ashford International (change for Canterbury) and Dover Priory from the **train station**. Stagecoach's **bus** No 510 stops here en route between Maidstone, Ashford International, Lenham and Harrietsham; see the public transport map and table, pp37-40.

The **Londis** (Mon-Sat 7am-8pm, Sun 9am-6pm) convenience store does **cash-back** for a 20p charge. **Richard's** (☎ 01233-713142; Mon-Fri 8am-5pm, Sat 8am-3pm) is both **butcher** and **baker**.

(cont'd on p152)

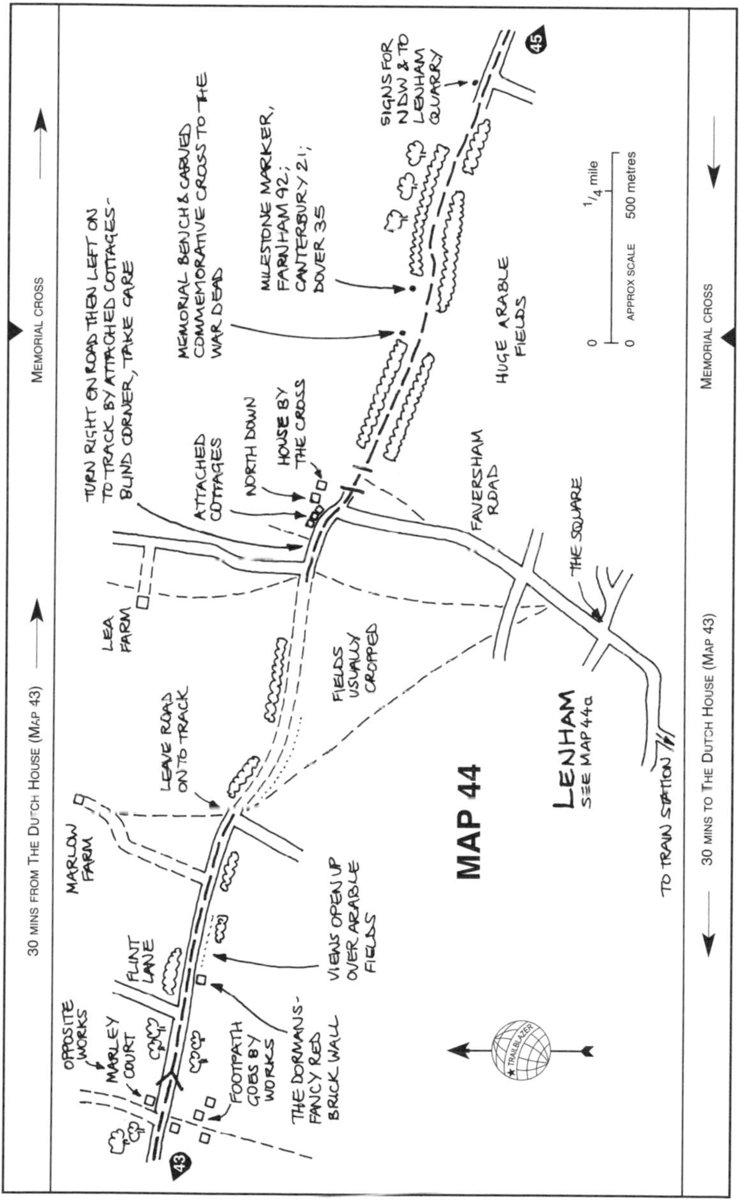

MAP 44
LENHAM
SEE MAP 44a
30 MINS FROM THE DUTCH HOUSE (MAP 43)
30 MINS TO THE DUTCH HOUSE (MAP 43)
MEMORIAL CROSS
MEMORIAL CROSS
43
45
OPPOSITE WORKS
MARLEY COURT
FOOTPATH GOES BY WORKS
THE DORMANS - FANCY RED BRICK WALL
FLINT LANE
VIEWS OPEN UP OVER ARABLE FIELDS
MARLOW FARM
LEAVE ROAD ONTO TRACK
FIELDS USUALLY CROPPED
LEA FARM
TURN RIGHT ON ROAD THEN LEFT ON TO TRACK BY ATTACHED COTTAGES - BLIND CORNER, TAKE CARE
ATTACHED COTTAGES
NORTH DOWN
HOUSE BY THE CROSS
FAVERSHAM ROAD
THE SQUARE
TO TRAIN STATION
MEMORIAL BENCH & CARVED COMMEMORATIVE CROSS TO THE WAR DEAD
MILESTONE MARKER, FARNHAM 92; CANTERBURY 21; DOVER 35
HUGE ARABLE FIELDS
SIGNS FOR NDW & TO LENHAM QUARRY
APPROX SCALE
0
1/4 mile
0
500 metres
TRAILBLAZER

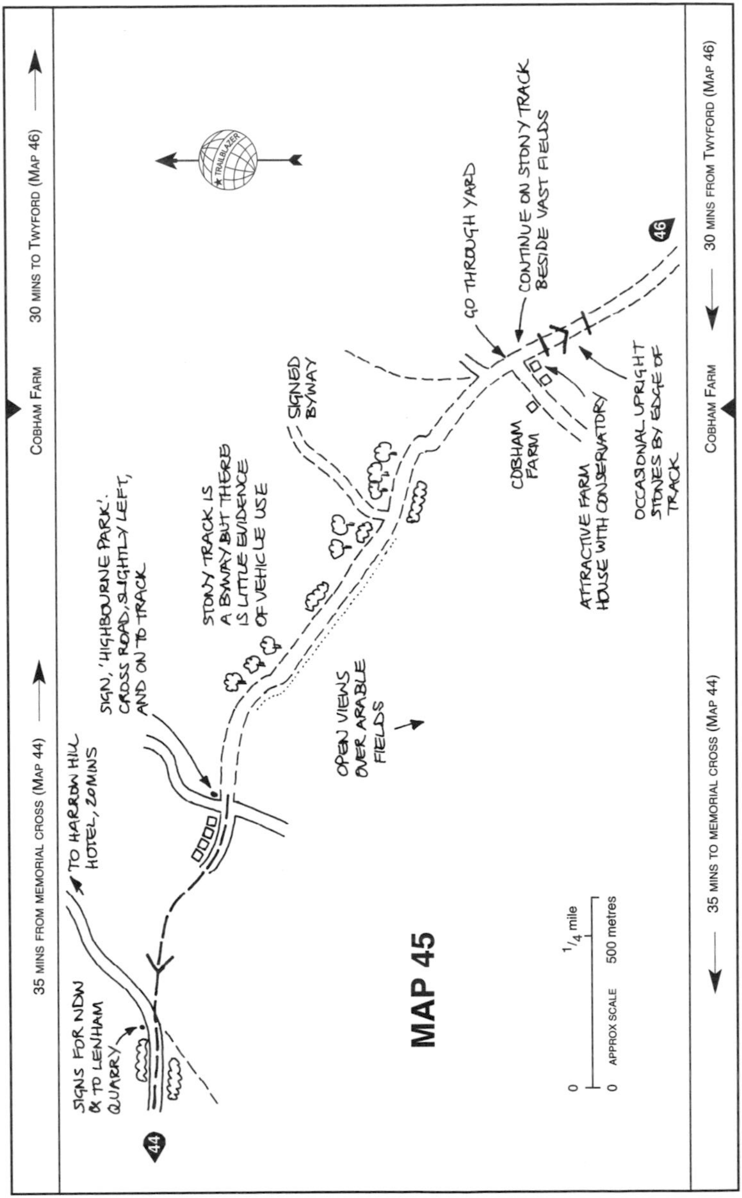
MAP 45
35 MINS FROM MEMORIAL CROSS (MAP 44)
COBHAM FARM
30 MINS TO TWYFORD (MAP 46)
35 MINS TO MEMORIAL CROSS (MAP 44)
30 MINS FROM TWYFORD (MAP 46)
TRAILBLAZER
44
46
SIGNS FOR NDW & TO LENHAM QUARRY
TO HARROW HILL HOTEL, 20MINS
SIGN, 'HIGHBOURNE PARK'. CROSS ROAD, SLIGHTLY LEFT, AND ON TO TRACK
STONY TRACK IS A BYWAY BUT THERE IS LITTLE EVIDENCE OF VEHICLE USE
OPEN VIEWS OVER ARABLE FIELDS
SIGNED BYWAY
COBHAM FARM
ATTRACTIVE FARM HOUSE WITH CONSERVATORY
OCCASIONAL UPRIGHT STONES BY EDGE OF TRACK
GO THROUGH YARD
CONTINUE ON STONY TRACK BESIDE VAST FIELDS
APPROX SCALE
0
1/4 mile
0
500 metres

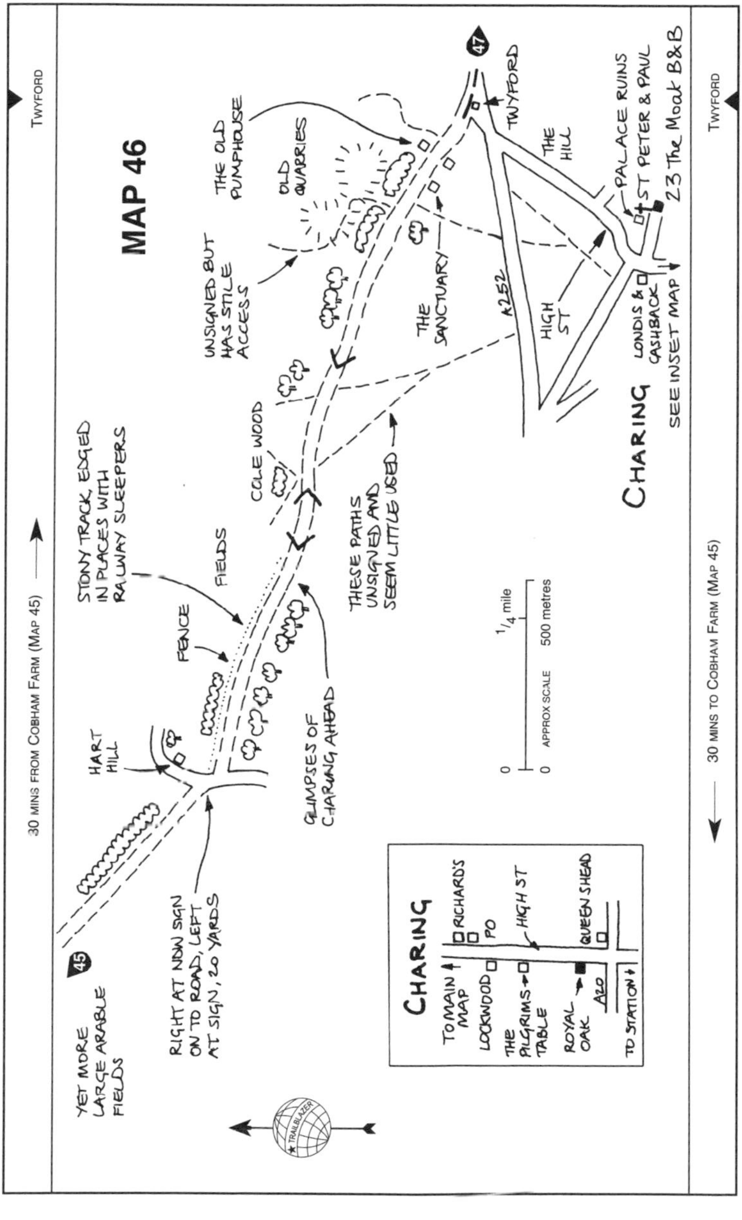
MAP 46
TWYFORD
30 MINS FROM COBHAM FARM (MAP 45)
TWYFORD
30 MINS TO COBHAM FARM (MAP 45)
45
47
YET MORE LARGE ARABLE FIELDS
RIGHT AT NDW SIGN ON TO ROAD, LEFT AT SIGN, 20 YARDS
HART HILL
FENCE
STONY TRACK, EDGED IN PLACES WITH RAILWAY SLEEPERS
FIELDS
GLIMPSES OF CHARING AHEAD
COLE WOOD
THESE PATHS UNSIGNED AND SEEM LITTLE USED
UNSIGNED BUT HAS STILE ACCESS
OLD QUARRIES
THE OLD PUMPHOUSE
THE SANCTUARY
A252
HIGH ST
THE HILL
TWYFORD
PALACE RUINS
ST PETER & PAUL
23 The Moat B&B
LONDIS & CASHBACK
SEE INSET MAP
CHARING
0
0
APPROX SCALE
1/4 mile
500 metres
CHARING
TO MAIN MAP
LOCKWOOD
THE PILGRIMS TABLE
ROYAL OAK
A20
TO STATION
RICHARD'S
PO
HIGH ST
QUEENS HEAD
TRAILBLAZER

(cont'd from p148) Next door is the **post office** (Mon-Fri 9am-5.30pm, Sat 9am-12.30pm). The **Lockwood Newsagent** (Mon-Fri 6.30am-5pm, Sat 7.30am-5pm, Sun 7.30am-11.30am) has a **cash machine** inside but closes for lunch (1-2pm).

23 The Moat (☎ 01233-713141; 1T en suite) is a well-kept modest bungalow behind the church where B&B is £28sgl/26dbl but it's only available April-September.

Timber Lodge (☎ 01233-713641; 1S/1D) is by the A252 about 320 metres north of the crossing to the Pilgrims' Way (see Map 47). B&B is £25sgl/25dbl. The single room has a private bathroom and the double is en suite.

The ***Royal Oak*** (☎ 01233-712612; 2S/2D/4T/1F) is a warm and inviting wood-floored pub with en suite rooms. B&B is £29.95sgl/20dbl/17fml. It has an extensive menu with a cheese ploughman's for £4.95, or grilled pork with cider apple sauce for £8.25.

The other pub, the ***Queens Head*** (☎ 01233-712253; food Mon-Fri noon-2pm only), is a darts-and-pool type of place and ***The Pilgrims Table*** (☎ 01233-712170; Wed-Sat noon-2.30pm) is open for lunches and from 6pm as a cozy wine bar; wines by the glass are £2.95.

CHARING TO CHILHAM [MAPS 47-52]

The trail continues to follow the route of the Pilgrims' Way, through the dense woods of Westwell Downs to cross the tranquil park landscape of Eastwell before arriving at Boughton Lees where the trail divides (see p183 for the alternative route). As there are no shops on the route and the accessible pubs are closed in the afternoon, stock up on water and snacks before leaving Charing on this **10¼mile/16.4km** section.

WESTWELL [MAP 48]

There's not much here but campers will find pitches for £4 per person at ***Dunn Street Farm*** (☎ 01233-712537) where there are 40 pitches; the route passes in front of the farm gates. ***The Wheel Inn*** (☎ 01233-712430) does pub grub and a roast on Sunday (daily 11.30am-2pm and 7-9.30pm).

EASTWELL [MAP 49]

The short walk to the ruins of **St Mary's** is worth it and if you bought a lottery ticket from the store in Charing and discover that you've won, part with some of your cash at ***Eastwell Manor Hotel*** (☎ 01233-213000, 🖳 www.eastwellmanor.co.uk; 23D). This is top-hole, glossy brochure stuff, carved panelled rooms with baronial-stone fireplaces. You'll pay from £95 for B&B. Some of the rooms have four posters. Jacket and tie is required in the dining room but the casually attired can go to the Brasserie, the hotel's 'alternative restaurant where informality is more than acceptable.'

The 'official' North Downs Way divides at **Boughton Lees** and we take the longer northern route through Canterbury with its wonderful cathedral (a World Heritage Site), across Kent orchard and hop country and on to Dover. The shorter direct route (see p183) has an escarpment view over the White Cliffs on the final day but we don't recommend it because it is bounded by the busy A20 and the Channel Tunnel marshalling yards and lacks the cultural riches that Canterbury offers.

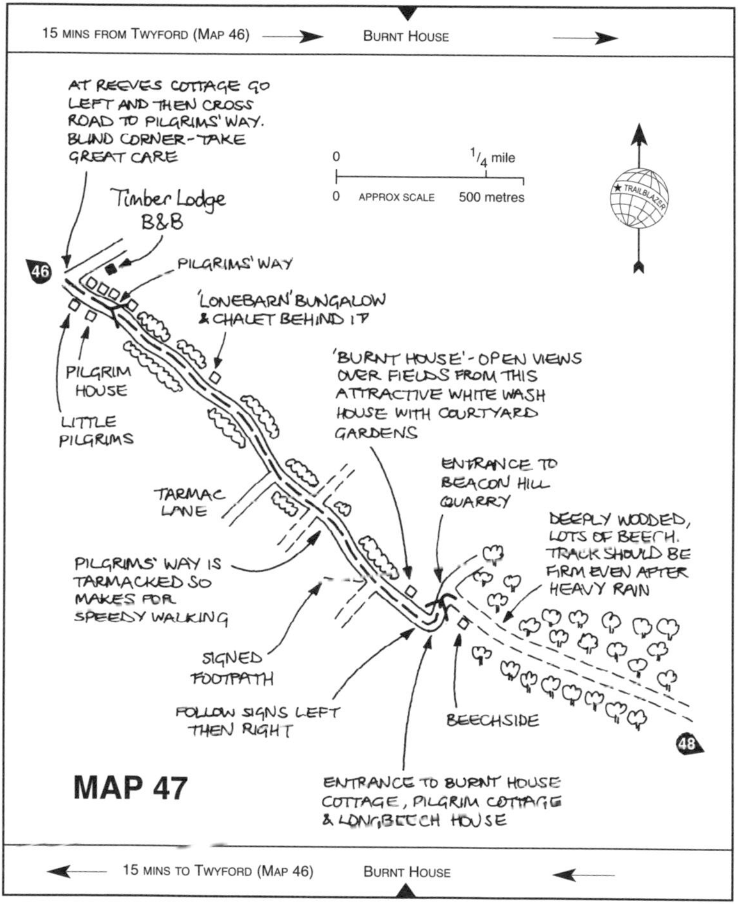

The ***Flying Horse Inn*** (Map 49; ☎ 01233-620914; food Mon-Sat noon-2.30pm, Tue-Sat 6-9pm, Sun 12.30-2.30pm) has a beautiful aspect overlooking the village cricket green where you can sup a pint over a few innings. The Sunday roast is £7.50.

Past **Boughton Aluph** (see Map 50) the trail cuts through the yard of ***Soakham Farm*** (☎ 01233-813509; 1S/1D/1T); B&B at this working farm is £30. It's in a lovely setting with uninterrupted views over the Great Stour Valley. They don't do an evening meal but you can order from a takeaway menu and the proprietor will go and collect the food, or they'll drive you to a local pub.

(cont'd on p158)

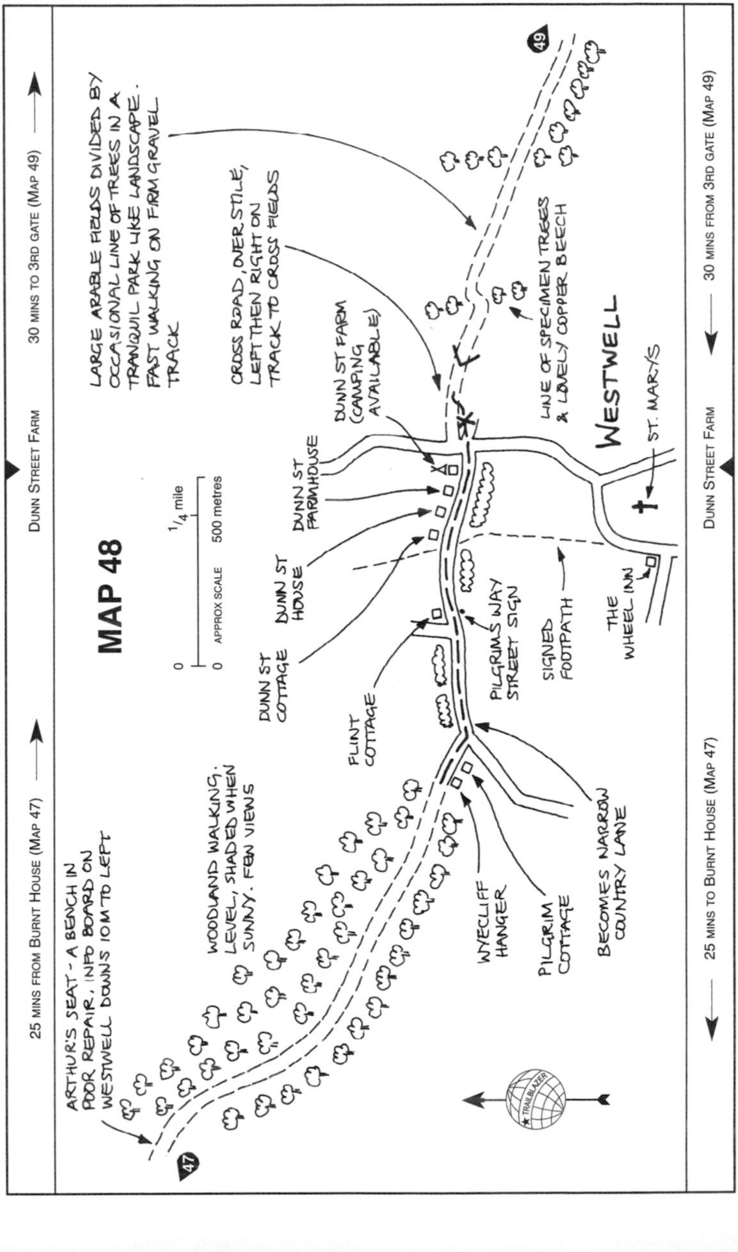
25 mins from Burnt House (Map 47)
Dunn Street Farm
30 mins to 3rd gate (Map 49)
MAP 48
0 1/4 mile
0 500 metres
APPROX SCALE
ARTHUR'S SEAT - A BENCH IN POOR REPAIR, INFO BOARD ON WESTWELL DOWNS 10M TO LEFT
WOODLAND WALKING, LEVEL, SHADED WHEN SUNNY. FEW VIEWS
WYECLIFF HANGER
PILGRIM COTTAGE
BECOMES NARROW COUNTRY LANE
FLINT COTTAGE
DUNN ST COTTAGE
DUNN ST HOUSE
DUNN ST FARMHOUSE
DUNN ST FARM (CAMPING AVAILABLE)
PILGRIMS WAY STREET SIGN
SIGNED FOOTPATH
THE WHEEL INN
ST. MARYS
WESTWELL
CROSS ROAD, OVER STILE, LEFT THEN RIGHT ON TRACK TO CROSS FIELDS
LARGE ARABLE FIELDS DIVIDED BY OCCASIONAL LINE OF TREES IN A TRANQUIL PARK LIKE LANDSCAPE. FAST WALKING ON FIRM GRAVEL TRACK
LINE OF SPECIMEN TREES & LOVELY COPPER BEECH
47
49
TRAILBLAZER
25 mins to Burnt House (Map 47)
Dunn Street Farm
30 mins from 3rd gate (Map 49)

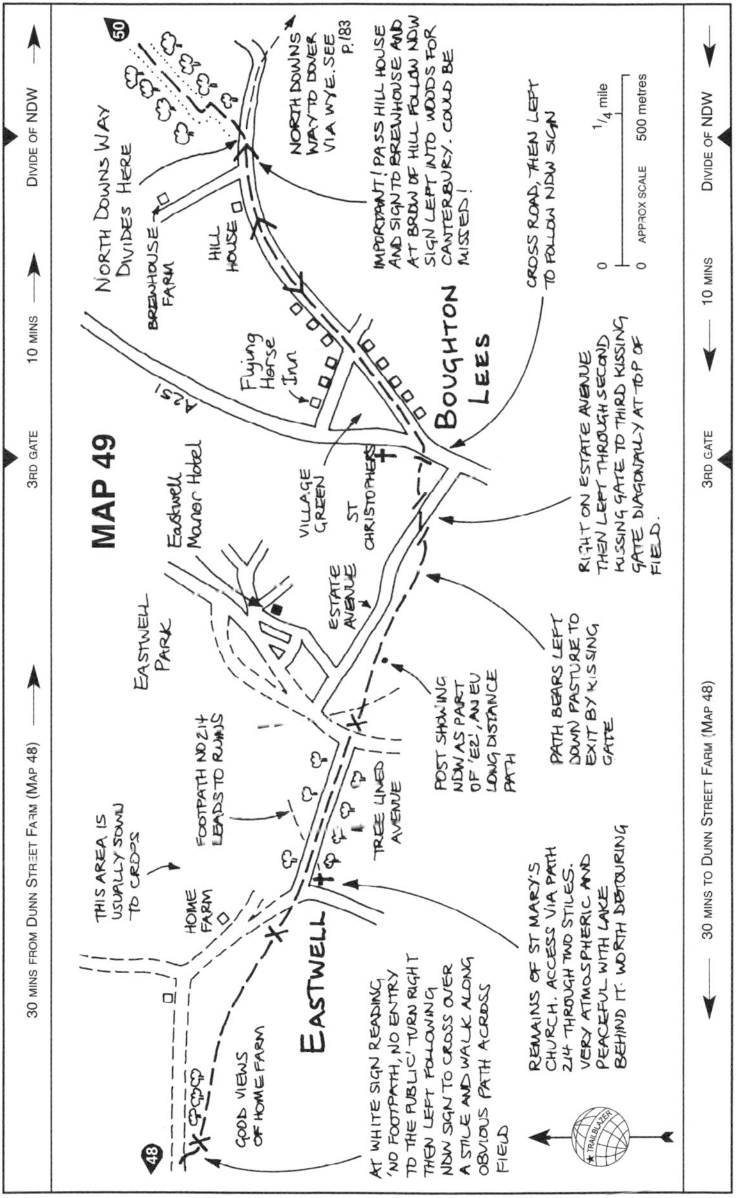
MAP 49
30 MINS FROM DUNN STREET FARM (MAP 48) →
3RD GATE
10 MINS →
DIVIDE OF NDW
← 30 MINS TO DUNN STREET FARM (MAP 48)
3RD GATE
← 10 MINS
DIVIDE OF NDW
48
50
GOOD VIEWS OF HOME FARM
AT WHITE SIGN READING 'NO FOOTPATH, NO ENTRY TO THE PUBLIC' TURN RIGHT THEN LEFT FOLLOWING NDW SIGN TO CROSS OVER A STILE AND WALK ALONG OBVIOUS PATH ACROSS FIELD
EASTWELL
HOME FARM
THIS AREA IS USUALLY SOWN TO CROPS
FOOTPATH NO 214 LEADS TO RUINS
TREE LINED AVENUE
REMAINS OF ST MARY'S CHURCH. ACCESS VIA PATH 214 THROUGH TWO STILES. VERY ATMOSPHERIC AND PEACEFUL WITH LAKE BEHIND IT. WORTH DETOURING
EASTWELL PARK
Eastwell Manor Hotel
ESTATE AVENUE
POST SHOWING NDW AS PART OF 'E2', AN EU LONG DISTANCE PATH
PATH BEARS LEFT DOWN PASTURE TO EXIT BY KISSING GATE
VILLAGE GREEN
ST CHRISTOPHERS
RIGHT ON ESTATE AVENUE THEN LEFT THROUGH SECOND KISSING GATE TO THIRD KISSING GATE DIAGONALLY AT TOP OF FIELD.
A251
Flying Horse Inn
BOUGHTON LEES
CROSS ROAD, THEN LEFT TO FOLLOW NDW SIGN
BREWHOUSE FARM
HILL HOUSE
NORTH DOWNS WAY DIVIDES HERE
IMPORTANT! PASS HILL HOUSE AND SIGN TO BREWHOUSE AND AT BROW OF HILL FOLLOW NDW SIGN LEFT INTO WOODS FOR CANTERBURY. COULD BE MISSED!
NORTH DOWNS WAY TO DOVER VIA WYE. SEE P.183
0
1/4 mile
0
APPROX SCALE
500 metres
TRAILBLAZER

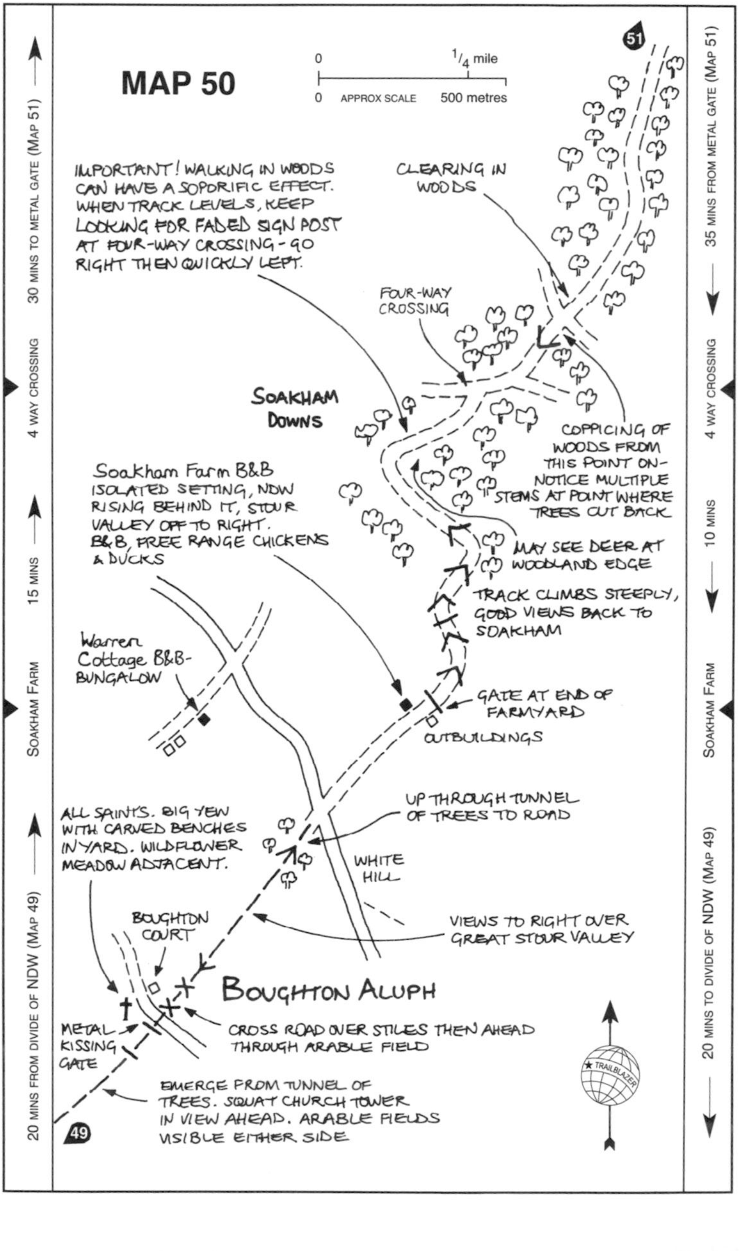
MAP 50
0 1/4 mile
0 APPROX SCALE 500 metres
30 MINS TO METAL GATE (MAP 51)
4 WAY CROSSING
15 MINS
SOAKHAM FARM
20 MINS FROM DIVIDE OF NDW (MAP 49)
35 MINS FROM METAL GATE (MAP 51)
4 WAY CROSSING
10 MINS
SOAKHAM FARM
20 MINS TO DIVIDE OF NDW (MAP 49)
51
49
IMPORTANT! WALKING IN WOODS CAN HAVE A SOPORIFIC EFFECT. WHEN TRACK LEVELS, KEEP LOOKING FOR FADED SIGN POST AT FOUR-WAY CROSSING - GO RIGHT THEN QUICKLY LEFT.
CLEARING IN WOODS
FOUR-WAY CROSSING
SOAKHAM DOWNS
COPPICING OF WOODS FROM THIS POINT ON - NOTICE MULTIPLE STEMS AT POINT WHERE TREES CUT BACK
Soakham Farm B&B
ISOLATED SETTING, NDW RISING BEHIND IT, STOUR VALLEY OFF TO RIGHT. B&B, FREE RANGE CHICKENS & DUCKS
MAY SEE DEER AT WOODLAND EDGE
TRACK CLIMBS STEEPLY, GOOD VIEWS BACK TO SOAKHAM
Warren Cottage B&B - BUNGALOW
GATE AT END OF FARMYARD
OUTBUILDINGS
ALL SAINTS. BIG YEW WITH CARVED BENCHES IN YARD. WILDFLOWER MEADOW ADJACENT.
UP THROUGH TUNNEL OF TREES TO ROAD
WHITE HILL
BOUGHTON COURT
VIEWS TO RIGHT OVER GREAT STOUR VALLEY
BOUGHTON ALUPH
METAL KISSING GATE
CROSS ROAD OVER STILES THEN AHEAD THROUGH ARABLE FIELD
EMERGE FROM TUNNEL OF TREES. SQUAT CHURCH TOWER IN VIEW AHEAD. ARABLE FIELDS VISIBLE EITHER SIDE
TRAILBLAZER

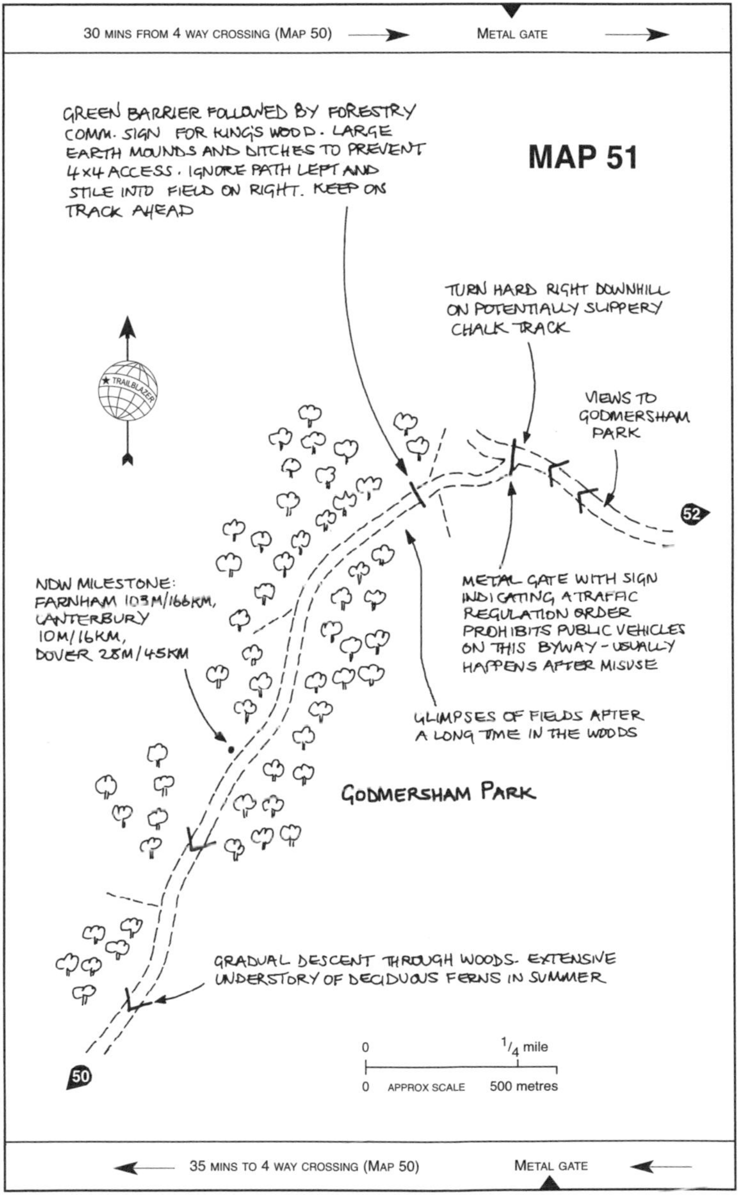
30 MINS FROM 4 WAY CROSSING (MAP 50)
METAL GATE
MAP 51
GREEN BARRIER FOLLOWED BY FORESTRY COMM. SIGN FOR KING'S WOOD. LARGE EARTH MOUNDS AND DITCHES TO PREVENT 4X4 ACCESS. IGNORE PATH LEFT AND STILE INTO FIELD ON RIGHT. KEEP ON TRACK AHEAD
TURN HARD RIGHT DOWNHILL ON POTENTIALLY SLIPPERY CHALK TRACK
VIEWS TO GODMERSHAM PARK
TRAILBLAZER
52
NDW MILESTONE: FARNHAM 103M/166KM, CANTERBURY 10M/16KM, DOVER 28M/45KM
METAL GATE WITH SIGN INDICATING A TRAFFIC REGULATION ORDER PROHIBITS PUBLIC VEHICLES ON THIS BYWAY - USUALLY HAPPENS AFTER MISUSE
GLIMPSES OF FIELDS AFTER A LONG TIME IN THE WOODS
GODMERSHAM PARK
GRADUAL DESCENT THROUGH WOODS. EXTENSIVE UNDERSTORY OF DECIDUOUS FERNS IN SUMMER
0
1/4 mile
0
APPROX SCALE
500 metres
50
35 MINS TO 4 WAY CROSSING (MAP 50)
METAL GATE

Godmersham Park

Godmersham Park (see Map 51) is an 18th-century park landscape. The mansion still exists but it may be difficult to see if the trees are in full leaf (ie in summer). At one time it was owned by the brother, Edward, of the 19th-century novelist Jane Austen and some say that it was the inspiration for *Mansfield Park*. Edward Austen was adopted by wealthy relatives, the Knights, owners of estates in Kent and Hampshire and he became heir to these in 1797, changing his name to Knight. In the 18th century this was not unusual; the dead were honoured and an inheritance received. It also explains a number of 'double-barrelled' surnames – the designated heir got the land; the family's name continued.

Since the mid-1980s it has been used as the training college of the Association of British Dispensing Opticians.

(cont'd from p153) At ***Warren Cottage*** (☎ 01233-740483; 1D/1T) Mrs Fearn does B&B for £25sgl occupancy/30dbl and has a similar arrangement for evening meals.

The trail climbs steeply on to **Soakham Downs** and then through attractive beech and chestnut forest, for the next hour or so, skirting **Godmersham Park** (see box above) and to follow a quiet tarmac road into Chilham.

CHILHAM **[MAP 52]**

Chilham is a very pretty village overlooked by a Jacobean castle, now a private residence. A previous owner replaced the brick wall with railings opening a pleasing view for the public. At the heart of the village is the medieval square bordered by black and white half-timbered buildings some of them faced with brick.

There is a **train station** with services to London Charing Cross (daily up to 3/hr), Ashford International and Canterbury (both Mon-Sat 2/hr, Sun 1/hr). Stagecoach **bus** No 652 (Mon-Sat only, up to 11/day) operates to Canterbury; see the public transport map and table pp37-40.

The **post office shop** (Mon-Sat 8am-5.30pm, Sun 8-10.30am shop only) has snacks and drinks.

The Old Alma Inn (☎ 01227-731913; 2D/1T), a former pub now a B&B, charges £25 per person for the en suite twin room and the double with shared bathroom and £27.50 for the en suite double. It's the closest to the train station and on the A28. Probably the most historic place is the ivy-clad ***Bagham Farmhouse*** (☎ 01227-730306; 2D/2T all en suite), built in 1460 and now standing off the A28. Rates are £25 and £27.50 for the larger of the doubles. The ***Woolpack Inn*** (☎ 01227-730351; 1S/7D/3T/3F) is an excellent pub with very comfortable en suite rooms charging £50sgl/£58 for single occupancy of a double and £40dbl/twin.

Woodchip House (☎ 01227-730386; 1S/1T/3D/1F) is across the A252 and you can't miss the large sign. Two of the doubles have their own bathroom, the family room is en suite and Mrs Phillips charges £25 for B&B.

The Copper Kettle Tea Shop (☎ 01227-730303; Tue-Sun 10am-5pm) on the square is dripping with hanging baskets in summer and does a fine poached salmon salad, or go for the ham, egg and chips; both are priced at £6.95. A pot of tea is £1.50 with an extra pot of hot water for good measure. The food at the ***Woolpack*** (see above; daily noon-2.30pm, 6.30-9.30pm) is top notch both in the bar and the pricier restaurant, with nice seasonal touches to the ploughman's (£6.95) and substantial portions of calves liver and bacon (£8.95). The ***White Horse Inn*** (☎ 01227-730355; food Tue-Sat noon-3pm/5.30-9pm, Sun & Mon noon-3pm) also does bar food and has occasional music nights.

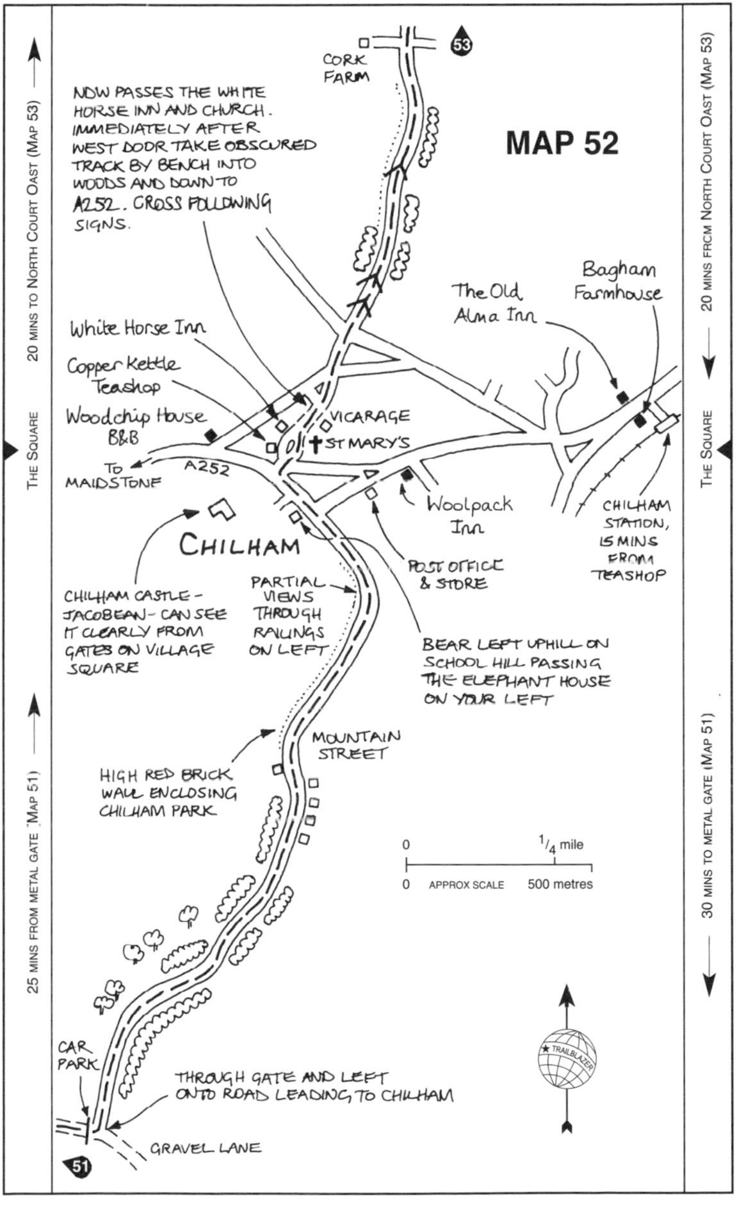
MAP 52
20 MINS TO NORTH COURT OAST (MAP 53)
THE SQUARE
25 MINS FROM METAL GATE (MAP 51)
20 MINS FROM NORTH COURT OAST (MAP 53)
30 MINS TO METAL GATE (MAP 51)
CORK FARM
NOW PASSES THE WHITE HORSE INN AND CHURCH. IMMEDIATELY AFTER WEST DOOR TAKE OBSCURED TRACK BY BENCH INTO WOODS AND DOWN TO A252. CROSS FOLLOWING SIGNS.
The Old Alma Inn
Bagham Farmhouse
White Horse Inn
Copper Kettle Teashop
Woodchip House B&B
VICARAGE
ST MARY'S
TO MAIDSTONE
A252
Woolpack Inn
CHILHAM STATION, 15 MINS FROM TEASHOP
CHILHAM
POST OFFICE & STORE
PARTIAL VIEWS THROUGH RAILINGS ON LEFT
CHILHAM CASTLE - JACOBEAN - CAN SEE IT CLEARLY FROM GATES ON VILLAGE SQUARE
BEAR LEFT UPHILL ON SCHOOL HILL PASSING THE ELEPHANT HOUSE ON YOUR LEFT
MOUNTAIN STREET
HIGH RED BRICK WALL ENCLOSING CHILHAM PARK
0 1/4 mile
0 APPROX SCALE 500 metres
TRAILBLAZER
CAR PARK
THROUGH GATE AND LEFT ONTO ROAD LEADING TO CHILHAM
GRAVEL LANE
53
51

Oast houses and hop gardens

© John Curtin

Oast houses are basically huge ovens used to dry hops, an ingredient in beer production. Now most have been converted into houses and often B&Bs. Usually consisting of four rooms, the oven and the store room downstairs, the drying room and the cooling room upstairs, when converted they make a spacious living area. The characteristic conical roof and pointed chimneys were designed to draw extra air through the kiln, increasing the amount of hops that could be dried in one go. Often oast houses were built near ponds – combining fire and wood is a risky business. We can see the remnants of a traditional Kent hop garden after Old Wives Lees (see Map 53) complete with a shelter belt of trees. The hop is a climbing plant and was traditionally grown on a system of poles and strings up to 20ft high. The female flower or cone is what gives beer a 'hoppy' bitter taste. At the height of the Kent hop industry up to 80,000 pickers would descend on the county for the September harvest but modern plants grow as 8ft hedges and now the crop is easily harvested by machine.

CHILHAM TO CANTERBURY [MAPS 52-55]

Leaving Chilham through the grounds of St Mary's the trail climbs gently to the curiously named **Old Wives Lees** at the start of this **7¼mile/11.5km** section through Kent's apple orchards. You can quench your thirst at the ***Star Inn*** (☎ 01227-730213; Mon-Fri 4-11pm, Sat 11am-midnight, Sun noon-10.30pm). Traversing a working orchard, you pass the entrance to ***The Barn Oast*** (☎ 01227-731255, 💻 www.thebarnoast.co.uk; 1T en suite/1D separate private bathroom) where B&B is £30 in this converted oast house (see Map 53 and box above), and continue climbing through woods and skirting orchards to arrive at Chartham Hatch. Next, the trail goes through No Man's Orchard (see p164 and Map 54) and through dense mixed woodland before crossing the A2 by a footbridge and emerging above Canterbury at Golden Hill, land managed by the National Trust (see Map 55).

CHARTHAM HATCH [MAP 54]

B&B at ***Wisteria Lodge*** (☎ 01227-738669; 1S/2D) is £24.50 for an en suite room and ***The Chapter Arms*** (☎ 01227-738340, 💻 www.chapterarms.com; food daily noon-2pm/7-9pm) next door is very welcoming. No smoking, except in the Pilgrim bar, it is more a restaurant with a bar attached, decorated with a collection of trumpet brasses. There's beef pudding made with suet (£7.50) at lunch or slow roast pork (£11.95) on the evening menu. On Sunday in summer clotted-cream teas are served (3-5pm) in the large flower-filled gardens.

(Opposite and overleaf) A highlight of this walk, **Canterbury Cathedral** (see p166) was founded in 597. After the murder of Archbishop Thomas à Becket in 1170 the cathedral became one of the most important pilgrimage centres in the medieval world. Following the Pilgrims' Way from London people came to make offerings at his tomb (see photo of stained glass window, **overleaf**), and the journey of one group and the stories they told became the subject of Chaucer's classic, *The Canterbury Tales*. The impressive Perpendicular nave (**overleaf, right**) was completed in 1405. (Photos © Bryn Thomas).

The Canterbury Tales

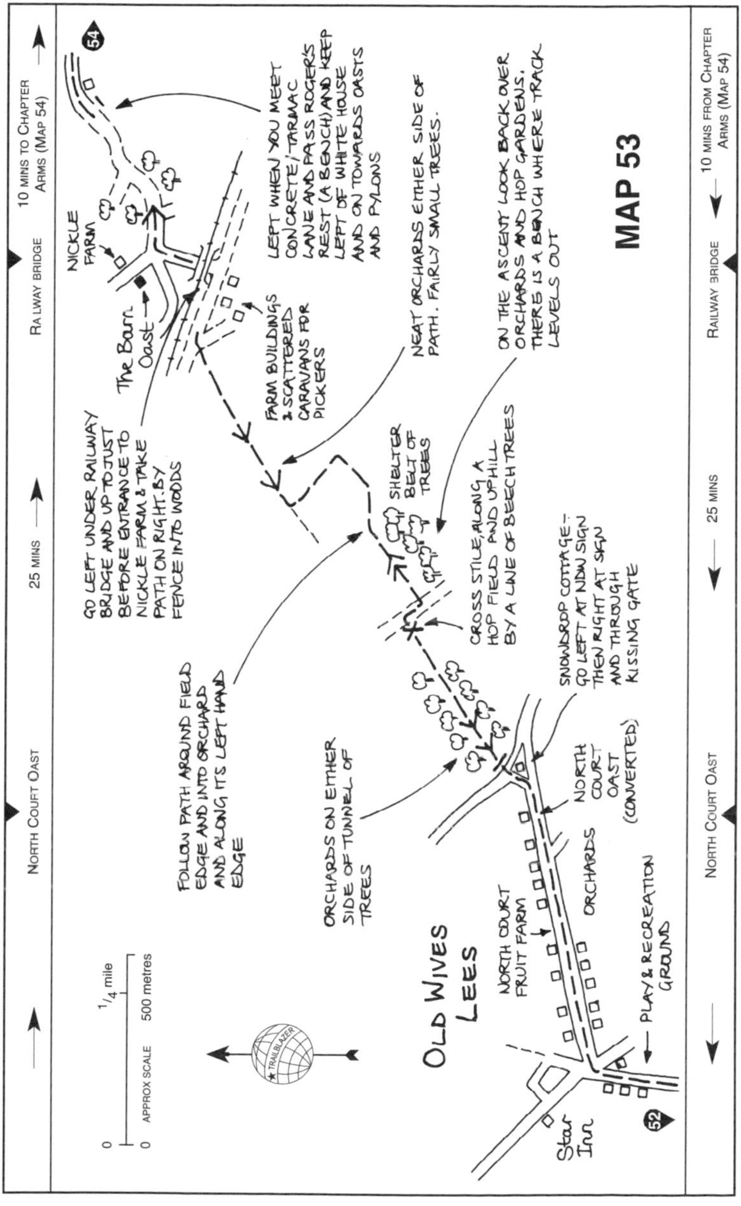
MAP 53
10 MINS TO CHAPTER ARMS (MAP 54)
RAILWAY BRIDGE
25 MINS
NORTH COURT OAST
10 MINS FROM CHAPTER ARMS (MAP 54)
APPROX SCALE
0 1/4 mile
0 500 metres
TRAILBLAZER
NICKLE FARM
The Barn Oast
LEFT WHEN YOU MEET CONCRETE/TARMAC LANE AND PASS ROGER'S REST (A BENCH) AND KEEP LEFT OF WHITE HOUSE AND ON TOWARDS OASTS AND PYLONS
FARM BUILDINGS & SCATTERED CARAVANS FOR PICKERS
NEAT ORCHARDS EITHER SIDE OF PATH. FAIRLY SMALL TREES.
ON THE ASCENT LOOK BACK OVER ORCHARDS AND HOP GARDENS. THERE IS A BENCH WHERE TRACK LEVELS OUT
GO LEFT UNDER RAILWAY BRIDGE AND UP TO JUST BEFORE ENTRANCE TO NICKLE FARM & TAKE PATH ON RIGHT. BY FENCE INTO WOODS
SHELTER BELT OF TREES
CROSS STILE, ALONG A HOP FIELD AND UPHILL BY A LINE OF BEECH TREES
FOLLOW PATH AROUND FIELD EDGE AND INTO ORCHARD AND ALONG ITS LEFT HAND EDGE
SNOWDROP COTTAGE - GO LEFT AT NDW SIGN THEN RIGHT AT SIGN AND THROUGH KISSING GATE
ORCHARDS ON EITHER SIDE OF TUNNEL OF TREES
NORTH COURT OAST (CONVERTED)
ORCHARDS
NORTH COURT FRUIT FARM
OLD WIVES LEES
PLAY & RECREATION GROUND
Star Inn
52
54

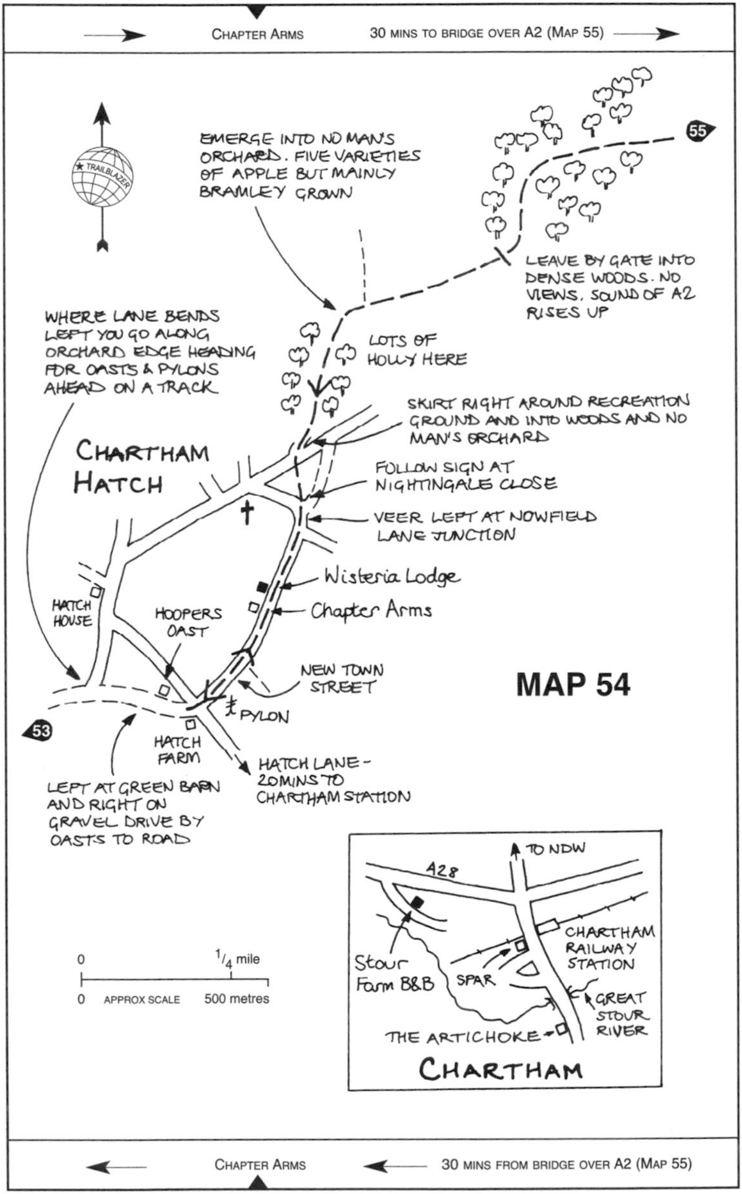

CHAPTER ARMS
30 MINS TO BRIDGE OVER A2 (MAP 55)
EMERGE INTO NO MAN'S ORCHARD. FIVE VARIETIES OF APPLE BUT MAINLY BRAMLEY GROWN
55
LEAVE BY GATE INTO DENSE WOODS. NO VIEWS, SOUND OF A2 RISES UP
WHERE LANE BENDS LEFT YOU GO ALONG ORCHARD EDGE HEADING FOR OASTS & PYLONS AHEAD ON A TRACK
LOTS OF HOLLY HERE
SKIRT RIGHT AROUND RECREATION GROUND AND INTO WOODS AND NO MAN'S ORCHARD
CHARTHAM HATCH
FOLLOW SIGN AT NIGHTINGALE CLOSE
VEER LEFT AT NOWFIELD LANE JUNCTION
Wisteria Lodge
Chapter Arms
HATCH HOUSE
HOOPERS OAST
NEW TOWN STREET
MAP 54
PYLON
53
HATCH FARM
HATCH LANE - 20MINS TO CHARTHAM STATION
LEFT AT GREEN BARN AND RIGHT ON GRAVEL DRIVE BY OASTS TO ROAD
0
1/4 mile
0
APPROX SCALE
500 metres
TO NDW
A28
Stour Farm B&B
SPAR
CHARTHAM RAILWAY STATION
GREAT STOUR RIVER
THE ARTICHOKE
CHARTHAM
CHAPTER ARMS
30 MINS FROM BRIDGE OVER A2 (MAP 55)

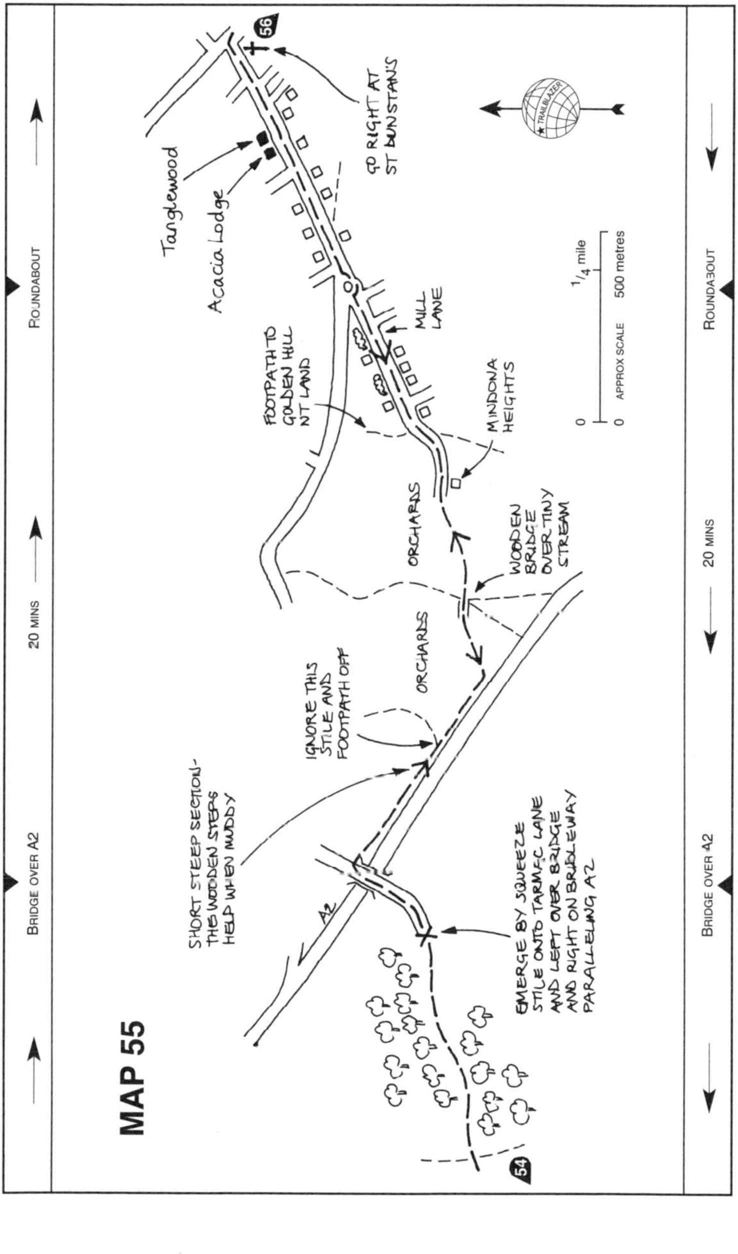
MAP 55
BRIDGE OVER A2
20 MINS
ROUNDABOUT
54
56
A2
EMERGE BY SQUEEZE STILE ONTO TARMAC LANE AND LEFT OVER BRIDGE AND RIGHT ON BRIDLEWAY PARALLELING A2
SHORT STEEP SECTION- THE WOODEN STEPS HELP WHEN MUDDY
IGNORE THIS STILE AND FOOTPATH OFF
ORCHARDS
WOODEN BRIDGE OVER TINY STREAM
ORCHARDS
FOOTPATH TO GOLDEN HILL NT LAND
MINDONA HEIGHTS
MILL LANE
Acacia Lodge
Tanglewood
GO RIGHT AT ST DUNSTAN'S
TRAILBLAZER
0
1/4 mile
0
APPROX SCALE
500 metres

❑ No Man's Orchard – a community orchard

This orchard (see Map 54) was planted in 1947 and purchased by Chartham and Harbledown parish councils becoming a community orchard in 1995. Orchards and fruit farms featured prominently in the landscape of Kent; with its mild climate and rich, deep soils the county came to be known as the garden of England. But experts reckon that 90% of its orchards have been lost in the last 50 years. No Man's Orchard is a traditional orchard planted with tall stemmed, large trees in contrast to modern dwarf varieties which are easier to harvest mechanically. The orchard is managed to attract birds with trees left to set blossom and windfall fruit left on the ground to attract wildlife.

CHARTHAM [MAP 54]

It is a 20-minute walk along Hatch Lane to the **train station** at Chartham. The station has services to London Charing Cross, Ashford International and Canterbury East (all daily, 2/hr). Stagecoach's **bus** No 652 operates to Canterbury from opposite the railway station; see the public transport map and table, pp37-40.

There is a **Spar** (daily 6am-9pm) convenience store with a bakery and deli counter. It does cashback; there is no charge on purchases over £5.

The ***Artichoke*** (☎ 01227-738316; food daily noon-2pm, Fri & Sat 7-9pm), just beyond the paper mill, is a fabulous timber-framed pub. B&B is available at ***Stour Farm*** (☎ 01227-731977, 🖳 www.stourfarm.co.uk; 1T/2D all en suite), with lovely views over the River Stour. Rates are £32.50 (£55 single occupancy) for the twin studio which has a kitchen and dining area but may be let for weekly self-catering. The rates for the double rooms are £27.50 (£45 single occupancy).

CANTERBURY [MAP 56]

Canterbury, home of the Mother Church for Anglicans, shrine of the martyr St Thomas à Becket and the destination of Chaucer's bawdy pilgrims, is worth at least a full day's visit and makes an ideal stop-over before the final leg to Dover. As one of England's top visitor attractions the demand for rooms is always high so it's best to book ahead.

The centre is car-free with a **medieval street pattern** surrounded by a ring road.

Services

There are two **train stations**: Canterbury East has services to London Victoria and Dover; Canterbury West has services to London Bridge and London Charing Cross (Mon-Sat up to 3/hr, Sun 1/hr).

The **bus station** is on St Georges Lane; Stagecoach's bus Nos 16/16A (daily, hourly) depart for Folkestone and the No 652 to Ashford via Chartham and Chilham. Jaycrest operate a service (No 335, Sun only) to Maidstone. **National Express** operates coach services to London Victoria Coach Station and Dover; see the public transport map and table, pp37-40.

The **tourist information centre** (TIC; ☎ 01227-378100, 🖳 www.canterbury.co.uk; Mon-Sat 9.30am-5.30pm and Sun 10am-4pm) is on Sun St opposite the cathedral. They have a currency exchange service for US dollars and euros. **Internet access** (£3/30 mins) is available at Debenhams Café Venue, the Buttermarket, just by the TIC. There are several banks with **cash machines** on the High St clustered near the corner of St Margaret's St and a **post office** (Mon-Sat 9am-5.30pm, Tue 9.15am-5.30pm).

There are three **outdoor shops**: Field & Trek (☎ 01227-470023; Mon-Sat 9am-5.30pm, Thur to 8pm, Sat to 6pm, Sun 10am-4pm), 3 Palace St; Blacks (☎ 01227-764385; Mon-Sat 9am-5.30pm, Sun 10am-4pm), 44 Burgate St; and Millets (☎ 01227-479698; Mon-Sat 9am-5.30pm, Sun 10am-

❑ The Pilgrims' Way

On 29 December 1170, Archbishop Thomas à Becket was murdered in Canterbury Cathedral by four knights, their swords scattering his brains on the floor. The spot where he was killed went on to become a shrine drawing thousands of pilgrims following Becket's swift elevation by the Pope to sainthood in 1173 and for the remainder of the Middle Ages it was one of the most popular and wealthiest of shrines.

It's doubtful that there was ever only one route by which pilgrims came to venerate at the cathedral and it was only after 1860 that the name Pilgrims' Way appeared on Ordnance Survey maps. The pilgrimages reached their height of popularity towards the end of the 14th century, at a time when Geoffrey Chaucer wrote *Canterbury Tales*. The North Downs Way coincides with the so-called Pilgrims' Way for much of its length in Kent. At Detling (Map 40 p143) the way is also marked by the traditional symbol of pilgrimage, the scallop shell, and behind the Tudor gate is thought to have been a pilgrim hospital or shelter for medieval pilgrims on their journey to Canterbury.

4pm) at No 47. Boots **chemist** (Mon-Sat 9.30am-5.30pm, Sun 10am-4pm) is on the Parade further up the High St and Morrison's **supermarket** at St Georges Centre opens Mon-Fri 8am-9pm, Sat 8am-8pm, Sun 11am-5pm.

Kingsmead Leisure Centre has a 32m indoor **swimming pool**; a swim costs £2.10.

Where to stay

Budget travellers have several choices. To the east of the city is ***Canterbury Youth Hostel*** (☎ 0870-7705744, 🖳 www.yha.org.uk; 69 dorm beds), 54 New Dover Rd, charging £17.50 including breakfast for members and popular with groups. Reception is open 7-10am/3-11pm. Walking here you pass ***Let's Stay*** (☎ 01227-463628), another hostel, with separate quarters for men and women of eight beds tightly squeezed in two rooms at £14. Convenient to Canterbury East station is ***Kipps Hostel*** (☎ 01227-786121, 🖳 www.kipps-hostel.com; 45 dorm beds), 40 Nunnery Fields, run by the young and enthusiastic Tony Oakey. Beds are £14 per person; there's a good atmosphere, a clean, well-equipped kitchen, a small shop and internet access for £1/half-hour. There's also a community noticeboard with essential travellers' intelligence like where to buy the cheapest pint and the latest clubs to open. There are three camping pitches (summer only) at Kipps; £7 per person.

Campers will find 200 pitches at ***St Martin's Camping and Caravanning Club*** (☎ 01227-463216) with a backpacker rate of £5.85 non member, £4.55 member. It's close to the North Downs Way as it leaves the city.

Arriving in the city the trail passes numerous B&Bs on London Rd, which is convenient for Canterbury West station. Two that stand out are: ***Acacia Lodge*** (☎ 01227-769955; 2D/1T en suite), 39 London Rd, and ***Tanglewood*** (☎ 01227-769955; 2D/ 1T), 30 London Rd. Both are under the same ownership and immaculately kept; the charge is £38sgl/£25dbl.

Part of ***Castle House*** (☎ 01227-761897; 1T/1D/1F), 28 Castle St, formed the medieval city walls, now near the busy Wincheap roundabout. Large en suite rooms are £60sgl/35dbl/32fml. And there's good value at the modest ***St John's Court Guest House*** (☎ 01227-456425; 1S/2T/4D/2F), St John's Lane, charging £25sgl/20dbl or twin/24 fml.

The Cathedral Gate Hotel (☎ 01227-464381, 🖳 www.cathgate.co.uk; 6S/7T/9D/5F) next to the Cathedral has a real medieval feel to it with sloping floors, low doorways and the hustle and bustle from the street below. Continental breakfast is included in the rates of £60sgl/45dbl/twin/ £30fml, all en suite. Rooms with

❑ The North Downs Way route through Canterbury

The path enters the city by Westgate and then bears left on to the pedestrianized High St. Turn left on Mercery Lane towards the cathedral and the TIC, then turn right. Walk past the cathedral and cross over Bridge St and keep straight on till you can turn right onto Monastery St then left along Burgate and on to Longport St, passing by the ruins of St Augustine's Abbey. Turn left at the roundabout onto the A257 (the direction marked is Littlebourne). Walk up the road and then turn right on Spring Lane past the sign to St Martin's and turn right onto Pilgrims' Way, opposite Hadlow College. Follow the North Downs Way marker post and pass the playing fields. Turn right over the railway bridge and on your right you will see a very well-kept and large allotment site. The way narrows at the end of the residential area and continues bordered by hedges to Barton Business Park.

shared bathrooms are £35sgl/30dbl/twin.

The former County Hotel has now been transformed into a luxurious designer hotel, ***Abode Canterbury*** (☎ 01227-766 266, 💻 www.abodehotels.co.uk), 30 High St. Rooms cost from £125 for a double and are classed Comfortable, Desirable, Envious and Fabulous. There's a champagne bar and 'an unrivalled range of Michael Caines dining and drinking experiences'.

Where to eat

Ferns Café & Restaurant (☎ 01227-781885; Mon-Fri 9.30am-4pm, Sat 9.30am-5pm & Sun 11am-4pm), above the TIC, has window seats with an unbeatable view of the cathedral. Toasted-cheese sandwiches are £2.95, flans £6.95, and a beautifully presented cream tea for two with a tower of sandwiches is £12.

All fish are cooked from fresh at ***No 7 The Borough*** (Mon-Fri 10am-10pm, Sat 10am-9.30pm) where you can also get a 'call the ambulance side order' of deep-fried Mars bar for 70p. Decent pub grub and a quiet pint can be had at the ***Thomas Becket*** (☎ 01227-464384; Mon-Fri noon-3pm, Mon-Thu 5-9pm, Fri 5-9.30pm, Sat noon-9.30pm, Sun noon-9pm), on Best Lane. For à la carte dining in a pub setting try ***The Dolphin*** (☎ 01227-455963; Mon-Fri noon-3pm, Sat 11am-10pm, Sun noon-10pm) where mozzarella-and-basil-stuffed chicken is £12.50. A three-course Sunday roast is £9.95 and afterwards you can while away the hours playing a variety of board games; ask at the bar.

Fans of the subcontinent will appreciate ***Kashmir*** (☎ 01227-462050; daily noon-2.30pm/6-10pm), on Palace St, where the ubiquitous chicken tikka masala is £6.95.

If you like fresh quality produce the chances are you'll want to eat at ***The Goods Shed*** (☎ 01227-459153; Tue-Sat 8-10.30am/noon-2.30pm, Sat to 3pm/6-9.30pm, Sun 9-10.30am, noon-3pm). England's first full-time farmers' market restaurant is housed in a revamped Victorian engine shed with high oak-beamed ceilings and huge windows. Bringing the kitchen to the market, the menu constantly changes using the produce available on the day so you can get the likes of pan-fried skate (£11.50) and pumpkin risotto (£8.50).

For modern Anglo-French cuisine ***Augustine's*** (☎ 01227-453063; Tue-Sat noon-1.30pm/6.30-9pm), Monastery St, close to the World Heritage site, St Augustine's Abbey (see p168), is not for those on a tight budget. New Romney lamb with rosemary mash is £15.90; expect to pay £25 a head without wine for two courses.

What to do and see

Canterbury Cathedral (☎ 01227-762862, 💻 www.canterbury-cathedral.org; admission £6, Mon-Fri 9am-6pm, Sat 9am-2.30pm summer, Mon-Sat 9am-4pm winter, Sun 12.30-2.30pm & August only 4.30-5.30pm) was founded in AD597 by St Augustine, a Catholic and the cathedral's first archbishop. It's now the seat of the Mother Church of the Anglican Communion or to give it its formal title The Cathedral

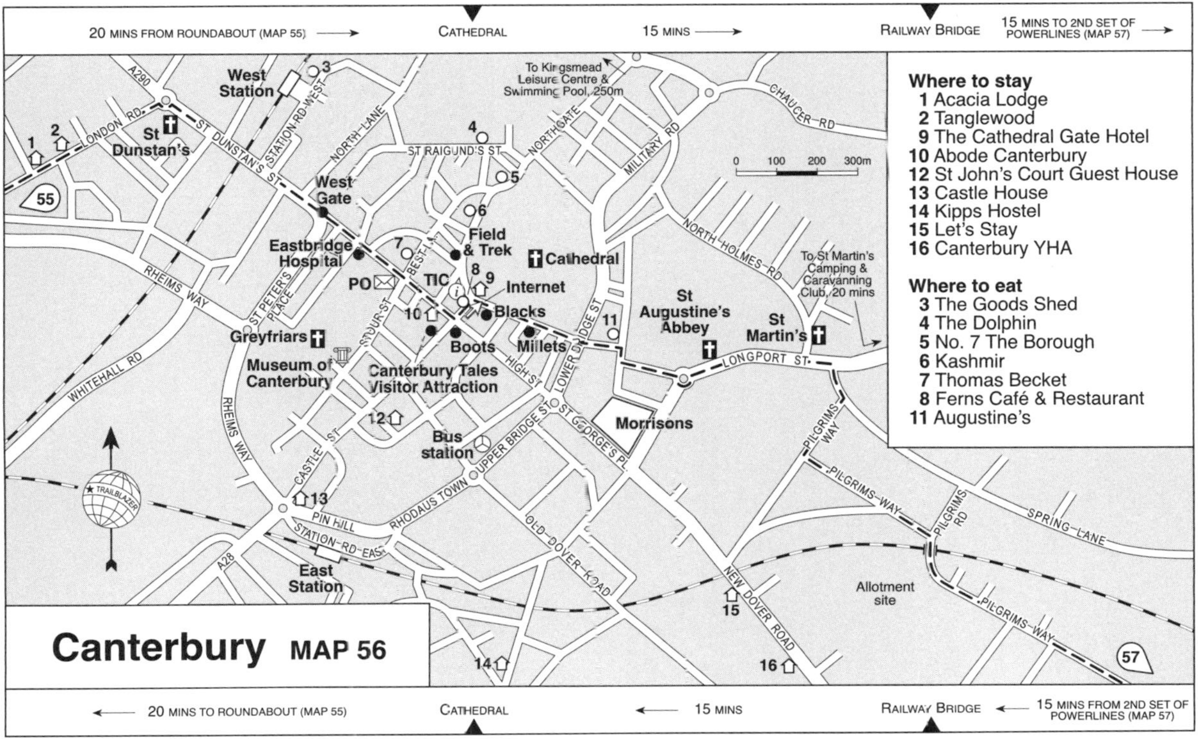
20 MINS FROM ROUNDABOUT (MAP 55) →
CATHEDRAL
15 MINS →
RAILWAY BRIDGE
15 MINS TO 2ND SET OF POWERLINES (MAP 57) →
Where to stay
1 Acacia Lodge
2 Tanglewood
9 The Cathedral Gate Hotel
10 Abode Canterbury
12 St John's Court Guest House
13 Castle House
14 Kipps Hostel
15 Let's Stay
16 Canterbury YHA
Where to eat
3 The Goods Shed
4 The Dolphin
5 No. 7 The Borough
6 Kashmir
7 Thomas Becket
8 Ferns Café & Restaurant
11 Augustine's
West Station
St Dunstan's
West Gate
Eastbridge Hospital
Greyfriars
Museum of Canterbury
PO
TIC
Field & Trek
Cathedral
Internet
Blacks
Boots
Millets
Canterbury Tales Visitor Attraction
Bus station
East Station
Morrisons
St Augustine's Abbey
St Martin's
To Kingsmead Leisure Centre & Swimming Pool, 250m
To St Martin's Camping & Caravanning Club, 20 mins
Allotment site
0 100 200 300m
A290
LONDON RD
ST DUNSTAN'S ST
STATION-RD-WEST
NORTH LANE
ST RAIGUND'S ST
NORTHGATE
MILITARY RD
CHAUCER RD
NORTH HOLMES RD
LONGPORT ST
LOWER BRIDGE ST
HIGH ST
BEST LA
STOUR ST
ST PETER'S PLACE
RHEIMS WAY
WHITEHALL RD
CASTLE ST
PIN HILL
STATION RD EAST
A28
RHODAUS TOWN
UPPER BRIDGE ST
ST GEORGE'S PL
OLD DOVER ROAD
NEW DOVER ROAD
PILGRIMS WAY
PILGRIMS RD
SPRING LANE
55
57
TRAILBLAZER
Canterbury MAP 56
← 20 MINS TO ROUNDABOUT (MAP 55)
CATHEDRAL
← 15 MINS
RAILWAY BRIDGE
← 15 MINS FROM 2ND SET OF POWERLINES (MAP 57)

and Metropolitical Church of Christ at Canterbury. On 29 December 1170 four knights burst through Canterbury Cathedral's doors and murdered the then Archbishop, Thomas à Becket (see box p165). He had been appointed by Henry II to bring the Church under the influence of the monarchy but set about defending its rights and paid the price. The spot where he was killed went on to become a shrine drawing thousands of pilgrims. The cathedral, the ruins of St Augustine's Abbey (see below) and St Martin's church (see below) make up the city's **UNESCO World Heritage** site. The cathedral has a wonderful Romanesque crypt, 12th-century quire and stained glass and of course the site and shrine of St Thomas à Becket's martyrdom. The best way to appreciate all that is there is to take a guided tour (£3.50) lasting about an hour. Tickets are available from the Welcome Centre on the day; tours leave Mon-Sat 10.30am, 12noon and 2.30pm (summer, 1.30pm on Sat) and 12 noon and 2pm (winter); there are no tours on Sunday.

English Heritage (EH) manages the ruins of **St Augustine's Abbey** (☎ 01227-767345; daily summer 10am-6pm, Wed-Sun winter 10am-4pm, £3.90, free to EH members); founded in AD598, it was thoroughly smashed by Henry VIII on the dissolution of the monasteries. There's a good audio tour. Off Longport lies England's oldest parish church, **St Martin's** (☎ 01227-768072; Tue, Thu & Sat 11am-4pm). **Greyfriars** (☎ 01227-471688; Mon-Sat 2-4pm summer, admission free), off Stour St, the first Franciscan church in England, was founded in 1267 and is so named for the colour of the monks' habits.

Today the private areas of **Eastbridge Hospital** (☎ 01227-471688; Mon-Sat 10am-5pm, £1), on St Peter's St, provide warden-assisted accommodation for Canterbury elderly. Originally a hospital for pilgrims, the Chantry chapel, the Pilgrims' Chapel and the medieval undercroft are fascinating.

For tales of medieval misadventure and humour the **Canterbury Tales Visitor Attraction** (☎ 01227-479227; daily 10am-5pm) brings to life Chaucer's larger than life characters with animated exhibits but it's the most expensive of the lot at £7.25.

The 1000-year-old **St Dunstan's Church** (☎ 01227-463654, open daily) is the first church passed on the way into Canterbury before the West Gate. Reputedly the head of Sir Thomas More lies in a lead vault in this church. More, a Catholic and Lord Chancellor of England refused to swear an oath of supremacy recognizing Henry VIII as head of the church in England. In 1535 on the orders of Henry he was charged with treason and beheaded.

Canterbury Walks (☎ 01227-459779; 💻 www.canterbury-walks.co.uk) offer daily walking tours lasting 90 minutes, Easter to October, departing from the Tourist Information Centre at 2pm and additionally daily at 11.30am July-Sep. The cost is £4.25/3.75/3 adult/concessions/child (family ticket £12.50).

CANTERBURY TO SHEPHERDSWELL [MAPS 56-62]

After leaving Canterbury along Pilgrims' Way you spend a long time crossing very large arable fields on this **10¼ mile/16.4km** stage and there is almost a prairie-like feel to it but for the A2 in the distance.

In case you've a sudden urge to get to London, Canterbury or Dover there is a **train station** at **Bekesbourne** (see Map 57) pronounced 'Beaksborn', which is about 15 minutes north-east of Patrixbourne. ***The Unicorn*** (☎ 01227-830210; food noon-1.45pm/7-9pm Wed-Sat, Sun noon-1.45pm, closed Sun evening, Mon & Tue) is good for a consoling pint if you've missed the train.

After passing St Mary's church in **Patrixbourne** (see Map 57) the road ahead leads to Bridge.

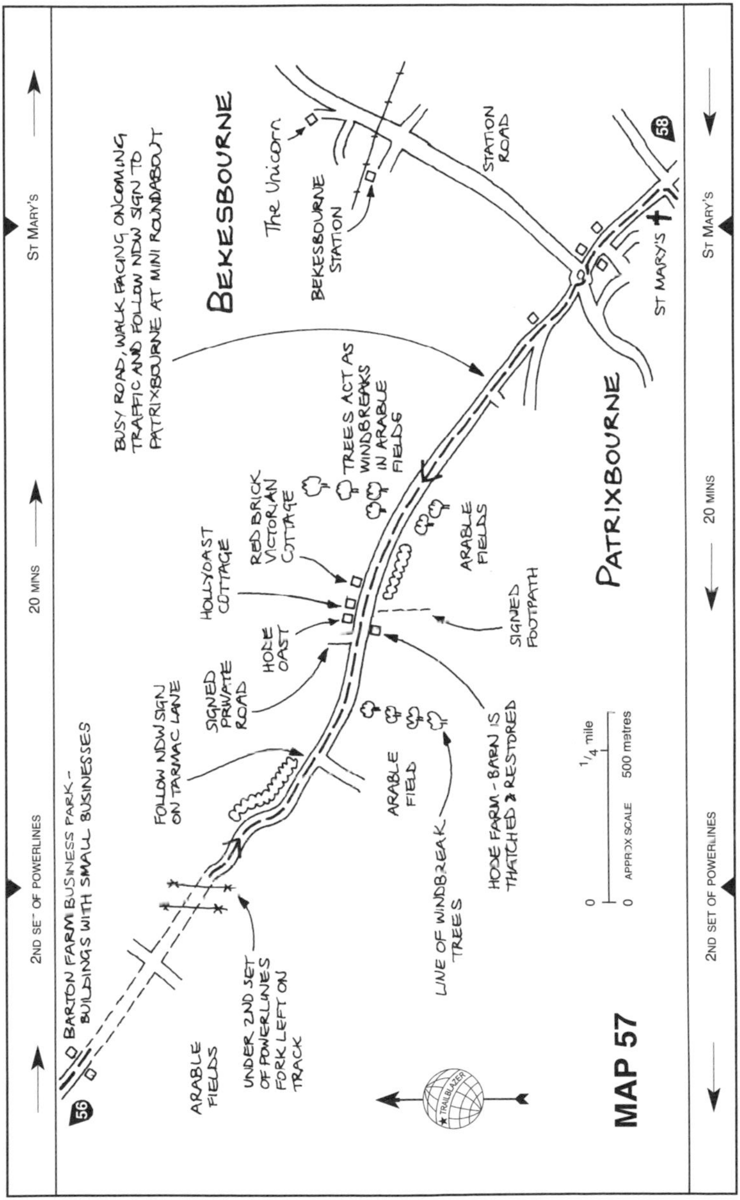
MAP 57
TRAILBLAZER
56
58
2ND SET OF POWERLINES
20 MINS
ST MARY'S
BARTON FARM BUSINESS PARK - BUILDINGS WITH SMALL BUSINESSES
ARABLE FIELDS
UNDER 2ND SET OF POWERLINES FORK LEFT ON TRACK
FOLLOW NDW SIGN ON TARMAC LANE
LINE OF WINDBREAK TREES
ARABLE FIELD
SIGNED PRIVATE ROAD
HODE OAST
HODE FARM - BARN IS THATCHED & RESTORED
HOLLYOAST COTTAGE
RED BRICK VICTORIAN COTTAGE
SIGNED FOOTPATH
ARABLE FIELDS
TREES ACT AS WINDBREAKS IN ARABLE FIELDS
BUSY ROAD, WALK FACING ONCOMING TRAFFIC AND FOLLOW NDW SIGN TO PATRIXBOURNE AT MINI ROUNDABOUT
BEKESBOURNE
The Unicorn
BEKESBOURNE STATION
STATION ROAD
ST MARY'S
PATRIXBOURNE
0 1/4 mile
0 500 metres
APPROX SCALE

BRIDGE [MAP 58]

Bridge has a **post office** (Mon-Fri 9am-5.30pm, Sat to 12.30pm), a **chemist** (Mon-Fri 9am-6pm, closed 1-2pm, Sat 9am-noon), a **bakery** (Mon-Fri 7.30am-4pm, Sat to 2pm) and a **Londis** (Mon-Sat 7am-8pm, Sun 8am-6pm) convenience store with an outdoor **cash machine**.

Stagecoach **bus** No 16A (Canterbury to Folkestone) stops by the White Horse on Sundays and Bank holidays; see the public transport map and table pp37-40.

There are fine rooms at ***Renville Oast*** (☎ 01227-830215; 1D/1T/1F) where B&B is £35 with two en suite rooms and one with private bath. But it's a good 15-minute walk uphill north of the post office and off the A2 slip road.

The ***White Horse Inn*** (☎ 01227-832814; food daily noon-2pm, Wed-Sat 6.30-9pm) proudly lists all its local and organic suppliers on its menu. A half-dozen Whitstable oysters is £6.75 and a fricassée of diced pear, parsnip and squash is £12.50. Simpler bar food is available; roast chicken is £7.75.

The landlady at the ***Plough & Harrow*** (Mon-Fri 11am-3pm, Sat 11am-11pm, Sun noon-10pm) doesn't mind you bringing your own sandwiches to have with a pint and dogs are welcome as well.

Across the road, at ***Skipper's*** (☎ 01227-830788, 🖳 www.skippersrestaurant.co.uk), a four-course supper will set you back £29.95 before you've even hit the bottle.

The ***Red Lion*** also does pub grub but was closed at the time of writing.

After Bridge you have to wait until Shepherdswell for easy access to refreshment, food and accommodation.

The path passes the entrance to **Higham Park and Gardens** (see box below and Map 58).

It's then over huge arable fields arriving at the quaint village of **Womenswold** (Map 60) and on to **Woolage Village** (Map 60), built for colliery workers on the Kent coalfields, after which the trail climbs through a tunnel of trees and hedgerow to drop along a country lane and farm track arriving in Shepherdswell.

(cont'd on p176)

❑ Chitty Chitty Bang Bang

The fine Palladian house at **Higham Park and Gardens** (see Map 58) is glimpsed from the North Downs Way and visitors come for the Italianate gardens designed by Harold Peto. But it was here in the 1920s that Polish count and dashing racing-car driver Louis Zborowski built three racing cars powered by aero engines and all called Chitty Chitty Bang Bang.

Inspired by the count and his cars, Ian Fleming wrote the children's story *Chitty Chitty Bang Bang* in 1964 and Roland Emett, sculptor and cartoonist, worked up the model of the car in the 1968 movie of the same name adapted from Roald Dahl's screenplay. One of the count's cars is displayed at the National Motor Museum, Beaulieu, Hampshire.

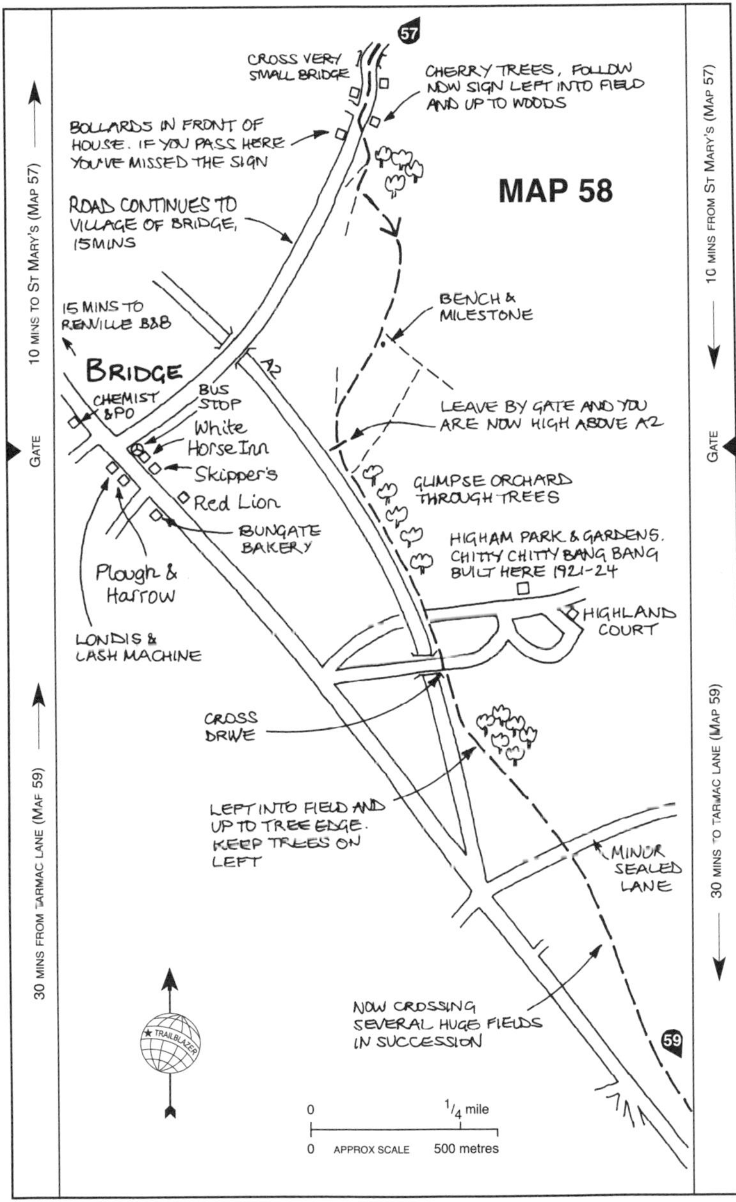
MAP 58
57
CROSS VERY SMALL BRIDGE
CHERRY TREES, FOLLOW NOW SIGN LEFT INTO FIELD AND UP TO WOODS
BOLLARDS IN FRONT OF HOUSE. IF YOU PASS HERE YOU'VE MISSED THE SIGN
ROAD CONTINUES TO VILLAGE OF BRIDGE, 15MINS
15 MINS TO RENVILLE B&B
BRIDGE
A2
BENCH & MILESTONE
CHEMIST &PO
BUS STOP
White Horse Inn
Skipper's
Red Lion
BUNGATE BAKERY
Plough & Harrow
LONDIS & CASH MACHINE
LEAVE BY GATE AND YOU ARE NOW HIGH ABOVE A2
GLIMPSE ORCHARD THROUGH TREES
HIGHAM PARK & GARDENS. CHITTY CHITTY BANG BANG BUILT HERE 1921-24
HIGHLAND COURT
CROSS DRIVE
LEFT INTO FIELD AND UP TO TREE EDGE. KEEP TREES ON LEFT
MINOR SEALED LANE
NOW CROSSING SEVERAL HUGE FIELDS IN SUCCESSION
59
TRAILBLAZER
0 1/4 mile
0 APPROX SCALE 500 metres
10 MINS TO ST MARY'S (MAP 57)
GATE
30 MINS FROM TARMAC LANE (MAP 59)
10 MINS FROM ST MARY'S (MAP 57)
GATE
30 MINS TO TARMAC LANE (MAP 59)

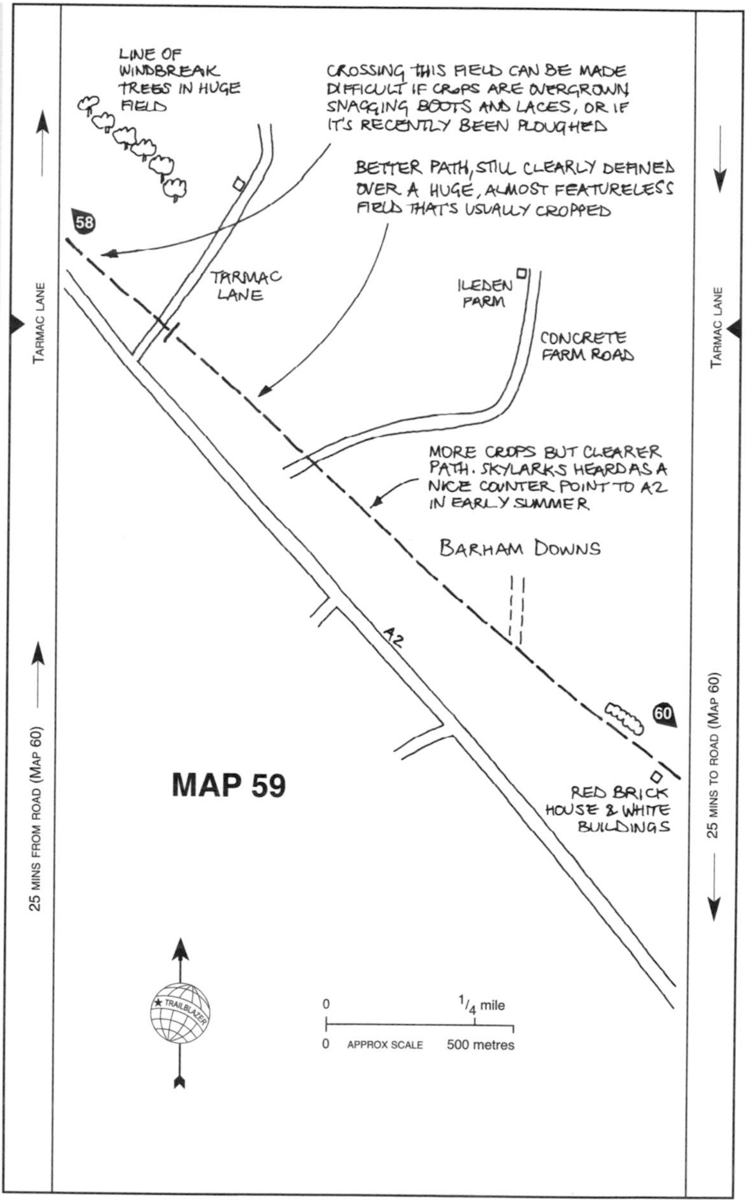
LINE OF WINDBREAK TREES IN HUGE FIELD
CROSSING THIS FIELD CAN BE MADE DIFFICULT IF CROPS ARE OVERGROWN SNAGGING BOOTS AND LACES, OR IF IT'S RECENTLY BEEN PLOUGHED
BETTER PATH, STILL CLEARLY DEFINED OVER A HUGE, ALMOST FEATURELESS FIELD THAT'S USUALLY CROPPED
58
TARMAC LANE
ILEDEN FARM
CONCRETE FARM ROAD
TARMAC LANE
TARMAC LANE
MORE CROPS BUT CLEARER PATH. SKYLARKS HEARD AS A NICE COUNTER POINT TO A2 IN EARLY SUMMER
BARHAM DOWNS
A2
60
RED BRICK HOUSE & WHITE BUILDINGS
25 MINS FROM ROAD (MAP 60)
25 MINS TO ROAD (MAP 60)
MAP 59
TRAILBLAZER
0
1/4 mile
0
APPROX SCALE
500 metres

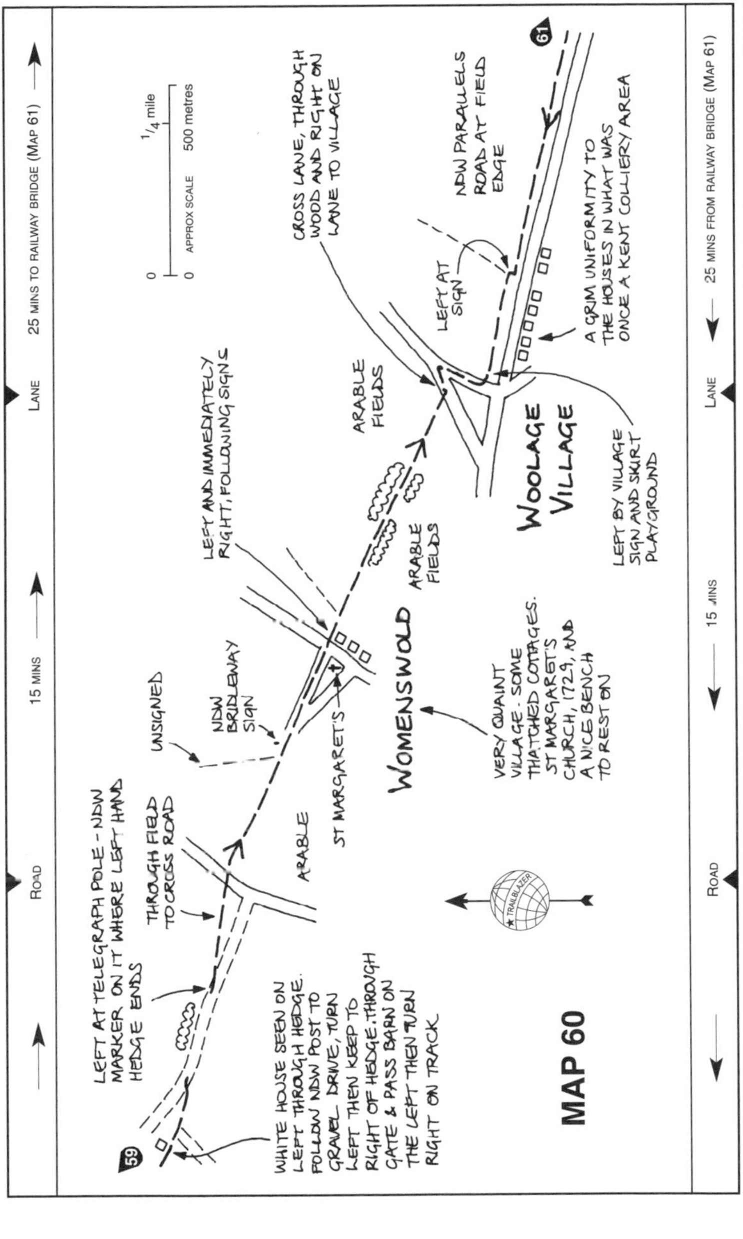
MAP 60
25 MINS TO RAILWAY BRIDGE (MAP 61)
ROAD
15 MINS
LANE
25 MINS FROM RAILWAY BRIDGE (MAP 61)
APPROX SCALE
0 1/4 mile
0 500 metres
59
61
WHITE HOUSE SEEN ON LEFT THROUGH HEDGE. FOLLOW NDW POST TO GRAVEL DRIVE, TURN LEFT THEN KEEP TO RIGHT OF HEDGE. THROUGH GATE & PASS BARN ON THE LEFT THEN TURN RIGHT ON TRACK
LEFT AT TELEGRAPH POLE - NDW MARKER ON IT WHERE LEFT HAND HEDGE ENDS
THROUGH FIELD TO CROSS ROAD
ARABLE
UNSIGNED
NDW BRIDLEWAY SIGN
ST MARGARET'S
WOMENSWOLD
VERY QUAINT VILLAGE. SOME THATCHED COTTAGES. ST MARGARET'S CHURCH, 1729, AND A NICE BENCH TO REST ON
LEFT AND IMMEDIATELY RIGHT, FOLLOWING SIGNS
ARABLE FIELDS
ARABLE FIELDS
WOOLAGE VILLAGE
LEFT BY VILLAGE SIGN AND SKIRT PLAYGROUND
CROSS LANE, THROUGH WOOD AND RIGHT ON LANE TO VILLAGE
LEFT AT SIGN
NDW PARALLELS ROAD AT FIELD EDGE
A GRIM UNIFORMITY TO THE HOUSES IN WHAT WAS ONCE A KENT COLLIERY AREA

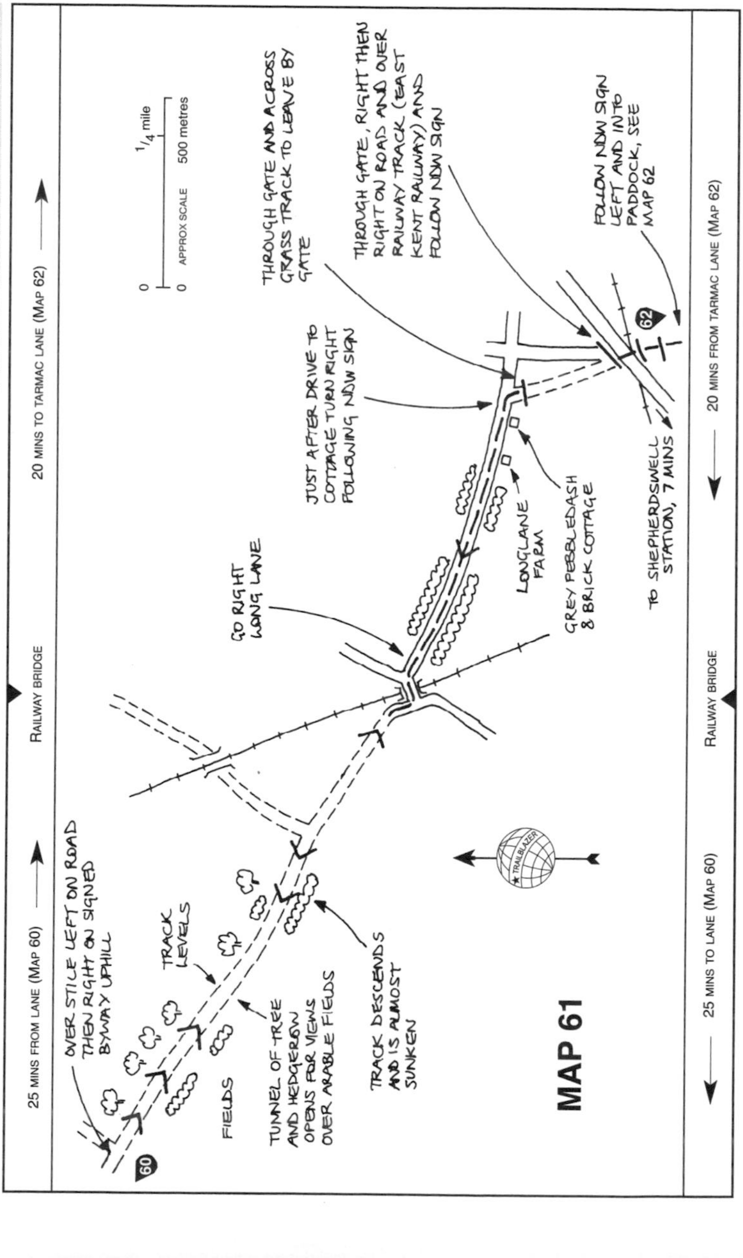
MAP 61
25 MINS FROM LANE (MAP 60)
20 MINS TO TARMAC LANE (MAP 62)
RAILWAY BRIDGE
APPROX SCALE
0
1/4 mile
0
500 metres
60
OVER STILE LEFT ON ROAD THEN RIGHT ON SIGNED BYWAY UPHILL
TRACK LEVELS
FIELDS
TUNNEL OF TREE AND HEDGEROW OPENS FOR VIEWS OVER ARABLE FIELDS
TRACK DESCENDS AND IS ALMOST SUNKEN
GO RIGHT LONG LANE
LONGLANE FARM
GREY PEBBLEDASH & BRICK COTTAGE
JUST AFTER DRIVE TO COTTAGE TURN RIGHT FOLLOWING NDW SIGN
THROUGH GATE AND ACROSS GRASS TRACK TO LEAVE BY GATE
THROUGH GATE, RIGHT THEN RIGHT ON ROAD AND OVER RAILWAY TRACK (EAST KENT RAILWAY) AND FOLLOW NDW SIGN
FOLLOW NDW SIGN LEFT AND INTO PADDOCK, SEE MAP 62
62
TO SHEPHERDSWELL STATION, 7 MINS
TRAILBLAZER
25 MINS TO LANE (MAP 60)
RAILWAY BRIDGE
20 MINS FROM TARMAC LANE (MAP 62)

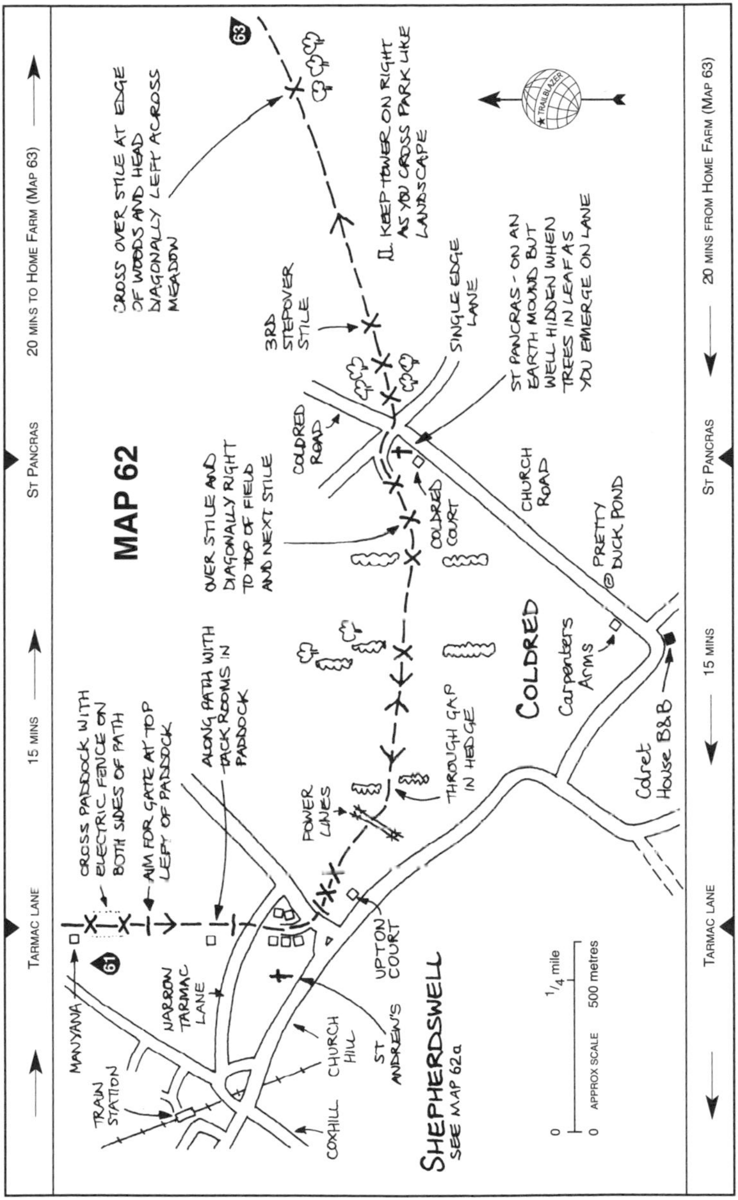
MAP 62
Tarmac Lane
15 mins
St Pancras
20 mins to Home Farm (Map 63)
20 mins from Home Farm (Map 63)
CROSS OVER STILE AT EDGE OF WOODS AND HEAD DIAGONALLY LEFT ACROSS MEADOW
KEEP TOWER ON RIGHT AS YOU CROSS PARK LIKE LANDSCAPE
3RD STEPOVER STILE
SINGLE EDGE LANE
ST PANCRAS - ON AN EARTH MOUND BUT WELL HIDDEN WHEN TREES IN LEAF AS YOU EMERGE ON LANE
COLDRED ROAD
CHURCH ROAD
COLDRED COURT
OVER STILE AND DIAGONALLY RIGHT TO TOP OF FIELD AND NEXT STILE
PRETTY DUCK POND
COLDRED
Carpenters Arms
Colret House B&B
THROUGH GAP IN HEDGE
ALONG PATH WITH TACK ROOMS IN PADDOCK
CROSS PADDOCK WITH ELECTRIC FENCE ON BOTH SIDES OF PATH
AIM FOR GATE AT TOP LEFT OF PADDOCK
POWER LINES
UPTON COURT
MANYANA
NARROW TARMAC LANE
TRAIN STATION
COXHILL
CHURCH HILL
ST ANDREW'S
SHEPHERDSWELL SEE MAP 62a
APPROX SCALE
1/4 mile
500 metres
TRAILBLAZER

SHEPHERDSWELL [MAP 62a]

This compact village has a **train station** with services to London Victoria (Mon-Fri, hourly) via Dover Priory and to London Charing Cross (Sat and Sun), the Dover Priory service is daily, hourly and takes ten minutes. Stagecoach **bus** No 93 (Mon-Sat 3-5/day) leaves from the station for Dover; see the public transport map and table, pp37-40.

The **Co-op** (Mon-Fri 7am-9pm, Sat/Sun 8am-9pm) has snacks and food for meals on the go and there is a **cash machine**. There is also a **post office** and **grocery store** (Mon-Fri 9am-5.30pm, closed for lunch 1-2pm, Thu 9am-1pm, Sat 9am-12.30pm).

Sunshine Cottage (☎ 01304-831359, 💻 www.sunshine-cottage.co.uk; 5D/1T) is a pretty 17th-century cottage near the church charging £30-45sgl and £30dbl. Two rooms have private bathrooms. For an evening meal the owners will drive walkers to the Lydden Bell, at Lydden (also run by the owners of The Dolphin, Canterbury, see p166) or The Crown, at Eythorne pronounced 'a thorne'. ***Oast Cottage*** (☎ 01304-831532, 💻 www.oastcottage.com; 1D/2T) does B&B for £30 in comfortable beamed rooms all en suite.

Of the two pubs ***The Bell*** (☎ 01304-830374; food daily noon-2.15pm, Thu-Sun 6.30-8.15pm) has seen better days and ***The Bricklayers Arms*** (☎ 01304-830323; food Mon-Fri 9am-7pm) is a Shepherd Neame house.

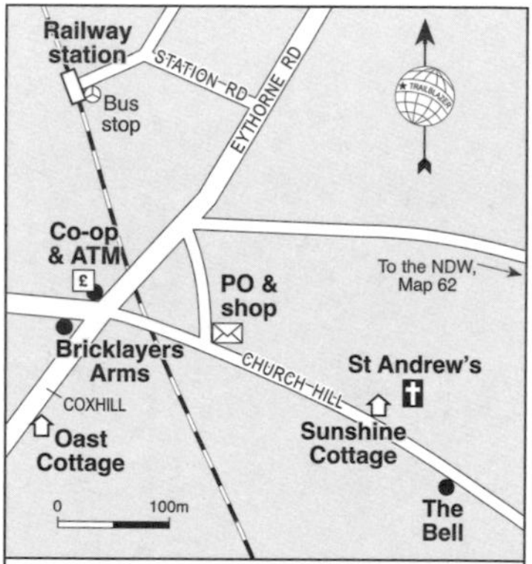

Shepherdswell MAP 62a

SHEPHERDSWELL TO DOVER [MAPS 62-66]

This last **8¾mile/14km** section is easy walking through park landscape and pockets of woodland with no villages en route until, before you know it, the trail descends the Roman road into Dover.

After Shepherdswell the trail weaves its way through undulating fields to **Coldred** where it's easy to miss the church of St Pancras. Stagecoach **bus** No 93 stops here en route between Shepherdswell and Dover.

Colret House B&B (☎ 01304-830388, 💻 www.colrethouse.co.uk; 2D en suite) is an elegant Edwardian house down Church Rd with accommodation (£30 per person) in a separate annex. They have plenty of drying room and will drive walkers to a local pub for an evening meal as the ***Carpenters Arms*** (Mon-Sat 11am-3pm/6-11pm, Sun noon-2pm/6-10pm) across the village green – complete with 'slow ducks crossing sign' – is a true local pub, drinks only no food, but worth a quick look at least.

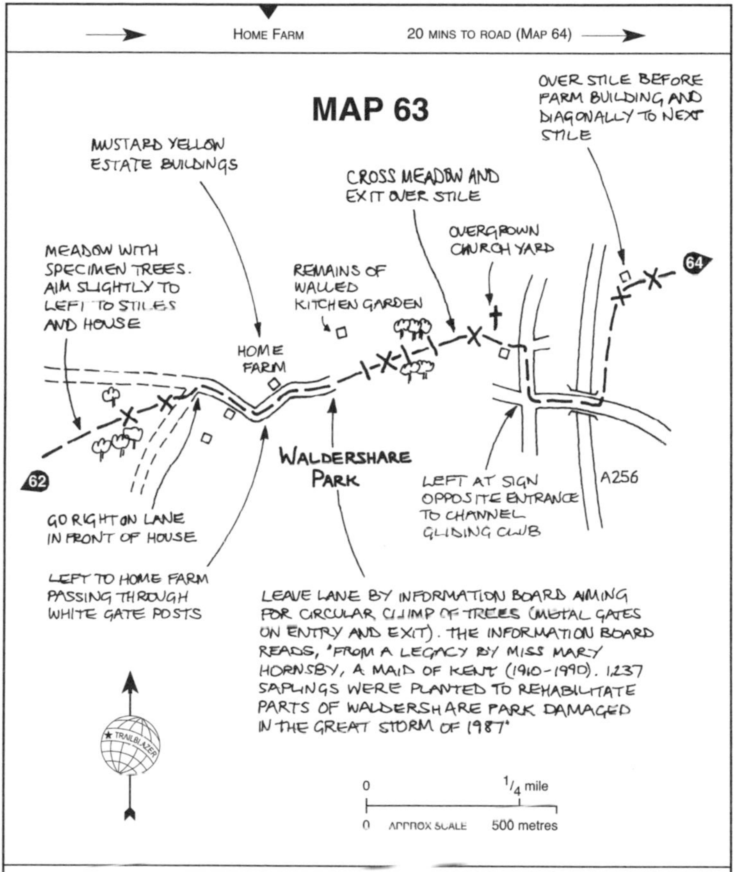
HOME FARM
20 MINS TO ROAD (MAP 64)
MAP 63
OVER STILE BEFORE FARM BUILDING AND DIAGONALLY TO NEXT STILE
MUSTARD YELLOW ESTATE BUILDINGS
CROSS MEADOW AND EXIT OVER STILE
OVERGROWN CHURCH YARD
MEADOW WITH SPECIMEN TREES. AIM SLIGHTLY TO LEFT TO STILES AND HOUSE
REMAINS OF WALLED KITCHEN GARDEN
64
HOME FARM
62
WALDERSHARE PARK
A256
LEFT AT SIGN OPPOSITE ENTRANCE TO CHANNEL GLIDING CLUB
GO RIGHT ON LANE IN FRONT OF HOUSE
LEFT TO HOME FARM PASSING THROUGH WHITE GATE POSTS
LEAVE LANE BY INFORMATION BOARD AIMING FOR CIRCULAR CLUMP OF TREES (METAL GATES ON ENTRY AND EXIT). THE INFORMATION BOARD READS, 'FROM A LEGACY BY MISS MARY HORNSBY, A MAID OF KENT (1910-1990). 1,237 SAPLINGS WERE PLANTED TO REHABILITATE PARTS OF WALDERSHARE PARK DAMAGED IN THE GREAT STORM OF 1987'
TRAILBLAZER
0
1/4 mile
0 APPROX SCALE 500 metres
HOME FARM
20 MINS FROM ROAD (MAP 64)

Stagecoach **bus** No 94 stops at **Waldershare Park** (Map 63) Mon-Sat only.

From Waldershare Park the trail climbs through Ashley (Map 64) to rise again to the A2 beyond Pineham (Map 65). A short detour ensures a safe crossing of the A2 to start shortly a descent along the Roman road to Dover and the satisfaction of having reached the end of the North Downs Way.

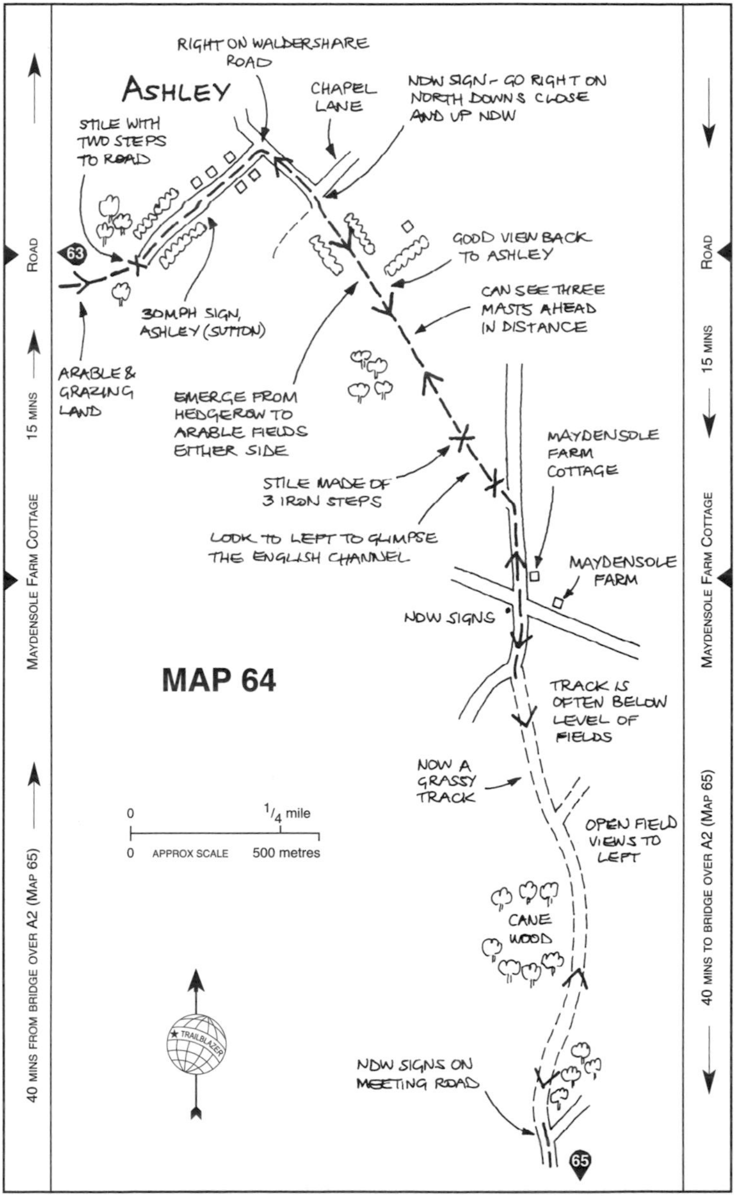

ASHLEY
RIGHT ON WALDERSHARE ROAD
CHAPEL LANE
NDW SIGN – GO RIGHT ON NORTH DOWNS CLOSE AND UP NDW
STILE WITH TWO STEPS TO ROAD
GOOD VIEW BACK TO ASHLEY
CAN SEE THREE MASTS AHEAD IN DISTANCE
30MPH SIGN, ASHLEY (SUTTON)
ARABLE & GRAZING LAND
EMERGE FROM HEDGEROW TO ARABLE FIELDS EITHER SIDE
MAYDENSOLE FARM COTTAGE
STILE MADE OF 3 IRON STEPS
LOOK TO LEFT TO GLIMPSE THE ENGLISH CHANNEL
MAYDENSOLE FARM
NDW SIGNS
MAP 64
TRACK IS OFTEN BELOW LEVEL OF FIELDS
NOW A GRASSY TRACK
0 1/4 mile
0 APPROX SCALE 500 metres
OPEN FIELD VIEWS TO LEFT
CANE WOOD
TRAILBLAZER
NDW SIGNS ON MEETING ROAD
63
65
ROAD
15 MINS
MAYDENSOLE FARM COTTAGE
40 MINS FROM BRIDGE OVER A2 (MAP 65)
40 MINS TO BRIDGE OVER A2 (MAP 65)

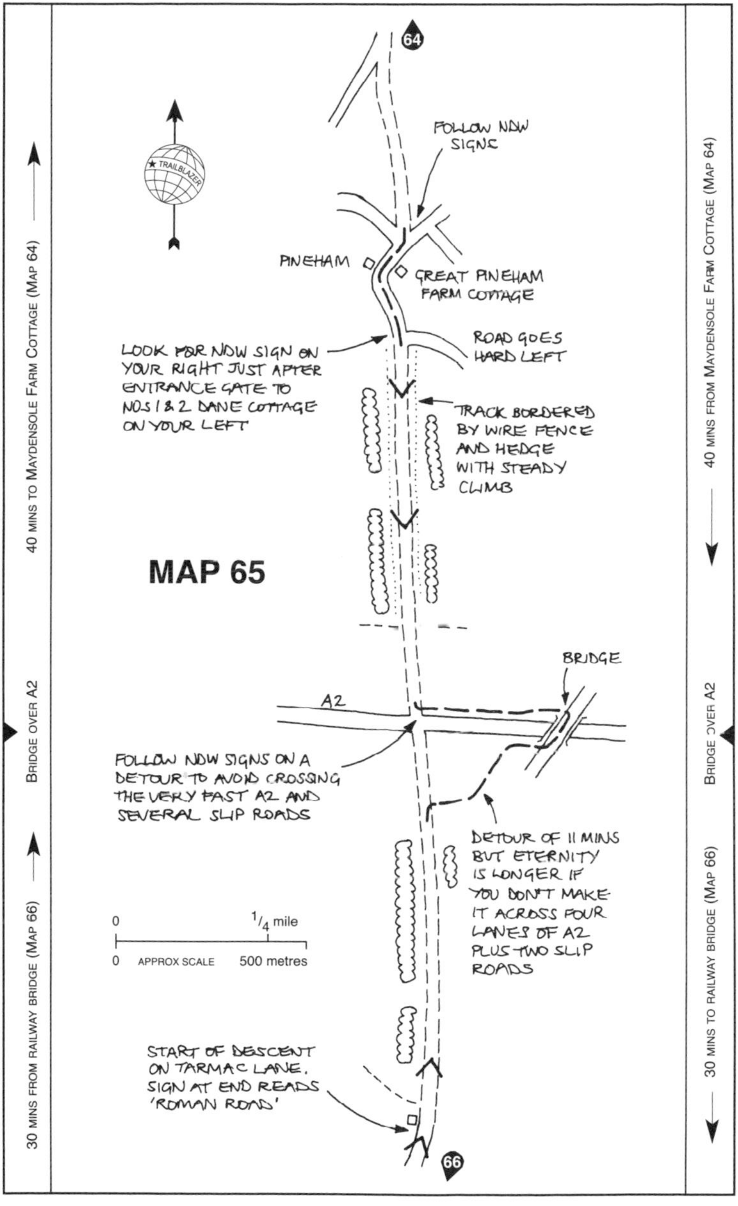
40 MINS TO MAYDENSOLE FARM COTTAGE (MAP 64)
40 MINS FROM MAYDENSOLE FARM COTTAGE (MAP 64)
BRIDGE OVER A2
BRIDGE OVER A2
30 MINS FROM RAILWAY BRIDGE (MAP 66)
30 MINS TO RAILWAY BRIDGE (MAP 66)
64
TRAILBLAZER
FOLLOW NDW SIGNS
PINEHAM
GREAT PINEHAM FARM COTTAGE
LOOK FOR NDW SIGN ON YOUR RIGHT JUST AFTER ENTRANCE GATE TO NOS 1 & 2 DANE COTTAGE ON YOUR LEFT
ROAD GOES HARD LEFT
TRACK BORDERED BY WIRE FENCE AND HEDGE WITH STEADY CLIMB
MAP 65
BRIDGE
A2
FOLLOW NDW SIGNS ON A DETOUR TO AVOID CROSSING THE VERY FAST A2 AND SEVERAL SLIP ROADS
DETOUR OF 11 MINS BUT ETERNITY IS LONGER IF YOU DON'T MAKE IT ACROSS FOUR LANES OF A2 PLUS TWO SLIP ROADS
0
1/4 mile
0
APPROX SCALE
500 metres
START OF DESCENT ON TARMAC LANE. SIGN AT END READS 'ROMAN ROAD'
66

DOVER [MAP 66]

Dover struggles as a destination. People pass through on the way to the Continent or use it as a gateway to somewhere else in England. As with any busy port town it has its fair share of life's flotsam and jetsam and after the cultural high point of Canterbury it's a disappointment. There's an impressive **castle**, a **museum**, a fine **Roman house** and a view of the **White Cliffs** from the Hoverport pier but little else to keep you longer than it takes to make for the train, bus or boat home.

Services

The **tourist information centre** (☎ 01304-205108, 💻 www.whitecliffscountry.org.uk; Mon-Fri 9am-5.30pm, Sat/Sun 10am-4pm, closed Sun Oct-Mar) is on Biggin St. The **chemist** Superdrug (Mon-Sat 8.30am-5.30pm, Sun 10am-4pm) is on Cannon St, above Market Sq, and there are two banks (Barclays and Lloyds TSB) with **cash machines** on Market Sq conveniently located at the end of the walk. **Internet access** at 21 High St (Mon-Thu 8.30am-10pm, Fri & Sat 8.30am-11pm, Sun 9am-10pm) costs £1.50 a half-hour and **free** internet access is available at **Dover Library** (☎ 01304-204241; Mon, Tue & Thur 9.30am-6pm, Wed, Fri & Sat 9.30am-5pm) on Market Sq. There is a **post office** (Mon-Sat 9.30am-5.30pm) on Pencester Rd as well as Alldays **supermarket** (Mon-Sat 8am-10pm, Sun 8.30am-10pm) and a Marks & Spencer (Mon-Thur 9.30am-5.30pm, Fri & Sat 8.30am-5.30pm) on Biggin St.

Trains from Dover Priory depart for London Victoria (Mon-Fri 2-3/hr, Sat 2/hr) and to London Charing Cross (Sun 2/hr) via Ashford International; services to Ashford International depart up to twice hourly (one via Canterbury) daily. National Express coaches to Canterbury and London (10/day) leave from Pencester Rd **bus station**. Stagecoach bus No 93 serves Coldred and Shepherdswell (Mon-Sat 3-5/day) and bus No 94 goes hourly (Mon-Sat only) to Waldershare Park; see also the public transport map and table, pp37-40.

Where to stay

Campers will find the closest pitch is three miles away at ***Hawthorn Farm*** (☎ 01304-852658; open Mar-Nov), Martin Mill, off the A258. It's best to take the train to Martin Mill station (eight minutes). Walkers pay £11.50 per person.

Dover Youth Hostel (☎ 0870-7705798, 💻 www.yha.org.uk; 120 beds), 306 London Rd, is open year-round and costs £17.50 inc breakfast. At the time of writing this was scheduled to relocate in September 2007 so check in advance.

On the trail coming into Dover on Park Avenue are several well-established B&Bs. ***Peverell House*** (☎ 01304-202573, 💻 www.peverellhouse.co.uk; 7D/3 en suite) is the first you come to. B&B at this large Victorian house is £26 en suite, £22 shared bathroom. Further down is ***Blériots*** (☎ 01304-211394, 💻 www.bleriots.net; 1S/3D/2T/2F all en suite) another Victorian property on this tree-lined road charging £27.

Turning left into Maison Dieu Rd there is ***Maison Dieu Guesthouse*** (☎ 01304-204033; 3S/1T/3F). All rooms except two of the singles are en suite and they charge £42sgl/21dbl/17fml plus £4 for breakfast.

St Albans (☎ 01304-206308, 💻 www.accommodation-dover.co.uk; 2S/4D/1T/1F all en suite) is closest to the train station and non-smoking. Rates are £45sgl/£27.50dbl or twin/25fml. Continental breakfast is included. Also close to the station is ***Mildmay Hotel*** (☎ 01304-204278, 💻 www.mildmayhoteldover.com; 1S/5T/12D/3F all en suite); rates, including a full English breakfast, are £60sgl/40dbl/26fml and the staff are friendly. The top-end hotel with a sea view is ***The Churchill*** (☎ 01304-203633, 💻 www.bw-churchillhotel.co.uk; 81 en suite rooms); rooms at this Best Western hotel cost from £45 plus £9 for buffet-style breakfast. Out on East Cliff on the sea front below the Castle is ***Loddington House Hotel*** (☎ 01304-201947; 6T) which is really an upmarket B&B charging from £37.50 per person. ***Blakes*** (☎ 01304-202194, 4D en suite), on Castle St, charges £22.50 per person plus

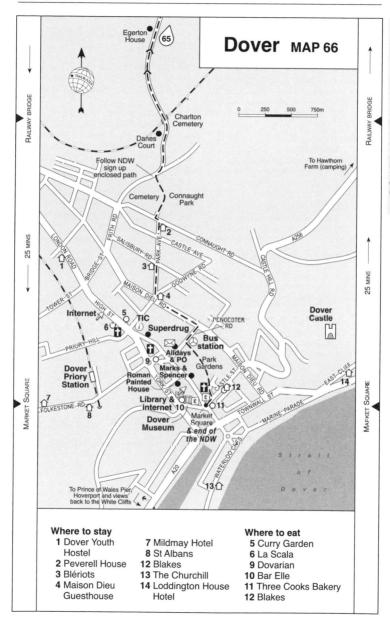

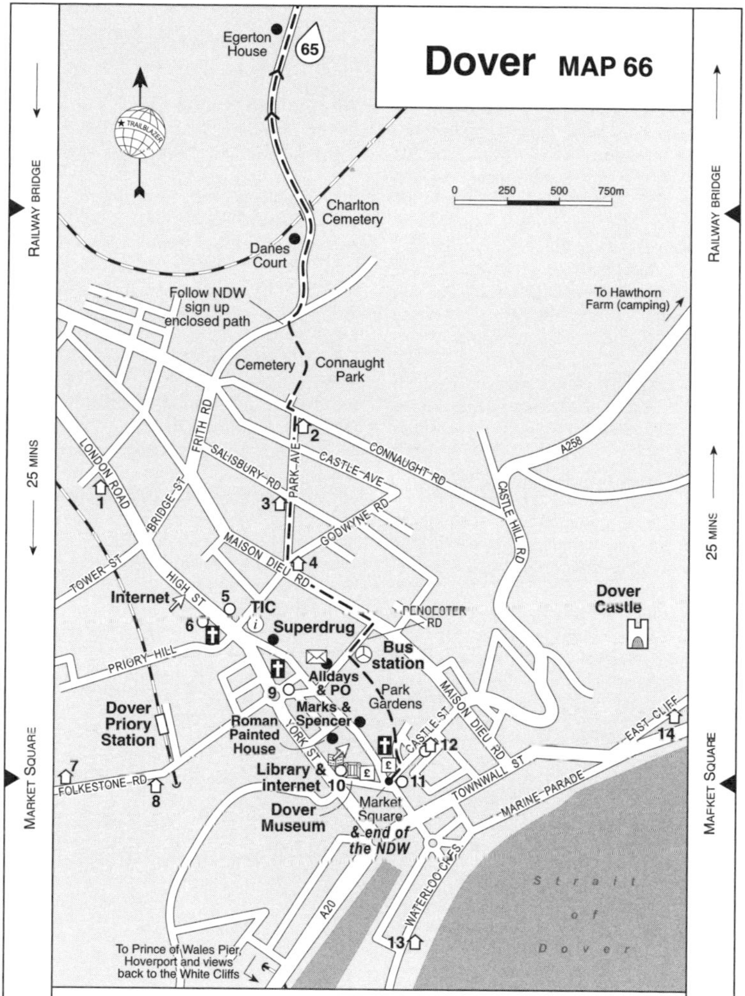

Where to stay
1 Dover Youth Hostel
2 Peverell House
3 Blériots
4 Maison Dieu Guesthouse
7 Mildmay Hotel
8 St Albans
12 Blakes
13 The Churchill
14 Loddington House Hotel

Where to eat
5 Curry Garden
6 La Scala
9 Dovarian
10 Bar Elle
11 Three Cooks Bakery
12 Blakes

£5.95 for breakfast. The climb to some rooms is vertiginous.

Where to eat

Dover is not a culinary magnet. But for simple no frills cafeteria-style food try the spotless ***Dovarian*** (Mon-Fri 9am-6pm, Sat 9am-5.30pm) on Worthington St. The Formica-topped tables fill up fast at lunch time when the blue-rinse brigade descend for large portions of chicken pie, peas and chips (£3.30). Plaice and chips is £3.50.

The ***Curry Garden*** (☎ 01304-206357; daily noon-3pm/6pm-12.30am), on High St, dishes out the standard repertoire of curries from £5.50 and ***La Scala*** (☎ 01304-208044; Mon-Sat noon-2pm/6-10.30pm) is a friendly Italian restaurant where a large tuna salad is £8.95 and bowls of pasta start at £5.95.

Bar Elle (☎ 01304-215685; food served daily 11am-2.30pm) has an outdoor seating area in summer, overlooking Market Sq, where you can sip a latte and munch on a pastry or knock back a beer to celebrate the end of the walk. Inside, the blaring music doesn't encourage you to linger. ***Three Cooks Bakery*** (Mon-Sat 8am-5pm), Market Sq, is the place for a celebration cake before heading home. And if it's a glass of wine you're after try ***Blakes*** (see p180) which serves food (Mon-Sat noon-2pm/6-9pm, Sun noon-2pm only) and has good beer and a cellar bar.

What to see and do

Dover Museum (☎ 01304-201066; Mon-Sat 10am-5.30pm, Sun 10am-5pm Apr-Sep, £2.20), on Market Square, has extensive exhibits on the town's history since 1066. **Dover Castle** (☎ 01304-211067; winter daily 10am-4pm, summer 10am-6pm, £8.95) 'guardian of the gateway to England' is strategically placed on the White Cliffs of Dover. It's a prime site for English Heritage and the tours of the secret tunnels used in the Napoleonic Wars and WWII are fascinating. **The Roman Painted House** (☎ 01304-203279; Apr-Sept, Tue-Sat 10am-5pm, Sun 2-5pm and Mon in Jul, Aug and Bank Holidays, £2) was discovered in 1970 and reckoned to be one of the best-preserved Roman buildings in England largely because it was buried to make way for a new building in AD270. Over 400 sq metres of painted plaster survive.

Finally, a good view of the **White Cliffs of Dover** is free from the Prince of Wales pier by the Hoverport.

APPENDIX: ALTERNATIVE ROUTE

Boughton Lees to Dover via Folkestone

The North Downs Way divides at Boughton Lees (see p152). We recommend taking the northern route as described on pp152-79, through Canterbury, across Kent orchard and hop country and on to Dover.

The alternative route to Dover via Folkestone is shorter and has escarpment views over the White Cliffs on the final day but it is bounded by the busy A20 and the Channel Tunnel marshalling yards and lacks the cultural riches that Canterbury offers.

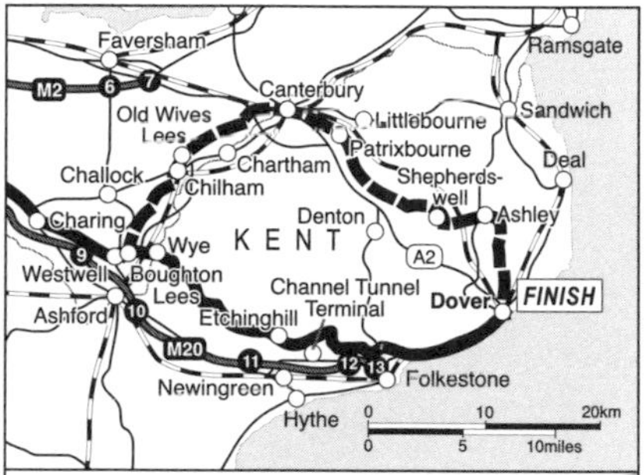

NORTH DOWNS WAY ALTERNATIVE ROUTE
Boughton Lees to Dover via Folkestone

BOUGHTON LEES – WYE – ETCHINGHILL

This **13 mile stage** passes through the pleasant town of **Wye**, famous for its agricultural college. There is a **farmers' market** (see p15) on the 1st and 3rd Saturday of each month, 9am-12noon, on The Green.

A useful source of pub, hotel and B&B **accommodation** in a variety of price brackets can be found at 💻 www.wye.org.

There are convenient **train services** from Wye to Canterbury, Ashford International and London and **bus services** to Canterbury and Ashford.

Shortly after leaving Wye the NDW enters a National Nature Reserve at **Wye Downs**. This rolling downland is habitat to cowslips, violets and many orchids as well as more common species such as ox-eye daisy.

ETCHINGHILL – FOLKESTONE – CAPEL-LE-FERNE – DOVER

With **12 miles** to go on the final stage there are good escarpment views over the sea and the Channel on a clear day.

The route skirts **Folkestone** above the motorway and the Channel Tunnel terminal. Descending to the town you will find a helpful **TIC** at Harbour St (☎ 01303-258594; 💻 www.discoverfolkestone.co.uk) and a useful accommodation booking service. Alternatively, 💻 www.thisisfolkestone.co.uk has a comprehensive listing.

Folkestone is the focus of cargo ferry services to the Continent and cars and vehicles are carried by train via the Channel Tunnel. Passenger services use Eurostar (p34) which stops only in Ashford, further up the line. Train services operate from Folkestone Central and Folkestone West, which may require changing at Dover, to London, Dover Priory and Canterbury. There are bus services to Ashford International, Canterbury and Dover.

After regaining the downland ridge beyond Folkestone, the route to Dover via **Capel-Le-Ferne** takes you by the cliff edge path with sea views, entering **Dover** (see pp180-2) through Western Heights. The trail ends at Market Square.

INDEX

Page references in bold type refer to maps

access rights 55
accommodation 11-14, 63, 65
see also place name
advance bookings 13
air services 34
Albury 82, **84**
Albury Downs 82, **85**
Albury Park 84
allotments 124
annual events 21
Areas of Outstanding Natural Beauty (AONBs) 42
Ashley 177, **178**
autumn 20
Aylesford 138, **138**, 140
Aylesford Friary 137

B&Bs 12-13, 19
B&B itinerary 25
Backpackers' Club 33
backpacks 28
Becket, Thomas à 165, 168
Bekesbourne 168, **169**
Betchworth 98
bibliography 32-3
birds 46-7
books on 33
blisters 61
Blue Bell Hill 138, **139**
bookings 13
boots 28-9
Borough Green 124
Borstal 137
Botley Hill 109, 111
Boughton Aluph 153, **156**
Boughton Lees 152, **155**
Box Hill **93**, 96, 98
Box Hill Village **97**, 98
Bridge 170, **171**
British Summer Time (BST) 17
budgeting 18-19
bunkhouses 11, 19
bunkhouse/hostel itinerary 26
Bunyan, John 76, 78
buses 34, 37-40
business hours 17
butterflies 48, 98

campaigning organizations 43-4
camping 11, 19
camping barns 11
camping gear 31
camping itinerary 25
camping supplies 14
Canterbury 164-6, **167**, 168
Capel-Le-Ferne 184
castles
Dover 182
Farnham 68
Guildford 81
Rochester 136
Thurnham 142
cathedrals
Canterbury 166, 168
Guildford 81
Rochester 136
Chalk Pit Lane 111
Charing 148, **151**, 152
Chartham **162**, 164
Chartham Hatch 160, **162**
Chartwell 111
Chevening House 115, **117**
Chilham 158, 159
Chilworth 82, **83**
Chitty Chitty Bang Bang 170
Christie, Agatha 86
churches
St Augustine's Abbey, Canterbury **167**, 168
St Barnabas 82, **91**
St Dunstan's, Canterbury **167**, 168
St James, Shere 86, **86**, 88
St Martin's, Canterbury **167**, 168
St Mary's 111, **112**
St Mary's, Eastwell (ruins) 152, **155**
St Martha's 82, **83**
St Mary the Virgin, Kemsing **121**, 122
St Mary the Virgin, Shalford 76, **76**
St Nicholas, Compton 72, **75**
Saxon Old Church, Albury Park 84
Watts Chapel, Compton 74, **75**
Church Hill 111, **112**
Churchill, Sir Winston 111
clothing 29-30
coaches 35-6
Cobbett, William 65
Coldred **175**, 176

Coldrum Stones 128
Colley Hill 96, 98, **99**
Compton 68, 72, 74, **75**
conservation 41-4
conservation organizations 43-4
Countryside Code 55-6
currency 17
Cuxton 128, **131**, **132**, 134

day walks 27
Denbies Wine Estate 92, **93**, 94
Detling 140, **143**, 165
Dickens, Charles 134, 135, 136
direction of walk 24
disabled access 18
Disabled Ramblers 18
dogs 18, 56
Domesday Book 82, 84
Dorking 82, **93**, 94-6, **95**
Dover 9, 177, 180, **181**, 182
drinks 14-15
drinking water 14
driving 34, 36
Dunton Green 115, 118
duration of walk 10

Eastwell 152, **155**
emergency services 17
equipment 26-31
erosion 58
Etchinghill 183
Europe: travelling from 34
European Health Insurance Card (EHIC) 17

Farnham 9, 27, 65-8, **67**, **69**
ferries 34
fires 60
first-aid kit 30-1
fish 45
flora and fauna 45-54
  guides 33
Folkestone 183-4
food 14-15
  see also place name
footwear 28-9

Godmersham Park **157**, 158
Godstone Vineyards **107**, 108
Gomshall 88
government agencies and schemes 41
Greenwich Meridian Line **109**, 111
Guildford 78-81, **79**

Harrietsham 146
heat exhaustion 61-2
heatstroke 62
Higham Park 170, **171**
history of route 9
Hollingbourne 142, **145**, 146
Holmbury St Mary 88, 90
hop gardens 160
hostels 11, 19
hostels/bunkhouse itinerary 26
hotels 14
hyperthermia 61-2
hypothermia 62

inns 13
insects 49
itineraries 24-6

Juniper Hill 96, 98, **99**

Kemsing 120, **121**, 122
Kent Downs AONB 42
Kentish Men 134
Kit's Coty 138, **139**
Knockholt 115, **116**
Knockholt Pound 115

Lenham 146, 148, **148**, **149**
litter 58
Littleton 74, **77**
local economy 57
local food and drink 15
local transport 36-40, 58
Long Distance Walkers' Association 33
Lutyens, Sir Edwin 88

Malthus, Thomas 92
mammals 45
map keys 64
maps 32
markets
  Dorking 96
  Farnham 68
  Guildford 81
  Redhill 100
Mears, Ray 51
Medway Bridge **132**, 134
Medway burial tombs 138
Merstham 103, **104**

minimum impact walking 55-7
money 16, 17, 32
More, Sir Thomas 168
Mullins, William 96
museums
  Dorking 96
  Dover 182
  Farnham 68
  Rochester 136
  Shere 86

national holidays 17
Natural England 41, 43
Newlands Corner 82, 84, **85**
No Man's Orchard **162**, 164

oast houses 160
Old Wives Lees 160, **161**
Olivier, Sir Lawrence 96
Otford 118, **118**, **119**, 120
outdoor safety 60-2
Oxted 108-11, **110**
Oxted Downs 108, **109**

Patrixbourne 168, **169**
Pearsall, Phyllis 124
personal safety 62
Peto, Harold 170
Pilgrims' Way 9, 128, 138, 146, 152, 165, 166, 168
Pilgrims Holt 98, **101**
Pineham 177, **179**
public transport 37-40, 58
pubs 13
Pugin, A.W. 82, 84
Puttenham 68, 72, **73**
Puttenham Heath 72

Quarry Hangers Nature Reserve 103, **105**
Quebec House 111, 114

rainfall 21
Ramblers' Association 33
Ranmore Common 82, **91**, 92
rates of exchange 17
Redhill 100-3, **102**
Reigate Fort 100, **101**
Reigate Hill 96, 98, **101**
restaurants *see place name*
reptiles 48
Rochester 134-6, **135**
Roman house: Dover 182
Roman snails 54
Roxley Warren Nature Reserve **139**, 140
Ryarsh 128

safety 56-8
school holidays 17
Scott, Sir George Gilbert 82
Seale 68, **71**, 72
seasons 19-20
services 16
Shalford 74, 76, **76**, **77**, 78
Shepherdswell **175**, 176, **176**
Shere 82, 86, **86**
Shoulder of Mutton Wood **133**, 138
side trips 24
Soakham Downs **156**, 158
spring 20
St Barnabas, church 82, **91**
St Martha, church 82, **83**
St Martha's Hill 82, **83**
statutory bodies 43
summer 20
sunburn 62
Surrey Hills AONB 42, 50
Surrey Maginot Line 100
swimming pools
  Guildford 78
  Oxted 108

Tandridge Hill **107**, 108
telephones 17
temperatures 20
theatres: Yvonne Arnaud 81
Thurnham 142, **143**
Titsey Plantation **109**, 111
Tourism South East 33
Tourist Information Centres (TICs) 33
town facilities table 22-3
town plan key 64
trail information 33
trail maps and map key 64
trains 34, 35, 38-9
  see also place name
travel insurance 17
trees 51-53
Trosley Country Park **127**, 128
Trottiscliffe 124, 126

Upper Bush 128

Vaughan Williams, Ralph 96
village facilities table 22-3

Waldershare Park 177, **177**
walking: time taken 63, 68
walking companies 16, 18
walking season 19
wartime defences 100
water pollution 60
Watts Cemetery Chapel 68, 74, **75**
Watts Gallery 68, 74, **75**
waymark posts 10
weather forecasts 60
weekend walks 27
weights and measures 17
Westcott 92
Westerham 111, 114-15, **114**
Westwell 152, **154**
Westwell Downs 152
White Horse Stone 138, **139**, 140
Whitehill Tower **105**, 106
wild camping 11, 61
winter 20
Wolfe, General James 111
Womenswold 170, **173**
Woolage Village 170, **173**
Wrotham 120, 122, **125**
Wye 183
Wye Downs 183

Youth Hostel Association 12
Yvonne Arnaud Theatre 81

TRAILBLAZER GUIDES – TITLE LIST

Adventure Cycle-Touring Handbook	1st edn out now
Adventure Motorcycling Handbook	5th edn out now
Australia by Rail	5th edn out now
Azerbaijan	3rd edn out now
The Blues Highway – New Orleans to Chicago	2nd edn out now
Coast to Coast (British Walking Guide)	2nd edn out now
Cornwall Coast Path (British Walking Guide)	2nd edn out now
Corsica Trekking – GR20	1st edn Apr 2007
Dolomites Trekking – AV1 & AV2	2nd edn out now
Himalaya by Bicycle – a route and planning guide	1st edn mid 2007
Inca Trail, Cusco & Machu Picchu	3rd edn out now
Indian Rail Handbook	1st edn mid 2007
Japan by Rail	2nd edn Apr 2007
Kilimanjaro – the trekking guide (with Mt Meru)	2nd edn out now
Mediterranean Handbook	1st edn out now
Nepal Mountaineering Guide	1st edn May 2007
New Zealand – The Great Walks	1st edn out now
North Downs Way (British Walking Guide)	1st edn out now
Norway's Arctic Highway	1st edn out now
Offa's Dyke Path (British Walking Guide)	1st edn out now
Pembrokeshire Coast Path (British Walking Guide)	1st edn out now
Pennine Way (British Walking Guide)	1st edn out now
The Ridgeway (British Walking Guide)	1st edn Dec 2006
Siberian BAM Guide – rail, rivers & road	2nd edn out now
The Silk Roads – a route and planning guide	1st end out now
Sahara Overland – a route and planning guide	2nd edn out now
Sahara Abenteuerhandbuch (German edition)	1st edn out now
Scottish Highlands – The Hillwalking Guide	1st edn out now
South Downs Way (British Walking Guide)	1st edn out now
South-East Asia – The Graphic Guide	1st edn out now
Tibet Overland – mountain biking & jeep touring	1st edn out now
Trans-Canada Rail Guide	4th edn Apr 2007
Trans-Siberian Handbook	7th edn Jan 2007
Trekking in the Annapurna Region	4th edn out now
Trekking in the Everest Region	4th edn out now
Trekking in Corsica	1st edn out now
Trekking in Ladakh	3rd edn out now
Trekking in the Moroccan Atlas	2nd edn May 2007
Trekking in the Pyrenees	3rd edn out now
West Highland Way (British Walking Guide)	2nd edn out now

For more information about Trailblazer, for where to find your nearest stockist, for guidebook updates or for credit card mail order sales visit:

www.trailblazer-guides.com

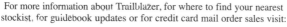

Europe
Trekking in Corsica
Corsica Trekking – GR20
Dolomites Trekking – AV1 & AV2
Trekking in the Pyrenees
Scottish Highlands – The Hillwalking Guide
(and British Walking Series: see p192)

Africa
Kilimanjaro
Trekking in the Moroccan Atlas

South America
Inca Trail, Cusco & Machu Picchu

Australasia
New Zealand – Great Walks

Asia
Trekking in the Annapurna Region
Trekking in the Everest Region
Trekking in Ladakh
Nepal Mountaineering Guide

Scottish Highlands – The Hillwalking Guide
Jim Manthorpe 1st edn 312pp, 86 maps 40 photos
ISBN 1 873756 84 4 £11.99, Can$26.95, US$19.95
This new guide covers 60 day-hikes in the following areas: • Loch Lomond, the Trossachs and Southern Highlands • Glen Coe and Ben Nevis • Central Highlands • Cairngorms and Eastern Highlands • Western Highlands • North-West Highlands • The Far North • The Islands. Plus: 3- to 4-day hikes linking some regions.

Trekking in the Pyrenees *Douglas Streatfeild-James*
3rd edition, 320pp, 97 maps, 60 colour photos
ISBN 1 873756 82 8, £11.99, Can$29.95, US$19.95
All the main trails along the France-Spain border including the GR10 (France) coast to coast trek and the GR11 (Spain) from Roncesvalles to Andorra, plus many shorter routes. 90 route maps include walking times and places to stay.
'Readily accessible, well-written' ***John Cleare***

Trekking in Ladakh *Charlie Loram*
3rd edition, 288 pages, 75 maps, 24 colour photos
ISBN 1 873756 75 5, £12.99, Can$27.95, US$18.95
Fully revised and extended 3rd edition of Charlie Loram's practical guide to trekking in this spectacular Himalayan region of India. Includes 75 detailed walking maps, guides to Leh, Manali and Delhi plus information on getting to Ladakh.
'Extensive...and well researched'. ***Climber Magazine***

New Zealand – The Great Walks *Alexander Stewart*
1st edn, 272pp, 60 maps, 40 colour photos
ISBN 1 873756 78 X, £11.99, Can$28.95, US$19.95
New Zealand is a wilderness paradise of incredibly beautiful landscapes. There is no better way to experience it than on one of the nine designated Great Walks, the country's premier walking tracks which provide outstanding hiking opportunities for people at all levels of fitness. Also includes detailed guides to Auckland, Wellington, National Park Village, Taumaranui, Nelson, Queenstown, Te Anau and Oban.

Kilimanjaro: the trekking guide to Africa's highest mountain
Henry Stedman, 2nd edition, 320pp, 40 maps, 30 photos
ISBN 1 873756 97 1, £11.99, Can$24.95, US$19.95
At 19,340ft the world's tallest freestanding mountain, Kilimanjaro is one of the most popular destinations for hikers visiting Africa. It's possible to walk up to the summit: no technical skills are necessary. Includes town guides to Nairobi and Dar-Es-Salaam, excursions in the region and a detailed colour guide to flora and fauna. **Includes Mount Meru.**' *Stedman's wonderfully down-to-earth, practical guide to the mountain'.* ***Longitude Books***

Himalaya by Bicycle – a route & planning guide
Laura Stone 336pp, 28 colour & 50 B&W photos, 60 maps
ISBN 1 905864 04 3, *1st edn,* £14.99, – due mid 2007
An all-in-one guide for Himalayan cycle-touring. Covers the Himalayan regions of Pakistan, Tibet, India, Nepal and Sikkim with detailed km-by-km guides to main routes including the Karakoram Highway and the Friendship Highway. Plus: town and city guides.

Adventure Cycle-Touring Handbook – a route & planning guide *Stephen Lord* 320pp, 28 colour & 100 B&W photos
ISBN 1 873756 89 5, *1st edition,* £13.99, US$19.95
New guide for anyone planning (or dreaming) about taking their bicycle on a long-distance adventure. This comprehensive manual will make that dream a reality whether it's cycling in Tibet or pedalling from Patagonia to Alaska. Presented in the same proven style as *Adventure Motorcycling Handbook.*

'The definitive guide to how, where, why and what to do on a cycle expedition' ***Adventure Travel***

Tibet Overland – a route & planning guide *Kym McConnell*
1st edition, 224pp, 16pp colour maps
ISBN 1 873756 41 0, £12.99, Can$29.95, US$19.95
Featuring 16pp of full colour mapping based on satellite photographs, this is a guide for mountain bikers and other road users in Tibet. Includes detailed information on over 9000km of overland routes across the world's highest and largest plateau. Includes Lhasa–Kathmandu route and the route to Everest North Base Camp. *'..a wealth of advice...'* ***HH The Dalai Lama***

Sahara Overland – a route & planning guide *Chris Scott*
2nd edition, 640 pages, 24 colour & 170 B&W photos
ISBN 1 873756 26 7 Hardback £19.99, Can$44.95 US$29.95
Fully-updated 2nd edition covers all aspects Saharan, from acquiring documentation to vehicle choice and preparation; from descriptions of the prehistoric art sites of the Libyan Fezzan to the ancient caravan cities of southern Mauritania. How to 'read' sand surfaces, using GPS – it's all here along with detailed off-road itineraries covering 26,000kms in nine countries. *''THE essential desert companion for anyone planning a Saharan trip on either two wheels or four.'* ***Trailbike Magazine***

The Silk Roads – a route & planning guide *Paul Wilson*
2nd edition, 352pp, 50 maps, 30 colour photos
ISBN 1 905864 00 0, £13.99, Can$29.95, US$19.95
The Silk Road was never a single thread but an intricate web of trade routes linking Asia and Europe. This guide follows all the routes with sections on Turkey, Syria, Iran, Turkmenistan, Uzbekistan, Kyrgyzstan, Pakistan and China. Fully revised new edition.

Trans-Siberian Handbook *Bryn Thomas*
7th edition, 448pp, 60 maps, 40 colour photos
ISBN 1 873756 94 1, £13.99, Can$29.95 US$19.95
First edition short-listed for the **Thomas Cook Guidebook Awards**. New seventh edition of the most popular guide to the world's longest rail journey. How to arrange a trip, plus a km-by-km guide to the routes. Updated and expanded to include extra information on travelling independently in Russia. New mapping.

'The best guidebook is Bryn Thomas's "Trans-Siberian Handbook"'
The Independent 28 Jan 2006